THE
MUSICAL WORLD
OF
JJ ohnson

studies in jazz

Institute of Jazz Studies
Rutgers—The State University of New Jersey
General Editors: Dan Morgenstern and Edward Berger

1. BENNY CARTER: A Life in American Music, *by Morroe Berger, Edward Berger, and James Patrick, 2 vols., 1982*
2. ART TATUM: A Guide to His Recorded Music, *by Arnold Laubich and Ray Spencer, 1982*
3. ERROLL GARNER: The Most Happy Piano, *by James M. Doran, 1995*
4. JAMES P. JOHNSON: A Case of Mistaken Identity, *by Scott E. Brown;* Discography 1917–1950, *by Robert Hilbert, 1986*
5. PEE WEE ERWIN: This Horn for Hire, *as told to Warren W. Vaché, Sr., 1987*
6. BENNY GOODMAN: Listen to His Legacy, *by D. Russell Connor, 1988*
7. ELLINGTONIA: The Recorded Music of Duke Ellington and His Sidemen, *by W. E. Timner, 1988; 4th ed., 1996*
8. THE GLENN MILLER ARMY AIR FORCE BAND: Sustineo Alas / I Sustain the Wings, *by Edward F. Polic;* Foreword *by George T. Simon, 1989*
9. SWING LEGACY, *by Chip Deffaa, 1989*
10. REMINISCING IN TEMPO: The Life and Times of a Jazz Hustler, *by Teddy Reig, with Edward Berger, 1990*
11. IN THE MAINSTREAM: 18 Portraits in Jazz, *by Chip Deffaa, 1992*
12. BUDDY DeFRANCO: A Biographical Portrait and Discography, *by John Kuehn and Arne Astrup, 1993*
13. PEE WEE SPEAKS: A Discography of Pee Wee Russell, *by Robert Hilbert, with David Niven, 1992*
14. SYLVESTER AHOLA: The Gloucester Gabriel, *by Dick Hill, 1993*
15. THE POLICE CARD DISCORD, *by Maxwell T. Cohen, 1993*
16. TRADITIONALISTS AND REVIVALISTS IN JAZZ, *by Chip Deffaa, 1993*
17. BASSICALLY SPEAKING: An Oral History of George Duvivier, *by Edward Berger;* Musical Analysis *by David Chevan, 1993*
18. TRAM: The Frank Trumbauer Story, *by Philip R. Evans and Larry F. Kiner, with William Trumbauer, 1994*
19. TOMMY DORSEY: On the Side, *by Robert L. Stockdale, 1995*
20. JOHN COLTRANE: A Discography and Musical Biography, *by Yasuhiro Fujioka, with Lewis Porter and Yoh-ichi Hamada, 1995*
21. RED HEAD: A Chronological Survey of "Red" Nichols and His Five Pennies, *by Stephen M. Stroff, 1996*
22. THE RED NICHOLS STORY: After Intermission 1942-1965, *by Philip R. Evans, Stanley Hester, Stephen Hester, and Linda Evans, 1997*
23. BENNY GOODMAN: Wrappin' It Up, *by D. Russell Connor, 1996*

THE MUSICAL WORLD OF

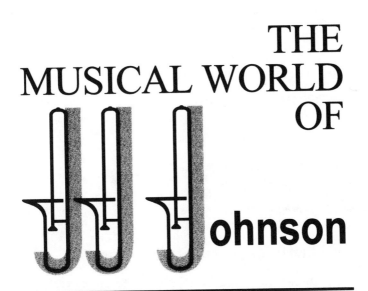

JJ ohnson

JOSHUA BERRETT

&

LOUIS G. BOURGOIS III

Studies in Jazz, No. 35

The Scarecrow Press, Inc.
Lanham, Maryland, and London
and
Institute of Jazz Studies
Rutgers—The State University of New Jersey
1999

SCARECROW PRESS, INC.

Published in the United States of America
by Scarecrow Press, Inc.
4720 Boston Way, Lanham, Maryland 20706
http://www.scarecrowpress.com

4 Pleydell Gardens, Folkestone
Kent CT20 2DN, England

British Library Cataloguing in Publication Information Available

Library of Congress Cataloging-in-Publication Data

Berrett, Joshua.
    The musical world of J.J. Johnson / Joshua Berrett and Louis G. Bourgois,
III.
        p. cm. -- (Studies in jazz ; no. 35)
    Includes bibliographical references and index.
    Filmography: p.
    "Catalog of compositions": p.
    Discography: p.
    ISBN 0-8108-3648-3 (cloth : alk. paper)
    1. Johnson, J. J., 1924-   . 2. Jazz musicians—United States Biography.
I. Bourgois, Louis G., 1956-   . II. Title. III. Series.
ML419.J62B47 1999
788.9'3165'09--dc21
[B]   99-10077
                                     CIP

To our wives—
Lynne Berrett and Robyn Bourgois

Contents

Figures

Foreword

J.J. Johnson is a magnificent instrumentalist and composer, and we are proud to be able to say that this monograph was produced with his cooperation. Johnson has been interviewed and profiled regularly in the literature of jazz, and David Baker published a valuable short volume of his transcribed solos with commentary. But Johnson has never been the subject of a full-length study. Since I am one of Johnson's biggest fans, it is my pleasure to have played a role in the development of this book.

Berrett and Bourgois bring an ideal combination of credentials to this project. Bourgois, a professional trombonist, analyzed Johnson's early style and compiled a discography as part of his doctoral dissertation. Berrett, a musicologist combining an interest in style analysis and cultural history, has published in the areas of both classical music and jazz, including a major article on Louis Armstrong and opera.

They present in this volume a number of surprises: details of Johnson's youth, including his school report card and his first compositions; interviews with Johnson, family members, and associates; a thorough investigation of Johnson's classical roots as a writer. Johnson is a marvelous writer, and it is one of the greatest strengths of this volume that his work as a composer is highlighted. In my opinion Johnson has not received his due in this regard, and this book should help rectify that.

In 1995 Johnson was voted into the *Down Beat Hall of Fame*, and in 1996 he won a National Endowment for the Arts Jazz Masters Award. This book is, therefore, a timely addition to the *Studies in Jazz Series*. Congratulations are due Berrett and Bourgois for an impressive achievement, and J.J. Johnson, the man of the hour, past, present, and future.

Lewis Porter, Guest Editor
Associate Professor of Music
Rutgers University at Newark

General Editors, *Studies in Jazz Series*:
Dan Morgenstern and Edward Berger

Preface

J.J. Johnson, spiritual father of modern trombone, has been a major presence on the international jazz scene for more than half a century. In 1946, during the heyday of 52nd Street, Johnson was overheard by Dizzy Gillespie working on "some of the sounds he'd been hearing from Gillespie, Parker, and Monk." The occasion was a defining moment, for it was with his comment that Gillespie in effect welcomed the Indianapolis native into the inner circle of beboppers and helped launch a career in which Johnson would soon become the supreme exponent of a "post-tailgate" style. "I've always known that a trombone could be played different, that somebody'd catch on one of these days. Man, you're elected."

In adapting his instrument to the bebop language, Johnson developed levels of accuracy, clarity, and speed that have never been surpassed. Yet unlike one misguided Philadelphia club owner, Johnson would be the last to characterize himself purely and simply as "the fastest trombone player alive." He is attuned to something a lot more subtle—the matter of syntax, a sense of style and taste appropriate to the nature of the musical utterance. For example, he has spoken with great affection about Dickie Wells and his great gift for playing very few but very well chosen notes. Similarly, the understated lyricism that Miles Davis achieved in "So What" has filled him with a sense of wonder.

J.J. Johnson, like many great artists, is his own severest critic, one who is forever on a journey of self-analysis and discovery. He has, with characteristic candor, spoken repeatedly of the need to avoid "just another day at the office," of the urge to "expand the envelope." His instrument has been but the means to an end in a career that, while identified with bebop, has exemplified jazz at its most elastic and inclusive; the trajectory of his career has intersected with virtually every major development in jazz over the past half-century. A lot more than a trombonist, he has also made his mark as an arranger and composer, one who has embodied influences from Basie to Bartók, funky blues to Britten, hard bop to Hindemith, swing to Stravinsky, disco to Schoenberg. Whether it is performing at Norman Granz's "Jazz at the Philharmonic," with members of the London Philharmonic, with Kai Winding, or as a member of Miles Davis's historic "Birth of the Cool" ensemble, or writing for blaxploitation movies, for TV series such as *Mike Hammer,* or composing for the concert hall in the third-stream mode, Johnson has done it all.

Over the span of some fifty years, J.J. Johnson has had his share of media attention in the form of polls conducted by *Metronome, Down Beat, Esquire,* and the French Jazz Academy, or as the recipient of an "American Jazz Masters" fellowship awarded in 1996 by the National Endowment for the Arts, and more. Then again, he has not completely escaped the pathologies that have afflicted the lives of jazzmen. In 1959 J.J. Johnson, arrested earlier in his career on a misdemeanor, was one of three "nominal plaintiffs" in a highly publicized, precedent-setting, cabaret card case argued in the New York State Supreme Court that forever changed the balance of power between nightclub jazz performers and the New York Police Department.

Yet Johnson has been the subject of only sporadic articles and book chapters covering various facets of his career—his style, his recordings, his preferences in instruments, his long-standing conflicted loyalties between being a composer-arranger and a performer. For all the fifty years or more that he has been before the public, there have been only two other extended critical studies. These are David N. Baker, *J.J. Johnson: Jazz Monograph Series* (New York: Shattinger International Music Corporation, 1979) and the unpublished doctoral dissertation of Louis G. Bourgois III, *Jazz Trombonist J.J. Johnson: A Comprehensive Discography and Study of the Early Evolution of His Style* (The Ohio State University, 1986).

The present book—the first-ever comprehensive biography, filmography, catalog of compositions, and discography of J.J. Johnson— therefore fills a major gap in jazz scholarship. It interweaves the many strands that define the man, his musical style, and the cultural contexts that have given meaning to his career. Although this has been a fully collaborative effort overall, the areas of individual responsibility in producing the actual book have been distinct and separate. The discography, filmography, catalog of compositions, typesetting of music and text, and editing of graphics and photographic images are the work of Louis G. Bourgois III. As primary author, Joshua Berrett is responsible for all other parts of the book, while at the same time clearly drawing upon the Bourgois dissertation in much of the discussion of Johnson's early style.

The indirect origins of the book date back to 1988, when Berrett received a grant to participate in the Summer Institute on Jazz Education, which was directed by Lewis Porter at Rutgers University (Newark Campus) and cosponsored by the Institute of Jazz Studies. It was Porter who strongly encouraged Berrett in his research of materials borrowed by jazzmen from nonjazz sources, what they reveal about the creative process, and what they signify about the larger cultural context. The happy outcome was Berrett's article "Louis Armstrong and Opera" published in *The Musical Quarterly*, vol. 76 (Summer 1992).

A short time later it was again Porter who brought to Berrett's attention the research that Bourgois had completed on J.J. Johnson, not to mention his eagerness to find an appropriate collaborator with whom he could develop the material into a full-length book. It is clear that Porter had the perspicacity to realize that the "fit" between Berrett and Bourgois was just right. Indeed, Bourgois responded most enthusiastically to the proposal for a collaboration, and one good thing led to another.

Much to Bourgois's credit and grant-writing savvy, a collaborative research grant was awarded by the National Endowment for the Humanities (NEH) for the period July 1991 to June 1993, with extensions granted through 1996. The Endowment committed itself to funding 80 percent of the award, with the respective grantee institutions—Kentucky State University and Mercy College—providing an equal share of the balance. This institutional support is hereby gratefully acknowledged, as is the invaluable help and encouragement received from Elizabeth Arndt at the NEH. Again, Lewis Porter's contributions as project consultant were vital to our success. The grant provided support for the conducting of archival research and personal oral history interviews in New York, Indianapolis, New Orleans, Los Angeles, and Chicago. Additional interviews were conducted by telephone with interviewees across the United States. Archives and public records searched include those of the Indiana Historical Society, the Crispus Attucks Center, the Indiana Humanities Council, the Public Records Office of the City of Indianapolis, the Indianapolis Public Library, the Film and Television Archives of the University of California–Los Angeles, the Hogan Jazz Archive (Tulane University), the Institute of Jazz Studies (Rutgers University), Indiana University, Broadcast Music Inc. (New York and Los Angeles), RCA Records archives of the Bertelsmann Music Group, Inc. (BMG), the New York Public Library, the New York Police Department, and the Museum of Television and Radio.

Oral history interviews were conducted in person or by telephone with George Avakian, David N. Baker, Rosemary Johnson Belcher, Benny Carter, Jimmy Coe, Maxwell T. Cohen, Robin Eubanks, Tommy Flanagan, Joy Nolcox Gaddie, Robert Gangel, Dizzy Gillespie, Benny Golson, Joe Gourdin, Dorothy Greenberg, Earle Hagen, Slide Hampton, Jimmy Heath, Conrad Herwig, Billy Johnson, J.J. Johnson, Kevin Johnson, Dick Katz, LaVon Kemp, Bert Kossow, Erma Levin, Walter Levinsky, Rod Levitt, Z. Richard Lieb, Peter Matz, Tommy Newsom, LaVerne E. Newsome, André Previn, Rufus Reid, Don Sickler, Gilbert Taylor, Mary Ann Topper, Steve Turré, and Josephine Weathers-Rogers. Edward Berger, Laura Calzolari, and Dan Morgenstern helped smooth the way for approaching specific interviewees. Our deepest thanks to one and all.

Finally, there are those individuals who generously provided access to rare material, particularly Gilbert Taylor (Crispus Attucks Center), Tom Everett (Harvard University Bands), Mary Ann Topper and her very special assistant, Anna Marta Sala (The Jazz Tree), Michael McGehee (BMI Artist Relations–Los

Angeles), David Sanjek (BMI Archives–New York), Don Sickler, Dick Katz, LaVon Kemp, Jamey Aebersold, Tina Vinces (archivist, CBS Records), Bernadette Holloway Moore (archivist, RCA Records), Benjamin Young (research coordinator, Verve Records), Marti Cuevas (Second Floor Music), Bobby Bryan (WKMS, Murray State University), Jack Nigoff, and Lowell Nigoff. Others volunteered valuable information, among them Bill Kirchner, David Demsey, Michael Fitzgerald, Krin Gabbard, Henry Martin, Martha Nochimson, Mark Tucker, and Hunt Butler.

The coauthors are deeply grateful to their wives, Lynne Berrett and Robyn Bourgois, for their support and encouragement. Joshua Berrett is grateful to his sons Jesse and Dan, his daughters-in-law, Susan and Julia, and to other family members for their unfailing support and interest. Emma Jane and George Bourgois are owed a debt of gratitude for their continuing support and encouragement of their son since his initial discographical study of J.J. Johnson began in 1973. Without a doubt, the moral support of close family has been indispensable in bringing a project of this scope to fruition.

Chapter 1

Early Years in Indianapolis, 1924–42

The summer of 1967 pulsed with a unique sense of excitement, what with such events as the release of the Beatles' *Sgt. Pepper's Lonely Hearts Club Band* album, the Monterey Pop Festival, the burgeoning of "flower power" and "love-ins." Far removed from this pop-rock world another kind of event was taking place in Indianapolis, Indiana—one filled with impressive dignity and enormous pride. In the late afternoon of Sunday, June 4, 1967, Crispus Attucks High School, the only public high school for blacks in Indianapolis, held vesper ceremonies as part of its fortieth anniversary year. James Louis (J.J.) Johnson, arguably the preeminent trombonist of modern jazz, was awarded the school's distinguished alumnus citation.[1] Surrounded by family, local colleagues, and the very teachers who had nurtured his musical growth at Crispus Attucks from 1937 to 1941, J.J. Johnson was clearly enjoying his own "love-in."

Norman L. Merrifield, music department head at Crispus Attucks from 1934 to 1942 and 1946 to 1967, who happened to be retiring that year, reminisced about his famous pupil for a local newspaper. He recalled that J.J. had been in the school band only six weeks when Merrifield realized that he had an exceptional talent on his hands. What astounded him was that the young teenager made as much progress in those six weeks on his school-supplied trombone "as the average boy makes in a year . . . [and] at the end of a year, he knew as much as I knew about the trombone."[2] The extent of the bonding between the young man and his "bent and beat-up" horn was plain for all to see, particularly his mother, Nina Gieger Johnson. "He'd lay that trombone right down beside him when he went to bed at night. In the morning . . . the first thing he'd do [was] blow a couple of toots on that trombone."[3] Johnson's sister, Rosemary Johnson Belcher, the first of two younger siblings, vividly recalled this phase of her brother's life with a slightly different twist. "He ate and slept with the horn. He was more concerned about the horn than he was [about] girls."[4]

Johnson's early years were spent in a world centered around church and home, a life dominated by two dramatically contrasting parents. Not only did they worship separately at different churches on opposite sides of the same street—James Horace

1

Johnson at the New Baptist Church and Nina Johnson at Phillips Temple, C.M.E. (subsequently renamed Grace Memorial Church, C.M.E.);[5] they were also opposites in terms of personality—the mother demonstrative, adoring of her son, and prone to be bossy, the father a man of very few words, stern, strict, and reportedly cruel at times. The children were brought up in both churches, attending Baptist Sunday school with the father and Methodist services with the mother; it was a "forced issue" that continued through their teenage years.

Even though Nina Johnson "couldn't tell one note from the other," it was she who encouraged the children in their music and hired a neighborhood male teacher to come to the house and give each child lessons on the family upright piano.[6] In recalling those years Nina Johnson remarked about her son, who must have been between about nine and eleven years of age at the time, " I never had to make him go to the piano and practice."[7] Memories of James Horace Johnson are far less flattering. Rosemary Belcher brought up an incident she said she could never forget that occurred around the same time.

> My father sang in the choir . . . my sister, my brother, and I were sitting together, and my brother broke wind and we laughed . . . you know, like kids, we thought it was funny. My father did not miss a note. He came out of that choir, down the aisle to where we were sitting, and popped crap out of my brother, and walked right on back up in the choir. And he [J.J.] did not cry out.[8]

Brother Johnson, as he was known to his Baptist brethren, wanted all to know that he was "really raising" his kids, even though it meant beating them. One can speculate that Johnson deeply internalized these strictures, coming to display in later life a certain "Mr. Clean" image, personifying a musician who for most of his career has resisted the temptations of drugs, alcohol, and womanizing.[9] Again, he has confided to his sister how cruel and unreasonable he found his father to have been, and how he could never raise his own sons that way. "You know I could hate my father. I could."[10] But later years seem to have brought father and son closer together.[11]

The Indianapolis world of family, school, church, and community that shaped J.J. Johnson's early life was touched by a sense of solidarity, a need to close ranks and clutch tightly that which it held dear. There was a special tension exerted by the Ku Klux Klan, which was approaching its peak of influence at the time J.J. Johnson was born on January 22, 1924. Grand Dragon David Curtis Stephenson ("I am the law in Indiana") was lording it over many areas of state government. At the Republican state convention that year many who were to win elective office—from school board candidates, to the mayor of Indianapolis, to the state governor—clearly owed allegiance to the Klan. But by 1928 Stephenson had been convicted of murder, many of his political cronies indicted, and the ranks of the Klan left in disarray. That same year the *Indianapolis Times* won the Pulitzer Prize for its exposé of political corruption, tainted by Klan connections. Yet despite its

Fig. 1.1   J.J. Johnson, two and a half to three years of age, seated on a pony in front of the house on Jon Drake Street where he was born (an unidentified man is in the background). Photograph courtesy of J.J. Johnson.

precipitous rise and fall within that decade, the Klan came to exert an effect on black public education in Indianapolis that was far-reaching and long-lasting.

In fact, the very origins of Crispus Attucks High School can be traced to a Klan-inspired petition by the White Supremacy League of 1922. On December 22 of that year the Indianapolis Board of School Commissioners passed a unanimous resolution authorizing the creation of a "colored high school." Named after Crispus Attucks, a runaway slave and the first martyr of the American Revolution in the Boston Massacre of March 5, 1770, the school opened its doors in September 1927.[12] As a result, the practice of allowing black children to attend integrated high schools, in effect since 1877, was overturned. This is not, however, to ignore the realities of day-to-day de facto segregation, which were in place well before. Coming in a steady northward stream since after the Civil War, the black population tended to cluster in the western part of the city toward White River and within a neighborhood of streets branching off from, and intersecting with, the artery of Indiana Avenue.[13]

Crispus Attucks was a revitalized school with an optimistic air about it when J.J. entered as freshman in September 1937. The tone of the decade had been set when Dr. Russell Adrian Lane, one of the school's original English teachers, was appointed acting principal in 1930 and named principal in 1932—a position in which he was to remain until 1957. Trained not only in English, Lane had also earned a degree from Howard University Law School and had undertaken graduate study at the University of Heidelberg. He was a man who viewed his assignment as a challenge and an opportunity, soon earning the plaudits of the local press, particularly for his communication skills—"He is a remarkably engaging conversationalist with a healthy hobby [*sic*] of looking his interviewer in the eye."[14] At the same time Lane was able to build on the tradition of excellence established by the formidable founding principal of Attucks, Matthias Nolcox, personal friend of Booker T. Washington and George Washington Carver, who had almost single-handedly recruited the school's teaching faculty from the midwest, the deep South, Florida, and the northeast. None was without a master's degree, and there were a number with doctorates.

Nolcox "did not allow excuses not to be educated" and was unshakable in his commitment that "anything less than the best" was simply not good enough for the school.[15] At the same time such a commitment could exact a heavy price. Joy Nolcox Gaddie has recounted an incident that more than likely cost her father his job or certainly helped precipitate his ouster as principal of Crispus Attucks. The school board had apparently ordered new auditorium chairs for Attucks, but had no intention of actually delivering them. Instead these chairs were to go to an elite local high school and the used ones brought over to Attucks. Undeterred, Nolcox stood in front of the doorway, arms outstretched and stopped the movers; he told them to take the chairs back where they came from and to bring the new ones to their rightful place.

Fig. 1.2 Crispus Attucks High School, November 1938, after construction of a new annex. The sign in the lower right proclaims, "Open House. American Education Week. Friday, November 11, 1938, 7:30 P.M. Come in. See your new building. Teachers, exhibits, etc." Photograph courtesy of the Indiana Historical Society, Indianapolis.

Less confrontational and more pragmatic, Russell Lane had the special gift of translating the ideals of Nolcox into action within an imperfect world where one sometimes had to be selective about the battles one fought—a world in which "separate but unequal" was the norm. Fortunately, battles were won fairly easily when it involved the physical plant or the recruitment and retention of highly qualified, dedicated faculty. For example, in 1937, the year J.J. Johnson entered, Dr. Lane was able to win a $275,000 appropriation for an annex to accommodate additional classrooms, music rooms, two laboratories, a gymnasium, and a new industrial arts section. This construction was driven largely by enrollment growth, with numbers in J.J.'s senior year almost doubling the total recorded for the school's initial year—2,450 students for the 1940–41 school year as compared with 1,354 for the 1927–28 school year. Even more important were the changes made in the curriculum and faculty of the music program. Two teachers, Norman L. Merrifield and LaVerne Newsome, hired by Dr. Lane in 1934 and 1936, respectively, were a fresh and vital presence, helping nurture J.J. Johnson's musical growth at Attucks from 1937 to 1941.

A graduate of Northwestern University who had studied elsewhere in the Midwest as well as at Trinity College of Music in London, Norman Merrifield headed the music department from 1934 to 1942 and resumed the position in 1946 (after service in the U.S. Army as a band director) to eventually retire in 1967. He was revered as an educator, pianist, choral director, band director, composer, and arranger of spirituals and Crispus Attucks songs. But above all he stood for quality. As Gilbert Taylor, curator of Crispus Attucks Center put it: "He established an excellent department. He required that anybody majoring in music or anyone taking music take harmony and theory; and he was very, very insistent on that. He was dedicated beyond any call of duty."[16] Merrifield's close colleague of many years, LaVerne E. Newsome, also a graduate of Northwestern, taught orchestra, string music class, and music appreciation, and team-taught a humanities course. Like Merrifield, he was dedicated to his students to a remarkable degree. On the occasion of his retirement in 1973 Newsome was presented with a plaque which read : "For outstanding leadership as an educator in the field of music, unselfish devotion in providing guidance, and exceptional teaching expertise which has produced many outstanding musicians."[17]

What made the musical learning experience at Attucks so special was the unique tension between the culture of commitment on the part of the faculty and the larger climate of discrimination. As LaVerne Newsome put it: "Our students didn't have the benefit of private teachers . . . most of the students got their instrumental experience through the school. That's the way they got their training. A youngster who was talented . . . we'd tell him to come back after school and we'd give him some extra help."[18] Gilbert Taylor said it even more pointedly: " Teachers were often at school until 9 o'clock doing private lessons. It wasn't anything they were paid for. But if they saw you had any potential at all, they would stay with you."[19]

When it came to the instruments themselves, "they tried a lot of things with Attucks; they tried to send all the new instruments to other schools and would send us the leftovers."[20] LaVerne Newsome recalled that the school often had to settle for even less than that.

> Before I came here Merrifield was asked by the principal to go around to the pawnshops, the various pawnshops on Indiana Avenue . . . then we were encouraged to go up to people's attics . . . But, at the same time, the other high schools were getting brand-new instruments, very shiny instruments. We wanted to know why, what was happening. We couldn't get a satisfactory answer.[21]

But LaVerne Newsome was undaunted. In 1940, the year in which J.J. Johnson entered his senior year, Newsome organized an orchestra–band parents club.

> One of the purposes of that group was to supply instruments, to buy instruments, to encourage youngsters to improve. They bought a number of instruments, I would say at least a thousand dollars of instruments, or more than that . . . the school board provided a core of instruments, a very small number of instruments. For some reason Attucks High School did not get . . . comparable treatment.[22]

Things could sometimes get absurd as when a budget request by Newsome was rejected and Norman Merrifield went to the downtown office of the superintendant and his assistant to raise "unholy hell."

> [The budget item in question] was a batch of liquid sterilizers costing less than $25.00 to be used for mouth pieces on wind instruments. . . . I explained that . . . Attucks had six trombone mouth pieces and 18 players. Without the sterilizers we were contributing daily to the epidemic of colds, sore throats and influenza that had recently hit the community. The item was accepted; in fact, the entire budget was hurriedly accepted . . . the only time in this teacher's tour of duty.[23]

This was the kind of world that J.J. Johnson entered in the fall of 1937, a world in which he was to bond with that "bent and beat-up" horn during Norman Merrifield's instrumental music course the following fall.[24] It was in this course that he received his earliest training on the trombone, astonishing Merrifield in the process, after having switched to the instrument following a frustrating time on the baritone saxophone. "The school had a baritone saxophone that I played that was in such miserable shape and in such horrible condition, and so unplayable, that I was encouraged to take up another instrument that the school owned, and it turned out to be trombone."[25] In a high school beset by acute shortages of adequate instruments, the baritone saxophone was, in fact, the closest available approximation to the tenor saxophone of his idol, Lester Young, to whom he was listening after school hours. Johnson elaborates:

During those same years I became involved with a circle of guys . . . who were into listening to Lunceford, to Basie, and Earl Hines . . . . I remember with fondness how joyous it was for all of us just to get together and listen to these records. . . . Pres was our hero. We were all big Lester Young freaks. We knew all of his solos, note for note. We couldn't play them, but we could sing them . . . we'd just get together and listen, listen, listen, listen, listen.[26]

And in a more analytical frame of mind, J.J. Johnson once remarked to Leonard Feather: "Lester was the forerunner of progressive jazz. My thing, maybe more than any other jazz musicians at that time, was the linear approach, and Lester epitomized that."[27]

During these impressionable high school years Johnson was profoundly affected by other players as well, particularly trombonist Fred Beckett (1917–1946). His was a lean, dry, clean, linear sound, similar to that of Lester Young. Johnson recalled to Leonard Feather: "Beckett was the first trombonist I ever heard play in a manner other than the usual sliding, slurring, lip trilling, or 'gutbucket' style. He had tremendous facilities [*sic*] for improvisation; in general, Beckett's playing made a lasting impression on me."[28]

Lead trombonist with the Kansas City band of Harlan Leonard and His Rockets (1939–40), Beckett vividly exemplified two contrasting "proto-Johnson" stylistic facets in two recordings from this period—"À la Bridges" and "Skee." Whereas "Skee," in its use of Pres-like motives, anticipates Johnson's detached, articulated style, "À la Bridges" illustrates the linear and triplet-filled approach that Johnson was to later follow in his 1944 recording of "Body and Soul." In the course of each phrase he generates melodic tension by ascending into the upper register, outlining the basic harmony in the process, while a sense of release comes with descending lines using scalar figures sprinkled with chromatic passing notes.

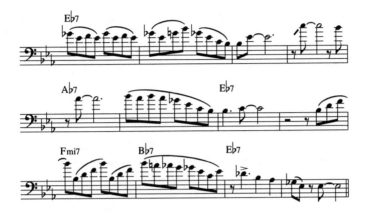

Fig. 1.3 "Skee," Fred Beckett solo, recorded January 11, 1940.

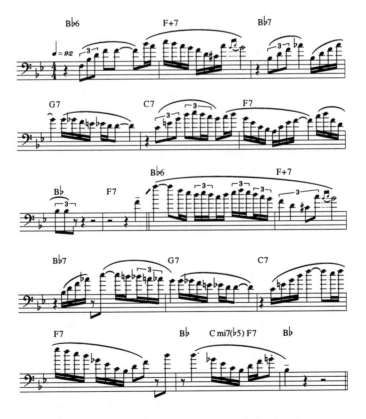

Fig. 1.4 "À la Bridges," Fred Beckett solo, recorded July 15, 1940.

The Kansas City background that is common to both Lester Young and Fred Beckett forms part of a larger context. Young's early association with bands such as those of Bennie Moten, Clarence Love, Count Basie, and Andy Kirk is rather well known—as is Fred Beckett's work with Harlan Leonard and His Rockets. What is also provocative, in terms of style dissemination and its analysis, is how the careers of Andy Kirk, Clarence Love, and those working with them on the Kansas City scene were soon to touch the life of Johnson shortly after he completed high school.

During these early formative years Johnson's roving ear was attracted to other trombonists as well, among them two fixtures in the bands of Count Basie and Jimmie Lunceford—Dickie Wells and Trummy Young. Speaking about Dickie Wells: "He was a guy who didn't play many notes. It wasn't exhibitionistic, it wasn't terribly dramatic. There was just something about it that grabbed you."[29] As for Trummy Young, he represented for Johnson not only remarkable trombone playing, but something more.

> I was particularly attracted to, and influenced by, in the early years, Trummy Young. There was something . . . that was very unique, very distinctive . . . . I'll never forget a recording he made, with Lunceford, I believe, on "My Gal Sal," where he took a four-bar break. This four-bar break was so outstanding that for a long time—I never heard it in person . . . only on the record—I thought it was a trumpet playing. I was amazed when someone said: "That's not a trumpet J.J., that's Trummy Young playing that break." He was playing so high on the horn, he was playing in the trumpet register . . . so clear and so articulate. That's what tricked me. He played with a great sense of humor. You could just hear the warmth and humor in his playing. . . . He was a beautiful person to know. To know Trummy was to love Trummy.[30]

Listening to these trombonists was an integral part of Johnson's early musical experience—included in the welter of multiple musical styles and impressions. And it is in this context that his course of formal music study in high school should be considered. Instrumental music was one of a roster of twelve courses that he took in order to fulfill his requirements as a music major. In fact, his complete transcript identifies him as a student with two majors (English and music) and two minors (Spanish and math). In addition, the transcript hints at some practical concerns as well—how to survive as a young black man in time of war—with courses taken in general shop (metalwork) and shoe repair.

Given the time and place, J.J. Johnson's formal musical education was almost exclusively centered around a Eurocentric classical repertoire, spirituals, hymns, and such. The bill of fare for senior vespers and commencement of May 1940 (on page 12) is illustrative.[31]

Adding to his kind of musical diet was the high school appearance every spring by Fabien Sevitzky and the Indianapolis Symphony Orchestra. LaVerne

Norman Merrifield		
Date	Course	Grade
1/38	A cappella I	B
6/38	A cappella II	B
1/39	Instrumental music	A+
1/39	A cappella III	B
6/39	A cappella IV	A
6/39	Band	A
6/39	Harmony I	C
1/40	Band	A
1/40	Harmony II	B

LaVerne Newsome		
Date	Course	Grade
1/40	Orchestra	B
6/40	Orchestra	B
6/41	Music appreciation I	B

Fig. 1.5   Music courses completed by J.J. Johnson at Crispus Attucks High School, separated according to teacher.

1938 Academic Year		
Date	Course	Grade
1/38	English I	C
1/38	Algebra I	B
1/38	Spanish I	A
1/38	Physical Training I	C
1/38	A cappella I	B
6/38	English II	C
6/38	Algebra II	B
6/38	Spanish II	B
6/38	Physical Training II	C
6/38	A cappella II	B

1939 Academic Year		
Date	Course	Grade
1/39	English III	C
1/39	Geometry I	C
1/39	Military Training I	A
1/39	General Shop I/Metal	B
1/39	Instrumental Music	A+
1/39	A cappella III	B
6/39	A cappella IV	A
6/39	Band	A
6/39	Harmony I	C
6/39	English IV	C
6/39	Geometry II	B

1940 Academic Year		
Date	Course	Grade
1/40	Spanish III	B
1/40	Orchestra	B
1/40	Band	A
1/40	Harmony II	B
3/40	English V	C
6/40	Orchestra	B
6/40	English VI	B
6/40	U.S. History VII	C
6/40	Spanish IV	B
6/40	Chemistry I	C

1941 Academic Year		
Date	Course	Grade
1/41	Mechanical Drawing I	B
1/41	U.S. History VIII	C
1/41	Civics-State	B
1/41	Chemistry II	C
6/41	Economics	C
6/41	Health	B
6/41	Mechanical Drawing II	B
6/41	Shoe Repair I	C
6/41	Music Appreciation I	B

Entered: September 7, 1937
Graduated: June 11, 1941
Rank: 109 of 230 in graduating class

Fig. 1.6   J.J. Johnson's official Crispus Attucks High School academic record.

Senior Vespers

SUNDAY, MAY TWENTY-SIXTH
5:00 P.M. SCHOOL AUDITORIUM

"Father, O Hear Me" (Handel-Christiansen) .... A Cappella Choir
Norman L. Merrifield, Director

Invocation ——"The Lord's Prayer" (Malotte) .... Anna Hearn
Marion Burch, Accompanist

"Break Forth O Beauteous Heavenly Light" (Bach) .... A Cappella Choir

Sermon ——"Resources for the Tasks We Must Face"............... Reverend R. T. Andrews

"Emitte Spirituum" (Schuetky) .... A Cappella Choir

Announcements .... Mr. Russell A. Lane

Benediction .... Reverend R. T. Andrews

★

Commencement Program

FRIDAY, MAY THIRTY-FIRST
CADLE TABERNACLE
PRECOMMENCEMENT CONCERT
CRISPUS ATTUCKS HIGH SCHOOL ORCHESTRA
7:30 TO 8:00 P.M.

"Triumphant March" (Sigurd Jorsalfar) .... Grieg
"Andante" (Surprise Symphony) .... Haydn
"Calif of Bagdad" .... Boildieu
LaVerne Newsome, Director

8:00 P.M.

Processional ——"War March of the Priests" (Mendelssohn) .... Orchestra
LaVerne Newsome, Director

Invocation ——"Prayer" (Arr. from Beethoven) .... A Cappella Choir
Norman L. Merrifield, Director

"Silver" (Harris) .... Girls' Glee Clubs
Hortense Bullock, Director
Marion Burch, Accompanist

Address ——"The Illusion of the Far" .... President Rufus Clement
Atlanta University

"I Must Go Down to the Sea" (Mitchell) .... Boys' Glee Clubs
Marion Burch, Director
Hortense Bullock, Accompanist

Presentation of Diplomas .... Mrs. Carl Manthei
Member of Board of School Commissioners

"Praise Ye the Lord" (Randegger) .... Combined Glee Clubs, Choir and Orchestra
Marion Burch, Director
Hortense Bullock, Accompanist

Scholarship Awards .... Mr. Russell A. Lane
Taps and Reveille
By Paul Overbey, '39
(Audience is asked to stand)

Fig. 1.7 Senior vespers and commencement programs of Crispus Attucks High School, Indianapolis, 1940.

Newsome made elaborate preparations for these events, knowing full well that this would probably be the only experience most students would have of hearing a symphony. He wrote program notes, distributed seating charts, played recordings of selections on the program (records were also loaned to any department heads who were interested), had students identify instruments, and presented biographical information on each composer.

All of these musical offerings are of a piece with the standards of intellectual rigor and artistic accomplishment that were characteristic of post-Reconstruction black American life. The prevailing attitude on the part of the black leadership encouraged a blending of the African heritage with European art music—a means of ennobling the "race" and lending it respectability.[32] It is in this context that we can appreciate anew the achievements of Matthias Nolcox, founding principal of Attucks and a man who moved in the social circle of Booker T. Washington and George Washington Carver, his successor Russell Lane, and musical mentors like Norman Merrifield and LaVerne Newsome. These values were, of course, hardly unique to the Indianapolis black community. In fact, what is compelling is how strong they were elsewhere as well, in Kansas City, for example, where the likes of Major N. Clark Smith and Charles T. Watts, among others, exerted a decisive musical influence of a similar sort on the early career of Clarence Love and many others.

Regardless of the type of repertoire involved in more formal high school events, however, Johnson displayed a personal seriousness and sense of commitment then that was prophetic of his later brand of meticulous professionalism. LaVerne Newsome has shared the following reminiscence about J.J. Johnson in his senior year, when Newsome conducted the orchestra:

> He came into the [orchestra] class as just another student. I didn't know a thing about him. But after he started playing I began to look at him a second and third time. A very good player, a rather quiet person in class. He was concerned about doing a good job and trying to meet the standard that you were expecting from him, which was kind of unusual. . . . He was amenable to suggestions you'd make, that you'd give him to improve his playing, or to get to a particular spot that you wanted to take it in that particular piece. . . . Very intense, very determined, and a hard worker. Worked quite hard after rehearsal. The next day, after rehearsal, he had it just the way you wanted it.[33]

As is already apparent from his early record-listening habits, what Johnson was doing outside of school was of far-reaching significance. LaVerne Newsome recalls, "J.J. Johnson and [later] David Baker . . . many of the other folks, the brass players, they would steal time after school and step down to the Avenue and sneak in there and listen and play. We weren't supposed to know what was going on."[34] Indiana Avenue, or the Avenue, was the city's Funky Broadway. In its heyday, the 1930s through the mid-1950s, it was an avenue with "soul," pure and unadulterated, an avenue revealing "the first and last kernel of naked humanity."[35] It was strung with nightclubs such as Henri's, the Cotton Club, Ritz Lounge, Trianon Ballroom, Red Keg, George's Bar, the Pink Poodle, and, last but not least, the Sunset Terrace. Noble Sissle, Ethel Waters, Josephine Baker, Cootie Williams, Tiny Bradshaw, Wes Montgomery, the Ink Spots, Count Basie, Duke Ellington, Jimmy Lunceford, and Benny Carter were among the many who appeared on the Avenue.

But the Avenue was a lot more than nightclubs. It was home to a cross-section of the black community, with its share of teachers, lawyers, doctors, dentists, postal clerks, custodians, merchants, cooks, and more. At the north-western end stood Lockefield Gardens, a twenty-two acre complex of fifteen apartment buildings, a community within a community accommodating 729 families bounded by Indiana Avenue and Blake, Locke, and Walnut Streets. A WPA project dating from 1932, it was once described by a resident as "one of the best things that's happened for colored people since Abraham Lincoln."[36] At the southeastern end of the Avenue stands an imposing four-story triangular Afro-Egyptian art deco building that has now taken on a new life—the Walker Center.[37] Originally built in 1927 by Madame C.J. Walker, the first black woman millionaire, it housed the national headquarters of her company, which manufactured ethnic beauty and hair care products. But it was, and remains, primarily for its theater and casino that the Walker Center holds musical and cultural interest as it dominates the landscape where North and West Streets and Indiana Avenue converge.

During these early impressionable years of J.J. Johnson's life, Indiana Avenue represented an avenue of dreams. Soon, however, during the period 1941–42, decisive events at the Sunset Terrace would change the course of his career. This could happen only after he had sufficiently internalized the sounds he heard on records, honed his skills outside of school in and around Indianapolis, and established a presence on the local jazz scene. Some of the earliest playing that resulted most likely started at home on the front porch. Rosemary Johnson Belcher has vivid memories:

> When we were kids I used to tell her, "Mom, I wish you'd make him stop all that noise." He'd be on the front porch playing loud, 'cause [the] trombone is loud anyway. And it used to get on my nerves and I'd tell her it would embarrass me, you know, never dreaming that he would grow up and be famous like he is. . . . He and Erroll Grandy, who played piano, and Eldridge Morrison, who played trumpet; and they would all be at the house.[38]

Erroll "Groundhog" Grandy, some six years Johnson's senior, is considered the "godfather" of Indianapolis jazz, the driving force behind the Naptown Sound.[39] Afflicted with cataracts and chronic eye problems while still in high school, Grandy was virtually blind for much of his life. This, however, did not deter him from becoming a beloved mentor to many jazz musicians who got their start in Indianapolis—among them Wes Montgomery, Freddie Hubbard, Slide Hampton,

J.J. Johnson, and his close local friend and fellow musician of many years, Jimmy Coe. As Clem Tiggs put it in his eloquent obituary: "Erroll just got another promotion in God's division."[40] Everyone who came his way had a unique chance to learn something about music. In fact, in the case of J.J. it seems that Grandy's blindness opened his own eyes to the world of arranging. According to Jimmy Coe, "This is the way J.J. got into arranging. Erroll would play the arrangements on the piano, and he had real long fingers. He could make excellent chords, and J.J. would write it out for him."[41]

During the 1938–39 academic year J.J. Johnson, joining Jimmy Coe and Erroll Grandy, began working after school hours with LaVon Kemp, another remarkable local mentor. He was ten years J.J.'s senior and also a Crispus Attucks graduate. Saxophonist, arranger, and bandleader LaVon Kemp had organized a band for young people at the community center on Fayette Street, one block over from Crispus Attucks High School and Indiana Avenue. Jimmy Coe recalled: "We . . . went into LaVon Kemp's band. At that time he was employing [musicians] who could read well."[42]

With the National Youth Administration as his sponsor, Kemp met with his group about three times a week, grooming his students to be good readers and ensemble players rather than promoting potential soloists.[43] It offered training opportunities to high school students who were both black and members of Indianapolis Local 3 of the American Federation of Musicians. Part of that training involved recreating charts off records by Jimmy Lunceford, Count Basie, Louis Armstrong, Fletcher and Horace Henderson, and Duke Ellington; it was an activity that sharply honed the skills of not only J.J. but also Jimmy Coe and fellow trombonist Robert Fisher. And the results were impressive. In the spring of 1939 the band began its own regular radio program, performing on WIBC every Saturday for several weeks. Longer-lived and more widely appreciated was the array of performances at such Indianapolis venues as the Walker Casino and Attucks auditorium as well as in outlying towns like Madison, Indiana, and Danville, in east central Illinois. An unidentified local newspaper reports enthusiastically about the band's return engagement on Labor Day 1939 in that Illinois town. "The Hiram Boosters Club and their friends swung until the wee hours at the beautiful and swanky country club in Harrison park." Most important, the review concludes with what must be one of the earliest references in newsprint to J.J. Johnson's playing:

> One of James Coe's latest arrangements, "By the River Saint Marie," was sung by Emerson Senior in his own inimitable style with Kemp taking a mellow chorus on his alto. Last, but not least, Robert Fisher and James Johnson were outstanding with their trombone duet on "Heaven Can Wait." The band is expected to return again soon.[44]

Fig. 1.8   Indianapolis's "Colored" YMCA Branch Building
(built in 1912), where the National Youth Administration-sponsored
LaVon Kemp Orchestra rehearsed. The signs in the windows state
"Some Doings. Colored YMCA. ?" Photograph courtesy of Indiana
Historical Society, Indianapolis.

Some time in the early 1940s J.J. Johnson was to pay tribute to his mentor by writing for him a theme song entitled "Kemptone" for which parts exist in manuscript—piano, trombone, trumpet, alto and tenor saxophones, bass, and drums. "Kemptone" is a snappy number replete with two-measure riffs, very much in the Basie mold. Cast mostly in B-flat, it consists of an introduction, a thirty-two-bar head, an interlude, and a full chorus blocked out for solo trumpet which, in turn, leads to a climactic eight-bar drum break. The concluding fifteen bars in D-flat, essentially a half out chorus, require the drummer to "push it."

Many of the other details of J.J. Johnson's high school years as well as the sixteen months spanning the time between his graduation in June 1941 and his joining the Benny Carter band in October 1942 remain sketchy at best. Nor is it clear just when it was that he last played with LaVon Kemp's group. It is, however, safe to assume that uncertainty about his professional future, not to mention anxiety about the war must have taken their toll.[45] At the same time he was edging into a faster-moving, more exciting world, one largely controlled by the Ferguson empire.

Denver Darius Ferguson and his younger brother, Sea H. Ferguson, embodied a special combination of business savvy, scandal, and civic leadership.[46] Married four times, Denver Ferguson, "a sepia Horatio Alger," set up a printing business in Indianapolis around 1919. He was soon involved in a "contract deal" for the production of lottery ticket coupons, including "number tickets," "baseball tickets," and such. The Ferguson organization eventually was to boast a catalog of over one hundred items in the "tally card" line, serving customers, among them big sporting figures, in thirty-odd states and abroad. As kingpin of the sporting world he built the Sunset Tavern on Indiana Avenue at Blake in the late 1930s, shortly thereafter adding the Sunset Terrace Club. At about the same time he organized the Ferguson Brothers Agency (also known as the Ferguson Booking Agency) located on Senate Avenue, the purpose of which was "to promote or book orchestras, bands, and popular artists of the amusement world." The bands of Duke Ellington, Count Basie, and many territory bands were among the groups handled by the agency. But by 1949 the federal government was hot on the trail of Denver Ferguson for income tax evasion, and "one of the big boys on the Avenue" found his properties being padlocked. Meanwhile, Sea H. Ferguson had his brush with the law as well. Owing some seven years' worth of taxes, he was one of the city's top gambling figures, owner of a bowling alley, liquor stores, rental properties, and the Cotton Club. He also sponsored a basketball team, furnished uniforms for a team at Attucks, and received a presidential citation for World War II service.

Intersecting with this local underworld were several bands moving through Indianapolis, appearing at Denver Ferguson's Sunset Terrace, that touched the lives of Johnson and his friends. Among them was the band of Tiny Bradshaw (1905–1958), singer and drummer who had previously performed with Horace

Kemptone

Fig. 1.9   Score to J.J. Johnson composition, "Kemptone."

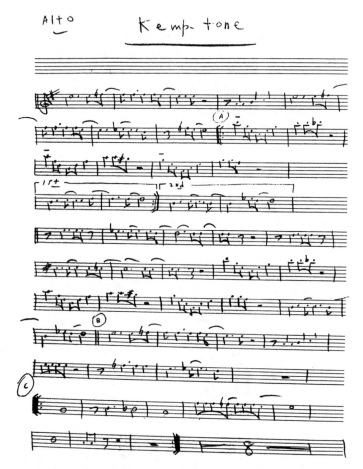

Fig. 1.10   Manuscript alto saxophone part to "Kemptone," mm. 1–58, in J.J. Johnson's hand. Manuscript courtesy of LaVon Kemp.

Henderson's Collegians at Wilberforce University, and with Marion Hardy's Alabamians, the Savoy Bearcats, and the Mills Blue Rhythm band in New York. Johnson elaborates:

> The activity was very fragmented as far as big bands coming to Indianapolis. They would come through now and again. But they weren't always the big-name big bands. For example, one of the better ones was not really a big-time, big name, but an excellent orchestra with excellent arrangements. We were all in love with that band—Tiny Bradshaw. He had a wonderful band that played at the Sunset Terrace. . . . I remember sitting in with people on Indiana Avenue at one time or another. . . . It brings back fond memories of some days gone by that I look back upon, and have an inner smile.[47]

Life behind the scenes, however, did not evoke such pleasant memories—certainly not for Joe Gourdin. He was a tenor saxophone and clarinet player with the Christine Chapman Orchestra, a group managed by the Ferguson Agency at about the same time that Johnson was playing with the Snookum Russell Orchestra.

> When I first got with the band, I came up [to Indianapolis] and they had a dormitory. On the second floor, they had a bunch of beds like this [Gourdin motions to his cot] with mattresses, no sheets or pillowcases, you know. And, I thought that you could always go into the crummiest town in the world and you would always see a sheet or a pillowcase. They didn't have any, and I thought "Damn, this is crude." But, anyway, I stayed there one night, and then, eventually—the second night—it wasn't too bad. We only stayed there about three nights. Duke Ellington came there too. We were staying on the second floor of a ballroom called the Sunset.[48]

In September 1941 Johnson was called for his first formal engagement at the Sunset Terrace Club—an appearance with the Clarence Love Orchestra performing under the direction of vocalist Pha Terrell. Even though it is quite unclear just how this all happened, general details of Clarence Love and Pha Terrell's backgrounds help provide some sense of context. Clarence Love was a musician with a checkered history. Born in Kansas City in 1905, Love had studied violin, piano, and mellophone there under such teachers as Charles T. Watts and William L. Dawson. His subsequent stints as a bandleader took him from Omaha, Nebraska, to the Southwest, to the Pacific. Probably one of his most successful spells was in the early 1930s in Kansas City, when he was working at the Blue Hill Gardens and El Torreon Ballroom in the battles of the bands. On those spring nights at the El Paseo some two hundred jazzmen, drawn from some ten or so bands, would wait their turn on the bandstand, staking their reputations on a single thirty-minute set. Tommy Douglas and Lester Young were among the many who passed through the ranks of the Clarence Love Orchestra. But a dispute over barbershop ownership—his father and the local union president had gotten into each other's hair—somehow forced Clarence Love out of Kansas City. He next worked in Dallas with Eddie Heywood as part of the band from 1934 to 1937. Meanwhile, Love's co-leader of the time, Orlando Roberson, a vocalist from Kansas City, had gotten a promise of a Decca recording contract whenever the group reached New York. But it was not to be. "No sooner did Love bring the band into New York than Roberson jumped them right into Danville, Virginia to start their tour."[49] In the course of 1936 this tour apparently broke up in Lansing, Michigan, and a few stalwart remnants returned with Love to Dallas. But within a few years Love was leading a reincarnated band through the South, eventually winding up in Indianapolis at the Sunset Terrace Club, where he joined the Ferguson Agency. Pha Terrell, his lead vocalist at the time, was something of a draw. A former bouncer, dancer, and onetime singer with Andy Kirk, Terrell was remembered by Buck Clayton as follows: "The ladies carried on, passed out like they did for Frank Sinatra. Pha was a dapper kind of guy, wore nice clothes. He wasn't big, but strong. And a nice person."[50] Shortly after Johnson appeared with his orchestra, Love moved on to fronting an "all-girl orchestra" and subsequently settled in Tulsa, where he booked name bands.

This footloose life of a rather feckless territory bandleader was not to be for J.J. Johnson. Yet he was able to turn this very lack of stability and tight organizational structure to advantage by trying out his own arrangements with this and other bands. Then again, the rigors of daily life in such orchestras and their frequent one-night stands often translated into problems of player retention—resulting in the very vacancies that proved to be Johnson's gain. As Joe Gourdin put it:

> The road was the closest thing you could get to being a hobo, and the guys who survived were the gentlemen. . . . [There were] a lot of bums out there, and they weakened to whatever their vices were. It'll eat you alive, and you have to be very, very strong. And without getting religious, you can say that the devil is alive and well out there.[51]

In March 1942, despite his father's reservations, Johnson joined yet another territory band managed by the Ferguson Agency—the Snookum Russell Orchestra. This group, it would seem, was one of Denver Ferguson's hottest properties. It was hyped in the local press as " the Nation's Number One swing band . . . positively the hottest dance band ever booked into the Terrace." The *Indianapolis Recorder* continues:

> Russell's Orchestra is considered one of the outstanding Negro groups in the country, in demand wherever swing is played. Among the better known engagements of Snookum Russell and his orchestra [are] The Famous Door, Savoy Ballroom in New York, Apollo Theater, Howard Theater, Rockland Palace, and every large theater in the country.[52]

Hired initially only to fill a vacancy, Johnson remained with Russell's group for close to eight months. During his tenure with the band he was able to hone his skills as an arranger even further; helping in this process was the opportunity to work alongside such musicians in this eleven-piece band as trumpeter Fats Navarro, tenor saxophonist Charlie Carmen, and bassist Ray Brown. Johnson's memories of Fats Navarro are especially fond: "Fats Navarro and myself became very, very dear friends. We sat together on the bus. We roomed together on many occasions. We were like brothers. He was a phenomenal player."[53] In any event, a variety of venues was the spice of these musicians' lives—whether in dance halls or tobacco warehouses. Joe Gourdin, whose tour of duty with the Christine Chapman Orchestra coincided more or less with Johnson's eight-month association with Russell, evoked the atmosphere of time and place.

> When you got down to North Carolina—they didn't have ballrooms—you got into the tobacco warehouses . . . there were white bands, too, that did that, like Hal McIntyre, not the Benny Goodmans or the Duke Ellingtons, but the seconds—the Louis Primas, the Hal McIntyres, the Ray Anthonys—people like that. Each town [on the circuit] had a night—like maybe Tuesday night might be the night for Winston Salem, North Carolina. The payroll was structured around a certain whatever—the booking agent and the tobacco warehouse people. If Tuesday was the night for Winston–Salem, then you could see a sign up there where it said: NEXT WEEK LUCKY MILLINDER.[54]

The Snookum Russell Orchestra was disbanded around the beginning of October 1942, and J.J. Johnson returned to Indianapolis. But the weekend of Saturday and Sunday, October 3 and 4, 1942, signaled one of the sweeping developments in his career, when, with band personnel constantly changing, the visiting Benny Carter found himself short of a trombonist. Thanks to a recommendation by vocalist Earl Coleman, Johnson played a couple of sets with the Benny Carter Orchestra at the Sunset Terrace. Carter was duly impressed, and this led to an association with the major jazz composer, arranger, and multi-instrumentalist that was to last some two and a half years.

Recently turned thirty-five—he was born August 7, 1905—Benny Carter had already established a compelling presence on the international jazz scene as leader and arranger. He had worked in that capacity with the bands of Fletcher Henderson and Don Redman, in addition to leading his own orchestra in New York. It was a group that included at various times sidemen at the cutting edge of early swing, such as Sid Catlett, Ben Webster, and Dickie Wells. From 1935 to 1938 Carter had worked in Europe, including serving as an arranger for the BBC and leading tours of England, France, Scandinavia, and the Netherlands. Upon his return to the United States in 1938 Carter had led a newly formed band at the Savoy Ballroom in Harlem. His subsequent appearance at the Sunset Terrace in October

1942 was with yet another big band that he had assembled the previous February. He had started at Harlem's Apollo with Billie Holiday as featured soloist and then swung through such cities as Syracuse, Boston, Baltimore, and Toledo. During the time that Johnson was with Carter's band he had the good fortune to work alongside musicians of the caliber of Curly Russell, Gerry Wiggins, and Max Roach. As Johnson has commented: "It was a continuous education in music."[55] There was, in addition, a special nurturing quality to Benny Carter that was legendary. Joe Gourdin spoke for many when he said:

> It's just that many guys at [that] age . . . don't get a chance to work with a guy like Benny Carter . . . a nurturing type, a fatherly-type man. . . . there's so much sleaze in this business and it [can be] a terrible occupation [with] a terrible bunch of people to work with.[56]

Initially, however, J.J. Johnson's parents had to be persuaded—a fact recalled by Benny Carter as he reminisced about his October 1942 visit to Indianapolis and his first meeting with them.

> He was eighteen when he joined my orchestra in Indianapolis. I met his parents because they had to okay his leaving home to go to California with me all the way from Indianapolis. They just wanted to see me and meet me, not really interview me . . . but see what kind of guy I was since I was taking their son miles away. I guess I passed scrutiny. He was more outgoing [than Miles Davis] . . . a very nice, well-educated young man. I don't remember him coming to me for advice [on arranging]. But we probably discussed music and arranging. But he had it then. We definitely played his charts with my band. He was already an arranger well on his way.[57]

Notes

1.   Although given the name James Louis Johnson shortly after birth, J.J. Johnson acquired the nickname "Jay Jay" or J.J. early on, certainly well before graduating from high school in 1941. J.J. Johnson is the name under which he has always been known throughout the musical world. Finally, on October 21, 1970, a formal petition to change his name from James Louis Johnson to J.J. Johnson was approved in Superior Court of the State of California, County of Los Angeles.

2.   Merrifield's comments have been excerpted from Fremont Power's column appearing in the *Indianapolis Star,* June 20, 1967. It should also be noted here that J.J. Johnson himself has identified this school-supplied instrument as the first trombone he ever played (Interview with Art Cromwell, Washington, D.C., ca. June 6, 1987). He therefore contradicts the version given by certain writers that his first instrument was bought for him by his father from a pawn shop.

3.   See Power, *Indianapolis Star.*

4. Interview with Rosemary Belcher, Chicago, June 26, 1993. Rosemary, the second of three Johnson children, was born in Indianapolis, July 12, 1925.

5. As of June 1993 both churches—street numbers 1211 and 1226, respectively—were still standing on Dr. Martin Luther King Jr. Street (formerly West Street).

6. The comment about Nina Johnson's tin ear occurs in the Rosemary Belcher interview, Chicago, June 26, 1993. The piano teacher, unnamed, could quite possibly have also served as organist at the Phillips Temple, C.M.E., the church with which Nina Johnson closely identified.

7. Power, *Indianapolis Star.*

8. Interview with Rosemary Belcher.

9. This is a topic to be more fully explored in later chapters.

10. Interview with Rosemary Belcher.

11. In a personal communication of September 22, 1998, J.J. Johnson maintains that once he became famous his father "boasted endlessly" to his friends about him. He adds that it was his father who came to the rescue in New York following his arrest by the New York police on a misdemeanor in 1946. Again, it was on his father's visit that he came to meet his beloved first wife, Vivian.

12. The originally proposed name for the school was Thomas Jefferson High School, but following petitions by black citizens in 1926, the name was changed to Crispus Attucks. In 1970, under a court-ordered desegregation plan, the school was integrated. Subsequently, in 1986, it became a junior high school, and three years later was entered in the National Register of Historic Places.

13. Built on level ground, Indianapolis is organized on an expansive, radial plan closely resembling that of Washington, D.C. Most of its streets intersect at right angles, although there are four great avenues that cut away like the spokes of a wheel from the hub of Monument Circle—Indiana, Massachusetts, Virginia, and Kentucky Avenues.

14. See Rosie Cheatham Mickey, *Russell Adrian Lane: Biography of an Urban Negro School Administrator* (Ph.D. diss., University of Akron, May 1983), 115.

15. Unpublished transcript of interview of Joy Nolcox Gaddie by Jeanne Killebrew, Indianapolis, 1985.

16. Interview with Gilbert Taylor, Indianapolis, October 23, 1992.

17. Among the more famous musicians, in addition to J.J. Johnson, to have graduated from Crispus Attucks are David Baker, Slide Hampton, and Freddie Hubbard. There are also a number of very gifted graduates whose impact has been more local, including Jimmy Coe, LaVon Kemp, and Erroll Grandy.

18. Interview with LaVerne Newsome, Indianapolis, June 22, 1993.

19. Interview with Gilbert Taylor.

20. *Ibid.*

21. Interview with LaVerne Newsome.

22. *Ibid.*

23. Unpublished manuscript by Norman Merrifield (1906–1993), *Music At Attucks.* One infers from a wry remark in the foreword that it was compiled some time in the course of 1990–91: "There are some errors and undoubtedly some unintended omissions which any two-fingered 84-year-old typist commits in the course of this kind of nostalgia."

24. Johnson's discovery of the trombone during his first year at Crispus Attucks High School takes on a deeper, more poignant meaning. His close, almost immediate

bonding with that school-supplied instrument, as implied by his mother, not to mention the profound impression he made on Norman Merrifield, stands in sharp contrast to what was a lackluster final semester in music at junior high school PS 87-42, when, according to his "scholarship record," it turned out to be his poorest subject.

25. Art Cromwell interview with J.J. Johnson, Washington, D.C., ca. June 6, 1987.

26. Interview with J.J. Johnson, Indianapolis, July 28, 1992. Pressed for further details, he singled out for special mention the following 1939–40 Lester Young performances as sideman with Count Basie: "Easy Does It," "Tickle Toe," and "Lester Leaps In." But given the time frame of Merrifield's instrumental music course (1938–39), it seems far more likely that Johnson's efforts on the baritone saxophone were directly inspired by earlier Lester Young recordings such as "Shoe Shine Boy" (1936), "Lady Be Good" (1936), "One O'Clock Jump" (1937), and "Jumpin' at the Woodside" (1938).

27. J.J. Johnson as quoted by Leonard Feather in liner notes to Savoy SJL-2232.

28. *Ibid.*

29. Art Cromwell interview with J.J. Johnson.

30. *Ibid.* In addition, in this same interview Johnson refers to J.C. Higginbotham as a "monster player." He has also spoken elsewhere of being touched by the distinctive timbre of Jimmy Knepper, "whose tone I have always admired because it does have a little bit of that French horn personality . . . [a] very dark, velvety kind of warm texture." Interview with J.J. Johnson, Indianapolis, May 4, 1994.

31. The commencement program contains a misspelling of the name of composer François-Adrien Boieldieu.

32. A window through which to view this musical order in historical perspective is provided by the celebrations marking the golden anniversary of the Emancipation Proclamation. See Joshua Berrett, "The Golden Anniversary of the Emancipation Proclamation," *The Black Perspective in Music,* vol. 16, no. 1 (1988) 63–80.

33. Interview with LaVerne Newsome, Indianapolis, June 22, 1993.

34. *Ibid.*

35. See "Grand Ol' Street at Turning Point," *Indianapolis News,* May 20, 1968.

36. See "Avenue Faces Poverty," *Indianapolis News,* September 7, 1970.

37. In 1991 the building was registered as a National Historic Landmark.

38. Interview with Rosemary Johnson Belcher, Chicago, June 26, 1993.

39. An exponent of "gospel jazz," Grandy, who died in 1991, always acknowledged the early influence of the music-making at Witherspoon United Presbyterian Church, where his father had once served as pastor. This also happens to be the church at which J.J. Johnson, who returned to settle in Indianapolis in 1987, and many of those closest to him now worship.

40. See *Indianapolis Recorder,* June 22, 1991.

41. Interview with Jimmy Coe, Indianapolis, August 6, 1992.

42. *Ibid.*

43. Eleanor Roosevelt was the force behind creation of the National Youth Administration. She was quoted in the *New York Times* (May 7, 1934) as saying: "I have moments of real terror when I think we may be losing this generation. We have got to bring these young people into the active life of the community and make them feel that they are necessary." The NYA was originally a relief project that would provide training of some kind that youth could later use in earning a living—"a fair deal all round as well as a new deal." Part-time public-service employment in government, hospitals, settlement houses,

libraries, and schools was the focus of the program. Established by the U.S. Congress in 1935 under the Works Progress Administration, its focus eventually shifted in 1942 to training for war work, and by 1944 the NYA was no more. In other words, J.J. Johnson's involvement with LaVon Kemp and his NYA-sponsored group was singularly propitious, providing a window of opportunity (1938–41) and coming as it did just on the eve of his joining territory bands and Benny Carter (1941–42).

44. This unattributed review is included among a scrapbook and assorted clippings generously shared by LaVon Kemp.

45. Also worthy of mention is the untimely death from rheumatic fever of the youngest of the three Johnson children, Ruth Pearl Johnson, on the day that Pearl Harbor was attacked. She was fourteen.

46. Much of the information presented on the Fergusons has been culled from the following local newspapers: *Indianapolis News*, March 11, 1974; *Indianapolis Recorder*, May 18, 1957; *Indianapolis Star*, December 14, 1951; May 11, 1957; March 12, 1974; *Indianapolis Times*, December 14, 1951.

47. Interview with J.J. Johnson, Indianapolis, July 28, 1992.

48. Interview with Joe Gourdin, New Orleans, June 12, 1991.

49. F.S. Driggs, "Kansas City and the Southwest," in *Jazz: New Perspectives on the History of Jazz by Twelve of the World's Foremost Jazz Critics and Scholars,* edited by Nat Hentoff and Albert J. McCarthy (New York and Toronto: Rinehart, 1959), 221.

50. Quoted in Leslie Gourse, *Louis' Children: American Jazz Singers* (New York: Morrow, 1984), 78.

51. Interview with Joe Gourdin.

52. See *Indianapolis Recorder*, June 28, 1941, 3.

53. Art Cromwell interview with J.J. Johnson.

54. Interview with Joe Gourdin.

55. George Hoefer, "Early J.J.," *Down Beat*, January 28, 1965, 16.

56. Interview with Joe Gourdin.

57. Edward Berger interview with Benny Carter on the occasion of his eighty-fifth birthday, August 8, 1992. It forms part of the Smithsonian Jazz Oral History Project.

Chapter 2

From Central Avenue to 52nd Street

The Los Angeles area, like much of the United States, was mobilizing for war when J.J. Johnson and the Benny Carter Orchestra arrived there in November 1942. This stark fact had profound implications for them in terms of audience receptivity as well as the making of recordings and movies. Understanding the larger societal context is immensely important here. The previous year President Roosevelt had urged conversion of the United States into "an arsenal of democracy" and under the Lend-Lease Act of March 1941 had authorized the "manufacture in arsenals, factories, and shipyards . . . [of] any defense article for the government of any country whose defense the President deems vital to the defense of the United States."[1] The manufacture of warplanes became a major industry in southern California with companies like Northrop, Lockheed, and Douglas dominating the scene. By the time of Pearl Harbor the industry was employing more than 34 percent of factory workers in the Los Angeles area and was soon producing more than a third of the nation's aircraft for the war effort.[2] During the 1940s national defense appropriations came to be institutionalized as tax resources were shifted from elsewhere in the country "to irrigate the Los Angeles area's aircraft plants and military bases."[3]

With defense industry plants operating around the clock there was an influx of thousands of black migrant workers from the southwest. Among them were a number of blues musicians from Texas, Oklahoma, Kansas, and Louisiana. It was from them that the leading exponents of the R&B sound in the city later in the decade were to emerge and help spawn the growth of independent studios. Along sections of Los Angeles like Central Avenue one could find "an elongated Harlem set down by the Pacific."[4] Nightspots like Club Alabam or the Downbeat were really jumping, and it was at venues such as these that "swing shift" dances were set up for late-night workers with bands playing until dawn.

Billy Berg, one of the enterprising nightclub owners of the day and a former vaudevillian, operated a series of clubs in Los Angeles. He had recently opened his Swing Club on Hollywood and Las Palmas, and it was there that the Benny Carter Orchestra opened on November 20, 1942, to rave reviews. *Metronome*

Fig. 2.1   A young J.J. Johnson in late 1942 or early 1943 after the
Benny Carter Orchestra's arrival in Los Angeles. The inscription
reads, "To Mom and Dad—from your loving son—James L. Johnson."
Photograph courtesy of J.J. Johnson.

wasted no words, declaring him a "big hit on his first visit to the West Coast . . . Benny's 17-piece jump band has the whole town excited."[5] In fact, two firsts were being celebrated: the first visit of Carter to California and the very first time that Billy Berg had presented a big band at his Swing Club. Then again, what gave their appearance special meaning was that Berg had not yet gotten a permit for dancing. As Carter put it, "We played what amounted to concerts for an attentive audience."[6] In fact, the *Down Beat* columnist claimed that fans, eager to hear Carter "at his best," were hoping that the club would do without the permit altogether.[7] After an eight-week stand at Billy Berg's, from November 20, 1942, through mid-January of 1943, the Benny Carter Orchestra had additional bookings at the Orpheum Theater in Los Angeles and at various other venues in Hollywood and Oakland.

Meanwhile, of far-reaching significance was their involvement in recording and, later, movie-making. Starting in December 1942 and continuing sporadically through June 1944, the orchestra, with J.J. Johnson as sideman, recorded some twenty-two sides for the Armed Forces Radio Service (AFRS). These represent J.J. Johnson's earliest recordings and include such titles as "Why Don't You Do Right," "Stompin' at the Savoy," and "Ol' Man River." This big-band repertoire epitomized the kind of fare broadcast to military bases abroad. Organized in 1942 as the Radio Section of the Office of Special Services within the War Department, the AFRS "was probably the largest single record operation anywhere in the world," with fully produced, prerecorded radio programs being distributed to the major networks.[8] Significantly, the very first session at which the band performed for AFRS, on December 18, 1942, was in its Jubilee series. First produced on October 9 of that year, this was a distinctive series which primarily featured jazz and was directed to largely African-American servicemen abroad. These were programs prompted by the feeling of AFRS planners "that the great pool of colored performers should be given a chance to make a wartime contribution."[9] There were over four hundred different half-hour Jubilee programs featuring such names as Duke Ellington, Jimmy Lunceford, Benny Goodman, Boyd Raeburn, Louis Armstrong, Lester Young, Charlie Parker, and Bud Powell. The value of these performances is considerable given the fact that in July 1942 James Petrillo and the American Federation of Musicians had put a ban on any commercial recording.

A parallel activity of the Benny Carter Orchestra was their performances at military camps and hospitals across the country during the period from 1943 to 1946. These were engagements sponsored by such agencies as the American Red Cross and the United Service Organizations. As Carter recalls:

> We would usually fit in these engagements along the routes of our regular tours. I can't make a big statement about it all—it was just something we wanted to do to help men in the service, who enjoyed it. Mostly, we played for segregated black troops but occasionally also for white audiences and racially mixed groups too.[10]

Regular tours criss-crossing the country and returning to Los Angeles became the norm during the periods of January through about April 1944 and again
from July 31, 1944, to March 1945. Locations could range from Hollywood to
Harlem with stands at such locales as Newark, Philadelphia, Kansas City, Detroit,
and Culver City. Although there were the inevitable stretches of numbing routine,
there were also moments of dramatic opportunity that were decisive in shaping
Johnson's career during these formative years. From May through July 1944, the
Benny Carter Orchestra, now back on home turf in Los Angeles, appeared at such
venues as the Orpheum Theater and the Hollywood Swing Club. It was during the
engagement at the Swing Club that J.J. Johnson was given his first big chance to
break out of the ranks of big-band sidemen. The previous fall, October 25, 1943, to
be exact, J.J. Johnson had recorded his first known solo to be included in a commercial release, a performance with Benny Carter and his orchestra of Cole Porter's
"Love for Sale." Thanks to an invitation from Norman Granz, he subsequently
appeared at the Embassy Theater in Los Angeles on July 2, 1944, in one of the
very first concerts that Granz had organized in what proved to be his historic Jazz
at the Philharmonic (JATP) series: all-star performances being recorded live in
the concert hall rather than in the studio.[11]

On this occasion Johnson performed as sole (and solo) trombonist in a septet
consisting of Illinois Jacquet and Jack McVea on tenor saxophones, Nat "King"
Cole on piano, Les Paul on guitar, Johnny Miller, alternating with Red Callender, on
bass, and Lee Young on drums. The session represents something of a cross-
roads. Aside from indicating Johnson's development at this point, it also features
others in a setting that contrasts sharply with more popular stereotypes about
these players. Cole was presumably still flush with excitement over his national hit
of 1943, "Straighten Up and Fly Right," while Les Paul, not especially noted for his
jazz contributions, was in the process of refining his prototype for the solid-body
electric guitar.

Johnson's solos in these sessions serve as valuable indicators of his growth
during this formative period and stand in bold relief against his first recorded solo
of the previous October as included in the Benny Carter band's rendition of Cole
Porter's "Love for Sale." All of twelve measures long, Johnson's solo here remains
very close to the original melody, showing minimal improvisation. But the JATP
session, which includes such standards as "Lester Leaps In," "Body and Soul,"
and "Tea for Two," offers the earliest extended examples of Johnson's developing
technique and swing-influenced concept of improvisation. Reminiscent of J.C.
Higginbotham's hard-swinging trombone, Johnson's solos typify a riff-based black

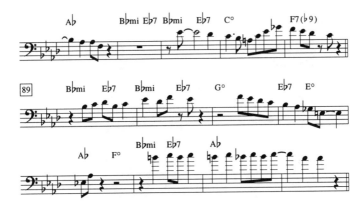

Fig. 2.2   "Tea for Two," J.J. Johnson solo, recorded July 2, 1944.

swing stylization whereby a number of riffs are strung together by means of repetition and minimal variation. His solo in "Tea for Two" is a case in point.

A standout is Johnson's rendition of "Body and Soul," one of the very few recorded ballad improvisations from his formative period. It is predictably derivative in its "Scotch-snap" rhythmic features (typically a dotted note directly preceded by its complementary short value), not to mention its melodic contour, which with its serpentine lines resemble the second chorus of tenor saxophonist Coleman Hawkins's 1939 recording of the title. Yet Johnson shows that he has internalized the linear conception of Fred Beckett to make this interpretation a moving individual statement that engages the listener.

Fig. 2.3 "Body and Soul," J.J. Johnson solo, recorded July 2, 1944.

Johnson's stint with Norman Granz and JATP could not obscure larger social problems of the day. The issue of black segregation during Johnson's wartime years with Benny Carter was mentioned earlier in our discussion of the AFRS Jubilee series, the scene at Billy Berg's clubs, and the performances in military camps and hospitals. But even more telling were two experiences that epitomized ongoing problems of racial integration, albeit on different levels. In October 1944, during a stand at the Plantation Club in St. Louis, an incident occurred that went beyond mere "Sambo" name-calling. This was a club that typically featured black bands catering to a white clientele. But when the band was integrated, as Carter's was, problems did erupt as when the band's pianist, Joe Albany, caught the attention of some dancers on the floor. Carter recalls: "I noticed one couple that kept looking up at us while they were dancing. They danced up to the bandstand and the lady leaned forward and said to me, 'Pardon me, Mr. Carter, but is your pianist white or black?' I looked over to Joe, turned to her and said, 'I don't know. I never asked him.' They seemed very surprised." That was not, however, the end of it. When other racial remarks were made later, none provoked by any band members, Carter went backstage to have a word with one of management's strong-arm men. "I mentioned these remarks to one of the goons. He pulled out a gun and pointed it at me, also giving me some advice. Just then J.J. [Johnson] came along and asked what was going on. The goon turned and hit him across the forehead with the butt of the gun. We didn't have a chance in that atmosphere. I pulled out the band, went to a lawyer and the union and we sued the club for several thousand dollars. I don't remember anything coming of it."[12] Meanwhile Johnson suffered a concussion for his efforts and had to be treated at a local hospital.

January 1944 saw the release of the MGM movie *Thousands Cheer.* Racism of a more subtle sort was at work here, impinging upon issues of racial stereotyping and how to incorporate black jazz musicians in an all-American wartime morale-booster movie. To see matters in context it is important to know the details of Carter's prior association with the Hollywood film industry. The previous January he had been invited by Twentieth Century-Fox to work on the film *Stormy Weather,* which had an all-black cast. Featured in the lineup were Bojangles Robinson and

Fig. 2.4   Benny Carter Orchestra at Loew's State, New York, 1944. Personnel includes Max Roach (drums) and J.J. Johnson (trombone, second from right). Photograph courtesy of Benny Carter.

Lena Horne. Given the showbiz story line, there were also cameo appearances by Fats Waller and Cab Calloway and his band. Music by Waller, Calloway, James P. Johnson, Nat "King" Cole, and Benny Carter was included in the soundtrack. But rather than appearing on screen, Carter received no screen credit at all and was confined to writing arrangements and playing on the soundtrack. As he succinctly put it: "That was a sideliner gig," referring to musicians on screen who only appear to be playing.[13]

Larger political pressures were at work as well. In his definitive study of blacks in American film through 1942, Thomas Cripps points out that *Stormy Weather* was the first significant black film made by a major studio following a March 1942 agreement between studio executives and representatives of the National Association for the Advancement of Colored People whereby they "codified some social changes and procedures." Pejorative racial roles were to be abandoned and Negroes were to be placed "in positions as extras they could reasonably be expected to occupy in society."[14] With old Southern stereotypes under assault, these codifications translated more often than not into segregated musical encapsulations, particularly in an all-star revue like *Thousands Cheer*, and the context within which the Benny Carter Orchestra makes its appearance there could not be a more compelling case in point.

Kathryn Jones (Kathryn Grayson), soprano daughter of an army colonel, has planned a camp entertainment to boost the morale of departing GIs. This turns out to be an all-star and virtually all-white revue, beginning with a rousing army band medley conducted by Jose Iturbi and culminating ten acts and forty-six and a half minutes later in a grand finale, which features Eddie Marsh (Gene Kelly), a disgruntled buck private now in his element, as he performs as king of the high trapeze with his aerialist family. The appearance (seventh "act") of the Benny Carter Band, with Lena Horne singing the Fats Waller–Andy Razaf standard "Honeysuckle Rose," takes slightly under three minutes, even including the introduction by Mickey Rooney. But it commands our interest for several reasons. Lena Horne, "the sepia songstress," the pedigree of black bourgeoisie traceable to Civil War days, and veteran already of such black films as *Stormy Weather* and *Cabin in the Sky,* clearly dominates the scene. Yet the camera work showing Benny Carter and his orchestra is striking for its sensitivity and imagination when compared to the corny conventional treatment visited upon other groups performing in the revue, such as those of Kay Kyser or Bob Crosby. The segment begins with a closeup of Carter playing his alto saxophone for the first half of the introduction. As the camera retreats for the balance of the introduction and the lead-in, sidemen on saxophone, trumpet, and trombone come into view in a rose window pattern, with Carter at the apex. Once Horne begins singing her two choruses and the tag, however, all attention is on her, except for two precious moments cutting away to the band. These occur at the turnaround coming at the end of the first chorus and during the tag. The second of these affords an especially clear view of the three-man trombone section, emerald derby mutes in hand, with J.J. Johnson in the top-left corner of the screen.

Two lesser-known vocalists brought Johnson into the recording studio in February 1945—Savannah Churchill and Timmie Rogers. Johnson's solo melody on Churchill's "Daddy Daddy" is something of an attention-getter, that in its use of nonharmonic tones, suggests a musician bridling at the confines of a swing arrangement.

Fig. 2.5 "Daddy Daddy," J.J. Johnson solo, recorded February 27, 1945.

By the spring of 1945 all indications are that J.J. Johnson felt that his "one continuous education in music" with Benny Carter was over and that it was now time to move on; he is accordingly not listed among the band's personnel after a recording session of April 2.[15] Yet, his presence very much remained with the band in the form of arrangements that are included in a series of AFRS Jubilee recordings made from May through July 1946.[16] These are surely the arrangements that

Benny Carter was invoking when, reminiscing about these years on the occasion of his eighty-fifth birthday, he recalled: "He was already an arranger well on his way."[17] The arrangements recorded during this three-month period embrace the competent but rather predictable "Without a Song" as well as the absolutely stunning "Polishin' Brass." This particular selection is in fact something of an oddity, being introduced by the emcee as follows: "Get set now for Benny Carter and his specialists handling a jump tune for which there is no title."[18] Compounding the riddle is the use of alternate titles on various other labels on which the recording was released.[19] In fact, in a recent interview J.J. Johnson was excited by the "dynamite arrangement" and was profoundly impressed by the "sure-handed conceptualizing for big band." Yet he was puzzled, incredulous that he might have possibly produced such an arrangement while in his early twenties. "I wonder did I in fact do that arrangement; and yet the feeling is so familiar. I said, 'Wow, I've heard that before.' Maybe I indeed did do that arrangement. I wish I knew that I did it, but I don't."[20]

Given the benefit of hindsight, one is drawn to what appear to be certain "proto-bebop" features in "Polishin' Brass," even though bebop was actually well established by the mid-1940s. For example, in the course of the three-measure introduction an octave figure appears on piano that bears an uncanny resemblance to the octave riff associated with Dizzy Gillespie's "Salt Peanuts." In this arrangement, however, it is no more than a dominant cue (on E-flat) for the catchy, uptempo, two-measure, eighth-note riff on muted trumpets that constitutes the head. This riff, with the underpinnings of the rhythm section, epitomizes Count Basie jump style to the hilt. In other respects, however, it is quite unique in being constructed of minor thirds and half steps exclusively.

Fig. 2.6 "Polishin' Brass," opening riff.

At the same time, this riff contains the seeds of many of the distinctive tonal and harmonic ideas that sprout in the course of "Polishin' Brass." Among these are: (1) a midsection in C-flat (enharmonic B), a minor third above the tonic of A-flat, which is the key of the head, out chorus and tag, and (2) a heavy use of chromaticism and diminished and extended chords.

The form of "Polishin' Brass" involves some idiosyncratic features as well. There are only two complete thirty-two-measure choruses: the head and the mid-section with its evenly distributed solos for piano, trumpet, saxophone, and trombone. Connecting these two sections are a dramatic half chorus, transition, and drum break, all of them combining dense chromaticism, contrasting timbres and registers, and punching syncopated tattoos for upper brass.

Taken by themselves, these tattoos generate the kind of rhythmic energy later seen in the head of Johnson's "Turnpike."

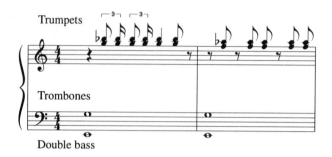

Fig. 2.7 "Polishin' Brass," syncopated tattoos.

The matching transition to the out chorus generates a real sense of climax in the course of its twenty-one measures as the trombones build in diminished chords upon the following riff:

Fig. 2.8 "Polishin' Brass," trombone riff in transition to out chorus.

A reprise of the opening four measures of the head is cut short by the tag, which is topped by a climactic E-flat on trumpet riding high on the band's A-flat final chord.

With its harmonic and formal daring, a piece like "Polishin' Brass" attests to the complex and often bewildering pace of change on the jazz scene in the mid-1940s; Johnson's personal doubts about even having written it in the first place, despite all evidence to the contrary, only underscores this very point. If anything, it provides further tangible proof of the daunting challenge one faces in attempting to disentangle the many threads connecting big-band jazz and bebop. By the same token, it underlines the importance of searching out continuities rather than perceiving bebop as a historically "inevitable" manifestation of some cycle of change. As David W. Stowe has succinctly put it: "Just as swing's luminaries were grounded in 1920s jazz, bop's leading practitioners had apprenticed in the big bands and smaller jump bands of the war years."[21]

In May 1945, when Johnson joined the Count Basie Orchestra, he began a period of critical transition, one marked by an unmistakable restlessness. There is even a hint of resentment in a comment by him to the effect that he was not being spotlighted often enough: "There are only about two recordings with the Basie band where I play. There's one original tune of mine called 'Rambo.' I solo on that and another thing called 'The King,' which featured Illinois Jacquet primarily."[22] In a session of August 2, 1945, with the Karl George Octet, Johnson lets loose with a kind of driving rhythmic energy that expresses with vivid clarity the reason he had recently bridled at being a swing-band sideman. A telling example is his solo on "Peekaboo," a fast tune based on the changes of "I Got Rhythm." Reflecting later on this phase of his career, Johnson remarked: "There was a time in my life—in the mid-1940s—when my aim was to play as fast as physically possible on the trombone." For some club owners this was apparently a very strong selling point. Johnson recalls a particular case: "In Philly, a ridiculous club owner had a sign outside which read FASTEST TROMBONE PLAYER ALIVE."[23] But in point of fact, Johnson has consistently placed the highest priority on tone, timbre, and clarity of articulation; a preoccupation with speed for its own sake is contrary to his musical nature.

Realizing that working in a swing band was blocking the career path that he envisioned for himself, Johnson made his next-to-last recordings in New York with Count Basie during January and February of 1946 and then eventually quit. His message was reportedly not lost on the veteran bandleader. As Bobby Tucker, musical director for Billy Eckstine, once confided: "Basie both loved and feared the things J.J. was saying in his last days with the band."[24]

Johnson was shifting his sights to 52nd Street, "the Street That Never Slept," "the Street" located between Fifth and Sixth Avenues. Historians of "the Street" like Arnold Shaw have made the point that during the Prohibition era this section of 52nd Street "had a larger concentration of speakeasies than any of its neighbors— and these became nightclubs or restaurants after Repeal."[25] It was a situation that proved highly conducive to the development of three major styles of jazz: small-combo Dixieland jazz of the speakeasy era, big-band swing of the New Deal thirties, and, with the end of World War II, small-combo bop and cool.

In early June 1987, shortly after participating in the seventieth-birthday concert at Wolf Trap for his great role model and mentor Dizzy Gillespie, J.J. Johnson shared some recollections of these formative 52nd Street years:

> I began to become aware of the fact that I wanted to participate in this thing that they were doing, if I could somehow . . . I didn't know how in the world I'd ever bring it off. But I got to talk to Dizzy a few times. And Dizzy was a great source of encouragement as far as how to go about bringing this off on the trombone, even though Dizzy is a trumpet player. He's so perceptive that he had ideas and suggestions that I pursued, and they worked out for me. I didn't know Bird quite as well as I knew Dizzy. They embraced me in a manner of speaking, saying: "Hey, man, you're elected," if I may use that kind of phraseology. It was like "You're it!" as far as the trombone is concerned. It was just a question of thinking

on it, absorbing what they were doing, absorbing the atmosphere of this new movement, and it became a way of life, just thinking about it, practicing it.[26]

Johnson's candor reflects his characteristic qualities of humility, diligence, and determination. By the same token, there is unlikely to have been any one "magic bullet" that made it possible for him to hit a bebopper's bull's-eye. Trial and error coupled with perseverance seem to have made possible for him the adaptation of the bebop language to the trombone, thanks in large measure to a certain generosity of spirit on the part of Dizzy Gillespie. With only interviews to provide a record of sorts as to what transpired between Johnson and Gillespie during that critical mentoring phase, we have to be satisfied with the following account of "ideas and suggestions . . . pursued" as given by Johnson to Tom Everett:

> There was something in my playing that gave Dizzy the impression that "Well, this guy could probably turn the trick, but he needs encouragement." And, man, he was so beautiful. He encouraged me. He embraced me, in a manner of speaking, like, "Hey, man, you're it. Just keep on doing what you're doing; try this." And he'd play something on his trumpet and I'd play it. I'd play it on the trombone and he'd say, "You're getting there; just stay at it." Dizzy was a great source of encouragement to me as far as the whole bebop syndrome was concerned. [27]

What strongly attracted Johnson to "the Street," aside from Gillespie and Parker themselves, was the opportunity for "sitting in," for playing music spontaneously and unrehearsed, and exchanging ideas with others. His experience at two clubs in particular made this possible: the Spotlite and the Downbeat, located at 56 and 66 West 52nd Street, respectively. In fact, it was at the Downbeat that Johnson became a nightly feature until Coleman Hawkins, the regular attraction, appeared.[28] A few doors away, at the Spotlite, one presumes sometime in the spring of 1946, Johnson, who was sitting in with Gillespie's quintet, was overheard by his mentor working between sets "on some sounds he'd been hearing from Gillespie, Parker, and Monk." His woodshedding efforts were impressive enough to prompt Gillespie to make a fateful endorsement: "I've always known that a trombone could be played different, that somebody'd catch on one of these days. Man, you're elected."[29]

Johnson's "election" was soon to be ratified when, on June 26, 1946, he made his recording debut as leader of a quintet called Jay Jay Johnson and his Beboppers. The other members included Bud Powell and Max Roach as well as Cecil Payne on alto saxophone and Leonard Gaskin on bass. Coincidentally, Powell, Roach, and Gaskin were hired around the same time to play in Gillespie's newly-formed big band at the Spotlite; Gaskin meanwhile had been performing at the Downbeat, where, of course, Johnson himself had very recently appeared. Johnson's quintet recorded four originals—"Jay Bird," "Jay Jay," "Mad Bebop" and "Coppin' the Bop."[30] This session for Savoy Records proved to be a defining moment for the young trombonist in that Johnson took the opportunity to record his longest studio improvisations up to that time. These include playing a complete solo chorus on all three takes of "Jay Bird," on "Mad Bebop," and on "Coppin' the Bop." On "Jay Jay" and its three takes one is able to hear the young trombonist reveling in his new found mastery and stamina as he plays two complete solo choruses for a total of sixty-four measures. Although Johnson's work on this date cannot be called mature—in the sense that there is little evidence of organic, motivic unity—it does reveal a number of important lessons learned on "the Street." Riff-based material has given way to more angular, typically bebop melodies that are supported by variable chord extensions and circle-of-fifths progressions; and associated with these features are more highly syncopated, less predictable rhythmic figures. A case in point is Johnson's solo, essentially the complete second chorus, of "Jay Bird" (take 1). Especially revealing here is the variety of treatment applied to the A phrases, with the very first of these quoting the popular song "Let's Fall in Love" in the opening five measures—a quotation from a song that, coincidentally, Lester Young, Johnson's youthful idol, would himself record in 1951. Then again, we see once more how the transition from swing and jump bands to bebop ensembles does not follow any simple, linear process of inevitable change. And in the case of Johnson's career there was an area of overlap that could not have been clearer. On July 31, 1946, a month and five days following the debut recording of his quintet, Jay Jay Johnson and his Beboppers, he was back in the studio for his final session with Count Basie and his Orchestra, a group with which he maintained only sporadic contact at this point in his career.

Fig. 2.9   "Jay Bird," take 1, J.J. Johnson solo, recorded June 26, 1946.

Johnson's final Basie session clearly represented the past for him; his sights were now turned to his newly formed quintet and its public reception. Indeed, critics and record buyers in general recognized the arrival of a new star. Ira Gitler claims that "Coppin' the Bop" and "Jay Jay," coupled as a single, "were soon in the hands of every young trombonist in New York. People who hadn't seen him refused to believe that he was playing a slide, not a valve, trombone."[31] It would seem that Johnson had already defined a quintessential bebop style that provided the basis for some important later critical insights. Thus, Don Heckman, placing Johnson in the larger context of trombone style and practice associated with Kid Ory, Jimmy Harrison, Jack Teagarden, and J.C. Higginbotham, offered the following assessment:

Few trombone players under the age of 30 have not incorporated important elements of the Johnson style and technique into their own playing. What Johnson did with Dizzy Gillespie's trumpet technique and Charlie Parker's alto saxophone innovations was not dissimilar to Harrison and Teagarden's adaptation of the Armstrong trumpet style.[32]

Others, such as Martin Williams, making a generalization applicable to bebop as a whole, suggested that J.J. Johnson "gave the trombone an almost abstract style that depended neither on the fact that a trombone can be made quite readily to imitate the human voice nor on the specific resources of the instrument." Williams, quoting Cannonball Adderley on the subject of Jimmy Knepper as contrasted with J.J. Johnson, maintained that you could play Johnson style on any horn, but that you could play Knepper style only on trombone. "Knepper, though he's very good, is too tied to the instrument. J.J., on the other hand, is a good soloist who happens to use the trombone." [33]

Notes

1. *Peace and War: United States Foreign Policy, 1931–41* (Washington, D.C.: 1943), 611. See also *United States Statutes at Large,* LV, 31–32.

2. Remi Nadeau, *Los Angeles: From Mission to Modern City* (New York and London: Longmans, Green, 1960), 202.

3. Mike Davis, *City of Quartz* (New York: Vintage Books, 1992), 120.

4. Ted Gioia, *West Coast Jazz* (New York: Oxford University Press, 1992), 4.

5. *Metronome,* December 1942, 21.

6. Morroe Berger, Edward Berger, and James Patrick, *Benny Carter: A Life in American Music,* 2 vols. (Metuchen, N.J.: Scarecrow Press, 1982), I, 212.

7. *Down Beat,* December 15, 1942, 8.

8. Jerry Valburn, "Armed Forces Transcriptions as Source Materials," *Studies in Jazz Discography,* 1971, 48.

9. Rainer E. Lotz and Ulrich Neuert, *The AFRS "Jubilee" Transcription Programs: An Exploratory Discography* (Frankfurt: Norbert Ruecker, 1985), xi. Our thanks to Lewis Porter for bringing this to our attention.

10. Berger et al., *Benny Carter,* I, 221.

11. An ardent political activist, Granz began his series as a fund-raiser by booking the Los Angeles Philharmonic Auditorium following a local Chicano riot. Around the same time (1944) he was approached by Billie Holiday, who complained that Billy Berg was not admitting some of her black friends to his Trouville Club in the Beverly Fairfax area. Granz made Berg an offer—he would guarantee a jam session and a crowd of paying customers on Sunday nights when the club was dark and the house band was off. But he insisted that Berg integrate the audience not only on Sundays, but on all other nights as well. In addition, he required him to put tables on the dance floor so that people would listen instead of dance. See John McDonough, "Norman Granz: JATP Pilot Driving Pablo Home," *Down Beat,* vol. 46, no. 16 (1979), 31. This chain of events also raises questions about the

conditions prevailing at Billy Berg's Swing Club, where the Benny Carter Orchestra had recently completed its eight-week stand.

12. Berger et al., *Benny Carter*, I, 230. According to the *Philadelphia Afro-American* of December 16, 1944, Benny Carter filed a $3,500 suit with the American Federation of Musicians against the Plantation Club. Our thanks to Lewis Porter for bringing this news item to our attention.

13. Berger et al., *Benny Carter*, I, 216.

14. Thomas Cripps, *Slow Fade to Black: The Negro in American Film, 1900–1942* (New York: Oxford University Press, 1977), 3.

15. Berger et al., *Benny Carter*, II, 117–118.

16. *Ibid.*, 126–128.

17. The full quotation appears at the end of chapter 1.

18. These remarks are included on Extreme Rarities 1007.

19. These titles can be found in Berger et al., *Benny Carter*, II, 127.

20. Interview with J.J. Johnson, New York, December 21, 1994.

21. David W. Stowe, *Swing Changes: Big Band Jazz in New Deal America* (Cambridge, Mass.: Harvard University Press, 1994), 206.

22. Ira Gitler, *Jazz Masters of the Forties* (New York and London: Collier Macmillan, 1966), 140. Johnson has often thought of "Rambo" as the first of his arrangements to have been recorded, even though Benny Carter and others have attributed the earlier "Polishin' Brass" to him. In an interview with David and Lida Baker (Indianapolis, February 26, 1994) Johnson recalls the piece as "my first-ever chance to have an original of mine recorded." Jazz composer Bill Kirchner pointed out in a separate interview (New York, May 16, 1995) that "Rambo" incorporates in highly simplified form many elements of orchestration and riff treatment that are broadly similar to what are found in "Polishin' Brass," but without any of the tonal and harmonic daring of Johnson's earlier work written for Benny Carter.

23. Gitler, *Jazz Masters of the Forties,* 146.

24. Raymond Horricks, "J.J. Johnson, Trombone Ultimate," in *These Jazzmen of Our Time* (London: The Jazz Book Club by arrangement with Victor Gollancz, 1959), 56.

25. Arnold Shaw, *52nd Street: The Street of Jazz* (New York: Da Capo, 1977), x.

26. Art Cromwell interview with J.J. Johnson, Washington, D.C., ca. June 6, 1987.

27. Tom Everett, "J.J. Johnson: On the Road Again," *Journal of the International Trombone Association,* vol. 16 (Summer 1988), 22–23.

28. In December of 1946 Johnson was hired by Coleman Hawkins to record as part of his septet that included a close friend from Johnson's Indianapolis days, Fats Navarro, as well as such musicians as Curly Russell on bass and Max Roach on drums. Two selections are especially valuable for J.J. Johnson solos : "I Mean You" and "Bean and the Boys."

29. George Hoefer, "Early J.J.," *Down Beat,* January 28, 1965, 16. The other members of Gillespie's quintet were Milt Jackson, Ray Brown, and Sonny Stitt. See Dizzy Gillespie and Al Fraser, *To Be or Not to Bop: Memoirs of Dizzy Gillespie* (Garden City, N.Y.: Doubleday, 1979), 251. Aside from winning high praise from Gillespie, Johnson was drawing the attention of fans who were impressed by his extraordinary "chops." See Gitler, *Jazz Masters of the Forties,* 140.

30. Max Roach is incorrectly listed as the composer of "Coppin' the Bop" in the original Savoy liner notes. Our thanks to David Baker for bringing this to our attention.

31. Gitler, *Jazz Masters of the Forties*, 140.

32. Don Heckman, "Jazz Trombone—Five Views," *Down Beat,* January 28, 1965, 19.

33. Martin Williams, "Thoughts on Jazz Trombone," *Down Beat,* January 18, 1962, 25–27.

Chapter 3

In the Inner Circle of Boppers

J.J. Johnson's arrival on the bebop scene in 1946 was signalled by yet another marker, one represented by the poll included in a report entitled "Esquire's All-American Jazz Band." A nonet featuring the trumpet duo of Charlie Shavers and Buck Clayton, this particular band also included such veterans as Coleman Hawkins, Harry Carney, and Teddy Wilson. The poll itself, one of Leonard Feather's creations, was based on balloting by previous winners who were asked to select "the best young, up-and-coming swing musicians they had heard during 1945." Significantly, "swing" is treated here as an elastic, inclusive category encompassing musicians from Louis Armstrong and Duke Ellington to Charlie Parker and J.J. Johnson. Put another way, the term "bop" or "bebop" is conspicuous by its absence. It is an omission vividly illustrated in the language used to describe both Parker and Johnson in the fourteen-category aggregation of "New Stars." At the same time the impression conveyed by the following descriptions clearly suggests two musicians on the cusp of change.

> It may seem strange to you, unless you've spent an awful lot of time around 52nd Street, that the musicians' first choice for the top new alto sax man of 1945 is an apparently obscure, unimportant character who has made few records and hardly ever appeared with a name band. Yet the thin, forlorn-faced young man known as "Yardbird," alias Charlie Parker, has had few competitors in his field. There's no way of describing Yardbird's frenetically fluent improvisations; the best thing one can say is, Jimmy Dorsey should live so long! Our find of the year on trombone, J.J. Johnson, known to fellow musicians simply as "Jay Jay," is a twenty-one-year-old Indianapolis product who graduated from Snookum Russell's band into the big time with Benny Carter and Count Basie. He plays the kind of fiery, rough trombone that made J.C. Higginbotham top man for years. [1]

By the time of the *Metronome* poll exactly two years later there is an unmistakable sense that a new jazz era is being born. While acknowledging the "low state of the band business," the magazine recognizes that times have changed with respect to both performance venue and recording. It is now a world in which "jazz musicians batter down the doors of obscure little night clubs, still more obscure record companies and their own back rooms to get their stuff heard." In a provocative skin metaphor readers are told that "the whole face of jazz has been made over" with bebop as "the biggest of the new cosmetics" and that it is doing as well as "Helena Rubinstein or Elizabeth Arden ever did with one of their fantasies of the epidermis."[2] Yet the actual polling embodies an undifferentiated critical mass; the top five vote-getters in the trombone category freely intermix players from the swing and bebop eras of jazz: Bill Harris, Kai Winding, Lawrence Brown, J.J. Johnson, and Tommy Dorsey, in that order.

The cosmetic/skin metaphor offers an apt image for characterizing bebop and its practice of giving a new melodic-rhythmic "face" to the harmonic skeleton of a pop standard. Coupled with the allusions to Helena Rubinstein or Elizabeth Arden, it also provides a smooth segue for introducing a vital feminine leitmotif into the larger drama of J.J. Johnson's life. On September 23, 1947, he married Vivian Elora Freeman in Indianapolis, an act that, given the benefit of hindsight, dramatizes a recurring theme in his life: being surrounded by a phalanx of strong women who can both nurture and take charge. The pattern, which began in his earliest years with his mother, Nina Johnson, continued with Vivian and her cousin Joy Nolcox Gaddie, and, as we shall see in later chapters, it is embodied in his present marriage to Carolyn Reid, who until his retirement in 1996, also served as his business manager, as well as his warm association with his artistic agent, Mary Ann Topper, who handled bookings and recordings.

First and foremost, Vivian exemplified the values of strong family pride and loyalty. As a niece of Matthias Nolcox, founding principal of Crispus Attucks High School, Vivian was a member of one of the most prominent and most tightly-knit black families in Indianapolis during the first half of the twentieth century. She and Matthias Nolcox's youngest daughter, Joy Nolcox Gaddie, were not only double cousins but were like loving sisters as well.

> Her mother and my father were brother and sister. So we were first cousins on my father's side. But her mother [married] my mother's first cousin. So therefore Vivian was my mother's second cousin because her father was my mom's first cousin. So we children were third cousins on my mother's side and first cousins on my dad's side because her mother married my mother's first cousin.[3]

Joy Gaddie has elaborated on this—"Vivian and I were more like sisters than first cousins"—but, even more importantly, she has brought attention to the distinctive close-knit loyalty that Vivian embodied in her role as wife to J.J. Johnson and as mother to their two sons, Billy and Kevin. Quite characteristically, when J. J. Johnson moved to California in 1970, after having lived in the New York area since 1946–47, both sons followed close behind him. Similarly, with the return of Johnson to Indianapolis in 1987, they made the move back to their father's hometown.   Again, the theme of the doting husband and J.J. Johnson the romantic has defined a good part of his family life. Mary Ann Topper has offered the

Fig. 3.1 Joy Nolcox Gaddie, *left,* and Vivian (Freeman) Johnson, *right,* in 1947. Photograph courtesy of Joy Gaddie.

Fig. 3.2   Undated (probably from the late 1940s) photograph of Vivian
Elora Johnson; dedication in the lower-right corner reads, "to Jay, with
all my love, Viv." Photograph courtesy of J.J. Johnson.

following observation: "Vivian was the great love of his life. She used to tell me J.J. would leave notes on her mirror in the morning, love notes, places where she would find them; and he was the total romantic, and I think that's part of his nature."[4] There is also a far more practical view of the whole family scene as suggested by J.J. Johnson's first son, Billy:

> Actually my mom ran everything. He was always on the road, more in my lifetime than in Kevin's. He was home more with Kevin in later years. But my mom usually ran everything. She was the banker and the disciplinarian. If something got too out of hand then he would step in. But basically she ran the show, and he wanted it that way. He didn't pay the bills; she paid the bills. She handled all the household chores, and he did his music. And that's something that I've always thought was a great thing because he was free to do that.[5]

Last but not least, there is the unique perspective, one of benign tolerance, of Rosemary Johnson Belcher, J.J. Johnson's younger sister and only surviving sibling: "All he knows is music. He loves it, he eats it, he sleeps it. And both wives [first, Vivian, and now Carolyn] had to be very understanding, very understanding, because he would go off in his studio, and they wouldn't see him . . . sometimes for days."[6]

In December 1947 the newlywed J.J. Johnson entered a period of frenetic recording activity in New York driven in part by the imminent ban by the American Federation of Musicians (AFM) that was due to take effect on New Year's Day 1948. At issue was the payment of record sale royalties to be made by companies to the union for use in supporting live music. A precedent had been set in 1943 when Decca and then various larger companies capitulated to the demands of the AFM. But the labor/management climate decisively changed in the course of 1947 with the passage of the Taft-Hartley Act. As a result, abusive practices by unions were outlawed and greater freedom for workers guaranteed, whether they joined a union or not. These developments help account for the establishment of the Recording Industries Music Performance Trust Fund to administer the payments. The AFM ban, in effect for all of 1948, was finally lifted on New Year's Day 1949.

Johnson's recording activity for December 1947, which was spread over five days—on December 11, 17, 18, 19, and 24—included sessions with the groups of Coleman Hawkins, Illinois Jacquet, Charlie Parker, baritone saxophonist Leo Parker, as well as Johnson's own quintet. Especially notable was his session on December 17 working at the cutting edge of bebop with the Charlie Parker Sextet which consisted of Parker, Johnson (going on twenty-four years of age), Miles Davis (a young twenty-one) as the front line, with Duke Jordan, Tommy Potter, and Max Roach on piano, bass, and drums, respectively. On that remarkable day six titles, all with multiple takes, were recorded within the prescribed AFM limit of three hours. This session, perhaps more than any other of the decade, epitomizes the adaptation of the trombone to bebop style, what with the punishing tempos, touches of melodic angularity, and advanced harmonic usage. These details are illustrated in the following three examples:

Fig. 3.3   Center label from Dial 1034-A, side A, "Crazeology," recorded December 17, 1947, by the Charlie Parker Sextet.

Fig. 3.4   "Drifting on a Reed," J.J. Johnson solo, recorded December 17, 1947.

Fig. 3.5 "Crazeology," take 3, J.J. Johnson solo, recorded December 17, 1947.

Fig. 3.6   "How Deep Is the Ocean," take 1, J.J. Johnson solo, recorded December 17, 1947.

When performing with his own quintet, as on December 24, Johnson was equally memorable. Aside from having the rather unusual sound of Leo Parker's baritone saxophone as part of his front line, Johnson displays some striking features of harmony and rhythm. Such is the case with "Boneology," which composer and jazz scholar Henry Martin has singled out for comment. Within its conventional thirty-two-bar structure and predictable use of the circle of fifths, Johnson injects some arresting details. As he launches into his solo chorus he not only introduces ♭VI⁷ harmony in the third measure, but also proceeds to tease the ear with his irregular phrase lengths as he lags behind the beat and "strikes a wonderful balance between the Parker-like sixteenth-note passages and the inventive, melodic eighth-note sections."[7]

Johnson's recording sessions with Illinois Jacquet on December 18 and 19, 1947, not to mention his touring with him during most of 1948, when the AFM ban was in effect, have generally been given short shrift. This represents an attitude that does little justice to either Johnson or Jacquet. There are admittedly instances, like the selection "Mutton Leg," in which a viscerally exciting performance replete with jagged-shaped predominantly chordal lines reflects far less concern for formal development.

Fig. 3.7 "Mutton Leg," J.J. Johnson solo, mm. 9–13, recorded December 19, 1947.

Although it is common to identify Jacquet with such solos as "Flying Home" and to dismiss him as one who "capitalised on his reputation as a purveyor of the frenetic," there is more to him than that.[8] There is certainly an avoidance of routine as is suggested by Jim Burns in his survey of 1940s bands:

> The Jacquet groups . . . did have a sound of their own, at least until the early 1950's when a drabness and a tendency towards routine performances became apparent. And the tunes, arrangements, and occasional brief solos by Russell Jacquet, Joe Newman, Henry Coker, J.J. Johnson, and others, are of interest, partly for their musical quality, and partly for their documentary value. The "Frantic Forties" come alive again when one listens to Jacquet and J.J. Johnson tearing through "Mutton Leg."[9]

Most important of all was something that was never documented on records, for which Johnson has acknowledged a deep debt.

> Jacquet would do all this honking and screaming on stage, but when he went backstage and noodled on his horn, Jacquet was playing pure bebop. He would never play it on the stage, but over in the corner, warming up, Jacquet was playing pure, unadulterated, good bebop. And he said, "Hey, J.J., let's jam such-

and-such," and I'd say, "No, I can't do that," and he'd say, "Yes, you can."
Jacquet was a great source of encouragement; we'd just get in the corner and just
start running lines and things. He'd say, "Come on, come on." He would just
encourage me to come along with him in this linear stuff he was doing, just
horsing around on his horn. It was amazing, because you don't think of Illinois
Jacquet and bebop; you think of . . . the showman, first and foremost. [10]

An index of Johnson's stature on the jazz scene as a whole was provided by the
Metronome readers' poll of January 1948. He won fourth place in the trombone
category, one like the others which was all-inclusive with its mixing of swing and
bebop players. A few years later Johnson was to provide a sobering assessment of
the whole polling phenomenon.

> I think, in a general sense, jazz polls are often misleading—I mean some of the
> polls in the music publications *Down Beat* and *Metronome*. They are, I think, for
> the most part, intended to be popularity polls, but there are those people . . . who size
> them up as something other than that. In other words, if so-and-so wins, they say
> that so-and-so must be the greatest, or something like that. [11]

It was in just this spirit that the editors of *Metronome* then proceeded to
assemble a band from poll winners and prepared for a recording date. Bill Harris,
however, who was first-place winner among the trombonists, was unavailable.
Eventually the two players needed to fill the trombone chairs were found in the
persons of Kai Winding (second-place winner) and J.J. Johnson. Finally, on
Monday, January 3, 1949—the first working day following the lifting of the AFM
ban—the RCA recording session took place. It had the quality of a stellar rebirth,
touting such players as Miles Davis, Dizzy Gillespie, Fats Navarro, Buddy
DeFranco, Charlie Parker, Charlie Ventura, and pianist–arranger Lennie Tristano.
Expressing himself in his characteristically colorful jive, Miles Davis has recalled:
"It was a bullshit record except for what me and Fats and Dizzy played. They were
limiting everybody because there were so many soloists and these were 78-rpm
recordings. But the shit that the trumpet section played I think was a
motherfucker."[12] We are also given to understand that "Bird was funny at that
session" in that he kept having to do extra takes under the pretense of not
understanding the arrangements. With a three-hour limit set by the union for the
new recording contract, anything beyond that was considered overtime. "So Bird
with his extra takes and shit stretched this session about three hours over the limit
and everybody made more money."[13] In fact, one of the titles from the session is
called "Overtime."

If one takes Davis at his word, the times spent with Johnson after hours seemed
like one wild ride. "After I started playing with Bird's band, me and Max Roach
got real tight. He, J.J. Johnson, and I used to run the streets all night until we
crashed in the early morning hours, either at Max's pad in Brooklyn or in Bird's
place."[14] His version of other incidents smacks of fiction rather than fact, bringing

Fig. 3.8   The 1948–49 *Metronome* All-Stars. Photograph courtesy of Institute of Jazz Studies, Rutgers University.

Fig. 3.9   Center label from RCA Victor 20-3361, side A, "Overtime," recorded by the 1948–49 *Metronome* All-Stars.

to mind the observation by Gary Giddins that Miles Davis is "a born hedgehog who believes in being a fox."[15] After a jam session at Minton's, Johnson reportedly turned up in the early morning at Davis's place, intent on checking a note in a Parker tune—Miles Davis, after all, had attended Juilliard and was the unimpeachable source when it came to such matters.

> I had gone home to sleep, there was this knock on my door. I got up and went to the door with sleep in my eyes, madder than a motherfucker. I opened the door and there was J.J. Johnson and Benny Carter standing there with pencils and paper in their hands. I asked them, "What do you motherfuckers want this early in the morning?" J.J. said,"'Confirmation.' Miles, do 'Confirmation' for me, hum it."[16]

Davis would have us believe that here was Johnson on his doorstep at six o'clock in the morning insisting that he hum "Confirmation" for him, obsessing about one note that he left out, promptly writing it down and then departing. Johnson himself, while subsequently questioning whether this particular incident ever actually occurred, has conceded that he was indeed in the habit at the time of dogging Davis for details.

> I read that in Miles's book, and for the life of me I could not recall that incident with Benny Carter taking place. I can say this, and . . . with conviction and honesty, that, yes, there were many occasions that I would harass and hound Miles to death about material. We sat in Penn Station on many occasions till the wee, small hours of the morning talking about a given tune . . . we were that tight.[17]

Johnson's point about their being so "tight" underscores the fact that Davis made Johnson his first choice for trombone when he began assembling his nonet for the historic "Birth of the Cool" sessions. But because of touring commitments with Illinois Jacquet and sporadic work with Babs Gonzales and Tadd Dameron, Johnson was unavailable for the initial session on January 21, 1949; Kai Winding substituted for him. In fact, on the previous day Johnson was in the studio recording with singer Babs Gonzales, who was one of the first to recognize the commercial potential of bebop. His work with Gonzales, while admittedly not all that significant to his overall career, is nevertheless illustrative of how he was modifying melodic materials to accommodate problems of slide position on his instrument. The following example juxtaposes an excerpt from Johnson's actual solo on "Capitolizing" with a hypothetical version that includes diatonic passing tones that might typically be present. The version with passing tones involves six problematic slide alternations indicated by brackets.[18] Johnson's solo itself, however, effectively eliminates four of the alternations by inserting staccato quarter notes—a circumvention typifying many of his improvised solos.

Fig. 3.10   "Capitolizing," J.J. Johnson solo, mm. 7–11, recorded January 20, 1949, compared with a hypothetical line (numbers indicate slide positions).

Yet there remain subtleties of Johnson's slide technique that elude clear or complete explanation, even by Johnson himself. An interview with Tom Everett bears this out:

> T.E: I noticed at the club last night that you use a very relaxed, loose wrist and finger contact on the slide.
>
> J.J: Right—you've got to!
>
> T.E: At times the slide is "floating" between fingers, not really in contact with any finger all the time. How did you develop that approach?
>
> J.J: It worked! It's the only way I could make it work.[19]

As for the subsequent "Birth of the Cool" sessions, Johnson was present on both April 22, 1949, and March 9, 1950. A figure of relative stability in a whirlwind of personnel changes, he played his part in a manner that was fully consistent with the aesthetic ideals of the ensemble. Thus, even though he has only one solo in the entire series, he functions as an exemplary member of what is essentially a chamber ensemble featuring one of each instrument. Gerry Mulligan has recalled:

> Miles and I had a lot of tastes in common. We both loved the Thornhill band, and we both loved the kind of orchestration that was represented in the band, and of course, the way Gil used that orchestration just flabbergasted us all. Really what we were doing wasn't revolutionary to us at all. It seemed perfectly logical. We picked instruments [with matching timbres] . . . and one of each. We had a high section with a trumpet and the alto, we had a middle section with the trombone and the French horn, and a low section with the baritone and tuba. So we had those . . . basic colors to work with. [20]

Johnson's one and only solo, occurring on "Deception," formed part of the final session on March 9, 1950. In a characteristic texture, instruments tend to move within a narrow compass in their midrange with noticeable homorhythm between or within sections as defined by Gil Evans and Gerry Mulligan. Johnson's solo in the bridge and the ensemble passage in measures 14–22 are illustrative.

Fig. 3.11   Miles Davis's "Deception," J.J. Johnson solo, mm. 96–117, recorded March 9, 1950.

Johnson's participation in the "Birth of the Cool" sessions was as significant in widening his socioprofessional network as it was in expanding his stylistic horizons. John Lewis and Gunther Schuller, in particular, were key figures in stimulating Johnson to move in the direction of third-stream composition. Later extended works such as *Poem for Brass*, *Perceptions*, or *Eurosuite* would have otherwise been unthinkable. Again, it was thanks to his association with John Lewis that his involvement with both the Monterey Jazz Festival and the Lenox School of Jazz was to later come about.

But Lewis would seem to have had an even more immediate effect on Johnson's growth. As a demonstration of formal development one cannot find a more compelling contemporaneous example than the "Fox Hunt" session with John Lewis. Recorded May 26, 1949, scarcely a month after the second of the "Birth of the Cool" sessions, "Fox Hunt" provides a vivid instance of a bebop selection in the "silent theme" category. Inspired by Frank Tirro, the "silent theme" epithet invokes

Fig. 3.12   Miles Davis's "Deception," mm. 14–21, transcribed by Mark Lopeman.

the notion of "musica reservata" and its identification with a Renaissance musical elite.[21] Tirro then proceeds to apply it to one of the essential characteristics of bebop, where the chord progressions (changes) from popular songs provide the harmonic foundation, "silent" and "secret," for the newly conceived bebop version. "It is a practice that operates on two levels, one sounded, and therefore open to the public, and one silent but implied, and therefore hidden and reserved for initiates who have been introduced to, and are capable of understanding, the secret."[22] The idea of a practice operating on these two levels is analogous to what is discussed earlier in this chapter where the *Metronome* poll of 1948 resorts to a skin metaphor: "the whole face of jazz has been made over" with bebop as "the biggest of the new cosmetics."

It is at this juncture that Johnson's career intersects with one of the most vital chapters in the history of the silent-theme tradition. Long before it was ever embraced by the beboppers, George and Ira Gershwin's "I Got Rhythm" (1930) was a favorite source of inspiration for jazz musicians. For example, by 1940 Fletcher Henderson, Jimmy Lunceford, Chick Webb, Benny Goodman, Count Basie, and Duke Ellington had trotted out this standard with their own distinctive trappings under such titles as "Yeah Man," "Stomp It Off," "Don't Be That Way," "Lester Leaps In," and "Cotton Tail."[23]

Johnson, starting in 1946, created some seven original compositions, all based on "Rhythm."[24] "Fox Hunt" is a case in point. It features Johnson in two complete choruses (the second and third) performing a solo that is striking for a sense of formal unity as achieved through melodic sequence (measures 21–23), variation (measures 1–4 and 9–12; measures 41–48 and 57–64), and motivic manipulation (measures 29–31 and 49–56).

Fig. 3.13   "Fox Hunt," J.J. Johnson solo, recorded May 26, 1949.

By the time of the "Birth of the Cool" and "Fox Hunt" sessions Johnson had developed a sizable repertoire—a "bag" of "licks," formulas, and more—the salient features of which help to more sharply define his place within the larger context of bebop. This repertoire, which takes shape within the culture of 52nd Street from around 1946 to 1950, is guided mostly by a distinctive adaptation of the trombone to the innovative language identified primarily with Parker and Gillespie. It will be examined in terms of characteristic harmony, melody, rhythm, and tone quality.[25]

Beginning with harmony, the elements present in Johnson's style and common to the bebop language as a whole, appear in four basic categories: (1) blues tunes; (2) popular songs; (3) silent-theme tunes; and (4) original tunes (not based on any recognizable, preexisting chord changes). Fig. 3.14 offers a sampling of forty-four titles from Johnson's early bebop period grouped accordingly. These groupings, however, should be placed in the larger context of a reservoir of memorized formulas. Lewis Porter's insights into Johnson's burgeoning style of the later 1940's are especially valuable in this regard.

> Johnson worked diligently ... to adapt bop patterns to the trombone, and his solos suffer from an emphasis on speed and an overreliance on memorized formulas incorporating such bop trademarks as the flatted fifth. His performances on both versions of "Crazeology" with Charlie Parker (1947) begin with the same phrase and contain other whole phrases in common. The same is true of the two renditions of Johnson's solo on "Blue Mode" (1949), despite their very different tempos.[26]

The twelve-measure blues tunes in the sample generally adhere to a harmonic convention typical of bebop practice: the secondary ii–V^7 progression is interpolated within the tonic to subdominant progression in measures 3–5, while the v/ii harmony in the eighth measure is typically followed by the ii–V–I progression in the final four measures.

Popular songs or standards such as "April in Paris," "Solitude," and "Yesterdays" form part of Johnson's early output. Ballads, in particular, become integral to his distinctive voice. They remain a vital expressive vehicle throughout his career, a case in point being the 1992 album *Vivian* dedicated to the memory of

Blues Tunes

Drifting on a Reed
Bird Feathers
Wee Dot
The Lion Roars
Riffette
St. Louis Blues
Goof Square
Bee Jay
Hilo
Blue Mode

Popular Songs

How Deep Is the Ocean
Yesterdays
Don't Blame Me

Original Tunes

I Mean You
Half Step Down, Please
Jumpin' for Jane
Mutton Leg
Down Vernon's Alley
Professor Bop
Capitolizing
Prelude to a Nightmare
John's Delight
Focus
Real Crazy
Audobon
Elysee
Opus V
Elora
Afternoon in Paris
Deception

Silent-Theme Tunes

Jay Bird (I Got Rhythm)
Coppin' the Bop (I Got Rhythm)
Jay Jay (I Got Rhythm)
Mad Bebop (Just You, Just Me)
Indiana Winter (How High the Moon)
Bean and the Boys (Lover Come Back to Me)
Quasimodo (Embraceable You)
Crazeology (I Got Rhythm)
Charlie's Wig (When I Grow Too Old to Dream)
Boneology (Riffin' at 24th Street)
Overtime (Love Me or Leave Me)
Victory Ball ('S Wonderful)
Fox Hunt (I Got Rhythm)
Teapot (Sweet Georgia Brown)

Of these forty-four titles, *Riffette, Bee Jay, Opus V, Elora, Jay Bird, Coppin' the Bop, Jay Jay, Mad Bebop, Boneology, Fox Hunt,* and *Teapot* are Johnson compositions.

Fig. 3.14   Categorized sample group titles from Johnson's early bebop period.

his beloved first wife. Within the quintessential bebop tradition of silent-theme usage, however, Johnson will often turn to such staples as "I Got Rhythm." It is therefore not at all surprising to find five titles within the sample of fourteen that are based on the changes of this Gershwin standard.

In the category of original tunes one finds a sophisticated harmonic usage involving the unusual and complex—a usage to be expected of one of bebop's pre-eminent practitioners. What is more predictable is the relatively common ii–V^7 progression, one that might appear in the following arpeggiated form.

Fig. 3.15   Arpeggiation to the ninth over ii–V^7–I in m.10 of J.J. Johnson's "Jay Bird" (take 1) solo.

Fig. 3.16   Arpeggiation to the sharp-ninth over ii–V^7–I in m.14 of J.J. Johnson's "Boneology" solo.

During the 1940s Johnson seldom used chord substitutions to increase harmonic motion in his melodic line, but when he did the chord substituted was most often a dominant seventh whose root was a tritone from the root of the primary chord, with both chords enharmonically sharing the same tritone.

Fig. 3.17   Primary chord and functional substitute chord with a shared tritone resolved down a fifth in mm.16–17 of J.J. Johnson's "Yesterdays" solo.

Fig. 3.18   Primary chord and functional substitute chord with a shared tritone resolved down a semitone in mm. 41–43 of J.J. Johnson's "Yesterdays" solo.

In developing a linear style in his improvisations, Johnson relied heavily on scales implied by the harmony. Four basic scale types occur again and again: (1) the major scale and its derivatives (dominant or Mixolydian), and minor forms like the Dorian and Aeolian; (2) the ascending melodic minor; (3) the blues scale (often with chromatic alteration); and (4) the half-step/whole-step diminished scale. At the same time, his melodic style is virtually inseparable from his approach to his instrument, whereby he was able to transcend its limitations by developing efficient slide movements. Two methods are especially important here: (1) use of the upper range of the instrument, where partials lie close together in each position and (2) playing in the middle range by exploiting the overlap of higher partials in the extended positions (five through seven) with the lower partials found in the first four positions. These methods allowed Johnson to minimize the amount of slide movement between many upper-register notes and to play more notes in the middle register within a single direction of slide movement. In general, he reserved the lowest range for ballads and the highest for brief expressive passages occurring in tunes of moderate to slow tempo. These methods also have a bearing on the contour of his melody. Lines can often change direction abruptly, with an initial ascending arpeggiated phrase being immediately followed by a descending scalar pattern.

Fig. 3.19   Ascending arpeggio with descending scalar motion, in mm. 19–21 of J.J. Johnson's "Bee Jay" (take 5) solo.

During his formative years on 52nd Street, from 1946 until 1949, Johnson sought to emulate features of not only Parker and Gillespie but also Fats Navarro. His friendship with Navarro, dating back to 1942 when they were together in the Snookum Russell Orchestra, continued on the Street through their ongoing professional contact. What is therefore provocative is to note some of the typical melodic coincidences among these musicians. More than that, respective recording dates point unequivocally to a cause–effect relationship.

Fats Navarro solo, "Calling Dr. Jazz," mm. 8–10 (December 20, 1946):

J.J. Johnson solo, "Drifting on a Reed" (take 5), mm. 12–13 (December 17, 1947):

J.J. Johnson solo, "Capitolizing" (take 5), mm. 1–5 (January 20, 1949):

Fats Navarro solo, "Wail," mm. 9–13 (August 8, 1949):

Charlie Parker solo, "Billie's Bounce," mm. 1–3 (November 26, 1945):

J.J. Johnson solo, "Jay Bird" (take 9), mm. 1–2 (June 26, 1946):

Charlie Parker solo, "The Street Beat," mm. 3–4 (September 4, 1945):

J.J. Johnson solo, "Indiana Winter," mm. 29–30 (December 4, 1946):

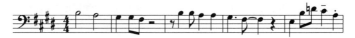

Fig. 3.20 Selected melodic coincidences in the recorded solos of J.J. Johnson, Fats Navarro, and Charlie Parker (1945–49).

Johnson's preoccupation with formal development and finding various means of tightly unifying his solos motivically—as is the case in the "Fox Hunt" solo of 1950 discussed earlier—would seem to have minimized the frequency of another phenomenon, namely, the quotation of themes from staples in the jazz and popular repertoires. About a dozen such instances occur during his formative years, drawn from such disparate sources as Parker's "Cool Blues," Gillespie's "Salt Peanuts," Fats Waller's "Honeysuckle Rose," and Gershwin's "Rhapsody in Blue," "High Society," and "Country Gardens."[27] It is a phenomenon that carries with it the risk of patchwork, a crazy quilt of multiple ideas that tends to militate against an overall unity.

Charlie Parker's "Cool Blues," in J.J. Johnson's "Charlie's Wig" (take 2) solo, mm. 1–3:

Dizzy Gillespie's "Salt Peanuts," in J.J. Johnson's *Indiana Winter* solo, mm. 1–2:

Fats Waller's "Honeysuckle Rose," in J.J. Johnson's "Jay Bird" (take 1) solo, mm. 17–18:

Johnny Dodds's 1923 "High Society" clarinet solo in J.J. Johnson's "Coppin' the Bop" solo, mm. 25–28:

Fig. 3.21   J.J. Johnson's quotation of themes from the jazz and popular repertoire.

As for rhythm, Johnson embraced the rhythmic elements of the bebop style, but in a manner well adapted to the trombone. The long melodic lines of uninterrupted eighth-notes, so characteristic of Parker and Gillespie, were well-nigh impossible to play on trombone in typically fast tempi because of the necessity for frequent slide alternations. Thanks to his facile technique and imaginative rhythmic constructions Johnson was able to overcome the natural limitations of his instrument. Thus we find that even though the eighth-note is the basic rhythmic unit in his style, groupings of more than sixteen of them (eight beats) rarely occur. What happens instead is that smaller groups of eighth-notes will occur, usually four to sixteen, interspersed with rests or passages in notes of longer value or in augmentation. This technique of interrupting rhythmic flow became a stock-in-trade throughout his career.

In describing Johnson's tone quality, we recall the points made in chapter 1 about his identification with Lester Young and Fred Beckett in his early Indianapolis years, as well as the critical assessments of Ira Gitler, Don Heckman, and Martin Williams as addressed at the end of chapter 2 that coincide with his arrival on the 52nd Street scene. What is especially compelling is not simply Johnson's cool, virtually vibratoless, abstract sound focusing on the musical line (Williams), but that, quoting Cannonball Adderley, you could play Johnson style on any horn and that Johnson is an exceptional soloist who happens to play the trombone without being tied to the instrument.

Meanwhile, during the late '40s and early '50s, the career of Johnson, like those of many fellow jazzmen, was being undermined by a process of decline in the quality of the nightclub scene on 52nd Street. With the proliferation of drugs and striptease joints a lurid form of Gresham's law was being visited upon the Street. Several factors conspired to cause its demise. Arnold Shaw has singled out World War II and a rash of attendant ills:

> World War II came to 52nd Street, bringing not only a curfew, entertainment tax, rationing and an influx of sailors and soldiers on leave, but a rash of striptease joints, tab padding and other sharp practices, fistfights and sluggings, racial conflict, and even attacks on the music. The war made The Street jump in a kind of desperate search for fun and forgetfulness, but it also accelerated its demise.[28]

Metronome deplored growing racial tensions, blaming them on aggressive police tactics that were fueled by tipsy white troops who were hostile to black musicians mingling with white girls. And the situation was not helped by the apparent pampering by musicians of "pimps, prostitutes, and tea [marijuana] peddlers."[29] There were, in fact, two groups with a large stake in the Street that contributed to its final downfall as an entertainment center—the city's landlords and the hoods. Arnold Shaw put it bluntly:

The former were not content to see a tenderloin threaten real-estate values in an area that could yield immeasurably greater revenues than the rundown brownstones. And the hoods who came as customers and stayed as partners demonstrated the relevance of Gresham's law about bad money driving out good.[30]

Billy Taylor has faulted the club owners themselves who, because of greed, would provide only small tables, demand big cover charges, and get into booking wars in a "battle of attractions."[31] As Joe Gourdin has recalled, these developments contributed to the failure of an increasing number of bands, particularly big bands:

The only bands that were going really great were small combos like Louis Jordan—six pieces—or Louis Prima—five pieces. Even Count Basie had a six-piece band . . . what I'm trying to say is that nationally, the big bands of guys like Basie were down from fourteen to six pieces, and even Woody Herman had retired, and Harry James had gone home to Betty Grable. [32]

It is only in this general context that one can begin to fully grasp why Johnson's career began to sputter in the early '50s with a series of short-term engagements and tours and only occasional, rather uneven recordings. In the spring of 1950, for example, the managers of Birdland (a club located at 1678 Broadway, just north of 52nd Street) tried to assemble an all-star band for a week-long engagement. The roster was certainly nothing short of stellar, what with Gillespie, Davis, Navarro, Dorham, Red Rodney, Johnson, Winding, Bennie Green, Mulligan, Konitz, and a rhythm section consisting of pianist Billy Taylor, drummer Art Blakey, and bassist Al McKibbon. Yet, despite the many brilliant players, the band proved to be both a commercial and a musical flop. After several names for the band were proposed by the management, including Dizzy Gillespie's Dream Band, and Symphony Sid's Dream Band, it was finally billed as the Birdland Dream Band since no one wanted to accept responsibility for it. Billy Taylor remembered:

The personnel consisted almost entirely of sidemen who wanted to be leaders, or had been leaders from time to time. . . . they were all marvelous musicians and the solos were the greatest. The only trouble was that when they tried to play the arrangements, using Dizzy's big band book, they sounded awful. They sounded so awful that no one wanted to be named as leader.[33]

Sporadic work became the norm after the Birdland stint in the spring of 1950. For the remainder of the year and throughout 1951 there was only occasional work in small groups, mainly sextets, fronted by Benny Carter, Miles Davis, and Dizzy Gillespie. To add insult to injury, conditions could sometimes be exacerbated by the violent temperament as well as bouts of paranoia and drunken behavior of a leader like Oscar Pettiford. In fact it was late in 1951 that Johnson joined an all-star sextet led by Pettiford on what was planned as a fifteen-thousand-mile United

Service Organizations (USO) tour through Korea, Japan, and the Pacific. But on January 7, 1952, following a six-day tour of Okinawa, Pettiford was relieved of his leadership and ordered by the commanding general to return to the United States with other band members continuing on to the Philippines.[34] Following a brief lackluster tour organized by "Symphony" Sid Torin, which concluded at the end of April 1952, Johnson joined a Miles Davis sextet on May 9 for a recording session.

But the fact that Johnson effectively withdrew from performing after this particular date cannot simply be attributed to the general conditions just described. Like many jazzmen of the time, Johnson had his bout with drugs, a situation that was almost inevitable on the 52nd Street scene. The general proliferation of drugs and striptease joints on the Street, mentioned earlier as contributing to its demise, was not likely the proximate cause of Johnson's problem as much as the overwhelming pressure of powerful role models. As Ross Russell observed:

> Booze and dope were the jazzman's escape hatches. Heroin was a hip, expensive substitute for alcohol. The high incidence of heroin users during the Forties can be explained in terms of a vogue—heroin as the "new thing." Its popularity in the bebop period was enhanced by Charlie's example . . . to play like Bird, you have to do like Bird![35]

Miles Davis recalls that upon his return to the United States in the summer of 1949 "some of the younger guys . . . started to get heavily into heroin," and proceeds to mention the following by name: Dexter Gordon, Tadd Dameron, Art Blakey, J.J. Johnson, Sonny Rollins, Jackie McLean, and himself.[36] Much of this heroin use seems to have been part of a larger ritual of initiation. Neil Leonard has perceptively written about the solitary nature of the jazzman's woodshedding efforts as he learns the intricate details of his parts, participates in "agonistic cutting sessions," sometimes suffers the trauma of "sitting in," and more. He adduces the case of California pianist Hampton Hawes, a man with a strong local reputation, who told of being frightened away from the bandstand at Minton's:

> It was like an initiation, a ceremonial rite . . . calling out fast tunes in strange keys with the hip changes at tempos so fast if you didn't fly you fell. . . . For a week I had watched these cats burning each other up, ambushing outsiders, fucking up their minds so bad they would fold and split the stand after one tune.[37]

It is a matter of public record that J.J. Johnson was arrested by the New York Police Department (NYPD) on December 27, 1946, on a misdemeanor. A hypodermic needle found in his apartment led to a conviction, a suspended sentence, and the revocation of his cabaret card. Even though this was his one and only arrest—he apparently never developed a narcotics addiction approaching that of Charlie Parker, Miles Davis, or Stan Getz, for example—Johnson's acute frustration and sense of humiliation at the hands of the NYPD was to fester for over twelve long years. During that trying time he was obliged to renew his cabaret card every six months because of the consistent denial of his applications for a permanent cabaret employee's identification card. Demeaning as his treatment by the NYPD was at the time, Johnson has also felt a sense of shame in more recent years as he has looked back and tried to make sense of this phase of his life.

> That was one of the dark cycles in my life that I prefer I don't remember in great detail. It did happen. We cannot undo what has happened. . . . I remember nothing about it other than I went through a very dark period in my life where I was involved with drugs. I readily admit that. There are many, many people who don't know that at one time J.J. Johnson was involved in drugs. Be that as it may, it did happen and I'm not trying to hide it.[38]

On the larger musical scene a painful message was beginning to sink in by the early 1950s, much of it identified with Charlie Parker. With the revocation of Parker's own New York cabaret license in 1951, his sharply declining health, his two suicide attempts in 1954, and his voluntary commitment to Bellevue Hospital, the ravages of drug abuse were becoming all too clear. When Parker died in March 1955 at the age of thirty-four the physician performing the autopsy estimated his age as fifty-five. And it was around 1954 that jazzmen in general began going public with confessions of drug addiction and its associated ills. No more compelling testimony can be found than that of Stan Getz, who wrote a highly publicized letter from Los Angeles county jail to Jack Tracy of *Down Beat*. Incarcerated after attempting to hold up a Seattle drugstore for narcotics, Getz had just come out of a three-day coma with a breathing tube inserted in his trachea. He was speaking for many of his colleagues when he concluded his letter with these words:

> I realize what I have done has hurt jazz music in general. To say I'm sorry is not nearly enough. I can't blame what I've done on the pressures of creative music in this country. Tell this boy from Seattle that it's pure and simple degeneracy of the mind, a lack of morals and personality short-comings I have . . . that the really good musicians are too smart to mess with it, and don't need it anyway.[39]

In a major study of drug use by jazz musicians conducted by Charles Winick during 1954 and 1955, 409 musicians were interviewed. Of these, 53 percent regarded heroin use as a serious health hazard. They were also more aware of the stiffer jail sentences meted out for heroin-related misdemeanors than any other drug. [40] The release in 1955 of Otto Preminger's movie *The Man with the Golden Arm* (with its memorable jazz score by Elmer Bernstein) did a great deal to heighten public awareness of the ravages of drug addiction. By 1957 the jazz community at large showed signs of lifting the curtain of silence when the Newport Jazz Festival organized a panel discussion that year entitled "Music and the Use of Habituating and Addicting Drugs."[41] That same summer Dizzy Gillespie contributed part of his fee at a jazz festival to a committee appointed by the City Council of New York to investigate all phases of the narcotics problem in the city.[42]

For his part, in August 1952 J.J. Johnson withdrew from the jazz scene and its underworld of hypodermic needles to begin working in the defense industry as a blueprint inspector. In the process he experienced a form of self-correction complemented toward the end of the decade—May 14, 1959—by the reinstatement of his permanent cabaret identification card. When Johnson began working for the Sperry Gyroscope Corporation in Great Neck, Long Island, he was surely acutely aware of Charlie Parker's contemporaneous sharp decline as he was mindful of his own recent brush with the law. While on one level the job provided a means of supporting his wife and children, the very fact of his being given it in the first place attests to the sure, guiding hand of Vivian.

Then again, it would seem that Sperry Gyroscope, upon vetting Johnson's background, sought to ignore his drug conviction or was unaware that it had ever occurred.

> I was screened for the job and got the job. How I got . . . the qualifications might be a bit of a story in itself. My wife . . . had worked for some kind of electronics company that made parts for the war effort . . . a job that required you to use precision measuring tools . . . she was like a parts inspector. She explained to me how a micrometer works, how precision machine tools work, and I read up on all that stuff and decided I had . . . nothing to lose. It was a challenge and a gamble, and I was damned if I didn't get the job. I had done my homework so well that I got the job based on my boning up . . . where I could put on a convincing, qualifying rap.[43]

So it was that Johnson began working for Sperry Gyroscope in August 1952, entering a growth industry at the height of the cold war in which the production of navigational computers, computing gun sights, automatic pilots, flight directors, and more was the norm. At the end of the following year the Instruments and Controls Division for which he worked could proudly claim in its annual report:

> The requirements of the defense program resulted in substantially increased activity in 1953 in our instruments and controls business. The increase occurred not only in production, but also in developmental work, and it was related to all three branches of the Armed Services.[44]

A former supervisor, Bob Gangel, has said that Johnson was part of a small group of about six inspectors operating in a company of several thousand. His responsibility as blueprint inspector was to catalog prints, making sure that the right print was being used, that it was up-to-date, that it was properly filed, and that design specifications were being followed.[45] These details of the job description, not to mention the way in which he was able to qualify for the position in the first place, all attest to Johnson's ability to distance himself from the addictive drug

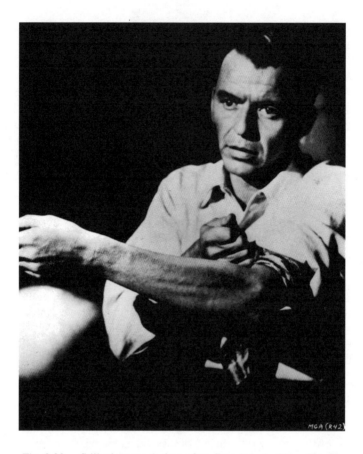

Fig. 3.22   Still photograph from Otto Preminger's film, *The Man with the Golden Arm* (1955), starring Frank Sinatra and Kim Novak. Photograph courtesy of United Artists.

atmosphere of 52nd Street and the grinding routine of performing to undertake a critical self-evaluation and personal stock-taking. It was by all accounts a phase of "self-prescribed rehabilitation," one in which he has admitted: "I felt like I was on a treadmill. I wanted to get off so I could look at myself more objectively."[46] At the same time he was able to bring to his work in the defense industry a capacity for adaptation and meticulous analysis, an asset that was to pay handsome dividends when he later ventured into third-stream composition and the writing of commercial jingles, movie and TV scores.

Fig. 3.23   The Johnson family—undated, though probably from the mid-1950s—in Teaneck, New Jersey. *Above left,* Vivian; *right,* J.J.; *below left,* Billy; *right,* Kevin. Photograph courtesy of J.J. Johnson.

Notes

1. *Esquire*, vol. 25, no. 1 (January 1946), 56–59.
2. *Metronome*, January 1948, 25. Mention of "still more obscure record companies" pertains to the time of the AFM recording ban, a topic to be addressed in due course.
3. Interview with Joy Nolcox Gaddie, Indianapolis, June 22, 1993.
4. Interview with Mary Ann Topper, New York, November 29, 1993.
5. Interview with Billy Johnson, Indianapolis, June 24, 1993.
6. Interview with Rosemary Johnson Belcher, Chicago, June 26, 1993.
7. Henry Martin, *Enjoying Jazz* (New York: Schirmer Books, 1986), 143 and 250.
8. Alun Morgan, "Illinois Jacquet," *Jazz Monthly*, vol. 9, no. 7 (September 1963), 9.
9. Jim Burns, "Lesser Known Bands of the Forties, No. 6: Illinois Jacquet, Roy Porter, Machito," *Jazz Monthly*, no. 164 (October 1968).
10. J.J. Johnson interviewed by Tom Everett, *International Trombone Association Journal*, vol. 16 (Summer 1988), 23.
11. "An Interview With Some All-Stars," *Playboy*, vol. 2 (November 1955), 44. This is a transcript of a radio interview with Dizzy Gillespie and Coleman Hawkins that was conducted by Jean Sheppard on WOR Mutual Radio, June 11, 1955.
12. Miles Davis with Quincy Troupe, *Miles: The Autobiography* (New York: Simon and Schuster, 1989), 125.
13. *Ibid.,* 124–125.

14. *Ibid.,* 82.

15. *The New York Times Book Review*, October 15, 1989, 7:1

16. Davis with Troupe, *Miles*, 61.

17. Interview with J.J. Johnson, New York, December 21, 1994. Reconstructing an accurate chronology of Johnson's after-hours social life with Miles Davis is well-nigh impossible, especially given Davis's propensity for "jive," not to mention the fallibility of human memory, Johnson's included. Nor does it help much to know that Parker recorded "Confirmation" in 1953.

18. "Capitolizing" is named for Capitol Records—a suggestion by Lewis Porter.

19. Interview with J.J. Johnson.

20. *The Miles Davis Radio Project*, produced by Steve Rowland with Quincy Troupe and Jay Allison. ZOUK Productions, 1990, Show 2.

21. Frank Tirro, "The Silent Theme Tradition in Jazz," *The Musical Quarterly*, vol. 53, no. 3 (July 1967), 313–334.

22. *Ibid.,* 313.

23. Richard Crawford has exhaustively examined the song's performance history in the final chapter of his magisterial book, *The American Musical Landscape* (Berkeley: University of California Press, 1993).

24. This aspect of Johnson's output is touched upon in David N. Baker, *J.J. Johnson: Trombone*, Jazz Monograph Series (New York: Shattinger International Music, 1979), 14.

25. More comprehensive treatment of these topics can be found in Louis G. Bourgois, III, *Jazz Trombonist J.J. Johnson: A Comprehensive Discography and Study of the Early Evolution of His Style* (D.M.A. dissertation, The Ohio State University, 1986) and David N. Baker, *J.J. Johnson: Trombone*, Jazz Monograph Series (New York: Shattinger International Music, 1979). Johnson's use of unifying devices in particular is a subject worthy of further study. From time to time *Jazz Educators Journal* has included transcriptions and analysis of Johnson solos where this facet of his style has been addressed. See, for example, *Jazz Educators Journal* (Winter 1989), 36–37, for a discussion by Lawrence McClellan, Jr. of the unifying triplets in Johnson's recording of "Walkin'" (Columbia CL 1161, recorded February 19, 1958).

26. *The New Grove Dictionary of Jazz*, Barry Kernfeld, ed., (London: Macmillan Press, 1988), I, 622.

27. The role of quotation in jazz is a fascinating one revealing a great deal about the cognitive process of the borrower and his or her relationship to the material borrowed. See, for example, Joshua Berrett, "Louis Armstrong and Opera," *The Musical Quarterly*, vol. 76, no. 2 (Summer 1992), 216–241. Also Krin Gabbard, "The Quoter and His Culture," in *Jazz in Mind*, edited by Reginald T. Buckner and Steven Weiland (Detroit: Wayne State University Press, 1991), 92–111.

28. Arnold Shaw, *52nd Street: The Street of Jazz* (New York: Da Capo, 1977), 251–252.

29. *Ibid.,* 256.

30. *Ibid.,* 350.

31. Nat Shapiro and Nat Hentoff, *Hear Me Talkin' to Ya* (New York: Dover Publications, 1966), 367–368.

32. Interview with Joe Gourdin, New Orleans, June 12, 1991.

33. Jack Chambers, *Milestones: The Music and Times of Miles Davis*, 2 vols.,

(Toronto: University of Toronto Press, 1983), I, 145. Chambers's text contains a misspelling of trombonist Bennie Green's name (Benny Green).

34. Ira Gitler, *Jazz Masters of the Forties* (New York: Collier Macmillan, 1966), 158–159.

35. Ross Russell, *Bird Lives! The High Life and Hard Times of Charlie (Yardbird) Parker* (London: Quartet Books, 1973), 260.

36. Davis with Troupe, *Miles*, 129.

37. Neil Leonard, *Jazz: Myth and Religion* (New York: Oxford University Press, 1987), 111–113.

38. Interview with J.J. Johnson, Indianapolis, February 1, 1995.

39. The letter of Stan Getz is featured by Jack Tracy in the column "Narcotics and Music," *Down Beat*, April 21, 1954, 3.

40. Charles Winick, "The Use of Drugs by Jazz Musicians," *Social Problems*, vol. 7, no. 3 (Winter 1959–60), 240–253.

41. Kenneth Allsop, "Jazz and Narcotics," *Encounter*, vol. 12 (June 1961), 55.

42. John Birks Gillespie, *To Be or Not . . . To Bop: Memoirs,* compiled by Al Frazier (Garden City, N.Y.: Doubleday, 1979), 444.

43. Interview with J.J. Johnson, Indianapolis, January 17, 1995.

44. *The Sperry Corporation. Twenty-first Annual Report* (for the year ended December 31, 1953), 11.

45. Interview with Bob Gangel, Babylon, New York, January 5, 1995.

46. Ira Gitler, "A Tranquil Frame of Mind: The Remarkable J.J. Johnson," *Down Beat*, May 11, 1961, 17.

Chapter 4

Once that record started happening . . .

Johnson's musical career was far from dormant during his nearly two-year stint (August 1952 to May 1954) with Sperry Gyroscope and for the balance of the decade. Even though his permanent cabaret card was not to be reinstated before 1959, he found ample opportunity to make recordings and perform in venues outside of the jurisdiction of the New York Police Department, whether in the United States or abroad. In the process he was able to leave his mark on hard bop, cool jazz, third-stream developments, and more.

Two sextet recording sessions, in April and June of 1953, and both for Blue Note, are telling in the sharp contrasts they offer. The first, featuring Miles Davis's sextet, is notable for the rhythmic tension generated by Art Blakey and the melodic sensitivity of Davis rather than any exceptional playing by Johnson. The session two months later, however, reveals Johnson in superb form fronting a group consisting of Clifford Brown, Jimmy Heath (on both tenor and baritone saxophone), John Lewis, Percy Heath, and Kenny Clarke.[1] Featuring elaborately arranged tunes, the session included the popular standards "Lover Man," "It Could Happen to You," and "Get Happy." But even more important were the original compositions recorded: Lewis's "Sketch One," Gigi Gryce's "Capri," and Johnson's own "Turnpike."

Played at a punishing tempo ($\quarternote = 160$), "Turnpike" opens with Kenny Clarke's highly charged ride cymbal work, which in turn introduces a passage for the front line having all the earmarks of the quartal-sound palette of Paul Hindemith.

As a composition from 1953 "Turnpike" is the artifact of a period when Paul Hindemith was at the height of his influence in the United States; he was, among other things, on the faculty of the Yale University School of Music from 1940 to 1953, he occupied the Charles Eliot Norton Chair at Harvard University from 1949 to 1950, and from 1945 to 1953 presented notable concerts of early music. Johnson has acknowledged the profound influence of Hindemith on his own writing, particularly on such later works as his *Poem for Brass* and *Perceptions*—a topic to be explored later in this chapter. What is worth noting here, however, is not simply the blurring of boundaries between jazz and classical music, but the relative weight that the

Fig. 4.1   Miles Davis's sextet at WOR studios in New York, May 9, 1952. Shown are Percy Heath, *left*; Miles Davis, *center*; J.J. Johnson, *right*. Photograph courtesy of J.J. Johnson.

Hindemith-inflected introduction imparts to "Turnpike" as a whole, affecting its larger proportions and overall conception.[2] In other words, it is more than simply another example of a silent-theme number, illustrating another turn in which musicians "run the changes" of Gershwin's all-time popular standard, "I Got Rhythm." By the same token, this is a multifaceted piece with its share of allusions to Paul Hindemith, Count Basie, and others. Thus the opening two-note riff of the head, something of a Johnson signature, suggests that the trombonist-composer has learned something from the earlier lessons of his Kansas City mentor, specifically from "Lester Leaps In" (1939), not to mention Thelonious Monk's "Thelonious" (1947).[3] In addition, the very title, "Turnpike," remains a provocative one, despite various disclaimers by Johnson.

> The title of Turnpike was like the titles of most of my tunes. As a matter of fact, I would say 98 percent of J.J. Johnson original compositions that have a title . . . the title comes about because you have to call the tune something. You just call it the first thing that comes into your mind. . . . the tendency is to hope that the title has some poetic or some . . . profound connection to the music. That's wonderful when it happens. In my case it never is the case. At the eleventh hour you grab a title out of thin air. Ninety-eight percent of all my titles are eleventh-hour desperation titles.[4]

Certain automotive imperatives, some driven by the facts of Johnson's personal life, others by larger events of the 1950s, lead one to question whether a title such as "Turnpike" can be dismissed as an eleventh-hour "desperation title" pure and simple. While there was apparently no conscious, immediate source of inspiration for the title, the work clearly was not conceived in a total vacuum. Put another way—and this is a daunting question for cognitive psychology in general—what is it that actually triggers "the first thing that comes into your mind"? It is most likely Miles Davis, and his driving habits and taste in cars, that provide some tantalizing clues. As noted in the previous chapter, there is little reason to doubt that, starting in the late 1940s, he and Johnson were "tight"—a word used by both Johnson himself and Miles Davis—and spent many of their off-hours together, whether in Penn Station or in Davis's car.

Thus the lure of high horsepower seems to have made its impact early on in their relationship. Some time later, after a gig in Philadelphia with Davis, the two of them decided to drive back to New York in Davis's car. Not quite sober, Davis could not make it past the toll booth and insisted that Johnson take the wheel. This he proceeded to do, only to be given a speeding ticket on the New Jersey Turnpike.[5] Reaching New York and delivering Miles home, Johnson was flabbergasted to be offered the car for two weeks to use as he wished. Offering what is part intimate confession, part an expression of ecstasy, he put his reactions to driving the twelve-cylinder Ferrari as follows:

Fig. 4.2 Excerpt from "Turnpike," front-line introduction, recorded
June 22, 1953.

Fig. 4.3   J.J. Johnson, the composer at work, at WOR studios in New York, June 22, 1953, during "The Eminent J.J. Johnson, vol. 1" recording session. Photograph courtesy of J.J. Johnson.

> There is no sensation that one can experience with all his clothes on that comes anywhere close to depressing the accelerator pedal of a Ferrari. Words cannot approach the sensation of applying your foot and pressure to the foot pedal of a Ferrari. If you think I'm exaggerating, multiply what I'm saying by a factor of about a hundred, and you'll be fairly close to what I'm really trying to say.[6]

Returning to the music itself, Conrad Herwig, one of the outstanding trombonists of the younger generation and one who, like many, acknowledges J.J. Johnson as the spiritual father of modern trombone, has said that the two volumes of the Blue Note release were the very first J.J. Johnson records that he ever bought. They profoundly influenced him during his own formative years in the early 1970s for their technical virtuosity and sense of compositional integrity. Speaking of individual titles, Herwig has singled out "a couple of ones that I think are unbelievable. There's a cut with Clifford Brown called 'Turnpike' and another one that has a phenomenal J.J. solo called 'Coffee Pot.' I was totally hooked on trombone."[7] Robin Eubanks, another major trombone talent of Herwig's generation, had a similar but more daunting experience with the album. "I put it on thinking I would learn one of these solos. The first one was 'Turnpike' and I took it off and put it away for a year because it scared me so much."[8]

The sense of a pre-eminent bebop musician almost constantly on the go as he was coming into his own is inescapable as one assesses Johnson's career during the balance of the 1950s. One is, in fact, tempted to think of it as a "turnpike period" of sorts in that he and his reputation were traveling as never before. A case in point is Johnson's recording with French pianist and producer Henri Renaud, who, in the early months of 1954 was working with tenor saxophonist Al Cohn in New York. Fully aware of the high esteem in which Johnson was held in Europe, Renaud called on him to join an all-star group to record for the French Vogue label. With such musicians as Milt Jackson on vibes, Percy Heath on bass, and Charlie Smith on drums, Johnson found himself collaborating with colleagues to produce sides of the highest quality in every respect. In fact, the album resulting from the session of March 7 was awarded the equivalent of an Oscar by the French Jazz Academy for the best record of 1954. The familiarity of the popular standards chosen was certainly no less a factor than the execution of musical ideas, what with such titles as "I'll Remember April," "There's No You," "Out of Nowhere," and "Indiana." Johnson's improvisations on this date attest to a compelling sense of unity and developmental structure—handsome dividends generated during the period of withdrawal associated with his working at Sperry Gyroscope.

His session of April 29, 1954, for Prestige with the Miles Davis sextet, serves as a defining moment in funky hard bop with its emphasis on blues material rather than popular song. Other members of the ensemble were tenor saxophonist Lucky Thompson, pianist Horace Silver, bassist Percy Heath, and drummer Kenny Clarke. The fact that Prestige would not pay for rehearsals put each player on his mettle, especially Miles Davis. Scholars such as Ian Carr have referred to this as the session in which "Miles produced his first full-scale masterpiece and did it in a most casual, almost accidental way."[9] He quotes Horace Silver as saying that Miles had a genius for spontaneous head arrangements, sitting with his head in his hands while the others were setting up. Davis would then show them voicings and rhythms, which the group would try a few times. This occasion, however, posed a special challenge in that the arrangement brought by Lucky Thompson to the session turned out to please no one. As Horace Silver put it: "We busked [prepared] a couple of head arrangements which turned out to be classics!"[10] These were the medium-tempo blues "Walkin'" and the faster-paced "Blue 'N' Boogie." What is memorable are not only such details of the head of "Walkin'" as the evocative flatted fifth and the stark sound of its call-and-response pattern; there is also a sense of symmetry and organic unity to the whole, with Davis's seven opening choruses leading logically to the seven of Johnson's, culminating in Lucky Thompson's saxophone solo, which at its climax is backed by a figure from the head played by Davis and Johnson. For his part, Johnson fondly remembers Horace Silver—he plays an interlude that eventually leads to the reprise—for his unique rhythmic sense.

> I loved the tapping of his feet as much as his playing. He had the most rhythmic foot tap of most musicians. The whole ball and toe of his shoe would come up about six inches off the floor with every beat of the piece. He was a one-man rhythm section.[11]

Almost four years later Johnson was to record "Walkin'" again, this time fronting a quintet that included Nat Adderley on cornet, Tommy Flanagan on piano, Wilbur Little on bass, and Albert Heath playing drums. Retaining the original F-minor head arrangement, Johnson's remake is in a brisker tempo and, at 6:33, clocks in at slightly less than half the time of the original 13:19. Johnson's later version is rather striking in the way that it dilutes the funky content, confining it to the head, the out chorus, and the tag. Taking a series of six fleet choruses directly after presentation of the head, Johnson offers a completely fresh take on the original; it is one that revels in a transcendent virtuosity all in the service of a solo that is tightly integrated by triplet motives and includes such "progressive" features as augmented passing chords descending by whole steps.[12]

Fig. 4.4   Augmented passing chords descending by whole steps in "Walkin'," mm. 27–31, J.J. Johnson solo, recorded February 19, 1958.

Returning to the Johnson/Renaud collaboration earlier in the decade and its enthusiastic reception by the French public brings up a critical issue of cultural context. The decade of the 1950s is striking for the degree to which African-American jazzmen were befriended and feted in centers like Paris, their recordings very much sought after. Coinciding with a period when racism was rampant in the United States, the mood of the time was poignantly expressed in the haunting rhetorical question, "What Did I Do to Be So Black and Blue?" as originally posed in the prologue to Ralph Ellison's *Invisible Man*.[13] Then again, a symptom of the explosive nature of race relations at the time was President Dwight D. Eisenhower dispatching federal troops to Little Rock, Arkansas, on September 24, 1957, to enforce a federal desegregation order. Meanwhile, what captures the Parisian jazz scene most vividly in the 1950s are such literary works as James Baldwin's semi-autobiographical account of transplanted jazzmen in the French capital, *Another Country*. And most compelling of all are the Paris sojourns of Bud Powell and Lester Young at the end of the decade. It is a phase reenacted in the semi-fictional conflation presented in Bertrand Tavernier's 1986 movie *'Round Midnight*, the soundtrack of which happens to include a selection ("Minuit Aux Champs Elysées") composed by Henri Renaud himself.

Johnson's own immediate career was rejuvenated by his success with the Renaud recordings and others in the spring of 1954. Indeed, it appears that a date with Savoy Records had a great deal to do with his decision to leave Sperry Gyroscope in May 1954. The dawning of the most commercially successful phase of his career was at hand with Johnson working in a small ensemble that had no precedent in its duetting trombone instrumentation—the J.J. Johnson/Kai Winding Quintet.

The circumstances which actually brought the two trombonists together are rather vague, and Johnson's own recollections are somewhat contradictory. In the April 1955 issue of *Metronome* Johnson offered this version:

> It's almost an accident that we got together. Our paths were always crossing after we first met in the clubs on 52nd Street . . . then Kai was booked into a Philadelphia club with a local rhythm section and the booker got the idea that it might be good to have two trombones for the job, and he called me.[14]

The popular notion, documented in the liner notes to Savoy SJL-2232 (a reissue LP) is that sometime in the summer of 1954 producer Ozzie Cadena, a Savoy A&R man, hit upon the idea for a duo trombone and rhythm section in his search for a "new sound." Johnson recalled:

> The original game plan called for me and Bennie Green, but Bennie at that time had a little hit going with his own combo, so he wasn't particularly interested. I think it was Ozzie Cadena who first introduced me to Kai Winding. I knew him, of course, but I had never known him personally.[15]

Yet more recently Johnson has given full credit to Teddy Reig, Savoy Records producer, for his initiative in forming the trombone partnership.

> Bennie Green opted not to become part of this unusual situation, so Teddy Reig said: "Let's try Kai Winding." I didn't know Kai personally at that time. I knew of him; I knew his work and that he was an excellent trombonist and I knew he was a nice person too. When we finally did get hold of Kai he was immediately interested in the idea.[16]

The two trombonists began working together in mid-August 1954 at the Blue Note club in Philadelphia, located at the time at 15th Street and Ridge Avenue.[17] Later that month—August 24 and 26—they entered the Savoy studios in New York to record eight sides. Those produced at the first session were unique in their use of a guitar, in the person of Billy Bauer, rather than a piano as a chording instrument. Johnson and Winding joined forces with Billy Bauer, bassist Charles Mingus, and drummer Kenny Clarke to record "Blues for Trombones," "What Is This Thing Called Love?," "The Major," and Johnson's own "Lament." The second session, on August 26, with pianist Wally Cirillo replacing Billy Bauer, saw the group recording the four remaining sides—"Bernie's Tune," "Reflections," "Co-op," and "Blues in Twos."

Despite the novelty of their sound, the group did not work together as a full-time unit until several months later. This phase was launched on October 17, 1954, when, before an invited audience, a reorganized Jay and Kai Quintet performed at Birdland. There was now a new rhythm section consisting of bassist Peck Morrison, drummer Al Harewood, and pianist Dick Katz. Although other rhythm personnel would come and go, Dick Katz remained with the group until it disbanded almost two years later.

Katz, who worked with Winding before the Jay and Kai Quintet years, has shared an amusing aside about Kai Winding's pre-Johnson career. It seems that Winding found that people in the United States, unlike those back home in Denmark, could not get the sound of his name quite right—mispronouncing it Kai (as in "pay") rather than Kai (as in "pie"). Rumor has it that a contretemps of sexual identity occurred when he showed up at a date to find that the benighted booking agent, who had presumably never heard of such bandleaders as Kay Kyser, had had the following posted in bold letters on the marquee: "Kai Winding and Her Orchestra." Winding lost no time in changing all of that.[18] Besides, according to Katz, to a man known for his sardonic humor and flashes of hot temper, it was perhaps par for the course.

Showing up at a gig could be fraught with other risks as well, as Johnson was to discover early on. Apparently Winding was a person who did not bother warming up and was in the habit of getting to a job "close to hitting time."[19] Johnson, who would have none of this, ended up having to buy his first car, a two-door Buick Roadmaster, so that he could arrive well ahead of time in order to warm his chops, taking anywhere from fifteen minutes to a full hour.

According to Katz, the Birdland event itself occurred at a point when Jay and Kai, acutely aware that their quintet book was still rather thin, realized that they had to fill up time. Consequently, four of the six selections recorded live at Birdland on that occasion range from almost six and a half to close to nine minutes. As their "book" gained in heft so did their live as well as studio performances come to average between two and a half and five minutes.[20] They didn't compromise the music at all, but the concession they made to the commercial world was to keep the performances short.[21]

Kai Winding, reportedly the one with the more commercial flair, had his eye on the cash register, entertained ambitions of becoming another writer like Nelson Riddle, and hoped to make it big in Hollywood someday.[22] Not that Johnson himself was totally immune to such temptation, as attested by his joining the New York commercial jingle firm of MBA Music, Inc., in 1967 and moving out to Hollywood three years later. More pointedly and immediately, it was the duo's hit arrangement of the Cole Porter standard "It's All Right with Me" that prompted the Johnson quip: "Once that record started happening, we decided to drop everything else and go out and do our thing together."[23] For Dick Katz, however, doing "our thing together" could take its toll. "We used to have to play that at least two or three times a night . . . and it was on jukeboxes . . . and I remember getting thoroughly sick of the tune."[24] Yet he does at the same time take pride in the piano part's touches of chordal and rhythmic counterpoint that clearly go beyond simple comping.

The general conception of the arrangements in their book belongs to a larger tradition that was concerned with ensemble performance, where the solo was but part of a larger whole. For Katz it was inseparable from the big-band practice associated with Henderson, Basie, Carter, Ellington, Lunceford, and others. With the advent of bebop and its emphasis on solo virtuosity in the small ensemble such a practice was undermined. Yet ironically, Parker, Gillespie, and Johnson exemplified a unique performance style.

> Their extreme improvising virtuosity seemed to take the focus off the need to play as a group. But herein lies the irony—the precision with which they played their complex *tours de force* was due in large measure to the extensive ensemble experience they gleaned as members of disciplined bands like Hines, Eckstine.[25]

Katz's observations are fully consistent with what writers have had to say more recently about the nature of stylistic change in jazz history—that bebop, rather than being part of the inexorable "cycle of change," drew its leading practitioners from those who had apprenticed in the big bands and smaller jump bands of the war years.[26] The apprenticeships of Dizzy Gillespie and Charlie Parker with Teddy Hill and Jay McShann, respectively, are among the best known. But then again there are the greater subtleties of big-band-inspired arranging just noted, not to mention the shaping of the kinds of riffs heard in the head of Johnson's "Turnpike."

Given all that has been said, it is not surprising that the Jay and Kai Quintet was to a large extent a formal group, with arrangements made of everything and little left to chance. Tight control extended to both music and the purse. "They split everything down the middle . . . and if there were fifty pieces in the book you can be sure that Kai wrote close to twenty-five of them and Jay the others."[27] Members of the rhythm section were kept on a tight leash as well, but it apparently had its virtues in that people learned when to play as much as when not to. "I got a free education in how a rhythm section is supposed to play because J.J. wrote out the rhythm section parts. A lot was not left to chance. There were the breaks. They were structured in some ways like big-band arrangements."[28]

The Jay and Kai Quintet discography includes some telling examples of big-band simulations. A case in point is the selection "It's Sand, Man," very much in the Count Basie mold, complete with plunger-mute shout chorus and a reworking of the familiar piano tag. Other instances, such as "Yes Sir, That's My Baby," feature lush barbershop-harmony voicings supported by three-note chords in the piano. Most characteristic of all is the sense of drama that Johnson and Winding impart in their treatment of the chase chorus. Many examples come to mind, among them "It's All Right with Me," "Side by Side," and "This Could Be the Start of Something." Such choruses make their impact not only because of differences in timbre on the open instruments—Winding tended to have a somewhat coarser, grainier sound—but also thanks to the virtuosic use of various mutes, as in "It's All Right with Me," "I Concentrate on You," and "Just for a Thrill."

Kai Winding addressed the challenge of maintaining musical interest without the benefit of reed color in the following words:

> We're always working on new ways of presentation. The two-trombone setup, to begin with, gives a lot of potential color changes and a range of sounds that don't clash. We also add variety by often splitting the lead, and from time to time, we alternate playing solos alone. J.J. plays, for example, tunes associated with him like "Capri," "Afternoon in Paris," or "Turnpike," and I'll do "Honey" or "Always" or "The Boy Next Door."[29]

Elsewhere, as in the introduction to "Mad about the Boy," one can find dark, intense writing. At a minor-seventh above Milt Hinton's D pedal point the horns begin a brooding, ascending chromatic line, their parts interlocking, and culminating in a whole-tone wash on the piano. It all serves perfectly to set the tone of the melancholy, F-minor-centered opening phrase of the head.

One of the more unusual phases of the Jay and Kai collaboration occurred in the spring and summer of 1956, primarily in the recording studio. As part of an effort to vary the timbre and texture of their ensemble they formed a trombone octet that included a rare specimen called a trombonium. This instrument, which is also featured in their final 1956 recording session as a quintet, is an upright valve trombone. It is similar in size to the nineteenth-century baritone horn that was

Fig. 4.5 The Jay and Kai Quintet during its June 24, 1955, recording session (Columbia CL742, *Trombone for Two*). Pictured are Dick Katz (piano and celesta), *below left*; Paul Chambers (bass), *above left*; Osie Johnson (drums and percussion), *above center*; producer George Avakian, *center*; Johnson, *right*, and Winding, *below right* (trombones). Photograph courtesy of Aram Avakian.

Fig. 4.6 An undated King Musical Instruments, Inc. advertisement for its King 3B Concert Trombone, featuring J.J. Johnson and Kai Winding. Courtesy of United Musical Instruments, Inc.

common in brass marching bands of the era and has been used in such bands until very recently. But unlike the baritone horn the trombonium has a cylindrical bore. In his liner notes for the final 1956 session, Charles Edward Smith writes about the instrument and its music with an engaging wit and panache, invoking the name of a star baseball pitcher known for his curveball.

> This brings us to the trombonium, an improbable-looking instrument with almost as many curves as Sal Maglie. . . . It is held upright, so that the bell seems to protrude from the fore-head, adding to its out-of-this-world appearance. The valves are pressed from the side . . . reminding one in its seeming awkwardness of the bunt position in baseball. . . . "Tromboniums," with its slurs and slides, has a brass band quality, especially in the whangy guttural tones . . . I hear delicate harmonies riding on that circus trombone sound.[30]

For all their superb technique and consummate artistry, the Jay and Kai ensemble would have been unlikely to succeed as well as it did without the backing of strong record production and distribution. Significantly, the ensemble was associated only briefly with the Savoy label, where A&R man Ozzie Cadena reportedly made the critical decision to bring them together in the first place. Their subsequent 1955 hit "It's All Right with Me," on the Bethlehem label, was the product of a young, aggressive start-up company that had been founded only two years before. What was ultimately invaluable, however, was their fourteen-month contract with Columbia Records, where they had the good fortune of working with pioneer producer George Avakian. It was he who was primarily responsible for producing some thirty-seven titles, including the selections recorded live at their final major public appearance at the Newport Jazz Festival on July 6, 1956.

Like many others, Avakian was taken with the Jay/Kai hit "It's All Right with Me" on Bethlehem. Though he had previously heard Johnson and Winding individually, he had never before realized how exciting a sound the duo could produce with their spectacular arrangements and playing. What is more, he was in a position to give them access to a much larger market than was available to an independent distributor like Bethlehem.

> One of the things that helped them was that at Columbia Records we were the pioneer company for the manufacture and distribution of the long-playing record. . . . So the market was wide open at that time. LP players were proliferating and Columbia had a head start in filling the demand. Also, at that time we started the Columbia Record Mail Order Club. I was in charge of popular albums, which meant that virtually everything, except classical recordings, came out of my department. So I had a great deal of say as to what product went into the Columbia Record Club. . . . There was a separate jazz category which gave especial attention to artists who had never been spotlighted before, unless they happened to be hugely popular on their own, like a Benny Goodman, a Duke Ellington or a Louis Armstrong. And Jay and Kai were the

Fig. 4.7   Manuscript leadsheet of "Lament" in J.J. Johnson's hand.

combination that profited from that because they shared the attention which the very biggest names in the business received through the Special Features of the booklet that went out every month.[31]

Avakian remembers what a delight it was working with them in that they knew exactly what they wanted. Ideas had usually already been tested on the road, and Johnson in particular instinctively knew how best to present his material. He was attuned to what went over well with his fans and was able to transfer that to the medium of the LP. Because they were almost invariably thoroughly prepared, there was minimal editing to do after a typical session. Above all, Avakian found that watching Jay and Kai at work during a recording session was almost as much fun as listening.

> When they trade off alternating muted phrases on a fast tune, as in "The Whiffenpoof Song," it's a wild sight to see them each keeping pace with the lightning routine of mute up, mute in, blow, mute out, mute down, new mute up, mute in, blow and so on. Never once did either ever fluff a phrase or even blow a bad one. Nor were there any easy clichés. Even under pressure, each listened carefully to what the other was playing and kept a logical line flowing.[32]

As a producer he was especially sensitive to the sequencing of titles on the LP, which usually consisted of ten titles averaging about four minutes in duration. Starting every LP with an attention-grabber, he structured the record in such a way as to avoid monotony, very much along the lines of a radio program. The end of the first side, corresponding to the half-time commercial break, had to persuade the listener to turn the record over. The second side would then ideally match the structure of the first. There was, however, a limit to what one could sell on trombone and, for Avakian, Jay and Kai showed savvy in each moving on to other things, as they did after some two years together. Every conceivable facet of duo trombone playing had been explored.

Meanwhile, the cumulative impact of Johnson's recent career on listeners, critics, and fellow musicians alike was immense. For the two consecutive years of 1955 and 1956 Johnson had led the trombone balloting in readers' polls conducted by *Down Beat* and *Metronome*. Enhancing his stature even more during this same period were not only the international *Down Beat* critics' polls, but also the pride of place given him some four years running in the Paris-based *Jazz Hot*. Finally, when Leonard Feather polled over one hundred jazzmen on their choice of trombonist for his 1956 publication *The Encyclopedia Yearbook of Jazz*, Johnson came in first.

It was in this heady atmosphere that Johnson made a major creative leap as he became involved in third-stream composition, an engagement that can be traced to his earlier association with Miles Davis and Gil Evans in the Birth of the Cool sessions. Now he was hanging out with a distinctive coterie of musicians who gravitated to Gil's place, "a room in a basement on 55th Street, near 5th Avenue . . . behind a Chinese laundry and [with] all the pipes for the building as well as a sink, a bed, a piano, a hot plate, and no heat."[33] Intent upon incorporating into jazz certain sonorities and compositional techniques of twentieth-century and baroque music, this group included such musicians as Gerry Mulligan, John Carisi, John Lewis, Max Roach, and Lee Konitz. Johnson has credited Carisi in particular for introducing him to such major scores as Stravinsky's *Rite of Spring* and *Firebird,* and Ravel's *Daphnis and Chloé,* not to mention seminal works by Richard Strauss, Bartók, and Bloch.[34] In addition, Johnson, through the influence of such mentors as Gunther Schuller, had become extremely familiar with such Hindemith works as *Mathis der Maler* and *Kleine Kammermusik,* Op. 24, No. 2. In fact, in the course of a 1994 interview, at a point when discussion was focused on his *Perceptions* (1961), Johnson offered the following observation before spontaneously singing the opening six measures of Hindemith's *Kleine Kammermusik*:

> If there's anything I discovered on listening to *Perceptions* after that long cycle of time, I heard in all its glory my fascination with Hindemith's treatment of brass harmonies. It's glaring that J.J. loves the way Hindemith writes for brass.
>
> [J.B.: Like *Mathis der Maler*?]
>
> For me that's the quintessential Hindemith, along with other pieces. His woodwind octet, it's masterful—*Kleine Kammermusik*—[sings opening six measures]. Oh, it's a marvelous work![35]

Johnson's *Poem for Brass*—also known as *Suite for Brass*—represents his first major third-stream essay, combining an unmistakable Central European sensibility with jazz idioms. Completed in 1956, it was, quite appropriately, premiered and recorded that year by the Brass Ensemble of the Jazz and Classical Music Society. Started in 1955 by John Lewis and Gunther Schuller, the society was an organization "to present authoritative and exemplary concert performances of rarely heard music. The emphasis was placed on contemporary music, including that written by composers in the jazz field who would not otherwise have an opportunity for their less conventional work to be presented under concert conditions."[36]

Running to very slightly under ten minutes' duration, *Poem for Brass* is Johnson's most extended composition prior to *Perceptions* and requires a sizable ensemble of twenty pieces, specifically solo flugelhorn and trombone (originally vehicles for Miles Davis and J.J. Johnson, respectively), six trumpets, four French horns, three trombones, two baritone saxophones, one tuba, one string bass, percussion. The work consists of an introduction joined to a body of seven interconnected sections with the following basic profile:

Introduction, Part 1:   mm. 1–12; 4/4, Largo cantabile

Introduction, Part 2:   mm. 13–28; 3/2, Moderately quick

A: mm. 1–52; 4/4, Gentle, with common material shared by the ensemble and Miles Davis on flugelhorn;

B: mm. 1–36; 4/4, without tempo marking;

C: mm. 1–44; 4/4, without tempo marking; comparable to **A** with Johnson on solo trombone;

mm. 45–47; 4/4, Slow (Transition to Interlude);

D: mm. 1–14; alternating meters of 4/4, 5/4, and 3/4;

Interlude; mm. 15–36; 4/4;

Ballad; a vehicle for Joe Wilder's trumpet, culminating in a lush show-band ending.

E: mm. 1–56; 4/4, medium swing tempo;

F: mm. 1–64; 2/2, without tempo marking; fugal exposition;

G: mm. 1–44; 2/2, without tempo marking; coda.

What is apparent from the score itself, rather than immediately heard in listening, is a charming contradiction between the Central European sensibility previously touched upon and Johnson's fidelity to jazz practice. On the one hand, he draws upon unifying motives in the Austro-German manner of a Brahms or Richard Strauss, anticipates his coda by working a climactic fugal exposition into the design, often uses a Hindemith-derived pentatonicism, and includes in his scoring a quartet of French horns—admittedly filtered through a Claude Thornhill/Gil Evans experience.[37] On the other hand, by providing a separate numbering of measures for the seven individual sections—obviously very practical for rehearsal purposes—Johnson tends to emphasize the episodic, accentuating the distinctive character and timbre of each such section, whether an interlude, ballad, or passage in swing tempo.

Johnson's introduction contains the seeds of many ideas that grow in the body of the work, helping unify the whole. For example, the falling-sixth motif, announced by unison trumpets and trombones in the opening four measures, not only launches section A but also, as it unfolds, provides the essential material supporting the subsequent solos of both Davis and Johnson.

POEM FOR BRASS

Fig. 4.8 Reproduction of page 1 of the score *Poem for Brass,* introduction, mm. 1–5.

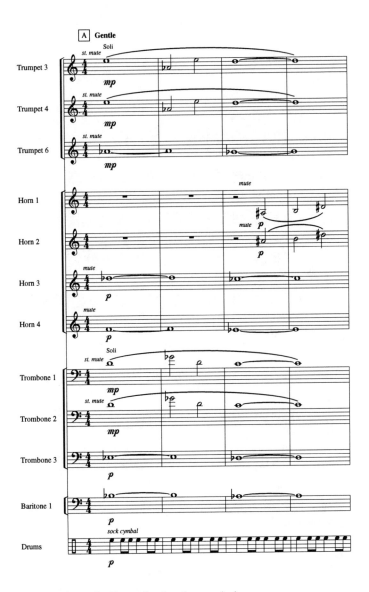

Fig. 4.9 *Poem for Brass,* Section A, mm. 1–4.

Fig. 4.10 *Poem for Brass,* Section B, mm. 41–44, and Section C, mm.1–3.

Then again Johnson's fugue subject, announced by unison trumpets, is essentially a transformation of material previously heard.

Fig. 4.11   *Poem for Brass,* Section A, mm. 9–13.

Fig. 4.12   *Poem for Brass,* Section F, mm. 1–4, prefiguration of fugue subject.

Hints of Hindemith's influence abound in Johnson's score from beginning to end. Consider, for example, the climactic close, which suggests a strong affinity with the parallel portion of *Mathis der Maler.*

Fig. 4.13   Hindemith, *Mathis der Maler,* "The Temptation of St. Anthony," "Alleluia," rehearsal no. 34, mm. 13–17.

Fig. 4.14   *Poem for Brass,* final 8 mm.

But the introduction itself provides some compelling instances. These include the following passage, with its characteristic pentatonic sonorities, which culminates in an ascending half-step, "decapitating" cadence—the third of three—directly followed by a roll.

Fig. 4.15   *Poem for Brass,* introduction, mm. 15–21.

Fig. 4.16   Hindemith, *Mathis der Maler,* "The Temptation of St. Anthony," mm. 13–18.

Rather than represent a slavish imitation of Hindemith, this particular cadential gesture, with its ascending half step, is part of a dynamic transformational process, one attesting to Johnson's immense skill in working it into the overall form, helping unify a large-scale structure. It is a process initiated in the form of a two-note seed first planted in measure 3, where third trombone and tuba move in parallel fifths, on D-E and A-B, respectively; and the work's climactic fugue and coda mark the culmination of the process.

Fig. 4.17   *Poem for Brass,* p. 35, mm. 41–47.

During the 1956–57 period, when he was riding the crest of a wave of critical and popular acclaim associated with the *Down Beat* and *Metronome* polls, Johnson was able to turn his attention to more standard jazz fare as well. His recording of the album *First Place* for Columbia in April 1957 provides a vivid example. It is one that posed a rather daunting challenge of having to provide some forty minutes' worth of music drawing upon the resources of only a quartet consisting of himself, with Max Roach, Paul Chambers, and Tommy Flanagan on drums, bass, and piano, respectively. This is an album that acquired a certain cachet among members of the younger set like Robin Eubanks. He has recalled that when he first came to New York and was hanging out at Slide Hampton's place people would sit around all day drinking in the sounds of *First Place*.[38]

By all accounts the recording of *First Place* turned out to be a joyous affair from start to finish and marked a distinct departure from the more controlled arrangements of the Jay/Kai sessions. According to Nat Hentoff, it was

> more of a blowing date, a suggestion by J.J. with which Columbia's head of jazz and popular albums, George Avakian, quickly concurred. There *were* sketches on each number—J.J. is so precise a spirit by temperament that he is not apt to leave all to luck, even on a blowing date. And in some cases there were even fuller arrangements. But basically, the four sessions that made up this and a succeeding album were conceived and executed as relatively free, almost entirely improvised conversations.[39]

First Place, while embodying a core repertory of the jazz market of the late 1950's, is nevertheless rather far-ranging. There are ballads, "reanimated" standards on the order of "It's Only a Paper Moon," a few originals, and a blues. Unmistakable throughout is the consummate artistry touching every aspect of form, phrase structure, deployment of instruments, timbre, articulation, and rhythm. In Sonny Rollins's piece "Paul's Pal," for example, there is a delicious duetting in thirds suggestive of a soft-shoe routine as heard between trombone and bass and then trombone and piano. Masterful too are such touches as Max Roach's drum break before the out chorus as it echoes distinctive melodic intervals of the head. "For Heaven's Sake," with its chimes, muted trombone, and brushes on drums, represents ballad playing at its best. The uptempo "Commutation," which directly follows, attests to the sure hand of George Avakian in producing an album of compelling contrasts. This number is interesting too for fact that Tommy Flanagan—freshly arrived from Detroit and at that time a relative neophyte on the New York scene—takes the opening chorus. Then again Roach's breaks with Johnson's trombone, and the bowed bass solo all contribute their share of color and drama. "Harvey's House," a blues tribute to New Jersey disk jockey and nightclub owner Harvey Husten, is a funky number striking for its perfectly nuanced and idiomatic solos on piano and trombone. Equally ear-bending, preceding the out chorus, is the dramatic trading of twos and ones between trombone and bass and between trombone and drums, respectively. "Be My Love" is largely a virtuoso solo vehicle for Johnson. A showstopper of the decade and identified with Mario Lanza in the movie *The Toast of New Orleans*, the song is given an uptempo treatment without compromising the piece's romantic significance.

An especially inspired touch involves the way in which the song's initial ascending half step is transmogrified in the course of the fourth chorus in the form of an allusion to the currently popular "Bali Hai" from Rodgers and Hammerstein's *South Pacific* only to reappear as a wistful memory in the tag, sounded on trombone and echoed on piano.

In June 1957, shortly after completing his sessions in New York with Columbia, Johnson set sail for Sweden on what was to be the start of his first European tour, with concerts in France, Belgium, Germany, and Holland.[40] No community felt a greater sense of pride than that of his hometown. Lagging slightly behind the actual course of events, the *Indianapolis Recorder* of June 22, 1957, positively gushed in a lead article about Naptown's famous son:

HOMEGROWN TROMBONIST OFF TO "FLOOR" SWEDEN

Indianapolis' own J.J. Johnson, this country's number one trombonist in practically every poll, recently set sail for Sweden where he and his quintet will "jazz it up" in a summer-long series of concerts under the auspices of the Swedish government. A 1941 graduate of Crispus Attucks, Johnson took up the trombone with his high school band and has been breathing through that elongated tubing ever since.[41]

Johnson had in fact already opened, June 14, in Stockholm's Kungstradgarden, attracting over twenty-thousand people.[42] In his report to *Down Beat* he is barely able to contain his excitement, speaking of the "reaction and response [as] quite overwhelming." He continues by talking about traveling all over Sweden in a series of one-night stands that took him from above the Arctic Circle to Malmo in the south. Although the roads themselves do not quite measure up, the scenery en route is "a photographer's paradise, so much so that we have acquired three new cameras in the band, and have increased the profits of Eastman-Kodak, etc. at the rate of some five to ten rolls of film per day."[43] He goes on to mention jam sessions with Swedish musicians, mostly at restaurants rather than nightclubs, and singles out trombonist Ake Persson and pianist–composer Bengt Hallberg as being the most impressive. At the same time, because everything closes down at midnight, members of the quintet are all apparently "getting too much sleep, which we probably need, since we do not get enough at home."[44]

Johnson's subsequent concerts in the other countries were accompanied by special pleasures. In Paris, in particular, rather than frequent the St. Germain jazz cellars, Johnson reportedly spent his free time strolling off the main boulevards, peering into darkened windows, contemplating the skyline, and hanging out at some bistro or other with an array of liqueurs in front of him. Raymond Horricks has given us a vivid description of J.J. Johnson's features at this point in his life.

His hair trimmed down close to the scalp emphasized the high, peaked forehead, which shone like mica. Otherwise his features were evenly rounded, and distinctly oriental. When he smiled he presented a kind of wise mandarin front: cheeks bunched outwards, crowding his eyes into two narrow cracks with wrinkles at the corners, and his lightly protective moustache spread equally above a knowing part of the lips.[45]

Shortly after his return to the United States, Johnson embarked on a series of Jazz at the Philharmonic concerts, produced and recorded by Norman Granz, with two of the icons of jazz: Stan Getz and Ella Fitzgerald. September 29, 1957, found Johnson at the Civic Opera House in Chicago sharing the front line with Stan Getz and joined by a quartet consisting of Oscar Peterson on piano, Herb Ellis on guitar, Ray Brown on bass, and Connie Kay on drums. Charlie Parker's "Billie's Bounce" served as their opener with ballads such as "Yesterdays" providing a foil (these are among the numbers they were to reprise thirty-one years later in a reunion on the same stage). In Los Angeles, on October 25, 1957, Johnson appeared in Philharmonic Hall with Ella Fitzgerald as part of the Jazz at the Philharmonic All-Stars. The Chicago sextet was augmented to include Roy Eldridge, Sonny Stitt, Lester Young, Illinois Jacquet, and Flip Phillips, all of them providing Fitzgerald with high-powered support in such staples as "Stompin' at the Savoy" and "Lady Be Good."

Johnson's association on records with singers, while highly sporadic, attests to his consummate skill in blending in seamlessly as a sideman as occasion demands. The selection "You've Changed" recorded the following February with Billie Holiday and the Ray Ellis Orchestra is aglow with a silken sheen, Johnson sharing trombone honors with Urbie Green and Tom Mitchell.

In September 1958 Johnson was the headline attraction in a tour of Great Britain organized by Harold Davison in his Jazz from Carnegie Hall series. Briefly reunited with Kai Winding, he was part of a lineup that also included Zoot Sims, Lee Konitz, Oscar Pettiford, Kenny Clarke, and Red Garland alternating with Phineas Newborn on piano. There were concerts in not only London, but twelve other cities as well, among them Sheffield, Glasgow, Liverpool, Birmingham, and Manchester. The sense of anticipation aroused by news of the tour was well captured by *Melody Maker.*

With the "Jazz from Carnegie Hall" package about to start a British tour, the Americans have whirled into our orbit a bunch of jazz satellites as swinging as any that have been launched under the exchange scheme.[46]

Notes

1.　Johnson's Blue Note session of June 22, 1953, was actually the first of three. The others were on September 24, 1954 and June 6, 1955, with Kenny Clarke as the only holdover. Selections were subsequently repackaged as *The Eminent Jay Jay Johnson, Volumes 1 and 2.*

2.   Even though Johnson claims to have known "absolutely nothing" about Hindemith at the time, the Hindemith-like sonorities are unmistakable—evidence of what was clearly in the air in the early 1950s. It might be instructive to examine the introductions of more jazz compositions of this sort, inviting a process of comparison with a time-honored practice in traditional musicology. Cases in point drawn from the Central European repertory, which have generated a vast body of commentary, include the introductions to such works as Mozart's "Dissonant" Quartet, Haydn's "The Creation," and Wagner's "Tristan and Isolde."

3.   Monk's piece, yet another Gershwin "Rhythm" contrafact, starts with a two-pitch pattern on the tonic and leading tone of B-flat. Aside from including F as a pick-up note, this pattern is identical to the riff making up the initial four measures of Johnson's head; but it is distinctly slower and harmonically quite different. Then again, even though Monk was a commanding presence at the Spotlite during Johnson's impressionable years on 52nd Street, his "Thelonious" is best thought of as but one of a number of possible subliminal influences on Johnson's creative process, one of several shards of musical memory. The point of comparison of Johnson's "Turnpike" with Monk's "Thelonious" was suggested by Mark Tucker. His insight is gratefully acknowledged.

4.   Interview with J.J. Johnson, Indianapolis, August 2, 1995.

5.   The New Jersey Turnpike, which opened around November 30, 1951, was touted as the "finest in the world." A great deal of press coverage in the early 1950s focused on both the creation of the Turnpike Authority and the opening of the Turnpike itself. It is inconceivable that J.J. Johnson, as a resident at the time of Brooklyn, New York, and later Teaneck, New Jersey, would not have heard or read something about these developments.

6.   Interview with David and Lida Baker, Indianapolis, February 26, 1994. The fascination during this general period with the power of cars was hardly unique to Miles Davis or J.J. Johnson. One thinks of Chuck Berry's "Maybellene" or of the fleet of rock 'n' roll's car groups—the Cadillacs, the Falcons, the Detroit Wheels, and so on—or of another pop icon, James Dean, who met his death in his Porsche in 1955. And it was the following year that President Dwight D. Eisenhower gave his official sanction to accelerated automobile travel by signing into law the Interstate Highway Act.

7.   Interview with Conrad Herwig, Brooklyn, N.Y., January 24, 1992.

8.   Interview with Robin Eubanks, Brooklyn, N.Y., June 23, 1992.

9.   Ian Carr, *Miles Davis, A Biography* (New York: William Morrow, 1982), 55.

10.   *Ibid.*

11.   Interview with David and Lida Baker, Indianapolis, February 26, 1994.

12.   *Jazz Educators Journal,* Winter 1989, 36–37, includes a transcription by Lawrence McClellan, Jr. of "Walkin'" and a discussion by him of unifying elements in Johnson's recording of February 19, 1958 (Columbia CL1161).

13.   The question was inspired by the song "Black and Blue," originally composed by Andy Razaf, Fats Waller, and Harry Brooks for the 1929 show *Hot Chocolates.* It was popularized by a recording made that same year by Louis Armstrong.

14.   Bill Coss, "J.J. Johnson and Kai Winding," *Metronome* (April 1955), 24.

15.   Leonard Feather, liner notes to Savoy SJL-2232, 1976.

16.   *The Trombonist* (British Trombone Society) (Summer 1994), 18. Compounding the mystery is the fact that Teddy Reig himself makes no mention at all of playing any part in bringing Johnson and Winding together as a duo. However, he clearly was acquainted with both trombonists and produced separate recordings of their work. See Teddy Reig

with Edward Berger, *Reminiscing in Tempo: The Life and Times of a Jazz Hustler* (Metuchen, N.J.: Scarecrow Press and the Institute of Jazz Studies, 1990).

17. This venue was the city's principal nightclub in the 1950s, noted for its presentation of bebop performers. After a fire, it was replaced by a club of the same name, but at a different location.

18. Interview with Dick Katz, New York, January 24, 1995.

19. Interview with David and Lida Baker, Indianapolis, February 26, 1994.

20. Interview with Dick Katz.

21. *Ibid.*

22. *Ibid.*

23. Leonard Feather, liner notes to Savoy SJL–2232.

24. Interview with Dick Katz.

25. Dick Katz, liner notes to Impulse MCA–29061.

26. David W. Stowe, *Swing Changes: Big Band Jazz in New Deal America* (Cambridge, Mass.: Harvard University Press, 1994), 205–206.

27. Interview with Dick Katz.

28. *Ibid.*

29. Nat Hentoff, "J.J., Kai Find Trombone Team is OK with Fans," *Down Beat,* January 12, 1955, 7.

30. Charles Edward Smith, liner notes to Columbia CL–973.

31. Interview with George Avakian, Riverdale, New York, January 5, 1995.

32. Raymond Horricks, "J.J. Johnson, Trombone Ultimate," in *These Jazzmen of Our Time* (London: The Jazz Book Club by arrangement with Victor Gollancz, 1959), 62–63.

33. Liner notes by Gerry Mulligan on *The Complete Birth of the Cool,* Capitol N–16168.

34. Lida and David Baker interview with J.J. Johnson, Indianapolis, February 26, 1994. Johnson's immersion in the scores of major twentieth–century composers is a topic to be explored more fully later.

35. Interview with J.J. Johnson, New York, December 21, 1994.

36. Liner notes by George Avakian and Gunther Schuller, Columbia CL941.

37. Fugal writing puts virtually all jazz musicians in alien territory, and J.J. Johnson is no exception; his five-part fugal exposition shows successive entrances being supported by largely static harmony without much evidence of imitative polyphony. At the same time, he is faithful to a tradition traceable to such works as the finale of Mozart's "Jupiter" Symphony, although one of his more immediate models is likely to have been Britten's *Young Person's Guide to the Orchestra,* otherwise known as "Variations and Fugue on a Theme of Purcell"—a score in his personal library.

38. Interview with Robin Eubanks.

39. Liner notes to Columbia JCL1030.

40. The other members of Johnson's quintet were: Tommy Flanagan on piano, the Belgian-born Bobby Jaspar on tenor saxophone, clarinet, and flute, Wilbur Little on bass, and Elvin Jones on drums.

41. *Indianapolis Recorder,* June 22, 1957.

42. This is the number cited in Horricks, "J.J. Johnson, Trombone Ultimate," 64. Horricks bases his information on a report written by J.J. Johnson about his travels as published in *Down Beat,* September 5, 1957, 11.

43. *Down Beat,* September 5, 1957, 11.
44. *Ibid.*
45. Horricks, "J.J. Johnson, Trombone Ultimate," 65.
46. *Melody Maker*, September 6, 1958, 2.

Chapter 5

Vindicated and in the Vanguard

"He came forward voluntarily saying he wanted to testify for those who didn't make it to court."[1] J.J. Johnson is remembered in this way for his quiet dignity and determination. They are qualities attributed to him by Maxwell T. Cohen, one of the most remarkable civil libertarian lawyers in the history of New York City. It was Max Cohen who, in the words of Dan Morgenstern, "succeeded in stripping New York's obscene cabaret card of its guise of legality [while] fighting vested political interests, prejudice, apathy and monumental stupidity."[2] And it was Johnson's willingness to testify as one of "three nominal plaintiffs" that was essential to the successful outcome of a trial heard in New York State Supreme Court on May 13 and 14, 1959—one that forever changed the balance of power between the New York Police Department (NYPD) and the thousands of musicians and entertainers seeking cabaret cards. At the same time, the case so fearlessly argued by Max Cohen placed jazz artists in the forefront of a fight against a flagrantly unfair and demonstrably illegal code. In effect, a remedy was provided for the many who had been victimized because of prior drug convictions despite clear evidence of their having undergone rehabilitation to reach the zenith of their profession, lead normal family lives, and maintain their own homes. J.J. Johnson was living proof of all of this. The present discussion, by focusing on Johnson's role in the legal challenge to the abuses of the cabaret card system, serves to counterbalance prior treatment in chapter 2, of the pathology of narcotics use and its effect on the individual lives of such musicians as Charlie Parker, Miles Davis, Johnson, and Stan Getz.

By the late 1950s Johnson's preeminence on the international jazz scene was beyond dispute and he was welcome to perform virtually anywhere in the world. Yet, he was unable to commit himself to any long-range planning for engagements at such New York cabarets as Birdland, the Village Vanguard, or Cafe Bohemia because the Division of Licenses of the NYPD consistently denied his applications for a permanent cabaret employee's identification card. In November 1956 he was issued a temporary card, which was good for six months and usually limited to one place of employment but subject to medical requirements virtually impossible to meet—a topic to be more fully explored in due course.[3] As noted earlier, on

December 27, 1946, Johnson had been arrested on a misdemeanor, convicted, and received a suspended sentence. It was a minor offense involving possession of a hypodermic needle, and no specific details beyond that were ever entered into the record. Arrested at a time when the courts were not especially sympathetic to blacks, Johnson‑pleaded guilty and, thanks to a plea bargain, was placed on probation. In any event, even though this was his one and only arrest, a thoroughly corrupt, self-aggrandizing police bureaucracy worked against him as it did against many of his colleagues, fostering a climate in which the very application process itself became an exercise in Kafkaesque absurdity.

The licensing laws that applied to cabarets owed their origins to controls that took shape during Prohibition. On June 17, 1926, Mayor James Walker introduced a local law "to regulate dance halls and cabarets." The bill contained no provisions for employees but focused instead on the requirement for the cabarets to have licenses. "Cabaret" was defined inclusively to refer to:

> any room, place or space in the city in which any musical entertainment, singing, dancing or other similar amusement is permitted in connection with the restaurant business or the business of directly or indirectly selling to the public food or drink.[4]

Even though "drink" here did not necessarily mean alcoholic beverages, it did lead to a troubling paradox. The Commissioner of Licenses of the City of New York, and later the police commissioner, were to supervise facilities, namely speakeasies, "directly or indirectly selling the public food or drink" at a time when, under Prohibition, the selling of alcoholic beverages was in clear violation of the law. It is therefore hardly surprising that a vice inquiry in 1932 disclosed that many men on the force were essentially accomplices, accepting bribes and condoning the selling of alcohol in thousands of speakeasies. Later, around 1940, the problem was compounded by a series of strikes and labor difficulties involving the Joint Board of Waiters and Chefs, a union that was thought to be Communist-dominated. These events coincided more or less with an antiradical directive from President Franklin Delano Roosevelt instructing the FBI to "prepare a list of those whose presence might be adverse to the security of the United States."[5] When the police later became involved in strike-breaking their work began to include passing judgment on the qualifications of waiters and chefs to work in restaurants. Anyone convicted of a felony or any offense, even as a minor, became highly vulnerable. Jazz musicians were placed in serious jeopardy in that around the same time (1941–43) a series of provisions in the state Alcoholic Beverage Control Law were enacted forbidding employment in a bar of anyone convicted of a felony or narcotics crime.[6] As a result, "the racist impulse to control the supposedly degrading abandon of black music was . . . absorbed into a vaguer purpose, more acceptable to contemporary tastes, of shielding patrons from 'undesirable' influences."[7] In the course of investigating the "police card" system and its procedures Cohen discovered that the police department "had arrogated to itself the authority to require the possession of identification cards as a requisite for employment, to impose a fee for the card, and to place the money so collected into a police pension fund."[8] This explains why the complaint dated October 28, 1958, with pianist Bill Rubenstein, J.J. Johnson, and composer Johnny Richards as plaintiffs and lodged in New York State Supreme Court, names as defendants not only the police commissioner and his deputy, but also the thirteen members constituting the board of trustees of the police pension fund.

J.J. Johnson's serving as one of the "three nominal plaintiffs" fits into the larger context of Max Cohen's earlier involvement in police card case law. It all started in 1951 with the case of Bud Powell, perhaps the most poignant example of how the law worked to undermine the career of a major musician. Shortly after his release from a psychiatric hospital Powell was offered employment by Birdland; this required his obtaining a cabaret employee's identification card. But upon applying to the NYPD for the card Powell, "An Alleged Incompetent," was rejected.[9] He then sought legal recourse from attorney Max Cohen, who had been recommended to him by Alan Morrison, a close mutual friend who was also an editor of *Jet* and *Ebony* magazines. What are important here are not so much the details of Powell's subsequent legal frustrations as the growing involvement in the card issue of Max Cohen, Alan Morrison, and Oscar Goodstein, who had left the practice of law to become manager of Birdland. Most crucial of all was Cohen's superb pioneering research of cabaret card history that had been prompted by the plight of Bud Powell. He proceeded to share his findings with Morrison and Goodstein. Vital information was then passed on to the editor of *Down Beat* and spread elsewhere in the jazz community. What Cohen's research revealed was nothing short of explosive.

> My thorough research and investigation had clearly and conclusively shown that there was no explicit statutory authority which unequivocally gave the New York City Police Department the power to demand the acquisition of a Cabaret Employee's Identification Card from Bud Powell (or from any other prospective employee) as a requisite for lawful employment in cabarets.[10]

As a corollary there was no statutory authority giving the NYPD the power to collect a "service charge" for such a card and place revenues so collected in its pension fund. Similarly it was against legislated public policy for the department to bar rehabilitated employees from working. Quite understandably, the pressure for change began to build, culminating in the 119-count complaint of October 28, 1958, lodged in the Supreme Court of the State of New York. The complaint named the "three nominal plaintiffs," people whose histories Cohen had gotten to know intimately, "who would make strong plaintiffs for different reasons."[11] They were Johnny Richards, composer, arranger, and bandleader; Bill Rubenstein, pianist, whom Richards wanted to hire; and J.J. Johnson.

SUPREME COURT OF THE STATE OF NEW YORK
                COUNTY OF NEW YORK

- X

BERIL W. RUBENSTEIN, for himself and others
similarly concerned and situated,
JAMES LOUIS JOHNSON, for himself and others
similarly concerned and situated, and
JOHNNY RICHARDS, for himself and other
employers and taxpayers similarly concerned
and situated,   Plaintiffs
                                                                        designate New
                                                                        York County as
                                              Plaintiffs,   the place of
                                                                        trial.
                - against -

STEPHEN P. KENNEDY, as Police Commissioner
of the City of New York, JAMES J. McELROY,
Deputy Police Commissioner of the City of
New York in Charge of Licenses,
STEPHEN P. KENNEDY, JOSEPH J. REGAN,
WILLIAM V. COSGROVE, GEORGE BLUMENTHAL,
JOHN E. CARTON, LAWRENCE E. GEROSA,
BERNARD J. RUGGIERI, PHILIP H. GILSTEN,
JOHN J. CASSESE, VINCENT J. STEIN,
PATRICK H. FITZPATRICK, JAMES F. SHEA,
JOHN J. HORAN, Constituting the Board of
Trustees of the Police Pension Fund,

                                              Defendants.

- X

TO THE ABOVE NAMED DEFENDANTS:

              YOU ARE HEREBY SUMMONED to answer the complaint

in this action, and to serve a copy of your answer, or, if the

complaint is not served with this summons, to serve a notice of

appearance, on the Plaintiffs' Attorney within twenty days after

the service of this summons, exclusive of the day of service; and

in case of your failure to appear, or answer, judgment will be

taken against you by default, for the relief demanded in the

complaint.

Dated: New York, New York
       October 28th, 1958.

                                    MAXWELL T. COHEN
                                    Attorney for Plaintiffs
                                    Office & P. O. Address
                                    505 Fifth Avenue
                                    Borough of Manhattan
                                    City of New York

BERIL W. RUBENSTEIN, being duly sworn, deposes and says that he is one of the plaintiffs in the within action; that he has read the foregoing Complaint and knows the contents thereof; that the same is true to his own knowledge, except as to the matters therein stated to be alleged on information and belief, and that as to those matters he believes it to be true.

Sworn to before me this

28th day of October, 1958.

Beril W. Rubenstein

MAXWELL T. COHN
Notary Public, State of New York
No. 31-5744300
Qualified in New York County

STATE OF NEW YORK)
COUNTY OF NEW YORK) ss. :

JAMES LOUIS JOHNSON, being duly sworn, deposes and says that he is one of the plaintiffs in the within action; that he has read the foregoing Complaint and knows the contents thereof; that the same is true to his own knowledge, except as to the matters therein stated to be alleged on information and belief, and that as to those matters he believes it to be true.

Sworn to before me this

28th day of October, 1958.

James Louis Johnson

MAXWELL T. COHN
Notary Public, State of New York
No. 31-5744300
Qualified in New York County

STATE OF NEW YORK)
COUNTY OF NEW YORK) ss. :

JOHNNY RICHARDS, being duly sworn, deposes and says that he is one of the plaintiffs in the within action; that he has read the foregoing Complaint and knows the contents thereof; that the same is true to his own knowledge, except as to the matters therein stated to be alleged on information and belief, and that as to those matters he believes it to be true.

Sworn to before me this

28th day of October, 1958.

Johnny Richards

MAXWELL T. COHN
Notary Public, State of New York
No. 31-5744300
Qualified in New York County
Certs. filed with N. Y. Co. Clk. & Reg.
Commission Expires March 30, 1952

Fig. 5.1 Complaint filed by Rubenstein, Johnson, and Richards in the New York State Supreme Court, October 28, 1958.

Johnson's treatment by the NYPD vividly illustrates the degree of arrogance, apathy, and "monumental stupidity" of which the department was capable, let alone their flouting of legislated public policy. Even though there were no convictions on his record since 1946, Johnson had consistently been denied a permanent cabaret employee's identification card. In November 1956 he had been issued a temporary card "conditioned upon his bringing proof from a City Hospital that he was not a narcotics addict."[12] (He never was a narcotics addict.) But no hospital had any facilities to conduct such examinations, which in any case were forbidden under the provision of the Mental Hygiene Law. When the NYPD was so informed they told Johnson to present a doctor's certificate every six months. Yet, on June 12, 1958, when Johnson appeared at the Division of Licenses with doctor's certificate in hand, his request for a permanent card was rejected; the rules had changed. As Cohen spells out in complaint:

> Plaintiff, Johnson, was on the aforementioned date interviewed by the Deputy Police Commissioner. Plaintiff, Johnson, was told in substance, by the Deputy Police Commissioner, that there are now "new policies"; new restrictions; that doctor's certificates would not be acceptable; that plaintiff, Johnson, would have to report to any New York City Hospital for an examination, and then obtain a certificate from the Hospital that he was not addicted to drugs; that upon doing so, a Temporary Card would be issued to him, but that the Card would restrict the plaintiff, Johnson, only to a particular and specific place of employment.[13]

In fact, the NYPD, specifically the Division of Licenses, was well aware that no New York City hospital would "examine any applicant with a view of certifying whether or not he is addicted to the use of narcotics."[14] As if matters were not already bizarre enough, a police department representative as well as the New York City Hospitals Commissioner had recently testified on this very point before the State of New York Joint Legislative Committee on Narcotic Study, the report of which had been widely distributed.

At the actual trial in New York State Supreme Court, May 13–14, 1959, Cohen brought forth some highly persuasive witnesses and plaintiffs to bolster the allegations in his 119-count complaint. Record producer John Hammond spoke of the humiliation suffered by musicians having to be fingerprinted like common criminals in the course of applying for the cards, cards that gave them the basic right to earn a livelihood in New York City. Hammond's testimony, in fact, touched on a key point developed by Cohen in his review of how police authority came to undermine constitutional and social principles. The plaintiffs were being "deprived of property without due process of law" and were being prevented from lawfully exercising their skills for compensation.[15] One source quoted in this regard was Shylock in Shakespeare's *The Merchant of Venice* (Act IV, scene 1): "you take my life when you do take the means whereby I live."

As for other testimony, the wives of Bill Rubenstein and J.J. Johnson spoke movingly of their husbands and their love of family and home. Writing of J.J. Johnson, Cohen observed that when he "testified with impressive dignity, one was aware of him as a human being and gifted artist."[16] Television star Steve Allen, whom Cohen has referred to as "extremely intelligent, an autodidact," testified that none of the people with past narcotics convictions on his show—Johnson had appeared on his TV program many times—had ever caused problems with either the sponsors or the viewing public.[17]

By far the most telling was the appearance of David Allen, a singer, recording artist, cabaret, and television performer. In September 1958 he had been engaged by The Den, a restaurant/cabaret. But because of a conviction in 1955, in order to work he needed permission from both the New York State Liquor Authority and the NYPD. Approved by the liquor authority, he went to work assuming that the police card would automatically be issued, only to be confronted by the police on his third night, when they proceeded to close down The Den. It would seem that the overwhelming evidence of Allen's rehabilitation or his history as a combat veteran who had been awarded the Purple Heart counted for naught in their eyes. Afflicted with malaria contracted during his war years, Allen suffered an acute attack in the court room.

> Dave's malaria attack in the court room added a new dimension to the trial—Dave, a plaintiff and an applicant for a Card, had suffered a war-consequent attack in full view of the judge and the public. Our plaintiffs and witnesses were no longer mere applicants before a Court, but human beings capable of suffering, agony, and tears.[18]

On the second and final day of the trial Judge Jacob Markowitz went into closed session with Max Cohen, Murray Rudman (representing the NYPD), and deputy commissioner James McElroy. Returning to the court room, he called on the police to issue cards to Johnson and Rubenstein immediately and to "liberalize" its policy on the cards, consistent with ideas of civil rights and humanity.

Asked about the larger significance of the ruling and Johnson's role in it, Cohen reflected: "It was exceedingly important. It was the first case that cracked the police wall. He got his card by direct order of the court and that's why the *New York Times* wrote about it—a directive right off the bench."[19] At the same time there was the disappointment that Cohen had won only a partial victory. He had been thwarted in his efforts to have the entire card system declared unconstitutional because of the "hands-off" and "pragmatic" attitude throughout the case on the part of the American Federation of Musicians Local 802 and the American Guild of Variety Artists.

> Jackie Bright, National Secretary of the American Guild of Variety Artists, the only union official in the entertainment industry who had volunteered to testify,

Fig. 5.2 *Left to right:* Maxwell T. Cohen, the author and the attorney who represented J.J. Johnson, Beril (Bill) Rubenstein, and Johnny Richards in "The Police Card Cases." Photograph courtesy of Maxwell T. Cohen.

stated in response to cross-examination by the Police Department's attorney that in his opinion it would be more appropriate that the Police screen the night club customers rather than the night club entertainers and employees.[20]

Buoyed by Judge Markowitz's directive of May 14, 1959, to the NYPD to issue him his card once and for all, Johnson was performing at the Village Vanguard twelve days later.[21] Max Gordon's nightclub had already established itself as a major venue not only for major jazz performers and folk musicians but also as a forum for poets to meet and to be heard. A vignette by Dan Wakefield graphically captures the contrasting personalities of Jack Kerouac and J.J. Johnson at the Village Vanguard around this time—Kerouac, the beat poet craving approval, and Johnson, forever the epitome of quiet dignity and dry humor.

> Kerouac started off his set by reading a piece about his pal the bartender at the Cellar in San Francisco, one of the beats' hangouts. I looked toward Lou, the bartender at the Vanguard, to get his reaction. When Kerouac finished, Lou shook his head and said, "He won't make many bartender friends if he keeps on usin' *that*." I drifted from my stool at the bar to try to hear other reactions. People who

I guessed were leftovers from an uptown office party were shifting restlessly at their table and speaking under their breath while Kerouac read, until one man shushed the others into quiet and explained, "Some people like this stuff." There was scattered, perfunctory applause when Kerouac finished, and I followed him to the room backstage where the trombone player J.J. Johnson and his sidemen were sitting around a table talking quietly—and soberly—at their break. Kerouac pulled up a chair to the edge of their group, but no one paid any attention to him until he asked Johnson, "What did you think of what I read?" Johnson, a dignified Negro from my hometown of Indianapolis, stared at the reeling [presumably drunken] writer a moment and asked politely if he had written it himself. Kerouac admitted he had, and after a pause Johnson said diplomatically, "It sounded very deep." Kerouac complimented Johnson's trombone playing and said he had always wanted to play saxophone himself: "Man, I could really work with a tenor sax." Johnson eyed him coolly and said, "You look more like a trumpet man to me." That was all Kerouac got from the pros.[22]

The trajectory of Johnson's career from March 1959 to December 1961 was epitomized by the title of one of his albums of the time, *Really Livin'*. One would indeed be hard pressed to find a comparable period in his life when so much was accomplished, from masterly arrangements of such intimate standards as "Stardust" or "Satin Doll" to the composing and recording of his large-scale *Perceptions,* to his teaching at the Lenox School of Jazz, to his creating of a Kurt Weill album with André Previn.

Really Livin', recorded in March 1959, just two months before his cabaret card case came to trial, features Johnson with members of his sextet: Nat Adderley, trumpet; Bobby Jaspar, flute and tenor saxophone; Cedar Walton, piano; James De Brest, bass; Albert Heath, drums. The album offers an impressive mix of original compositions, arrangements of popular standards, and blues; and the performing forces are deployed with unerring instinct. Johnson's composition, "Me Too," is a good example of his fascination with modal jazz in general and with Davis's contemporaneous "So What," in particular. It is a finely wrought score of contrasting elements: the opening gentle Lydian riff on piano, followed by the Aeolian melody played by Johnson, then transformed into a refrain for the front line as part of an uptempo treatment, the reprise of the opening material as part of the tag—all attest to a mastery of form and content.

"Sidewinder," another Johnson composition, this one in F minor, is a testament to his urge to avoid business as usual, to often pose new challenges for himself and his ensemble.[23] True to its name—it refers to a kind of rattlesnake—the piece is highly unpredictable, yet tightly integrated, allusive in its serpentine lines with their frequent tendency to slither down chromatically, drawing upon the half-step diminished scale.[24] The opening six measures of the introduction (the introduction as a whole is reprised at the end) are illustrative (Fig. 5.3).

Starting in measure 16 and continuing until measure 22, there is a descending sequence emphasizing the minor third (derived from the work's first two measures).

Fig. 5.3 "Sidewinder" score, introduction, mm. 1–6.

The head itself expands upon this intervallic idea as it briefly wends its way upward only to suddenly slip down a diminished fifth (mm. 34–40).

Johnson's solos and those of the others draw upon characteristic motivic and harmonic materials contained in these measures of the introduction and head. They provide a perfect fit for the strong Aeolian profile of Gershwin's "Summertime," which Johnson proceeds to quote in the second chorus and again, following a series of trombone/drum breaks, before the out chorus (Fig. 5.4).

Among other selections on *Really Livin'* are a virtuosic treatment of the Sonny Rollins blues "Decision," a version of "Red Cross" (vintage 1944 Charlie Parker), a loving tribute to Billie Holiday in "God Bless' the Child" (she passed away four months after the recording session), and a gently swinging rendition of Hoagy Carmichael's ballad "Stardust."

During the weekend of September 18–20, 1959, Johnson premiered two of his newly commissioned works at the Monterey Jazz Festival. While his *Sketch for*

Fig. 5.4   "Sidewinder" score, mm. 34–40.

Trombone and Orchestra has not enjoyed repeat performances, his *El Camino Real* has become something of a repertoire item, particularly at band clinics. Scored for fifteen pieces, the work calls for a saxophone quintet, trumpet quartet, trombone trio, solo trombone, bass, and drums. The allusive title refers to the Golden Road, California's Spanish Mission Trail that began in Mexico and eventually reached as far north as the Oregon border. The work, particularly in its introduction and A section, embellishes and expands upon a theme in the e Phrygian mode that imparts a distinctive Spanish flavor. The opening four measures on solo trombone set the tone with their emphasis on the characteristic whole step, minor third, and half-step intervals associated with the seventh, first, and second degrees of the Phrygian mode (Fig. 5.5).

The ethnic authenticity of this sound was dramatized many years earlier in the shrill parallel passage of Manuel De Falla's 1915 ballet score *El Amor Brujo* (Fig. 5.6). It is worth noting that this very same score served as a common source of

Fig. 5.5   *El Camino Real* score, mm. 1–5.

inspiration around the same time for two close colleagues of Johnson's, Gil Evans
and Miles Davis, as they were preparing to produce their album *Sketches of Spain*;
it happens to include the title "Will o' the Wisp," an adaptation of a section so
named from Falla's ballet. Recorded in New York on November 20, 1959, and
March 10–11, 1960, *Sketches of Spain* exudes much of the same aroma that seems
to have been in the air when Johnson premiered his *El Camino Real* at Monterey
the previous September. But Johnson's fascination with this kind of "Spanish
tinge," as we shall presently see, does not end here. In his slightly later
Perceptions (1961) the opening trumpet solo written for Dizzy Gillespie, which is
saturated with the Spanish Phrygian mode, shows a strong affinity to "Solea,"
another title on the *Sketches of Spain* album.[25]

For the rest, *El Camino Real*, with its prevailing buoyant duple swing feel, is
driven largely by such riffs as the following as they occur in a series of call-and-
response patterns. Other telling touches enhancing the overall effect include
quintal parallelisms between solo trombone and trumpet quartet (mm. 12–13) and a

EL AMOR BRUJO

Introduccion y Escena

MANUEL DE FALLA

Fig. 5.6   Manuel De Falla, *El Amor Brujo*, score, mm. 1–8.

Fig. 5.7   *El Camino Real* score, mm. 128–130.

final chord, far-removed from the initial pitch center of e, a metaphor describing an open-ended journey on *El Camino Real* (Fig. 5.7).[26]

With the release of his next sextet album, *J.J. Inc.,* recorded at the beginning of August 1960, Johnson attained an ideal he has often sought—having his original compositions recorded by a group that has come to intimately know his scores through repeated performance. *J.J. Inc.* retains Cedar Walton and Albert Heath on piano and drums but makes changes in the front line and bass positions;

Clifford Jordan, Freddie Hubbard, and Arthur Harper are featured on tenor saxophone, trumpet, and bass, respectively. As Johnson put it:

> This album was made under conditions which I consider ideal . . . The material for this album was composed and arranged eight months before the scheduled recording session. It was performed nightly in clubs, at jazz concerts and elsewhere during the intervening period by the same musicians who ultimately appeared on the record date. Naturally it isn't always possible to have such tailor-made conditions. But when it is, WOW! What a pleasure![27]

Consisting of six Johnson compositions, *J.J. Inc.* is an album that is true to its name, embodying a vivid portrait of Johnson's multiple musical states as of 1960. It evokes a mix of associations as diverse elements are juxtaposed or fused—cool jazz, blues, funk, and more. "Shutterbug"—possibly a self-referential allusion to Johnson's relatively recent Swedish experience of "photographer's paradise"—is a twenty-four-bar minor blues. The head, a clipped staccato riff suggestive of Miles Davis's "Miles" (1958)—which subsequently came to be known as "Milestones"—is played by the front line in close modal harmony and punctuated by a half-step Phrygian gesture in parallel fifths against the walking bass of Arthur Harper and the backbeat of Albert Heath. "Mohawk," a pentatonic quasi-Indian piece, is essentially a twelve-bar blues in 6/4 time, but one distinctively colored by an F Aeolian sound replete with quartal/quintal sonorities. Horace Silver's influence is apparent on "In Walked Horace," and the blues entitled "Fatback" is described by Johnson as "two-beat funk."[28]

By far the most progressive and complex selection here is "Aquarius." Although it is a traditional blues form, "Aquarius" departs from the norm in its harmonic usage. Interpolations and substitutions, very much a function of Johnson's reliance on the diminished scale on C in both whole-step and half-step forms, involve principally the following: (1) substituting in the second phrase a vii minor seventh chord for the more conventional IV–I progression; (2) starting the third phrase with two submediant chords—A^7 and A major seventh—before the ii–V–i (Cmi 9) cadence.[29] Especially striking in this regard is Johnson's first solo chorus in which the ninth measure features a touch of bitonality as he plays a C triad over an A^7 ensemble chord, a product of the diminished (half-step) scale specifically.

Tension is further heightened rhythmically, by a conflict between the 12/8 meter of the ensemble as a whole and the prevailing 4/4 of Johnson's solo, thereby "creating a three-against-two hemiola," which in its own way suggests a kind of swing feeling.[30] Johnson has put it in more psychological terms, calling it a "schizophrenic" effect, perhaps hinting at the delicate balancing act of the eponymous water-carrier himself.

The balance of Johnson's 1960 summer, from around mid-August to September 3, was spent at the Lenox School of Jazz in Massachusetts, at a location very close to Tanglewood, the renowned summer home of the Boston Symphony Orchestra and the Tanglewood Music Center. [31] Once the regular classical summer program was over in mid-August, the school would move in and hold its three-week session through around Labor Day. This particular summer, however, proved to be the fourth and final one of a remarkable school that had set a major precedent in offering an all-jazz curriculum based on a master–teacher, student–apprentice relationship. [32] Incorporated as a nonprofit organization the school had attracted scholarship and endowment funds from such disparate sources as the Schaefer Brewing Company, Broadcast Music, Inc., Associated Booking Corporation, Dizzy Gillespie, and Leonard Bernstein. Yet without a full-time year-round staff it had been unable to properly focus on curriculum planning, student recruitment and additional fund-raising.

In the course of its four years of existence the school, under the directorship of John Lewis, could boast of having on its faculty, in addition to Johnson, such stellar names as Dizzy Gillespie, Jimmy Giuffre, Kenny Dorham, Percy Heath, Oscar Peterson, George Russell, Bill Russo, Gunther Schuller, and Marshall Stearns. Courses in composition, history, and small ensemble playing were supplemented by at least two private instrumental lessons a week, a lecture series on specialized topics such as problems in jazz recording, management, or the relationship of jazz to classical music. Concerts were presented every Thursday and Saturday evening. Among the school's alumni were Ornette Coleman, David Baker, Jamey Aebersold, Don Ellis (a member of Johnson's ensemble at the School in 1960), and various others who went on to join the bands of Woody Herman, Quincy Jones, and groups led by George Russell and Kenny Dorham. All students were strongly urged to develop as composers and many cited Bill Russo's method of instruction by immersion as the highlight of their stay.

Johnson's role at the school was that of master teacher and clinician. David Baker, whom Johnson met for the first time that summer and who was then active as a trombonist, has some vivid memories to share:

> He was always prepared to the final degree. . . . I can remember him talking to me about how to organize material, how to approach tunes, how to play . . . I can remember him getting on me because when I would play the whole floor of the tent would move, and he would play in the most vigorous manner, and there would be no wasted motion, nothing. You hardly felt the breeze being stirred. I can remember admonitions like "Everything you play has to get out the end of the horn. . . . If it doesn't come out the end of the horn, it's of no value to the listener." So a lot of it was philosophical, a lot of it was technical, and a lot of it was . . . empirical kind of knowledge . . . that he could share through demonstration. [33]

In many respects it was the semi-weekly concerts that best exemplified the school's pedagogical philosophy of encouraging all student performers to be composers. This is well illustrated by a set led by Johnson on a concert program at

Lenox on Thursday, September 1, 1960, when his septet of piano, bass, drums, saxophone, trombone, trumpet, and vibraharp performed five selections, three of them by student members of the ensemble. One of these students, Don Ellis, who went on to considerable fame, offered an original composition entitled "Homeless." Later that evening Johnson was heard as "guest soloist" with string ensemble and rhythm section in two selections: Bob Brookmeyer's "Champagne Blues" and Gary McFarland's "Piece for Strings."

In September 1960, after completing his residency at the Lenox School of Jazz, Johnson made his final appearances leading his sextet. Increasingly preoccupied with arranging and composing, he was finding the responsibilities of leading a group too much of a burden and accordingly soon disbanded the ensemble. He recalled: "It suddenly occurred to me that I needed a change, and I even began to wonder was it possible that a musician or artist could be much too dedicated—so much so that he lived in a very narrow world."[34]

But, even when he was relieved of the pressures of having to lead a group, as was the case with his eighteen-month tenure with the Miles Davis sextet (ca. June 1961– December 1962), Johnson found the demands of travel too time consuming, remarking in an interview with Leonard Feather: "It's very frustrating, this business of writing vs. playing. I have to concentrate on one at a time . . . for a year and a half I hardly picked up a pen, because traveling makes it hard to write; writing is more demanding than playing."[35] Consequently, during the balance of the decade, most of Johnson's live and recording studio performances, usually as guest soloist, reflect ad hoc personnel arrangements rather than any long-term commitment. One of the notable exceptions was Johnson's full-time working quartet that he organized in the summer of 1963, only to disband it a little more than a year later.

Despite the undeniable frustrations that were visited upon his efforts as arranger and composer, Johnson continued an impressive career as live performer and recording artist. There are moments of contagious buoyant energy and inspiration, to say nothing of a thoroughgoing versatility. Evidence of this is provided by a Jazz at the Philharmonic (JATP) European tour and a follow-up recording session in New York. Late November 1960 found Johnson performing with Norman Granz's troupe in a lineup that featured Dizzy Gillespie and Stan Getz as well as Leo Wright on alto saxophone and flute, Art Davis on bass, Chuck Lampkin on drums, Lalo Schifrin on piano, and Candido Camero on congas. Others on the tour included Victor Feldman, Sam Jones, and Louis Hayes on piano, bass, and drums, respectively.[36] Following an approach now standard for Granz, the musicians were encouraged to treat performances as jam sessions, "to see what happens when the individual style of one is used as the whetstone for the individual style of another. The audiences in Europe heard improvised music in the moment of its creation."[37] By all accounts, this was very much a fun-filled series of "blowing" dates, and what was provided, above all, was a sense of theater and exotic color.

Gillespie's "Kush," recorded at the concert of November 21 in Stockholm is a case in point. Running to just under eighteen minutes, it is rich in its spectrum of timbres and textures. An evocative mood is established at the outset with an impressionistic, chromatic flute solo that is punctuated by a series of percussive outbursts. What follows, after some washes of piano color, is essentially a highly exotic blues (C Aeolian) anchored by the following bass ostinato punctuated by shifts to the IV chord:

Fig. 5.8 Dizzy Gillespie's "Kush," bass ostinato.

Sounds of muted and open trumpet, passages for Gillespie and Getz in quartal harmony, and a quasi-tropical, polyrhythmic, uptempo section energized by trilling saxophone riffs all add to the excitement and lead to the cresting solos of Getz and Johnson. One other selection performed that night, "Wheatleigh Hall," is riveting for the breakneck solos by Gillespie, Getz, and Johnson, culminating in the climactic, attention-grabbing conga playing of Candido.

Back in New York, Johnson assembled a quartet for his next Columbia recording sessions by hiring the three members of Cannonball Adderley's rhythm section—Victor Feldman, Sam Jones, and Louis Hayes—all of whom had participated in the recent JATP tour. The resulting album, *A Touch of Satin,* has proven to be Johnson's personal favorite, with each member of the ensemble on his mettle performing a series of selections of considerable stylistic scope. These include popular standards like "Satin Doll," "Gigi," and "Sophisticated Lady," adaptations of classical music such as "Full Moon and Empty Arms" (based on the lyrical second theme from the final movement of Rachmaninoff's Second Piano Concerto), Thelonious Monk's "Jackie-ing," and original Johnson compositions "Flat Black" and "Bloozineff."

Commenting more pointedly on individual selections, one can begin by singling out Monk's "Jackie-ing." Cast in the B-flat Lydian mode and clearly the most "progressive" piece on the album, "Jackie-ing" has a typically jagged melodic head; it generates distinctive material such as the following variation that becomes a vital part of Johnson's tightly integrated solo.

Fig. 5.9 "Jackie-ing" melodic motive.

Drawing upon such devices as motivic fragmentation, and rhythmic and registral displacement, Johnson imparts an impressive unity to the whole (Fig 5.10).

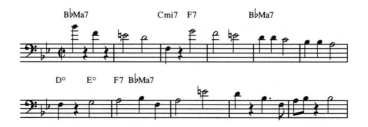

Fig. 5.10   J.J. Johnson solo on "Jackie-ing," mm. 85–95, recorded January 12, 1961.

Ellington's standard "Satin Doll" casts Johnson in a strikingly different light as he offers a seductively swinging performance marked by expressive slurs, caressing sequences, an appropriately high tessitura, and a predominantly conjunct line, all communicating the sense of delicacy and smoothness signified by the title. Finally, mention should be made of Johnson's original "Flat Black," a reworking of the standard "What Is This Thing Called Love?," and hence an example of a piece in the silent-theme tradition. The head with its tango beat, Johnson's uptempo stop-and-go rhythm in the subsequent choruses, and the dramatic drum breaks all contribute to a highly charged performance.

Notes

1.   Interview with Maxwell T. Cohen, Minisink Hills, Pa., July 23, 1994.

2.   Maxwell T. Cohen, *The Police Card Discord* (Metuchen, N.J.: Scarecrow Press, 1993), ix.

3.   It was under these conditions that Johnson appeared with his quintet at Cafe Bohemia, February 2, 1957.

4.   Cohen, *The Police Card Discord*, 17.

5.   Maxwell Cohen as quoted in Michael Ullman, *Jazz Lives* (Washington, D.C: New Republic, 1980), 32.

6.   Paul Chevigny, *Gigs: Jazz and the Cabaret Laws in New York City* (New York: Routledge, Chapman, and Hall, 1991), 58–59, 195.

7.   *Ibid.*, 59.

8.   Cohen, *The Police Card Discord,* xv.

9.   *Ibid.*, xi.

10.   *Ibid.*,1.

11.   Interview with Maxwell T. Cohen.

12. Cohen, *The Police Card Discord,* 7.

13. *Ibid.,* 11–12.

14. *Ibid.,* 12.

15. *Ibid.,* 25.

16. *Ibid.,* 37.

17. Interview with Maxwell T. Cohen.

18. Cohen, *The Police Card Discord,* 37.

19. Interview with Maxwell T. Cohen. Also see *The New York Times,* May 15, 1959, 24.

20. Cohen, *The Police Card Discord,* 50.

21.   The coup de grâce to the entire cabaret card system was to come some eighteen months later with the rally of support following the death on November 12, 1960, of noted monologist Lord Buckley. A high-powered Citizen's Emergency Committee was formed determined to fight the police department cabaret card system to the death. By the end of that month "law and order" police commissioner Stephen P. Kennedy was in serious trouble amid disclosures that his department had illegally funnelled around $1 million into its pension fund from cabaret card fees. Commissioner Kennedy, who at one point had been considered by the White House of John F. Kennedy (no relation) as a successor to J. Edgar Hoover at the FBI, was soon to resign in disgrace and leave New York City for good.

22.   Dan Wakefield, *New York in the Fifties* (Boston: Houghton Mifflin/Seymour Lawrence, 1992), 168–169. Wakefield, incidentally, covered Johnson's cabaret card test case in *The Nation.* Our thanks to Lewis Porter for bringing this material to our attention.

23.   Johnson's piece should not be confused with Lee Morgan's 1963 boogaloo blues hit, "The Sidewinder."

24.   The diminished half-step scale, with its characteristic alternation of half and whole steps, is sometimes referred to by other names. For example, in his *Lydian Chromatic Concept of Tonal Organization,* George Russell calls this scale an "auxiliary-diminished blues scale," whereas other theorists speak of it as an octatonic scale.

25.   Our thanks to Bill Kirchner for drawing our attention to this connection.

26.   The pitches of the final chord are all drawn from the minor pentatonic scale of E-flat but are anchored by an A-flat in the bass.

27.   Comments by J.J. Johnson as included in liner notes by Teo Macero for the recording *J.J., Inc.,* Columbia CL 1606.

28.   Liner notes to Columbia CL 1606.

29.   Johnson's solo is analyzed in some detail in Scott D. Reeves, *Creative Jazz Improvisation* (Englewood Cliffs, N.J.: Prentice-Hall, 1989), 173–175. The previous discussion has been adapted from his work.

30.   *Ibid.,* 174.

31.   Jazz pianist Michael Fitzgerald has generously shared the results of his research on the Lenox School of Jazz. His help is very gratefully acknowledged.

32.   The school formally began as a three-week session in the summer of 1957. It was sparked by a series of jazz panel discussions the previous summer. *Down Beat,* August 31, 1961, 11.

33.   Interview with David Baker, Bloomington, Indiana, June 23, 1993.

34.   Ira Gitler, "The Remarkable J.J. Johnson," *Down Beat,* May 11, 1961, 18.

35.   Leonard Feather, "J.J. Johnson: Blindfold Test," *Down Beat,* January 30, 1964, 30.

36.   These particular three musicians, all members of Cannonball Adderley's rhythm

section, were later hired by Johnson for his recording of the album *A Touch of Satin,*
Columbia CS 8537.

    37.   Liner notes by Bennie Green, Verve V–8542.

Chapter 6

A Shift in Focus

After recording his album *A Touch of Satin* Johnson became increasingly preoccupied with arranging and composing. As noted in the previous chapter, his decision to disband his sextet in the fall of 1960 shortly after completing his residency at the Lenox School of Jazz was driven by a deep-seated desire for a change. Rather than undertake the burden of leading a working group, Johnson came to concentrate his energies on writing for the balance of the 1960s, continuing in this way through his Hollywood years until well into the 1980s. This is not to deny the impact of his appearances at Newport (July 4, 1964) in a Charlie Parker tribute, his performances later that month with Sonny Stitt and Clark Terry in Tokyo as part of the World Jazz Festival, or those situations in which he assumed the role of guest soloist or leader with ad hoc ensembles. His first priority became writing for two distinct audiences: (1) an elite nurtured on third-stream composition in general and on such Johnson works in particular as *Poem for Brass* and (2) a commercial market associated with Broadway show tunes, television variety shows, jingles, soundtracks for TV cops-and-robbers shows, and full-length movies.

Dizzy Gillespie once briefly commented on his own efforts "to establish jazz as a concert music, a form of art, not just music you hear in clubs or places where they serve whiskey."[1] He proceeded to mention several venues, such as Circle in the Square, the Museum of Modern Art in New York, and the Monterey Jazz Festival, where, particularly in the late 1950s and early 1960s, he had promoted the cause. It was in this context that he commissioned J.J. Johnson in 1960 to write *Perceptions* after hearing his *Poem for Brass*. Running to about thirty-five minutes, *Perceptions* remains Johnson's most ambitious and extended composition. It was recorded on May 22, 1961 for Verve by Gillespie with an ensemble conducted by Gunther Schuller, some four months prior to their presenting the world premiere on September 24, 1961, at the Monterey Jazz Festival. Recalling the experience, Gillespie has referred to the work as "the most difficult piece I'd ever played."[2] But, the nature of the difficulty, it turns out, has far less to do with complex meters or rhythms or unusual demands on the trumpet

141

as much as the simple fact that Gillespie, for most of his solo, is required to read from a fully notated part, much in the tradition of conventional classical music. Indeed, *Perceptions* stands as a vivid example of how ideas of orchestration and harmonic language have been borrowed from such sources as Johnson's Hindemith-inspired *Poem for Brass*, the slightly earlier "Solea" from the Miles Davis/Gil Evans album *Sketches of Spain* (replete with its own appropriations of Manuel De Falla and Joaquin Rodrigo), Igor Stravinsky and Ernest Bloch.

In his holograph score Johnson has subtitled *Perceptions* "suite for solo trumpet, brass ensemble, two harps, bass violin, and percussion." The word "suite" here describes what is a work of six interconnected movements of contrasting moods with the pictorial titles of: (1) The Sword of Orion; (2) Jubelo; (3) Blue Mist; (4) Fantasia; (5) Horn of Plenty; and (6) Ballade.[3] His brass ensemble is closely modeled after *Poem* in its use of six trumpets and four horns. But Johnson treats the trumpets this time with a much greater sense of timbre and nuance, requiring them, like Gillespie himself, to use straight, cup, and Harmon mutes. The lower brass choir here, which omits the two baritone saxophones of the earlier work, consists of three tenor trombones, one bass trombone, and two tubas. What stand out in Johnson's ensemble, however, are the two harps. These instruments impart, particularly in the second and fourth movements, a distinctive atmosphere evocative of Ravel and Stravinsky. Indeed, they are crucial overall in projecting the exotic pitch materials and timbres of the score, helping realize something of what is implied by the visually suggestive main title and the names given to the individual movements. Most compelling of all, given what is known about Johnson's subsequent career in Hollywood, *Perceptions* is perhaps best heard as a quasi movie soundtrack accompanying a drama in one's mind's eye.

The opening movement is a case in point. While it does hint at a rondo structure with what Gunther Schuller has called "a free somewhat responsorial alternation of solo trumpet and brass ensemble," something more is communicated.[4] It might or might not be purely coincidental that roughly the first thirty seconds of both *Perceptions* and the prelude (main title music) of Miklós Rózsa's soundtrack to the 1959 blockbuster movie *Ben-Hur* begin in strikingly similar fashion—a brassy epic sound, full of pentatonic parallelisms. Johnson realizes this perfectly in his opening seven measures that are scored as a six-trumpet fanfare (Fig. 6.1).

The other brass and two harps then join in, dramatizing the mood further in a transitional passage that culminates in a climactic wash of two chords—one derived from the half-step diminished scale on A-flat followed by a half diminished chord on A over an A-flat pedal point. But no sooner has that happened than everything dissolves to a slow pulse on the pitch of E, analogous to cutting away with the camera to a contrasting scene. Indeed, what comes to dominate this movement is anything but epic or grandiose. Gillespie's solo—its initial pitch happens to be E as well—has a poignant, vulnerable quality, much of it inseparable from Johnson's use of the Spanish Phrygian scale on A. It is a sound very much akin to that of "Solea" from the *Sketches of Spain* album, but with subliminal Hebraic suggestions as well, inspired by Bloch's

Fig. 6.1 *Perceptions,* score p. 1, opening fanfare, mm. 1–3.

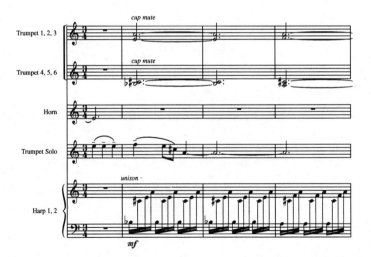

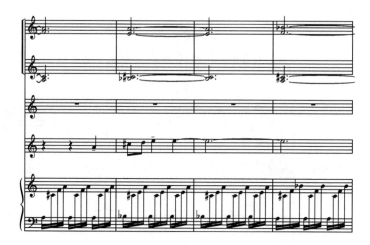

Fig. 6.2 *Perceptions,* reprise of trumpet solo, score pp. 5–6.

Schelomo. This becomes especially strong with the return of the trumpet solo to the accompaniment of the two harps (Fig. 6.2).[5]

"Jubelo," Johnson's second movement, is something of a dreamscape, much of it unfolding from a gently rocking d-Phrygian vamp—an allusion to the Phrygian gestures of the first movement—introduced here by harp harmonics. This is a sound

Fig. 6.3 Stravinsky, "Berceuse" from *Firebird,* Kalmus edition score, p. 67, mm.1–4.

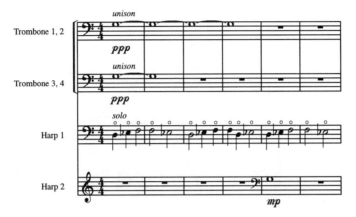

Fig. 6.4 *Perceptions,* score p. 19, mm. 1–6.

reminiscent of the "Berceuse" from Stravinsky's *Firebird,* in which a similar minor third ostinato in harp and violas cradles the bassoon solo (Figs. 6.3 and 6.4).

The mood is sustained by the tone of Gillespie's solo, which is performed with a Harmon mute and notated for the most part by only chord symbols. These are marked "Quasi ad lib," explained in a footnote as "meaning rather sparse and subdued," as the solo instrument spins out its yarn against a "bed" of muted trumpets and lower brass. Gradually and very skillfully, Johnson builds a carefully plotted crescendo, accelerating his rhythm to arrive at a climax of quartal harmony à la Hindemith and a passage of pentatonic parallelisms. The G-Phrygian close of this movement is seamlessly joined to the E-pentatonic opening of the third movement.

This movement, "Blue Mist," brings the percussion group to life, particularly the woodblock and top cymbal as they add energy and spice to the bass ostinato. More importantly, "Blue Mist" is unique among the six movements in its dependence upon traditional thirty-two-bar popular song form. There is a twist, however, in that Johnson's prevailing 7/4 meter alternates with a waltzlike bridge in 6/4. Yet within this structure he provides an element of freedom in that there are passages for solo trumpet, bass, and percussion marked "6/4 jazz free style." Then again, faithful to tradition, Johnson concludes with a climactic shout chorus, but in dissonant parallel harmonies evocative of Gil Evans's most intense scoring for full brass choir (Fig. 6.5).

"Fantasia," Johnson's fourth movement, is, as its title implies, rather loose and rhapsodic. Most of the attention focuses on the solo trumpet and two harps, with occasional interjections from the brass choir. Included are splashes of harp color in the form of the half-diminished seventh chord and the whole-tone scale that leave no doubt as to Johnson's fascination with the sonorities of Debussy and Ravel. The movement's midsection gains in intensity as the solo trumpet, against

Fig. 6.5 *Perceptions,* score p. 84, mm. 1–4.

Fig. 6.6   *Perceptions,* score pp. 95–97.

Fig. 6.7 Bloch, *Schelomo,* Schirmer edition score pp. 18–19, rehearsal 7, mm. 1–4.

an augmented-Lydian "bed" provided by the brass choir and plangent harp sounds, evokes a characteristic sonority of Ernest Bloch's "Hebraic Rhapsody," *Schelomo* (Figs. 6.6 and 6.7).

A varied reprise of the opening material acquires greater pungency as it is rescored, with secundal writing in the trumpets in particular and brass parallelisms in general. But as a movement showing overall minimal repetition or development of thematic material, this fourth segment of the work reveals anew the play of Johnson's timbral and harmonic imagination. At the same time, it provides a foil for the following movement, "Horn of Plenty," perhaps the most charming, extroverted, and conventional-sounding of the movements. The several hints at Gershwin's "There's a Boat Dat's Leaving Soon for New York"—one of the selections on what was the then-recent Gil Evans/Miles Davis *Porgy and Bess* album—are unmistakable. Then again, this movement is the one that swings the hardest, most notably in the passages for solo trumpet and rhythm section.

The concluding movement, the rather bittersweet "Ballade," assumes a burden that is crucial to the substantive aesthetic discussion of any creative work— how to convincingly impart a sense of closure to the composition as a whole. It is a challenge especially daunting in the case of *Perceptions,* with its super- abundance of ideas. What is more, unlike most of his Central European counterparts past and present, Johnson composes a final movement that is the shortest of the entire work. It was in this general context that Max Harrison, reviewing the recording of *Perceptions* after its initial release, remarked:

> Formally the results are not always entirely convincing and there is a little too much of the "free fantasia" about several of the movements for a work of this size. . . . Johnson has gone to the other extreme from those writers who are unable to extend their ideas, and he gives us rather too much that is new in each movement; one could have done with a little more repetition of thematic material. But he will undoubtedly win greater formal control with further composition.[6]

What Johnson does incorporate in "Ballade" are wisps of harmonic and melodic material that allude to what has come before. The pentatonicism and the half-step ascending Phrygian gestures are especially compelling, hinting at the first movement in particular (Fig. 6.8).

In addition, there are whole-tone and Lydian-augmented structures—the closing measures are a case in point—that color the movement. Finally, the sweeping closing line of the solo trumpet itself suggests a bell-like curve, seemingly all-encompassing in its gesture. If *Perceptions* is properly perceived as a series of tableaux, each in its own way evocative and visually suggestive, and expressed by a rich harmonic and timbral imagination, then one has to recognize that Johnson has succeeded brilliantly in prefiguring much of what he was to later do, particularly in film and TV scoring.

As noted earlier, when Dizzy Gillespie commissioned J.J. Johnson to write *Perceptions* he was doing so as part of a larger agenda. A very high priority for Gillespie was to impart a certain legitimacy to jazz by moving it out of the nightclub into the venues of the concert hall, major museums, and festivals such as those at Monterey. A larger drama was being played out that owed its origins to developments in third-stream jazz, the 1957 Brandeis University Festival of the Arts, and other influences. It was a process that by its very nature redefined jazz, simultaneously blurring categories of jazz, classical, and other music.

The career of J.J. Johnson, most vividly in the 1960s and beyond, epitomizes this kind of development. *Perceptions,* with its allusive, pictorial qualities, exemplifies a crossover work with resonances of classical music, jazz, and movie score writing.

Fig. 6.8 *Perceptions,* score p. 98.

Similarly, Johnson's collaboration with André Previn in late 1961 in an album of Kurt Weill selections from *The Threepenny Opera* and other works that Weill wrote for the musical theater typifies a phase.[7] Jazz versions of Broadway show tunes were highly popular while at the same time drawing upon the talents of musicians who embodied overlapping musical traditions and areas of training.

The general tenor of André Previn's career at the time of this recording is illustrative. Although he was classically trained at the Berlin Hochschule für Musik and the Paris Conservatoire, much of his early musical career in the United States was spent in the Hollywood studios of MGM. It was there that he started working in the 1940s as jazz pianist and orchestrator while still in high school. After leaving MGM he garnered a series of Oscars in the late '50s and early '60s for scores to such movies as *Gigi, Porgy and Bess, Irma La Douce,* and *My Fair Lady.* He also collaborated (1956) with drummer Shelly Manne in a highly successful album of *My Fair Lady* selections that initiated a trend featuring jazz albums based on Broadway musicals. Riding the crest of this wave, Previn was asked by *Down Beat* to serve as judge in one of its Blindfold Tests. [8] There were eight selections from an equal number of shows displaying the talents of Tony Scott, Pee-Wee Hunt, Jimmy Giuffre, Manny Albam, Wilbur De Paris, and others.

The one-time collaboration of André Previn and J.J. Johnson on the Kurt Weill album involved a repertoire with which Johnson had never previously been associated and to which he was never to return. Then again, the session appears to have been the idea of André Previn, at the possible urging of Columbia's Irving Townsend. By all accounts Johnson assumed a largely passive role, performing arrangements conceived by Previn, including the much touted writing in "Moritat" (alias "Mack the Knife")—a relatively extended form of bitonality that is unique in the entire Johnson discography. [9]

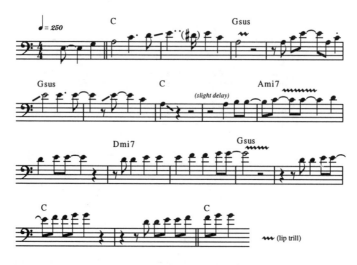

Fig. 6.9   J.J. Johnson solo on Moritat ("Mack the Knife"), from Kurt Weill's *Threepenny Opera,* recorded December 31, 1961. Transcribed by Lewis Porter.

Johnson's memories of the session indicate that this was for him essentially a studio call, a response to a challenge posed by Previn.

> I got a call about this. It intrigued me. When I talked to André he was very nice about it . . . neither of us knew how it would turn out. We were from such different backgrounds. . . . I did it as a challenge . . . to see if we could bring any chemistry to it. And we did. [10]

By contrast, Previn's detailed account of events puts things in perspective and leaves little doubt as to his primary role in the whole undertaking.

> I had had that kind of freak success with those Broadway show things starting with *My Fair Lady*. . . . I forget whose suggestion Kurt Weill was. I don't know whether I thought of it or whether Irv Townsend at Columbia thought of it. But I know that once I examined Kurt Weill's songs I realized that very few of them actually lend themselves to free improvisation, because very few of them are in the accepted thirty-two-bar mold, and a lot of them, even though they're fascinating, are harmonically very limited. So I also knew that if we were going to make a Kurt Weill album it would take a certain amount of arranging . . . it wasn't going to be as straightforward as a normal tune. . . . So once I got to that realization I then also thought of . . . the German songs of Kurt Weill, which are even more blowsy and low-life sounding than the later American ones. And because I wanted them to have that sort of feel it became obvious to me that a trombone was a good instrument to use. . . . J.J. was the most obvious because I knew I was going to write some things that were slightly off the beaten track. And since he was an arranger himself I knew he'd have absolutely not the slightest problem identifying with them and being able to figure out what I wanted. So I guess I must have made that request to Columbia Records and I suppose they found him and asked him, and he was nice enough to say yes.[11]

The chemistry that Johnson imparts to the overall performance is unmistakable. Examples range from the muted tango-inflected ballad entitled "Barbara Song," to the open-horn contrast he is able to project against Previn's secundal backdrop à la Thelonious Monk in "Bilbao Song," to the countermelodies in the "Overture" from *The Threepenny Opera,* to the evocative cops-and-robbers sound of "Pirate Jenny," to the bitonality in "Moritat" ("Mack the Knife").

Taking his cue from André Previn and other jazz colleagues, Johnson was to fairly soon record two of his own albums of standards from Broadway musicals. Rather than undertake a virtually complete recomposition of material, as was the case with Miles Davis and Gil Evans in their *Porgy and Bess* album, Johnson strikes a balance between borrowed and original material. The album *J.J.'s Broadway* is illustrative. It features a collection of highly arranged solo vehicles such as "Lovely," "My Favorite Things," and "Put on a Happy Face." His timbres, textures, and meters, to say nothing of the integration of his own freshly composed material, are all conveyed with great skill by the forces of an accompanying ensemble of four trombones and rhythm on some, and only a rhythm section on others. In all of this Johnson was responding to a challenge of his own, somewhat analogous to what André Previn had previously faced with Kurt Weill's music. As he put it to Nat Hentoff:

> The challenge in this kind of venture is that there are many good show tunes which are really effective only with their lyrics or in Broadway-style treatments.

Amazingly, in some cases when you take away the lyrics, there's nothing there. I searched out those songs with interesting melodic and/or harmonic content—songs that can stand on their own.[12]

Building on this experience, Johnson turned his attention to arranging for large ensemble in a series of recording sessions for RCA from August 1964 to December 1966. A fine illustration of his work during this period is provided by the album *J.J.!* of December 7–9, 1964, his first-ever album fronting a big band. What he assembled for the first two sessions was an aggregation consisting of two trumpets, two trombones, three reeds, piano, bass, and drums. For the third and final session the instrumentation consisted of four trumpets, three trombones, four reeds, French horn, tuba, and rhythm. Such generalities, however, do not convey the subtlety of Johnson's orchestral timbres, let alone the stellar quality and versatility of his sidemen. In the course of the three days his trumpet section, for example, drew upon the talents of Clark Terry, Ernie Royal, and Thad Jones (all doubling on flugelhorn), as well as James Maxwell and Joe Wilder. Other players, such as Harvey Estrin, were heard on soprano saxophone and doubling on four other instruments—alto saxophone, flute, alto flute, and clarinet.

Nine of Johnson's favorite works are featured, six of them in arrangements by Johnson himself. The others are by one of Johnson's reedmen, Oliver Nelson ("Stolen Moments"), while Gary McFarland contributes "Train Samba" and "Winter's Waif." Johnson's arrangements comprise Miles Davis's "Swing Spring," Thelonious Monk's "Bemsha Swing," Charlie Parker's "My Little Suede Shoes," Miles Davis's "So What," George Russell's "Stratusphunk," and his own *El Camino Real*. *El Camino Real* was discussed in the previous chapter in terms of both its musical content and its connection with the 1959 Monterey Jazz Festival. What is therefore appropriate here is to make some observations about other representative Johnson arrangements on the album.

Johnson's brilliance as an orchestrator, animated by an infallible instinct for mood, is apparent throughout. The buoyant, uptempo "Swing Spring" finds a fitting metaphor in the ascending scalar head. This, in turn, provides an apt foil for Johnson's solo with the rhythm section, to which are then added the interjections from trombones, trumpets, and reeds. Trombone pedal points, Hank Jones's piano, and a reorchestrated out-chorus all impart a certain ebullience to the whole. "Bemsha Swing" is a swaggering, funky number. The overblown, folksy flute of Jerome Richardson, the modal parallelisms of reeds and muted brass, and the piano solo of Hank Jones, with its witty ripostes and wry Basie allusion in the tag, all contribute to the sense of fun. "So What" provides a fascinating example of virtual recomposition. The uptempo, swinging quality, the countermelodies to Davis's stark Dorian riff, and the transformation of Paul Chambers's original pizzicato bass into an airy utterance for flutes are among the memorable touches.

Also included is George Russell's "Stratusphunk"—once characterized as "a medium-tempoed blues that intimates atonality though it maintains an essential tonality—Blues in F."[13] Johnson's treatment of the score is filled with original strokes. These range from the introductory falling minor seventh motif on solo trombone against walking bass, to the development of this as Johnson plays out the idea against the full band, to Oliver Nelson's tenor saxophone solo, to the bebopper version of Dixieland polyphony in the climax. It is a climax that serves as a dramatic foil for the original out chorus as things unwind, leaving the lone bass of Bob Cranshaw to pick up bits and pieces. "My Little Suede Shoes" transports one to another universe. The introduction alone is a compelling study in witty, pointillistic touches and registral shifts as Cranshaw's bass solo, initially supported by rhythm only, is contrasted with responses from trombones and flutes. The suggestive samba beat, antiphonal muted effects in trumpets, and the original sonority of flute and muted solo trombone and then of flute and muted trumpets all serve to epitomize the humor and impeccable taste that are the essence of J.J. Johnson.

Johnson has the fondest memories of the 1960s New York studio scene and the good times spent with fellow musicians. In an electronic mail posting of July 28, 1998, he shared this about his friendship with trombonist Urbie Green:

> Friends, has anyone seen Urban Clifford Green lately? Does he have a Web page? What a gifted trombonist. I have great respect for him and his gargantuan talents. Also, we were good friends. . . . we became good friends back in the 60's when I did the New York studio scene for a spell (my sightreading savvy had to improve, but quick, very quick, and it did). Back then Urbie was the #1 "first-call" trombonist for all of the big-time contractors. The so-called studio scene in NY was throbbing and thriving at that time. I'll have you know that I even did the Broadway musical pit orchestra scene once, playing 2nd trombone in the musical, "Flora, the Red Menace" starring Liza Minnelli; but that's another story for another post. Back to Urbie. In addition to his considerable talents and warm, friendly persona, he had a dry, wry sense of humor that cracked me up at times. When I sat next to him in the 'bone section on a studio call, he would lean over and whisper in my ear things like: "J.J., this conductor is drunk with power; don't trust his upbeat," and other such witticisms. One night, after a rather grueling recording session, he and I decided to just "hang out" together. We hit almost every bar in midtown NY until almost daybreak. What a hangover!!!!

It was around January 1965, a few months into his RCA contract, that Johnson received a call to play on Quincy Jones's soundtrack to the Sydney Lumet movie *The Pawnbroker*.[14] Filmed on location in Harlem and released in 1965, the movie tells the haunting story of a Jewish survivor of the Nazi death camps who is eking out his existence in the world of the African-American ghetto. Performing the riveting score, with its melding of Old and New World elements, and seeing first-hand how Jones met the challenges of synchronizing the music with film footage proved to be a turning point for Johnson. It was this experience more than any other that convinced him to set his sights on composing for the Hollywood studios.[15]

Being a member of Quincy Jones's orchestra for the recording of *The Pawnbroker* soundtrack provided Johnson with the stimulus of contact with colleagues such as Freddie Hubbard and Oliver Nelson. It was Oliver Nelson and his accomplishments as composer and arranger that goaded Johnson into more sharply honing his own skills. Saxophonist Phil Woods, a regular on the studio scene of the day and one who worked with Johnson on a variety of other dates, has recalled: "J.J. was always checking out Oliver's scores. Whenever there was a break and we'd go out for coffee, J.J. would be hovering around the podium checking out how Oliver wrote this, how he voiced it."[16]

The first four months of 1966 found Johnson answering a studio call of a different sort when he was hired to play in the trombone section of the *Sammy Davis, Jr. Show*. The show, which ran from January 7 to April 22, also involved his serving as co–principal arranger with O.B. Massingill.[17] This was a sizable thirty-piece ensemble composed of eleven strings, five reeds (doubling on various woodwinds), four trumpets, four trombones, drums, two percussion, guitar, piano, and harp. The sixteen one-hour weekly programs of this NBC TV variety show, with their range of vocals, dance routines, and other production numbers, introduced Johnson to a world of commercial assignments and one largely devoid of jazz content.[18] Guests on the show could range from Richard Burton and Elizabeth Taylor to the Andrews Sisters, Mel Tormé, the Supremes, or Judy Garland. There were also very tight deadlines. In a typical week the director, writers, and arrangers would meet on a Tuesday to decide what musical material was going to be required. Starting the next day, pencilled arrangements in full score would begin coming in. Parts had to then be prepared within some forty-eight hours so as to be ready for a full day of rehearsal on Saturday, which often continued into the evening. Last-minute changes, additions, substitutions and the like were a fact of this fast-paced life. Sunday was the day for taping the show at NBC's main color studio at 13th and Avenue M in the Flatbush section of Brooklyn. If anything, this work situation, where so much was ruled by the clock, served as a prelude to the bigger acts to follow in Johnson's professional career— writing commercials for MBA Music and underscoring in Hollywood motion pictures and television series.

Then again, Johnson was able to indulge his creative urges, flirting with ideas inspired by Stravinsky, for example, and trying them out on the orchestra. Bert Kosow, supervising copyist on the show, fondly remembers how much Johnson relished being nicknamed "Igor," especially after Johnson's fellow arranger, O.B. Massingill, a man of more traditional stripe, once remarked to him: "Man, you sound like Igor Stravinsky!"[19] Johnson took it as a high compliment, and around this time was seen at the Bums Ball, an annual fund-raiser for inner-city black kids, attired in a tattered vest with "Igor" written in bold letters across the back and a broad smile on his face.[20]

Equally revealing about overlapping musical categories in Johnson's life at this point, not to mention the pace of events, is that on May 5, 1966, some two weeks after the last *Sammy Davis, Jr. Show* was aired, he wrote a check to Bert Kosow. Johnson was paying him in advance for preparing parts of his *Eurosuite,* a commission from Friedrich Gulda and his Eurojazz Orchestra, which was recorded that summer. Even though the title of *Eurosuite* might well suggest some affinity with Ellington's travelogues of the same general period, notably *The Far East Suite* (1966) and *The Latin American Suite* (1968), Johnson's work is "Euro" primarily because of the players involved. Gulda's group was indeed true to its name, with J.J. Johnson, Ernie Royal, Ron Carter, and Mel Lewis as the only American personnel. Writing for a seventeen-piece ensemble, including himself on trombone and Joe Zawinul on piano, Johnson successfully addressed some special challenges. Unlike other big bands, Gulda's aggregation had three instead of four saxophones, and a small brass section of three trumpets and two trombones. Yet adding to the unique darker timbre was the presence of tuba (bass and tenor), bass clarinet, and the bass trumpet.[21]

Johnson's introduction to the first movement, with its evocative bass clarinet solo and rich brass scoring, makes an association with Harry Carney and Duke Ellington difficult to avoid. What directly follows, however, is a hard swinging ballad for trombone solo supported largely by rhythm with occasional responses from the full ensemble. The opening of the second movement is similarly atmospheric, with telling touches by muted trumpets, bass clarinet, and washes of color on the piano. What follows is a bluesy affair showcasing the flute, alto saxophone, and baritone saxophone. The third movement is driven by the rhythm of piano, bass, and cymbal work. Johnson's fragmented, stop-and-go, repeated-note riff recalls his early connection with Count Basie, not to mention his own later works such as "Turnpike" and "Fox Hunt." His brief fourth and final movement conveys the effect of a tag, an out chorus for the full ensemble.

Johnson's only other primarily classical essay during this period was his 1968 commission from Robert A. Boudreau, music director of the American Wind Symphony Orchestra in Pittsburgh. *Diversions,* a work for six trombones, celesta, harp, and percussion, is part of a body of some four hundred works commissioned by Boudreau since the founding of his ensemble around 1957.[22] Contributing composers have been highly diverse, including Henk Badings, Alan Hovhaness, David Amram, Jacques Castérède, Robert Russell Bennett, Heitor Villa-Lobos, Paul Creston, Krzystof Penderecki, and William Bolcom.

Diversions is true to its name in one basic respect. It represents a diversion for Johnson from his more accustomed mode of orchestration in that much of his attention is focused on his percussion group. Although the writing for the trombones, celesta, and harp contains few surprises, it is his marshaling here of large percussion forces that is unique in his output. There are, in fact, five subgroups specified in the score containing an array of timpani of various sizes (twenty-one to thirty inches), marimba, vibraphone, xylophone, chimes, orchestral bells, cymbals (as well as pairs of small metal cymbals called crotales), Japanese woodblock and temple bells, and more. The inclusion of the rather exotic Japanese instruments reflects the relatively recent discoveries Johnson made in the course of his visit to Japan in July 1964 when he toured the country with Sonny Stitt and Clark Terry in an all-star sextet. Then again, the emphasis on the percussion group as a whole must also be attributed to the commission itself and its association with an ensemble identified with outdoor performance.

Commercial studio work, however, remained Johnson's principal livelihood at this time. It was around 1966 that he met up with Marc Brown, studio violinist and flamboyant entrepreneur extraordinaire, who was starting the production house for radio and TV jingles of Marc Brown Associates, otherwise known as MBA Music, Inc. Johnson was made an offer he simply could not refuse—the opportunity to advance his ambitions as a composer while earning a good steady income plus residuals. It was hard to resist Marc Brown. Here was a man who reportedly walked up thirty-two flights of stairs during an elevator strike to sign a highly lucrative Chevrolet account with the advertising agency of Campbell Ewald. Dorothy Greenberg, a close childhood friend and onetime treasurer of MBA Music, put it this way: "Marc was a very fascinating, very crazy young man . . . he had a lot of charisma, and he was very enchanting. He could sell ice to Eskimoes."[23] Epitomizing the image of dressing for success—he had grown up very poor and as one of the unwashed—Marc Brown had closets full of expensive Italian shoes and custom-tailored suits and he drove around with a personal chauffeur.

Even more to the point, Marc Brown had an uncanny instinct for matching client with musical concept and product. His was a musical antenna tuned to the latest trends yet at the same time wired to an older classical tradition. He had in fact been a violin prodigy and continued performing in public until at least the late 1960s. This was a man who had the savvy to be among the first to include the Fifth Dimension, the Swingle Singers, or the Moog synthesizer in commercials, and who could also be heard in recital at Town Hall performing sonatas of Schubert, Beethoven, Brahms, and Piston with his childhood friend Elmer Bernstein. [24]

Ensconced in three converted apartments at 8 East 48th Street, Marc Brown Associates was for a while in a feeding frenzy. There was a boom for commercials, including station identifications involving TV and radio that promoted such clients as American Airlines, Ford, Alcoa, and Heinz. The firm was garnering Clio Awards, money was pouring in, and the sky was the limit.

At its height, MBA Music had six writers on staff, each with their own clients, offices, and secretaries. But, the pressure to work under frequent overnight deadlines, while intense, was not without its moments of mischievous humor. Walt Levinsky, alto saxophone veteran of the Tommy Dorsey and Benny Goodman bands, and assistant conductor of the *Tonight Show* band, joined MBA Music shortly before J.J. Johnson and has shared the following anecdote. It appears that one evening, when he was on the verge of walking out of the lobby and going home for dinner, a vice president from Gray Advertising showed up, film footage in hand,

and insisted on having a commercial composed and ready for recording the very next morning. Levinsky had to return upstairs, look at the film, take timings, compose original music, and call people to get an orchestra and studio booked. Before leaving, the man from Gray said: "Listen, I want to hear the music before we record it . . . call me tonight when you're done and play it over the phone."[25] But Levinsky replied: "Look, I might not be done before midnight." The client was not deterred. "Doesn't matter. Call me." Levinsky actually did finish the piece around midnight, but decided to set his alarm for four A.M. and call the Gray man when he knew he was sound asleep and play it for him then. Now, as primarily a reed player, Levinsky was not all that proficient at the keyboard, yet he was able to make the most of this moment of mischief by playing "nonsense chords" and singing "totally out of context." He let this go on for about thirty seconds, stopped, and then asked: "What do you think ?" There was a long silence. Finally there came a sleepy reply: "I guess it will sound better when the orchestra plays it."[26]

For his part, Johnson has offered a somewhat more sober assessment of his years at MBA Music. While fondly remembering the lavish daily in-house lunches for clients and staff, Marc Brown's closets crammed with shoes and more, or how Dorothy Greenberg arrived at work every day in midtown Manhattan on a bicycle, he has focused on what it all meant to his larger musical development. He relished

Fig. 6.10   Stock certificate issued by Marc Brown Associates (MBA Music). Certificate courtesy of Dorothy Greenberg.

the idea of having his own office, with scores, reference books, metronome, access to a Moviola, and whatever else he wanted. His creative juices were flowing—at times like ketchup. Indeed, one of his major successes was a Heinz ketchup commercial with the slogan "It's slow good." And what Johnson wrote was a romantic ballad played by none other than Bobby Hackett on cornet.[27] It was, however, only incidental to Johnson's larger agenda. As he put it,

> J.J. went into the MBA Music thing knowing that he would go from that someday into Hollywood film scoring because at MBA he learned the craft and mathematics of film production . . . in both arenas, whether it be television commercials or . . . doing *Jurassic Park,* the same film mathematics applies.[28]

Coinciding with these developments was Johnson's discovery of the Moog synthesizer and multitrack recording.[29] Then again, a number of MBA Music competitors were beginning to use the Moog synthesizer. Marc Brown, not to be outdone, promptly purchased one as well and dispatched J.J. Johnson to Trumansburg, New York, to take a three-day cram course with Robert A. Moog himself. What he learned there came to benefit not only MBA Music but also Johnson in his subsequent career, both in Hollywood and in his home studio.

By the fall of 1968, however, changes were under way at MBA Music that did not bode well as boom was changing to bust. Ever eager to expand, Marc Brown suffered from the fatal flaw of not knowing his limits and became involved in recording and publishing projects, two enterprises in which he had no experience. Purported experts were brought in from Motown and Atlantic Records, heads began to roll, and the sense of positive morale and trust was soon eroded. What is more, a close lifelong friend like Dorothy Greenberg has said that skulduggery was most probably at work in that staff composers or arrangers like J.J. Johnson, Walt Levinsky, or Tommy Newsom were not given a fair fifty-fifty split of the profits. In fact, it became a typical ploy of Marc Brown to seduce staff members with titles like "vice president" or "president" rather than pay them fair and square. One therefore has to approach the following announcement in *Variety* with a certain degree of cynicism.

NAME JAZZMAN JOHNSON PRESIDENT OF MBA MUSIC
Top jazz trombonist J.J. Johnson has been named president of MBA Music, New York firm specializing in radio and television music tracks. For the past two years, Johnson has been staff composer, arranger, and conductor at MBA. Johnson is believed to be the first Negro heading such an operation. Marc Brown, founder of the company, is board chairman.[30]

Johnson was to leave a little over a year later. While wrapping up his affairs at MBA Music he was invited to participate in the White House celebration on April 29, 1969, when President Richard M. Nixon honored Duke Ellington with the Medal of Freedom on the occasion of his seventieth birthday.[31] Johnson and

Fig. 6.11   Seventieth birthday celebration for Duke Ellington hosted by President and Mrs. Richard M. Nixon. *Left to right:* Dave Brubeck; Hank Jones; Jim Hall; Tom Whaley; Paul Desmond; Earl "Fatha" Hines; Gerry Mulligan; Billy Taylor; Mary Mayo; Milt Hinton; Willis Conover; Richard M. Nixon; Louie Bellson, hidden behind Conover and Nixon; Clark Terry; Duke Ellington; Joe Williams; Urbie Green; J.J. Johnson; Bill Berry. Photograph courtesy of Institute of Jazz Studies.

his wife, Vivian, were part of a guest list that included Dizzy Gillespie, Harold Arlen, Mary Mayo, Joe Williams, Benny Goodman, Cab Calloway, Billy Eckstine, Earl Hines, Milt Hinton, Billy Taylor, Gerry Mulligan, Clark Terry, Urbie Green, and Paul Desmond. A formal program featuring many of Ellington's compositions was followed by a massive jam session that reportedly included Vice President Spiro Agnew doing a turn on "Sophisticated Lady."

A seventieth-birthday celebration, whether of a jazz immortal or not, resonates with a certain biblical meaning. Indeed, attaining the age of three-score years and ten can often serve as a moment of deep introspection as much as of joyous affirmation. What is compelling about Johnson's career is the way it was to intersect with that of another jazz immortal eighteen years later, once again in the area of Washington, D.C. It was on June 5, 1987, that Johnson participated in the seventieth-birthday celebration of Dizzy Gillespie at Wolf Trap. Only on this occasion, instead being about to head west to seek fame and fortune in Hollywood, he was returning home to Indianapolis, a far more sober man reconnecting with his past and trying to find his musical compass once again.

Notes

1.   Dizzy Gillespie and Al Fraser, *To Be or Not to Bop: Memoirs of Dizzy Gillespie* (Garden City, N. Y.: Doubleday, 1979), 448.

2.   *Ibid.*

3.   Johnson has claimed that the titles of the first two movements were inspired by a period when he was briefly active as a member of the Shriners. Interview with J.J. Johnson, Indianapolis, July 24, 1992. Although widely known as a fraternal and charitable organization, the Shriners (founded in 1872) have a more formal name expressing a sense of history that is lost in the mists of an exotic past: "Ancient Imperial Council of the Ancient Arabic Order of the Nobles of the Mystic Shrine for North America." See *Encyclopedia of Associations* (Detroit: Gale Research, 1995), Vol. I, Part 2, 2218.

4.   Schuller's comment is excerpted from his liner notes to Verve recording V6-8411.

5.   Johnson's immersion in major twentieth-century scores is discussed in chapter 4 as part of his larger involvement in the third-stream genre and his being nourished by the stylistic tributaries represented by John Carisi, Gunther Schuller, and others. Bloch's *Schelomo* is mentioned as one of the works introduced to him during this immersion. Interview with David and Lida Baker, Indianapolis, February 26, 1994. The Bloch work is cited again, this time in the context of an answer by J.J. Johnson to a question about the impact of Jewish music on the evolution of jazz. "One of my favorite pieces is *Schelomo,* a concerto for 'cello, very sad, that brings me to the point of tears." *Musica Jazz* (January 1995), 25.

6.   Max Harrison, "*Perceptions* and a question of unity," *Jazz Monthly* (July 1962), 25.

7.   There was a larger context giving meaning to all of this. The decade of the 1950s had not only witnessed the rampant hysteria of McCarthyism; it was also in 1952 that Marc Blitzstein, a blacklisted composer, gained considerable acclaim for his translation and adaptation of *The Threepenny Opera.*

8. *Down Beat,* January 8, 1959, 35.

9. There is no evidence to support the assumption sometimes made that Johnson conceived of the bitonal idea of having the piano and trombone simultaneously play in G-flat and C respectively. In fact, the liner notes to the Columbia album (stereo 32 160260) singled out this particular number as posing the greatest challenge because of the daunting precedents set by earlier musicians, but that "André had the answer . . . it came in the shape of a delightful exercise in bitonality." At the same time, there is no denying the mature sophistication of Johnson's solo per se.

10. Interview with J.J. Johnson, Indianapolis, July 24, 1992.

11. Interview with André Previn, Bedford Hills, New York, August 5, 1992. Of course, the fact that Johnson was a Columbia artist at the time simplified matters considerably.

12. Nat Hentoff, liner notes to Verve V-8530.

13. These are the words of Burt Korall writing in a 1960 BMI promotional brochure.

14. Although Quincy Jones was credited with composing the "explosive motion picture score," his soundtrack was not entirely his work alone. According to the notes accompanying the compact disc reissue on Verve (314 531 233-2), Billy Byers and Dick Hazard were responsible for the writing of unspecified arrangements.

15. Interview with Lida and David Baker.

16. Phil Woods interviewed by Bill Kirchner, Delaware Water Gap, Pennsylvania, March 18, 1995. Bill Kirchner's sharing of this interview excerpt is gratefully acknowledged.

17. Dates of the Sammy Davis, Jr. Show were provided by the Museum of Television and Radio, New York.

18. In the late 1960s and continuing into his early years in California, Johnson was involved with other sporadic commercial TV ventures as well. Important in this connection was his association with Peter Matz, who was instrumental in getting him work as section man and arranger on such shows as *Hullabaloo, The Kraft Music Hall,* and *The Carol Burnett Show.*

19. Interview with Bert Kosow, Flushing, New York, August 14, 1995.

20. *Ibid.* At the time, Vivian Johnson was apparently involved in a prominent women's social organization called the Continentals, a group that sponsored the annual Bums Ball.

21. Johnson's inclusion of bass trumpet harks back to his familiarity with such scores as Strauss's *Ein Heldenleben* and Stravinsky's *Rite of Spring.*

22. All commissioned works are published by C.F. Peters Corporation.

23. Interview with Dorothy Greenberg, New York, January 31, 1995.

24. Elmer Bernstein was a childhood friend of both Marc Brown and Dorothy Greenberg dating from their summers in Woodstock, New York, and from their years together at the Walden School; the Town Hall recital of October 22, 1967, was for the benefit of their alma mater. At the same time, the recital revealed Elmer Bernstein in an unfamiliar pianistic guise rather than as a composer of jazz film scores such as *The Man with the Golden Arm* and *Walk on the Wild Side.* It was Bernstein who was a short time later to help Johnson make contacts in the Hollywood film industry.

25. Interview with Walt Levinsky, Sarasota, Florida, December 4, 1994.

26. *Ibid.*

27. Johnson's Heinz ketchup commercial is not to be confused with a slightly later version adapting Carly Simon's song "Anticipation" (1971).

28. Interview with J.J. Johnson, New York, December 21, 1994. Johnson's reference to "film mathematics" is based on the fact that the standard speed at which a thirty-five millimeter film is run through a projector is twenty-four frames per second. Johnson's major film scoring mentor in Hollywood, Earle Hagen, would always quote the formula $3 = 2$, that is, three feet of film is equivalent to two seconds of music. Incidentally, J.J. Johnson will often refer to himself in the third person, epitomizing a certain characteristic sense of detachment.

29. In addition, Johnson found himself drawn in the early 1970s to Isao Tomita's album *Snowflakes Are Dancing* as well as his electronic versions of Mussorgsky's *Night on Bald Mountain* and *Pictures at an Exhibition.*

30. *Variety,* Wednesday, September 11, 1968, 87.

31. Information on the Duke Ellington celebration was culled from various sources: *Jet,* May 15, 1969; the Billy Taylor interview appearing in *The New York Times,* April 30, 1969; and Elise K. Kirk, *Music at the White House* (Urbana and Chicago: University of Illinois Press, 1986).

Chapter 7

The Hollywood Years, 1970–87

By 1970 Johnson had attained a supremacy as trombonist on the international jazz scene that was beyond question. At the same time he had made his mark as a highly skilled arranger and composer, from his earliest efforts for the Benny Carter Orchestra to his most recent achievements on the staff of MBA Music, Inc. But his move to Hollywood was fraught with uncertainty and was to ultimately prove profoundly disappointing. For all his accomplishments, Johnson was ill prepared for a movie and TV industry that operated by a set of stereotypes involving black jazzmen. His transition into the industry was daunting challenge and difficulties were compounded by the stark facts of his career. Now forty-six years of age, and without any experience as a conservatory-trained opera or ballet composer, as a composer of pop songs, or as a seasoned veteran who had worked in such areas as musical theater or vaudeville in the capacity of conductor or rehearsal pianist, he was hoping to enter a highly competitive arena and learn firsthand the craft of integrating music with dramatic visual images and action. The path of his career thus departed sharply from those of Erich Wolfgang Korngold, Max Steiner, Bernard Herrmann, Franz Waxman, Miklós Rózsa, David Raksin, Alfred Newman, Elmer Bernstein, Jerry Goldsmith, André Previn, Oliver Nelson, Lalo Schifrin, or Marvin Hamlisch.

One is therefore struck by a certain plucky naiveté on Johnson's part, even though he did have a contact or two to whom to turn. Elmer Bernstein, whom he knew from his prior association with Marc Brown, introduced him to Al Bart and his partner, Stan Millander—agents who had an impressive record of pitching film composers. There were other connections that proved valuable as well.

> I came out here not knowing very many people who were in a position to recommend me. Quincy Jones was particularly helpful. I had been out here a little while when I worked with him and Ray Brown on an album they recorded of music from *The Adventurers*. Quincy got me to do some of the orchestrating on that. . . . Another very good friend was Herb Eisenmann, who was a Broadcast Music, Inc. representative when I came to Los Angeles. I went to him because friends had recommended me to him. He immediately called the late Leith

Stevens, and this led directly to my being assigned to write for *Barefoot in the Park*. That was how I got my feet wet in television, and it was an invaluable experience.[1]

But it was Earle Hagen, above all, who was Johnson's principal mentor. A veteran of the Hollywood studios, he was sufficiently impressed by Johnson's *Poem for Brass* and his experience in writing commercial jingles to assign him work on some of the most popular television shows in the industry. These included *Mayberry R.F.D., The Danny Thomas Show, That Girl, Mod Squad, Starsky and Hutch, The Six Million Dollar Man,* and *Mike Hammer*. Earle Hagen represented a long-standing tradition of composing film cues to be performed on a sound stage, all of them tightly controlled by the "mathematics" of film scoring.[2] A trombonist–arranger of the big band era—he had worked with Tommy Dorsey, Benny Goodman, and Ray Noble, among others—Hagen became an apprentice in 1946 to Alfred Newman at Twentieth Century-Fox Studios, where he remained for seven years. Working in the afterglow of composers such as Korngold and Steiner, he had in 1967 won an "Emmy" for the TV series *I Spy,* was offering classes in film scoring, and was gathering material for a definitive book, *Scoring for Films* (1971).[3] Johnson summed up his association with Earle Hagen as follows:

> Hagen is a veteran film scorer and I learned a great deal from him and his staff. Above and beyond being my boss, he took a liking to me and spent a lot of time helping me. This was a very beneficial period; I learned a lot about the mechanics, the whole philosophy involved in this kind of writing.[4]

It was in film rather than television that Johnson scored his first and most conspicuous successes. From 1971 to 1973 he served as composer or orchestrator for seven films, all of them examples of the blaxploitation genre. These black action adventures, generally set in the urban ghetto, were the rage between 1969 and 1974, when some sixty such films were produced. As such they signify larger issues in the drama of African-American culture that reduced Johnson to little more than a bit player. Ed Guerrero has suggested that the blaxploitation genre "emerged out of the dialectical interactions of three broad, overdetermining conditions of possibility."[5] There was for him, first and foremost, a heightened nationalist impulse arising from the civil rights movement that translated into a deep-seated need to see a "full humanity" portrayed on the screen. Associated with this was the outspoken criticism of the Hollywood practice of persistently degrading African-Americans. Third, and coinciding with this criticism, was the virtual collapse of the film industry in the late 1960s, which in turn caused it to focus on black-oriented features in an act of financial and moral redemption. But, the process of change did not occur without the tarring and feathering of black actors. Sidney Poitier is the most egregious example, the butt of criticism and even ridicule for his role in "integrationist film narrative." Guerrero argues his point by quoting black dramatist Clifford Mason, who attacks Poitier for his hypocrisy in "regretting" his roles in *Porgy and Bess* (1959), *The Long Ships* (1963), not to mention *Lilies of the Field* (1963), *A Patch of Blue* (1965), and *To Sir with Love* (1967). Poitier is dismissed as "a showcase nigger, who is given a clean suit and a complete purity of motivation so that like a mistreated puppy, he has all the sympathy on his side and all mean whites are just so many Simon Legrees."[6] To counter the "Sidney Poitier syndrome" and the image of the "good boy in a totally white world" helping the white man solve the problems of that world, there emerged the image of the more assertive black, macho, athletic hero as epitomized in the blaxploitation movie genre.[7]

As a black James Bond–type action film, *Shaft* (1971) focuses on the exploits of private eye John Shaft (Richard Roundtree), who is hired by Harlem mobster Bumpy Jonas (Moses Gunn) to find his kidnapped daughter. But infiltrating the mob before finding the girl is only part of the story. As an industry-backed moneymaking venture, *Shaft* refined certain conventions of the "superspade" protagonist that had recently been realized in *Sweet Sweetback* of Melvin Van Peebles.[8] John Shaft is a private eye capable of negotiating "the tensions of functioning in a white-dominated world while still portraying the sexploitative, aggressive, black *macho* image served up for consumption by young, urban black audiences."[9] Three urban locations define the action. Shaft occupies a townhouse in Greenwich Village and maintains an office in midtown Manhattan where he monitors the turf wars in Harlem. Then again, he mediates in a case of gang warfare between the black uptown mob and the white downtown Mafia. Last, but not least, this is a man of sexual prowess in a win-win situation. Although he has a black girlfriend, he is not above having random sex in his shower with a white woman picked up at a neighborhood bar in Greenwich Village.

Johnson's first venture into the blaxploitation genre was in this 1971 film—a major commercial success for the principals involved. Johnson's actual role was a rather limited one, confined to providing miscellaneous cues—precise details of his involvement remain elusive—and cowriting only one selection with Isaac Hayes. The soundtrack was in fact very much a celebration of Isaac Hayes and his special mix of soul, rhythm and blues, and early disco. He was flush with the success of his 1969 gold-record *Hot Buttered Soul* album and widely known for his work with the Memphis-based company of Stax Records, not to mention his serving as keyboard accompanist to the recently deceased soul singer and songwriter Otis Redding. The *Shaft* theme song by Isaac Hayes not only rose to number one on the pop charts but also garnered an Academy Award, a Golden Globe, and two Grammy Awards. Even more important, *Shaft* won an Oscar for the soundtrack and proved to be a distinct triumph for MGM. Costing $1.2 million to produce, it earned over $10.8 million in its first year of distribution.[10] But *Shaft* was significant in other ways: it was the first major Hollywood film of black director Gordon Parks, a man who had earlier broken racial barriers as a staff photographer at *Life* magazine.

None of this is meant to belittle Johnson's contributions in any way. By the same token, it reveals in the starkest light the daunting, ultimately insurmountable challenge he faced in trying to become established as a Hollywood composer in his own right, even within the genre of the blaxploitation movie. At the same time, Johnson's writing for the *Shaft* soundtrack is to a large extent generic, illustrative of what he was to do subsequently in his six other blaxploitation films. Comparison of various cues indicates an adroit melding of underscoring and the use of source music, that is, sounds coming from the scene being shot and heard by the actors themselves. Even though such melding is done by a sound editor, it does nevertheless help place Johnson's actual cues in the proper context.

The cue "Shaft and Ben," which begins at 40:44 into the film and has a running time of 1:27, readily lends itself to narrative description. It is an especially effective example of underscoring that flows directly from the ambient sound sources of machine-gun fire, a woman's screams, police sirens, and screeching tires. Shaft and Ben Buford—they "put in a lot of street time" together—are making their escape from an upper Amsterdam Avenue tenement where five of Ben's buddies have just been machine-gunned to death by Bumpy Jonas's men. The cue generates much of its tension from the progressive layering of the ride cymbal rhythm, sequencer ostinato, and bass guitar riff. Unison flutes in a low register coupled with pointillistic trombones against horns add to the overall impact.

Cowritten with Isaac Hayes, the cue "Walk from Reggio's" shows another aspect of Johnson's work on the *Shaft* soundtrack. It is a piece of underscoring that accompanies a Greenwich Village scene in which a ruse of Shaft's pays off. Shaft, led by one of the Mafia flunkies, makes his way from the cafe on MacDougal Street to an apartment hideaway a few blocks away where Bumpy Jonas's daughter Marcy is being held hostage by the mob. Starting at 76:27 and running for 2:21, this particular cue coincides with the approaching climax of the movie. There is a pointillistic quality to the writing combined with a five-layer effect of sharply differentiated timbres, with a bass guitar riff, bongos, muted trumpets, trombones, and chords on electric piano. This is disco music featuring a catchy dorian theme coupled with a contrasting mixolydian tumbling strain (on IV). The edge to the music serves as a perfect segue from the preceding cafe scene that includes the following sharp exchange between Shaft and the unnamed Mafia flunky as they trade insults:

"I'm looking for a nigger named John Shaft."

"You just found him, wop! Sit down."

"I'm supposed to take you to visit a lady. Come on."

"I haven't finished my espresso. Why don't you have some ? Maybe they'll put a little garlic in it . . ."

SPOT ON FILM	CUE TIMINGS	DESCRIPTION
Office Fight		
9:00		Long shot of lobby of Shaft's office building. Shaft about to enter when he notices one of "bad cats" sent by mobster Jonas leaning against coffee counter.
9:16	0:00	Shaft enters from rear of lobby accompanied by ominous notes in low piano register outlining tritone, ascending fourths in bass, and secundal flute riffs in an ascending pattern.
9:40	0:24	Stalks "cat" and gives him a sharp jab in lower back.
	0:29	Drags him to elevator.
	0:41	Shaft disarms him while they ride up to Shaft's office. Flute riffs keep rising; also bongo breaks. Cut to office shows accomplice waiting.
10:25	1:11	Plunge through office door to accompaniment of bass guitar riff. Find accomplice (Leroy) in office. Fight and thud of coat tree, shattering of glass.
	1:25	Further shattering of glass as Leroy is hurled out window. Bass guitar ostinato.
10:57	1:43	Brass crescendo segues into shrieks of pedestrians as cue ends.

Fig. 7.1   Music cue from the motion picture *Shaft* (1971).

"Walk from Reggio's" perfectly complements the ensuing street scene, which is virtually without dialogue and is concerned almost entirely with the physical act of walking. There is frequent cross-cutting, including many reaction shots involving Shaft and the mafioso on the one hand and Ben Buford and his two buddies on the other, who are bringing up the rear guard and providing tactical support. Extreme close-ups, low-angle shots, and panning are all critical to the jagged overall rhythm of the scene, which, rather like the writing of the cue itself, centers on the action of a quintet.

After completing his *Shaft* assignment Johnson became involved in six other blaxploitation films. Four of these were released in 1972: *Across 110th Street*, *Man and Boy*, *Trouble Man*, and *Top of the Heap*. But his status as a film composer recognized in his own right was far from assured. It is revealing that with *Trouble Man* Johnson once again found himself in the shadow of another musician with major box-office appeal, Marvin Gaye. And in the case of *Man and Boy,* even though he composed and orchestrated his own music, it was Quincy Jones who was given screen credit for "musical supervision." While Jones had long since been given screen credit, as in the case of the 1965 movie *The Pawnbroker,* Johnson was in effect still treated as a journeyman. To a large extent, this reflected an industrywide practice in that only known, "safe" quantities were given due credit; a whole army of unsung heroes—orchestrators as well as composers—would be paid but not credited. Full screen credit was to come with such releases as *Across 110th Street* (1972), a case where Johnson shares billing with gospel singer–songwriter Bobby Womack. The details of their respective contributions are quite explicit: "score composed and conducted by J.J. Johnson"; "title song composed by Bobby Womack and J.J. Johnson"; "additional songs composed by Bobby Womack and performed by him."

Across 110th Street, arguably the most violent film of gang warfare with which Johnson was ever associated, afforded him the opportunity to write sharply drawn cues and bridges. It is a movie in which, within the first twelve minutes, the stage is set for the ensuing wave of intimidation, torture, castration, and revenge killing. The cycle of violence begins as two black hoods disguised as cops "jive" their way into a rendezvous at a Harlem tenement where two of Don Gennarro's henchmen and their three black flunkies are counting the week's take from a Mafia-controlled Harlem numbers bank. After machine-gunning all five men the two black hoods—Jim Harris (Paul Benjamin) and his accomplice, Joe Logart (Ed Bernard)—escape with $300,000 in loot, but not before fatally shooting a cop on the street and running over another in the getaway car. The action then shifts to a celebration of the Don Gennarro clan where word of the Harlem carnage has gotten out. As the don tells his son-in-law, punk errand boy Nick D'Salvio (Anthony Franciosa), "we have to teach them a lesson," it becomes clear that a lot more than the stolen $300,000 is at stake; it is a matter of family prestige, *"l'onore."* What then unfolds is a drama of escalating violence, with D'Salvio and his hoods on the one hand, and New York police captain Mattelli (Anthony Quinn) and detective lieutenant Pope (Yaphet Kotto) on the other, converging on the black gangleader Jim Harris and his accomplices. Adding to the tension are episodes of friction between Mattelli, who feels he is being passed over because of age and affirmative action guidelines, and the younger Pope, who is put in charge of the investigation. Compounding Mattelli's problems is the fact that he is a cop on the take, beholden to the Mafia and their hired black flunkies, Doc Johnson (Richard Ward) and Shevvy (Gilbert Lewis). Then again, there is not much love lost between Doc Johnson and Nick D'Salvio, who holds Doc Johnson responsible for the initial carnage by not providing proper protection.

What all of this translates into is dialogue often saturated with obscenities and swearing that in turn makes for more incisive and vivid underscoring and source music. All of J.J. Johnson's cues are telling in their impact while often drawing upon common riffs. Specifically, the riff heard as part of the main title is recycled elsewhere in the movie in such cues as "Harlem Clavinette" and "Harlem Love Theme, " thereby imparting a certain motivic unity to the whole. At the same time, Johnson is following a procedure roughly analogous to what was typical practice in such TV series as *Mike Hammer* or *Starsky and Hutch,* in which various individual cues or bridges were based on material from the main title.[11] The "opening sequence" and "killing" cues are illustrative of Johnson's work in *Across 110th Street* (Fig. 7.2).

Bridging individual scenes, each with its mood-setting music, provides Johnson an occasion for demonstrating his skills in underscoring as well as developmental writing. Some thirty-five minutes into the movie we find ourselves in the tenement of Jim Harris, who is baring his soul to his girlfriend, Gloria Roberts (Norma Donaldson). He refuses her wish that he give the money back and try to get an honest job; all he says he can hope for is "an asshole job like a janitor." Here he is, "a 42-year-old ex con nigger with no schooling, no trade, and a medical problem" (epilepsy). Now emotionally drained after arguing, Jim and Gloria are at a loss for words and this is precisely where Johnson, in a master stroke, introduces the distinctive sound of the clavinet to convey the vulnerable, feminine side of Jim Harris. Indeed, it is an instrument he reserves exclusively for such intimate moments (Fig. 7.3).[12]

The closing minutes of *Across 110th Street* are awash in irony. In his dying moments Harris drags himself to the edge of the roof to toss the loot over, only to receive the coup de grâce from Lieutenant Pope. Clutching Pope's hand in what is a final bonding, Mattelli is then fatally shot from afar by Shevvy's silencer. He sinks to the roof in slow motion as the credits being to roll. A reprise of the clavinet music is heard—an evocation of Harris's inherent fragility and a commentary on the futility of violence.

The year 1973 saw the release of Johnson's two final blaxploitation films: *Willie Dynamite* and *Cleopatra Jones.* These particular movies are noteworthy for

SPOT ON FILM	CUE TIMINGS	DESCRIPTION
Opening Sequence		
0:00	0:00	A helicopter shot of Manhattan's West Side is followed by zoom and dolly shots (shot from a dolly-mounted camera) of a black coupe carrying Mafiosi. The high-pitched, snappy rhythms of bongos and congas provide background for the three-note pentatonic main title riff in upper brass—material to be reworked in later cues.
0:51	0:51	As the car passes the sign for 110th Street Bobby Womack launches into the gospel-styled theme song. The camera meanwhile pans Harlem's streets while keeping the car in constant focus.
3:27	3:27	The car pulls up at the curb on sustained notes in low strings and brass punctuated by timpani strokes. Cue ends with a low-angle camera on feet of Mafia henchmen as they walk from car to building entrance.
Killing		
6:36	0:00	Thick, dark-textured sound of low brass in sustained notes, overlaid with synthesizer, as camera pans scene of carnage then cuts to street as driver of getaway car is heard revving the engine.
6:58	0:22	

Fig. 7.2 "Opening Sequence" and "Killing" music cues from the motion picture *Across 110th Street* (1972), composed by J.J. Johnson.

SPOT ON FILM	CUE TIMINGS	DESCRIPTION

Clavinet Music

Harlem Clavinette; Harlem Love Theme [13]

38:19   0:00

Writing for the clavinet at the top of its range, where its timbre approximates that of the celesta, Johnson conveys a sense of fragility unique to the soundtrack. Camera work meanwhile involves two shots as well as extreme close-ups of Jim and Gloria. The delicate melody here, a minor b-pentatonic, is an augmentation of the riff first heard as part of the main title. Segue to next cue.

Recovery of Getaway Car

39:13   0:54

The camera directly shifts from the tenement to a scene where the getaway car is being hauled out of the river. Crane, cops, Lieutenant Pope, and the car itself are all panned as Johnson's underscoring works its special effect on a scene that approaches a kind of bizarre pantomime in that there is no source sound at all. His scoring is of a dark, thick texture with layering of percussion, violin trills, sustained low strings, reeds, and brass. An octave bass ostinato grows more insistent and sounds become more disjointed as dialogue about taking the car to a precinct garage becomes more audible. The cue

41:44   2:31

dissolves in sounds of traffic.

Attack on Jackson

49:01	0:00	The driver of the getaway car, Henry J. Jackson (Antonio Fargas), is tracked down by D'Salvio to a sleazy nightclub where he is whooping it up. Jackson is left sprawled on the floor badly beaten. Johnson
49:01	0:00	now introduces a cue that is telling in its disjointed, pointillistic quality—low sustained brass here, a strumming mandolin there, a hint of English horn, fluttertonguing on flute, and a suggestion of the opening bass ostinato from
49:55	0:54	Stravinsky's *Firebird*.

Final Shootout

94:45	0:00	The camera pans the rooftop of a Harlem tenement as police sharpshooters Captain Mattelli and Lieutenant Pope, not to mention the mob's hired black thug, Shevvy, all converge on fugitive Jim Harris. A polyrhythmic crescendo builds, replete with bongos, conga, maracas, brass riffs, trills, and wa-wa synthesizer effects, all punctuated by sounds of sirens and gunfire.
97:55	3:10	The cue culminates in a low sustained chord as Harris is shot.

Fig. 7.3   "Love Scene," "Recovery of Getaway Car," "Attack on Jackson," and "Final Shootout" music cues from the motion picture *Across 110th Street* (1972), composed by J.J. Johnson.

Fig. 7.4 Anthony Quinn (Captain Mattelli) and Yaphet Kotto (Detective Lieutenant Pope), still photograph from the motion picture *Across 110th Street* (1972). Courtesy of United Artists.

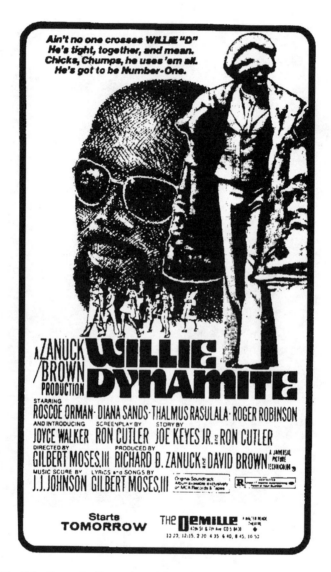

Fig. 7.5 Poster for the motion picture *Willie Dynamite* (1973).

Fig. 7.6   Still photograph from the motion picture *Cleopatra Jones* (1973). Photograph courtesy of Warner Bros., Inc.

a certain feminist perspective, viewing violence from a critical distance. *Willie Dynamite* depicts the rise and fall of a black pimp whose efforts to groom a sweet young thing for the big time on the streets are foiled by a former streetwalker. *Cleopatra Jones,* which grossed over $3.25 million upon commercial release, focuses on the exploits of the eponymous six-foot-two Amazonian secret agent (Tamara Dobson) acting in an idealized improbable world of reversed sexual stereotypes; she fights and ultimately destroys a heroin cartel operated by a lesbian queen called Mommy (Shelley Winters) that preys on the Watts ghetto of Los Angeles.[14]

In the case of *Cleopatra Jones* Johnson shares musical credits with three others; there is the title theme by Joe Simon as well as additional music attributed to Carl Brandt and Brad Shapiro. Johnson is credited with five cues, all of them sharply differentiated.[15] "Desert Sunrise," with which the movie opens, is a highly evocative tone poem in miniature running to just under one minute. It underscores a mountainous semidesert panorama in Turkey close to a region of poppy fields. Johnson has borrowed here from Benjamin Britten's opera *Peter Grimes* to provide a compelling metaphor describing the sweep of desert desolation.[16] What particularly inspired him in this musical landscape was the scoring of Britten's

"Dawn," the first of the four "Sea Interludes," in which high unison flutes and violins suggest the vast spaces of a deserted beach. Johnson's juxtaposition of registral extremes, of high flutes and violins contrasted with English horn, bass clarinet, and low brass and strings, is similarly telling in its impact.

"Go Chase Cleo," coming at the movie's midpoint, underscores a scene in which Cleo is chased by Mommy's hoods on the outskirts of Los Angeles near the city aqueduct. Johnson has written a disco-inflected cue replete with the layering of bongos, congas, bass guitar, and agitato strings that provide an underpinning for a two-note riff in the upper brass. Lasting 3:25, the cue epitomizes much of what was Johnson's stock-in-trade, whether in his blaxploitation movies or subsequent commercial cop shows. By contrast, the slowly waltzing love music, "Cleo and Reuben," with its dark reeds, sustained flute sounds, and lyric string writing, suggests the hand of Robert Farnon—a sound that was to be fully realized in Johnson's *Tangence* (1995) album.[17]

Yet despite the reported commercial success of the soundtrack album, Johnson's prospects were quite bleak at this point.[18] For reasons already articulated, his position in the movie industry had never been more than tenuous and, what is more, there were already larger forces at work within the African-American community that were to make his shift to commercial TV assignments inevitable. The winds of change were already blowing, even prior to the release of *Cleopatra Jones*, when, on July 29, 1972, in Chicago, Reverend Jesse Jackson held the inaugural conference of his organization PUSH (People United to Save Humanity). Movie studios came under assault for their exploitation of black images and their failure to provide jobs for African-Americans in all areas of the film industry. Rallying his troops in the tradition of the civil rights movement, Jackson went on to declare:

> Since we're organized in 30 key cities, the language we will use, if we are not heard, will not be obscenity and vulgarity. It will be at the box offices of the major theaters in those cities. Picket and boycott will be one form of protest. When and if we strike, it will not be secret. We are prepared to move on major studios with black films in production, those with films in the planning stages, and, if necessary, those already in distribution.[19]

Others added their voices to the chorus of criticism. Cicely Tyson of *Sounder* (1972) took exception to the deluge of cheaply made "totally unreal" black films and their potentially adverse effect on children. Feelings were intensified with the release of *Superfly* in August 1972, when a coalition of prominent civil rights groups such as the Congress of Racial Equality (CORE), the National Association for the Advancement of Colored People (NAACP), and the Southern Christian Leadership Conference (SCLC) banded together to form the Coalition Against Blaxploitation (CAB). One of the former presidents of the Beverly Hills/Hollywood chapter of the NAACP did not mince any words when he said:

We will not tolerate the continued warping of our black children's minds with the filth, violence and cultural lies that are all pervasive in current productions of so called black movies. The transformation from the stereotyped Stepin' Fetchit to Super Nigger on the screen is just another form of cultural genocide. The black community should deal with this problem by whatever means necessary. [20]

Changes on-screen were inevitable, as typified by *Sounder* with its more subtle treatment of a black humanity. It was a process that came to mean the production of more "crossover" films, ones with more universal themes. Indicative of the shift was a *Jet* magazine article in January 1974 that noted a dramatic decline in the release of black-oriented films between August and December 1973. Invoking the names of Bill Cosby and Billy Dee Williams, *Jet* proceeded to predict a change of approach that would incorporate issues unique to the black experience while at the same time being able to meet white expectations.[21]

The balance of Johnson's career on the Hollywood scene was devoted primarily to cop show assignments on commercial television. There were, however, some conspicuous exceptions in the cases of such shows as the sitcom *That Girl* and the science fiction series *The Six Million Dollar Man*. Others, such as *The Big Easy*, *Future Cop*, or *Travels with Flip*, were pilots or were presented as miniseries, while dismal ratings doomed such shows as *Harris and Company* and *Barefoot in the Park* (based on the play and film) to runs of four weeks and four months, respectively. In any event, the norm for Johnson was to work on multiple-composer shows.

I was one of four or five rotating composers on shows like *Harry O*, *The Bold Ones*, *Barefoot in the Park*, and *Mod Squad*, sometimes writing just one episode, sometimes more. I think that's one of the reasons there's a grey area around the period of my career from 1970 up to the present. Things were so unpredictable that you just couldn't pinpoint my activities or whereabouts. Yet, there I was in Hollywood wearing the hat of a film composer as it were.[22]

With the longest running series—among them *The Six Million Dollar Man*, *Mod Squad*, and *Mike Hammer*—Johnson was able to enjoy fairly steady employment even though, again, he was by no means the only one composing music for them. Earle Hagen, Lalo Schifrin, and Oliver Nelson were among a number of other writers responsible for various episodes. Furthermore, for major shows like *Mike Hammer* and *The Six Million Dollar Man*, Earle Hagen and Oliver Nelson enjoyed the enormous financial advantage of being credited with writing the themes or main titles. Consequently, Johnson's income was derived from individual episodes only.[23] In the case of *Mike Hammer*, for example, Earle Hagen's "Harlem Nocturne" serves as the theme for each and every episode, whereas Johnson's cues for a given episode will often augment or incorporate material from that main title. For this reason, profits for each such cue would have to be apportioned on the basis of the number of seconds of identifiably Hagen and Johnson music.

Illustrative episodes from two representative series have been selected for more detailed comment—*The Six Million Dollar Man* and *Mike Hammer*. The double episode entitled "The Lost Island," which comes from the series featuring the bionic former U.S. Air Force astronaut Steve Austin (Lee Majors), is part of a string of 100 fifty-minute episodes spanning the five-year run of the show (1973–78). A brief description of relevant segments of the episode is helpful for appreciating Johnson's treatment of cues.

"The Lost Island" deals with efforts to recover a neutron-powered satellite carrying top classified material that somehow has been lost in the vicinity of Hawaii. Aboard the recovery ship, a Dr. Rudy Wells has just gotten off the phone with Washington when, at 4:38, Johnson's one-minute cue begins. It essentially accompanies the landing aboard the vessel of a helicopter carrying Steve Austin. What Johnson writes is an augmentation of Oliver Nelson's theme (flute unisons) with an urgent undercurrent of motor rhythms in strings punctuated by brass interjections. Much of the music, however, is drowned out by the ambient sound of chopper blades and dialogue.

It appears that the recovery ship is visible to the occupants of "the lost island," where for the past twenty years a "famous anthropologist and amateur yachtsman," together with his daughter and plucky band of followers, have all effectively been prisoners. Because of "force fields reflecting back," they are invisible to the outside world and, lacking immunity to disease, dare not ask for any help. Meanwhile a seemingly mysterious fire has just erupted on the island, caused by the crash landing of nothing less than the satellite itself. At 10:02 a bridge cue in flutes and upper strings links a scene aboard the recovery vessel (Steve Austin is complaining that his "bionics" have been affected by something inexplicable to him) as we cut to a tense series of events on the island accompanied by 'cellos and vibraphone pulsations in a low register. As the camera pans the shoreline we see anthropologist Jenson's yacht bobbing up and down to the accompaniment of the theremin in unison with strings presenting an eerie augmentation of the theme.[24] At 10:25 the camera zooms in on a clearing showing our anthropologist, his daughter, and their close companions anxiously awaiting the return of three men sent to scout the island for the source of the trouble. There is an insistent accompanying string ostinato in secundal harmony overlaid with a modal bassoon solo fragment. The camera then cuts between the astonished daughter ("Torg, what has happened to your face?") and Torg himself, now disfigured by having stared too long at the radiation-emitting satellite. At 10:56 we are given a close-up of Torg's face to the accompaniment of an undulating F-minor ostinato of a protominimalist sort. At 11:37 the cue ends as we learn the painful truth that Torg's character has undergone analogous disfigurement; he will neither take orders nor be a follower anymore, and he flatly refuses to give any details of the fire.

Turning to one of the episodes—"Seven Dead Eyes"—from *Mike Hammer*, we are able to recreate more completely than in any prior instance the context within which Johnson wrote his cues. Cue sheets prepared by music editor Erma Levin, a kind of item rarely preserved in the movie and television industries, have been fleshed out and correlated with pertinent details of camera work and dramatic action.[25] Close examination of Johnson's work for this series, the last with which he was to be associated, serves to elaborate on some of the key points regarding general operating procedure that were touched upon at the beginning of this chapter.

Erma Levin, a veteran music editor on the Hollywood scene during Johnson's years there, would typically go through several sometimes overlapping steps that were crucial to the eventual shaping of the underscoring, whether for film or commercial television:

1.   She would begin by viewing the film and jotting down abbreviated notes specifying what music sounded most appropriate at precise locations on the film.

2.   A composer like J.J. Johnson would then see the film and along with the editor, decide upon scenes calling for music and what "sound" to compose for those scenes.

3.   The composer would then write the musical cues appropriate to the mood or character of the scene, making sure that they fit exactly into the allotted time.

4.   This music would then be performed and recorded, often at sight, by studio musicians.

5.   The music editor would then take these recorded cues and either direct the engineer to dub them in or edit them to fit a scene that may have been cut or expanded by the film editor in the interim, and then dub them in as indicated.

6.   The music editor would then have to ensure through the audio mixdown process that the music indeed properly underscored a given scene. For example, it could not, on the one hand, overpower a scene containing dialogue deemed important by the director or film editor; on the other hand, with a chase scene it would make perfect sense to have the music in the foreground.

7.   In general, Johnson or anyone else writing television or movie cues would not see these editorial notes in that their primary function as writers was to facilitate the job of the music editor.

What follow are the cues written for the "Seven Dead Eyes" episode. The spot on the film marking the start of each cue, its title, and its duration are all specified. A detailed description is given for each cue, including information on the music and its relation to the dramatic action.

Spot on Film	Cue Title	Cue Duration

0:00   **Main Title**   1:22

To the accompaniment of "Harlem Nocturne" the credits roll against a background montage of generic scenes from episodes.

1:23   **Pennsylvania 6-5000**   1:23

An example of diegetic (source) music, the Glenn Miller standard, which is played to a final cadence (complete end), serves as background to a scene one fall afternoon in Hammer's favorite Greenwich Village bar. He is shown meeting with private investigator Ridge Grundy, who comments approvingly, if laconically, on the music. There is a congruent sense of old-time loyalty that Hammer confesses to having toward Grundy—a man who helped him "shake the snakes out" when he got back from "Nam" and taught him to be a private eye. Grundy has apparently stumbled onto something and needs Hammer to be on hand the next day at a private eye convention at the Gramercy Park Hotel.

2:56   **Whatever**   1:55

As Grundy gets up to leave, a more subdued sound directly follows, very much in the style of the George Shearing quintet of piano, drums, bass, guitar, and vibes. Again played to a final cadence, this cue helps bridge the scene in the bar with the fatal explosion on the street that kills Grundy. The cue continues as the camera cuts back to the bar for a shot of patrons reacting to the explosion.

4:50   **Hollow Ache**   0:23

Hammer calls for an ambulance as Grundy breathes his last. He feels a "hollow ache" much like the one he felt when his father died. Low, slow, sustained sound, including a paraphrase of "Harlem Nocturne," features synthesizer and English horn as the music ends on a fermata.

5:48   **Hat Toss**   0:26

Music underscores motion as Hammer travels uptown to his office and tosses his hat on a coat tree. A 12-second paraphrase of "Harlem Nocturne" brings the cue to an end on a fermata.

7:15   **Edna**   2:31

Low-sounding drums begin the cue as the camera pans the street outside the apartment building of Grundy's widow. The cue continues to develop slowly with sad, romantic undertones evoked by the English horn solo. Close-ups of Hammer and Edna as she reminisces about twenty-seven years of marriage. Her reference to their honeymoon in Atlantic City is accompanied by a shift to a high register. Then her mention of his dying away from home marks a return to the slow, low sustained sound. "Harlem Nocturne" is quoted at 1:36 into the cue but is left unresolved as the cue serves to bridge the apartment scene with the panning of the street showing Hammer approaching the entrance to Grundy's office building. The music takes on a dark, foreboding quality at 2:10 into the cue with reeds, low brass, and synthesizer being predominant. It underscores Hammer's walking down the corridor to find Grundy's office door suspiciously open; he walks in pointing his gun at a stranger standing at Grundy's desk.

12:12   **Revolving Door (The Look)**   0:18

As Hammer enters through the revolving door at the Gramercy Park Hotel his eye catches a brunette who is exiting. The lyrical soprano saxophone melody is superimposed on gently rolling piano chords and synthesized strings. The cue continues to a fermata.

16:11   **Unknown Man**   0:34

Low-angle camera on stalker in the hotel suite of one Ari Artel. There is a tritone/ Lydian sound of brass and synthesizer in a low register. The moment of Artel's strangulation is underscored by an incisive rhythm evoking the fateful trumpet call ushering in the "Tuba Mirum" portion of Verdi's *Requiem*. Fade-out to black for a commercial break.

18:50   **Almost Finished**   1:50

Generic cocktail piano bar sounds (diegetic) at Gramercy Park Hotel begin the cue. They provide background to Velda (Hammer's secretary) and one Harry McCambridge (a suspect), who is coming on to her at the bar. Hammer approaches, distracts McCambridge, and is directed away by Velda to another suspect (Don Foreman) who also is drinking at the bar a few feet away.

23:40   **Cannot Give Back**   1:36

This bridge cue begins with low sound underscoring a scene in Hammer's office. News has just been received of the murder of Don Foreman. The camera cuts to the dark office building corridor where Hammer is picking the lock to the door of Foreman's office. At 1:07 low drums are heard as well as a half-step French horn riff. Music becomes darkly expressionist with sounds of bass clarinet and low brass. A high-angle shot shows Hammer being struck from behind while he is going through office files. He falls to the floor unconscious. The attacker spreads papers on and around Hammer. These he proceeds to set on fire underscored by strident trumpet sound as the music builds to a fermata.

25:25   **Flaming Mike**   0:28

Drums begin the cue and build in sound to 0:20, when the brasses play a very quick crescendo (flare) followed by a fall-off. This is essentially a fast glissando from high to low that underscores Hammer's plunge out the window to safety.

26:13   **Harlem Nocturne**   0:15

A slow, sad-sounding saxophone quotation of the main title. There is a fade-out to black for a commercial break.

26:28   **Killer Killer**   3:30

This exceptionally long bridge cue begins with "low melodic character" as the camera pans the sidewalk showing Velda approaching her basement apartment. Cut to stalker in her apartment as "danger" music develops. Velda is seen undressing to accompaniment of low-register piano, French horn, and wash of harpsichord sound. The telephone rings with segue of sustained synthesizer string sound. "Low shriek" of sustained string sound underscores stalker's removal of light bulb over bathroom sink. As Velda returns to use sink and try to turn on light she is grabbed from behind. The attempt to strangle her is aborted as she jabs the stalker in the ribs. He escapes.

Bridge to Hammer approaching the open door to his own apartment where he finds a shaken Velda on the couch. Lyrical oboe against synthesized background. Cut to next morning where, to accompaniment of French horns, flute, and piano, Velda is preparing breakfast for Hammer. The music continues to a fermata.

33:20   **Joyce Brothers Love Scene**   1:22
Hammer is in the apartment of Kim Warren, making love to her. She is a blonde private investigator who, it turns out, has valuable information to share on the case. The scene is one of gentle humor, combining features of the diegetic with standard underscoring. Dr. Joyce Brothers is holding forth on some TV "Midday Report," speaking about "attention and closeness" between the sexes. Hammer and Warren meanwhile are in a passionate clutch directly in front of the TV set; their actions are underscored by woodwind-flute sound with a bluesy feel. At 0:38 a celesta is heard in the foreground. Woodwinds predominate from 1:03 to the fermata.

35:02   **Goodbye, Kim**   0:38
The cue begins with a point of view shot through the telescopic sight of a sniper on the rooftop. Hammer and Warren are on their way to dinner on the opposite side of the street when Warren is hit by sniper fire. At 0:07 there is a sweep—e", f", a"-flat, b"-flat—up to a trill. Punctuating predominantly brass chords follow. At 0:26 "Harlem Nocturne" is paraphrased through to the end. Fade-out to black for commercial break.

35:40   **A Few Inches More**   0:36
Hammer is back at Kim Warren's apartment looking over minutes of meeting of "secret admissions committee." Soft orchestral chords provide a "bed" for guitar tritone ostinato—g-sharp, a, b, c'—with touches of brass and French horn in the background. With Hammer's comment regarding the minutes ("first paragraph a shocker") the cue bridges to Bellevue Hospital where Warren has been taken. The music continues to a fermata.

37:10   **Dumb Killer**   1:17
The scene is Kim Warren's hospital room. Underscoring of drums, low-register piano and "dark, snarly, growly" music accompanies a mad slasher intent on stabbing Kim in bed. But Hammer has been lying in wait for him. To the sound of shrieking trumpet he fatally shoots the intruder with the comment, "Congratulations, dummy, you just killed a dummy!" The music continues to a fermata.

40:15   **Harlem Nocturne**   0:42
The cue begins with a slow version of the main title featuring synthesizer, reeds, and English horn. At 0:13 a rhythm becomes prominent and at 0:32 the tempo speeds up as the fermata is approached.

43:49   **Pennsylvania 6-5000**   0:47
Hammer is back in Ridge Grundy's office fitting together the pieces of the puzzle. He has also set a trap for prime suspect Harry McCambridge, who duly shows up with two of his flunkies. McCambridge threatens to "take care of" Hammer, but is caught off guard when Hammer fires at him with his 45 cocked under the desk. After putting an LP of the Glenn Miller standard on the record player he proceeds to punch out McCambridge and company.[26]

| 44:57 | **Harlem Nocturne** | 0:44 |

This is a stock version of the main title, including saxophone solo, synthesizer, and electric guitar. It underscores a panning shot of the street showing a rear view of Hammer in trench coat walking off. The music continues to fade-out to black for a commercial break.

| 45:41 | **Harlem Nocturne** | 0:30 |

A stock but shorter version accompanying the final credits.

Fig. 7.7   Music cues for the *Mike Hammer* episode, "Seven Dead Eyes," composed by J.J. Johnson.

Johnson's final years in Hollywood were undermined by several forces, virtually all of them beyond his control. For one thing, his hopes of ever becoming fully established as a film composer had long since been tainted by the stereotypical view of him as a black jazzman composing for only blaxploitation movies. It was a situation compounded by the very nature of his pre-Hollywood career—a topic addressed at the beginning of this chapter. Johnson's younger son, Kevin, has painted a rather bleak picture of the final phase of his father's Hollywood career: "Actually there was a long period in L.A. . . . the phone wasn't ringing a whole lot. He wasn't the first guy they called and he just kind of sat in the chair for a long time."[27]

Another contributing factor was the change that the industry itself was undergoing, a process that proved daunting to all but the likes of John Williams or Jerry Goldsmith. Erma Levin recalls attending a seminar on movie scoring around this time at which the head of the music department at one of the major studios was heard to say in all seriousness: "I get the script and I read it. Then I go to the producer and we discuss how many songs we might be able to make out of this picture."[28]

The larger implications of this song-studded approach to the movie soundtrack clearly lie beyond the scope of the present discussion, and it is a phenomenon by no means confined to the Hollywood establishment. Barry Levinson's *Diner* (1982), his *Good Morning, Vietnam* (1987), or more recently Jonathan Demme's *Philadelphia* (1993) and Robert Zemeckis's *Forrest Gump* (1994) are but a few examples. Combine that with the proliferation of explicitly ethnic movies such as Reginald Hudlin's *House Party* (1990) with its hip-hop/rap soundtrack or Spike Lee's *Do the Right Thing* of the previous year, or Arne Glimcher's *The Mambo Kings* (1992), and we are dealing with soundtracks in which traditional narrative underscoring has all but disappeared or is greatly undervalued. Finally, the popularity of such TV series as *Miami Vice*, (which premiered in 1984) signaled the arrival of a world of glittering lime-green walls, hot pink neon signs, sunny beaches, and clothes of liquid blue, fuchsia, or pastels, all accompanied by synthesized music and strings of songs by Tina Turner, Lionel Ritchie, and the Pointer Sisters.

Johnson's anchor throughout this change, and indeed throughout his Hollywood years, continued to be his jazz and his trombone, even though his general musical priorities had shifted. Given the benefit of hindsight and Johnson's ultimate disillusionment, however, one cannot avoid discerning a certain sad irony in the following remarks he made to Leonard Feather shortly after his arrival in Hollywood:

> I still do play on sessions . . . but not as a soloist. I just keep my head above water doing studio gigs or playing with Quincy once in a while in the trombone section. But, I don't want to be caught up in that daily studio playing grind. If things go as they should, and I become firmly established as a composer, then it will be worth my while to pick up the trombone and play jazz again for kicks. By that time I hope I won't have to be worried about having the wrong identification by doing so.[29]

These comments should be tempered by the feelings he had shared slightly earlier with *Melody Maker* (1970), when he confessed that he did not expect the television and movie producers to fall over one another besieging him with offers.[30] It was also a time when he did some playing with Oliver Nelson and assumed responsibility for the music on the Academy Awards telecast that year. This meant contracting the house band for the refurbished Cocoanut Grove on Wilshire Boulevard when it reopened with Sammy Davis, Jr. Johnson now had the happy opportunity to work once more with a familiar face or two in an interracial setting that included a precedent-breaking "five salt, five pepper" string section. As Johnson put it:

> The band at the Grove was a gas. The leader is Sammy's regular musical director, George Rhodes. Some of the sidemen . . . were Al Aarons on trumpet and Marshall Royal as lead saxophone—both ex-Basie men; Jimmy Cleveland, one of the great all-round trombonists; and Don Menza, who played in Buddy Rich's sax section.[31]

Johnson's sporadic activity as a performing jazzman during his seventeen-odd years in Hollywood cannot be attributed simply to his preoccupation with writing for film and television. The truth of the matter is that the jazz scene as a whole was under assault from many sides. The inroads made by rock 'n' roll, free jazz, and a heightened Afrocentrism, for example, were closely associated with symptoms of disorientation, disillusionment, alienation, efforts to define new political alignments, and experimentation with electronic instruments, exotic rhythms, and timbres. When Sonny Rollins reappeared in 1972 after a withdrawal on a spiritual quest lasting over two years, he confessed: "I had got into a very disillusioned attitude by 1969, a despondent attitude. The first time I dropped out [August 1959], it was to write and study. This time it was disillusionment with the music scene."[32] Dexter Gordon, who spent most of the 1960s and early 1970s working in

Europe and living in Denmark, was profoundly pessimistic about the very future of jazz, "didn't dig . . . the Beatles thing," and felt himself to be a victim of racial discrimination, and unappreciated as a musician. "Copenhagen's like my home base. . . . Of course, there was no racial discrimination or anything like that. And the fact that you're an artist in Europe means something . . . over there it's an entirely different mentality."[33]

The general pattern of Johnson's performing during his Hollywood years is largely consistent with these observations. A "different mentality" for jazz outside the United States, though by no means unique to this period, clearly helped determine where he typically played, however sporadically that was. There is a smattering of performances at such Japanese venues as Yokohama (1977), the Aurex Jazz Festival (1982), Norman Granz's 1983 Jazz at the Philharmonic All-Star series "Live in Japan" (where he is essentially a sideman to Ella Fitzgerald), followed by appearances in France and Italy during the summer of 1984. Each experience was quite different.

The Yokohama concert, recorded live April 20, 1977, at Kanagawa Kenritsu Ongakudo, Yokohama, is a standout, revealing Johnson in top form. His playing has an incandescence that is matched at every turn by the musicians joining him. With him in the front line is Nat Adderley on trumpet, and in the rhythm section there are Billy Childs on keyboards, Tony Dumas on bass, and, in a unique appearance, Johnson's younger son, Kevin, on drums. Most of the selections, six of the eleven, are freshly composed originals by Johnson, with the exception of his classic ballad "Lament" from 1954. Enjoying similar status on the program is another title originally recorded that same year by Johnson as a member of the Miles Davis All-Star Sextet—"Walkin'."

Taken as a whole, including the pieces by Nat Adderley and Tony Dumas, the Yokohama concert shows the unmistakable hard-bop influences of Horace Silver and Art Blakey. Cases in point are Johnson's allusive "Horace" and his "Why Not" as well as Adderley's "Cyclops," with its funky gospel touches and two-note riff. These works all have a propulsive intensity with aggressive drumming to match. "Why Not," in particular, is in fact a fascinating eclectic piece consisting of a wealth of driving hard bop elements, including what David Baker once referred to as Johnson's characteristic "fragmented, stop-and-go rhythmic effects."[34] Serving as a highly effective foil is also the evocative, quasi-impressionistic introduction on synthesizer, which attests to Johnson's fascination with the work of Isao Tomita—something dating back to his MBA Music years and discussed earlier. Then the head itself, with its rugged quartal profile, demonstrates anew Johnson's admitted love of Hindemith's sonorities. This material serves not only to frame the total piece by dominating the head and out chorus, but also functions as a refrain and point of reference within the whole, thereby suggesting a rondo form and demarcating the respective solos by Nat Adderley and Billy Childs.

Contributing immensely to the energy of these performances is the playing of

Kevin Johnson. His propulsive off-beat accents, aggressive use of the ride cymbal, and palette of colors all provide vivid testimony to the influence of Art Blakey, among others. Especially dramatic are the younger Johnson's extended solos, both in "Splashes" (lasting almost three out of a total of seven minutes) and in the portmanteau-named piece celebrating the collaboration of father and son, "Jevin." Yet as Kevin Johnson has recalled, there were some moments of friction when he had to be brought into line by a father demanding tighter control. "I was playing all kind of crazy stuff, all over the bar line. . . . I was playing way too much for the tune. It wasn't what the tune needed. So afterward he lit into me!"[35]

Indeed, J.J. Johnson would have none of this, and after the performance made his feelings known in no uncertain terms:

> "Look, get your own fucking band if you're going to play this kind of stuff. You have to be a team player. We all need to know where 'one' is. If you're the only one out of five people who knows where 'one' is, that doesn't help us." After that I got real timid. [36]

By the same token, J.J. Johnson's 1977 Yokohama concert had a youthful exuberance, most vividly exuded by rhythm section members Tony Dumas (b. 1955) and Kevin Johnson (b. 1951). By contrast, the Aurex Jazz Festival All Star Jam (September 1, 2, and 5, 1982, in Tokyo, Osaka, and Yokohama, respectively) represented more of a meeting of the elder statesmen of jazz. Included in the line-up with Johnson were Kai Winding on trombone (he was to die the following May), Clark Terry on trumpet and flugelhorn, Dexter Gordon on tenor saxophone, Tommy Flanagan on piano, Kenny Burrell on guitar, Richard Davis on bass, and Roy Haynes on drums. The "All Star Jam" billing is in fact rather misleading in that most of the numbers feature duos, quartets or quintets. Johnson's playing seldom rises above the perfunctory, and he is heard on only six out of fourteen selections performing largely "golden oldies" on the order of "Autumn Leaves" and the hit of his Jay/Kai years, "It's All Right with Me."

The summer of 1984 brought Johnson to Europe. On July 6 and 10—there were two separate performances each evening—the J.J. Johnson All-Star Sextet appeared in France at the JVC Grande Parade du Jazz Nice, an event produced by George Wein and held in the Jardin des Arènes de Cimiez.[37] The occasion was an especially happy one, marking the revival of the kind of ensemble with which Johnson had been associated between 1954 and 1960—one that had come to signify several defining moments in his career. Cases in point included "Walkin'" (1954) with the Miles Davis All-Star Sextet and "Aquarius" (1960) with the J.J. Johnson Sextet. And now, in 1984, he was fortunate to have on hand two original ensemble members—Nat Adderley on cornet and Cedar Walton on piano. Joining Johnson in the front line was Harold Land on tenor saxophone, while the rhythm section was completed by Richard Davis on bass and Roy McCurdy on drums;

both Land and McCurdy, incidentally, were California-based musicians who were veterans of the Hollywood movie and television scenes.

The music offered that summer represented a mix of the old and the new, of hard bop, traditional blues, and a kind of third-stream fusion. For example, the July 6 concert offered the premiere of Johnson's "Toots Suite," an extended piece building on the following ostinato and quoting liberally from the bassoon solo in the "Berceuse" of Stravinsky's *Firebird*.

Fig. 7.8   "Toots Suite," opening bass ostinato.

By contrast, the treatment of Monk's classic blues from 1947, "Misterioso," includes a torrent of notes from Adderley's cornet in the opening solo chorus matched by a hot, intense solo by Johnson before the out chorus. Other numbers, like "What Is This Thing Called Love?," have a brash hard bop intensity, replete with explosive drumming and piano playing. Then again, Johnson can be heard in a rare unbuttoned mood announcing: "That was our clambake version of 'A Blues Walk'"—a quirky number buttressed by a unison head and out chorus, but featuring some daring efforts at "free" imitative counterpoint by trombone, cornet, and saxophone in the body of the piece.

At the ten P.M. concert on July 6 Johnson was joined in the front line by a trio of trombonists—Al Grey, Slide Hampton, and George Masso, who replaced Nat Adderley and Harold Land. The result was some hard-swinging performances of Miles Davis's "Milestones" and Ellington's "In a Mellotone," including some striking drum solos by Roy McCurdy doing honor to Art Blakey. In a walk down memory lane, Johnson featured one of his signatures from 1954, "Walkin'," a rendition incorporating a vivid solo by Cedar Walton, the climactic trading of fours by McCurdy and Davis on drums and bass, and a refreshing reharmonization by the front line in the out chorus. But what tops off the evening is a rarity in Johnson's recorded legacy—a true "blowing session" where the four trombonists have the time of their lives with the changes of a twelve-bar blues entitled simply "Improvisation." In the course of thirty-five choruses, including a solo by Cedar Walton and a quotation from Gershwin's *Rhapsody in Blue*, virtually every conceivable trombone style can be heard, from the impeccably clean to "gutbucket" and the growl-and-plunger "jungle" sound associated with Joe (Tricky Sam) Nanton.

Johnson's ebullient European performances in the summer of 1984 are far removed from another side of the man that came into view during his Hollywood years. Both of his sons have remarked on his periods of deep introspection, on his expression of disenchantment with performing, and that the dream he most cherished was to be recognized as a composer.[38] There is therefore a certain poignant symbolism in a 1979 recording Johnson made entitled *Pinnacles*, which signifies setting one's musical sights as high as one can without any regard for commercial success. In a way, he was ascending his own magic mountain. As Johnson put it in an interview coinciding with the release of the recording:

> I wanted to do the "Pinnacles" project to satisfy myself. That's why I spent so long writing the music and arrangements, and that's why I wanted to choose very special musicians for the session—a fantastic group, the best. And I must say I'm very pleased with the results.[39]

The *Pinnacles* album is significant for its music, both the issued and unissued selections, as well as the instrumental resources, electronic and acoustic, that are drawn upon. Johnson is pushing the envelope, driven in part by what he had previously been inspired to do by the examples of Isao Tomita, Robert A. Moog, and the theremin. In a more immediate sense there was also the precedent set, starting in the late 1960s and continuing into the mid-1970s, by jazzmen such as Don Ellis, Ornette Coleman (and his fusion group Prime Time), Joe Zawinul, and Herbie Hancock. In other words, Johnson's integration of synthesizer and electric piano into his ensemble is symptomatic of a larger phenomenon that helped define the nature of jazz during the decade and earlier.

The recording sessions for *Pinnacles*, as well as the subsequent mixing and mastering, took place at Fantasy Studios, Berkeley, California, on September 17–19, 1979. Thanks to work notes provided by producer Edward Michel, we are able to reconstruct something of what transpired over the course of the three days. It was a recording process that came with more than the usual share of frustration. Although twelve selections were recorded, only half of them were eventually issued—a telling statistic attesting to Johnson's characteristic blend of risk taking and rigorous self-criticism in his multiple capacity here as trombonist, composer, arranger, and leader. For example, on the first day there were three takes completed of "It Was a Very Good Year," yet none of these was ever issued; the following day only two out of five selections recorded were actually released. Among the rejected items that day was a fascinating oddity entitled "Ballad from Tremblay," a piece honoring Los Angeles composer and pianist George Tremblay, a Schoenberg disciple with whom Johnson had studied twelve-tone composition.[40] What, however, typifies virtually all of the selections, both issued and unissued, is a special combination of acoustic and electronic instruments, with extensive use being made of synthesis, overdubbing, and intercuts (Fig. 7.9).

"Night Flight," issued after only one take, features Tommy Flanagan playing electric piano and overdubbing on clavinet—an instrument Johnson had previously used on the soundtrack for *Across 110th Street*. The ensemble for this selection is completed by Johnson on trombone, Joe Henderson on tenor

edward michel productions   5051 grove street   cambria, ca 93428

PROJECT #5046

MONDAY, SEPTEMBER, 17, 1979

J.J. Johnson (trombone, composer, arranger, leader); Tommy Flanagan (keyboards); Ron Carter (bass); Billy Higgins (drums)

Selection–1:　　It Was a Very Good Year

3 takes completed, use 3b; Flanagan plays acoustic piano; Johnson plays trombone with a 101 Compressor/bass chorus, overdubs string synthesizer and ARP with echoplex; unused track.

Selection–2:　　Don't Buzz Me, I'll Buzz You

J.J. Johnson, composer; 1 take completed, use 1a; Flanagan plays electric piano; Johnson plays trombone with buzz-mute; Carter plays electric bass with Mu–Tron III; later overdub Oscar Brashear, trumpet, on ensemble line; Johnson overdubs string synthesizer with phaser; unused track.

Selection–3:　　Chant City (original title, changed to Pinnacles)

J.J. Johnson, composer; at this point in session add Joe Henderson, tenor saxophone; 4 takes completed, use 1 with opening phrase re-intercut from last chorus; Flanagan plays acoustic piano.

Selection–4:　　Nite Flite (original title, changed to Night Flight)

J.J. Johnson, composer; 1 take completed, use 1a with one phrase replaced by edits; Flanagan plays electric piano and overdubs clavinet.

TUESDAY, SEPTEMBER, 18, 1979

J.J. Johnson (trombone, composer, arranger, leader); Tommy Flanagan (keyboards); Ron Carter (bass); Billy Higgins (drums)

Selection–5:　　Better Days

J.J. Johnson, composer; 2 takes completed, use 2; Flanagan plays acoustic piano; later overdub Oscar Brashear, trumpet,on ensemble line; unused track.

Selection–6:　　Ballad from Tremblay

J.J. Johnson, composer; Johnson notes that Tremblay was a composition teacher who dealt with 12-tone technique and with whom Johnson studied; 1 take completed, use 1; Johnson overdubs ARP synthesizer; Michel overdubs string synthesizer; unused track.

Selection–7:   <u>Cannonball Junction</u>

J.J. Johnson, composer; at this point in session add Joe Henderson, tenor saxophone, and Oscar Brashear, trumpet; Flanagan plays acoustic piano; Johnson plays trombone and ARP synthesizer; Carter uses phaser on bass; 3 takes completed, use 3a; overdub Flanagan on clavinet.

Selection–8:   <u>Soul Van</u> (original title, change to <u>Deak</u>)

J.J. Johnson, composer; 2 takes completed, use 2; Flanagan plays Yamaha electronic grand piano.

Selection–9:   <u>Etheros</u>

J.J. Johnson, composer; introduction only; 1 take completed, use 1; Flanagan plays piano; 2 complete takes, use 2; Johnson overdubs ARP synthesizer; Michel overdubs string synthesizer; unused track.

WEDNESDAY, SEPTEMBER, 19, 1979

J.J. Johnson (trombone, composer, arranger, leader); Tommy Flanagan (keyboards); Ron Carter (bass); Billy Higgins (drums); Oscar Brashear (trumpet); Kenneth Nash (percussion).

Selection–10:   <u>See See Rider</u>

2 takes completed, use 2; Flanagan plays acoustic piano; Nash plays percussion.

Selection–11:   <u>Mr. Clean</u>

2 takes completed, use 2; Flanagan plays piano; Johnson plays trombone with Gentle Electric pitch follower, Barcus-Berry pickup, Oberheim Expander Module, and ARP 2600 synthesizer; Carter plays bass with phaser; Nash plays percussion, bongos, and congas.

Selection–12:   Untitled synthesizer cue

J.J. Johnson, composer; 1 take completed, use 1; personnel is only Flanagan, electric piano, and Johnson, programming of 3 synthesizers (ARP 2600 with 2 sequencers); unused track.

Fig. 7.9 Engineering notes from J.J. Johnson's *Pinnacles* recording sessions. Courtesy of Edward Michel.

saxophone, and a rhythm section consisting of Ron Carter on bass and Billy Higgins on drums. "Deak," originally entitled "Soul Van," is once again of primarily keyboard interest, with Flanagan playing the Yamaha electronic grand piano. The piece is actually a funky twelve-bar blues offering a distillation of much of what Johnson did in that vein in the 1950s, including the celebrated "Walkin'." "Cannonball Junction" begins with the attention-grabbing bass riff of Ron Carter, marked by a phasing (or flanging) effect achieved by electronically mixing a continually varying delay of a signal with its original; characteristics of pitch, amplitude, and harmonic distribution are inevitably affected. For the rest, the playing of Joe Henderson, Oscar Brashear, and Johnson on tenor saxophone, trumpet, and trombone, respectively, holds no special surprises. Tommy Flanagan, for his part, can be heard playing acoustic piano with some overdubbing on clavinet.

The title cut, "Pinnacles," is ironically the most conventional of all—a swinging number entirely on acoustic instruments with solid solos by Flanagan, Johnson, and Henderson, a strong walking bass by Carter, all buttressed by a unison head and out chorus. "See See Rider," a traditional blues associated with Bessie Smith in the 1920s, is given a gently rocking treatment with idiomatic solos by Johnson, Brashear, and Flanagan. However, the final cut, "Mr. Clean" (original by Weldon Irvine), is by far the most daring on the album. Against the rhythm of Ron Carter with his phasing effects, and the bongos and congas of Kenneth Nash, Johnson and Brashear do outstanding work in the front line. Johnson's performance is impressive for its use of a pitch-to-voltage converter. With one of his mouthpieces wired, Johnson was able to trigger a series of voltages in an Oberheim Expander Module corresponding to pitch frequencies on his instrument; the Oberheim, in turn, was patched into an ARP 2600 synthesizer. The result was a three-part parallel texture with pitches stacked in fourths—an evocation of a pentatonically based sound dating back to Johnson's fascination with Hindemith.

As we have seen, Johnson's remaining years in Hollywood were fitful at best. His life was admittedly given a lift by the exuberant festival appearances abroad. But, there was little if anything on the domestic front to match what he had experienced at the JVC Grande Parade du Jazz Nice, earlier at Yokohama, or at Perugia or Pescara. And once his work on the *Mike Hammer* series began to wind down his career clearly reached a plateau.

Johnson's beloved first wife, Vivian, was his salvation at this point. Sensing an acute need to reaffirm her own earlier bond with the church and reconnect with close family, she served as the instigator of the move back home to Indianapolis, an event coinciding with the declining health of J.J. Johnson's father, James Horace Johnson.

Notes

1.   Leonard Feather, "From Pen to Screen: J.J. Johnson," *International Musician*, vol. 71 (July 1972), 26.

2.   Working for Hagen gave Johnson the opportunity to hone his skills in underscoring, that is, writing supporting or accompanying music heard by the audience, not by the actors. Controlling the precise coordination of film and music was the mathematics of the formula $3 = 2$, that is, three feet of film corresponding to two seconds of music. Achieving such precision depended on the devices of the streamer and the punch.The streamer, a line moving from left to right across the screen, indicated where to start and end a cue; the punch, originally a burst of light, represented the "spotting" of a picture, showing where exactly each cue was to start and end. Working closely with a film editor and music editor was essential, whether in the case of dialogue cues, timed to within two-thirds of a second, or picture cues. Various refinements have since superseded some of these techniques.

3.   Hagen was not without his charming quirks. Reluctant to take money from "the guys in the orchestra studying composition," he charged the fee of "three dozen golf balls for eight weeks of classes." Interview with Earle Hagen, Rancho Mirage, California, December 17, 1991.

4.   Feather, *From Pen to Screen*.

5.   Ed Guerrero, *Framing Blackness: The African American Image in Film* (Philadelphia: Temple University Press, 1993), 69.

6.   *Ibid*, 73.

7.   *Ibid.*

8.   *Ibid*, 92.

9.   *Ibid.*

10.   Bonnie Allen, "The Macho Men, What Ever Happened to Them?" *Essence*, vol. 9 (January 1979), 90. Daniel J. Leab, *From Sambo to Superspade* (Boston: Houghton Mifflin, 1976), 248.

11.   Erma Levin was one of the veteran music editors in the film industry at the time; included among her many credits are *I Remember Mama* (1948), *Who's Afraid of Virginia Woolf?* (1966), *The Taking of Pelham One Two Three* (1974), and *'night Mother* (1986). Levin has pointed out that in the case of *Mike Hammer*, for example, Johnson would write his cues by elaborating on material from the main title composed by Earle Hagen. For this he would typically earn partial royalties for, say, fourteen out of twenty-two seconds. Interview with Erma Levin, Calabasas, California, December 16, 1991.

12.   The clavinet is a five-octave electric keyboard most typically used as an alternative to rhythm guitar in funk and rock. Johnson, however, departs quite markedly from this norm.

13.   These are the titles included in Johnson's BMI Participant Catalog Listing. BMI Archivist David Sanjek's help in generating this information is much appreciated.

14.   Guerrero, *Framing Blackness*, 98. The amount in gross earnings quoted by Guerrero is based on information provided by James Robert Parish and George H. Hill, *Black Action Films* (Jefferson, N.C.: McFarland, 1989), 94–96.

15.   Johnson's BMI Participant Catalog Listing includes the following five cues: "Cleo and Reuben," "Desert Sunrise," "Emdee," "Go Chase Cleo," and "Goin' to the Chase."

16. Johnson's personal library happens to include a copy of the score of Britten's "Four Sea Interludes" from *Peter Grimes*.

17. Johnson was smitten with the lush sound of Farnon's writing for the movie *Captain Horatio Hornblower* (1951), in particular the number "Lady Barbara." Born in Toronto, Robert Farnon first came into prominence as an arranger for Percy Faith on the Canadian Broadcasting Corporation. He settled in the United Kingdom following World War II, where he wrote arrangements for the bands of Ted Heath and Geraldo. He has since written original scores to a number of BBC radio shows as well as for some fourteen movies. His credits also include many recordings of his own music and albums made with singers. His richly scored accompaniments can be heard backing such singers as Sarah Vaughan, Frank Sinatra, Johnny Mathis, Tony Bennett, Lena Horne, Sheila Southern, and Eileen Farrell.

18. Estimates vary, but Ed Guerrero claims that the *Cleopatra Jones* soundtrack album sold over half a million copies. His information is based on Parish and Hill, *Black Action Films*.

19. B.J. Mason, "The New Films: Culture or Con Game?," *Ebony* 28 (December 1972), 62.

20. Paul Delaney, "Jesse Jackson," *The New York Times*, July 30, 1972, 39.

21. "Black Oriented Films Seen Losing Ground," *Jet*, January 17, 1974, 88.

22. David Franklin, "J.J. It's Back to Playing," *JazzTimes* (May 1988), 11.

23. Johnson began composing for *The Six Million Dollar Man* very shortly after Oliver Nelson's death (October 28, 1975) and continued for about a year and a half, until the show ended.

24. Johnson's choice of the theremin is part of a long-standing tradition in the underscoring of movies dealing with science fiction and themes of the paranormal. Two striking earlier examples include Miklós Rózsa's music for Alfred Hitchcock's *Spellbound* (1945) and Bernard Herrmann's score to Robert Wise's *The Day the Earth Stood Still* (1951).

25. The description of cues used in the "Seven Dead Eyes" episode of *Mike Hammer* expands upon notes originally provided by Erma Levin and edited by Louis G. Bourgois III.

26. The playing of "Pennsylvania 6–5000" serves as a reminiscence device providing a sense of unity to the episode as a whole. It harks back to the opening scene showing Hammer in his favorite Greenwich Village bar where he is meeting with Ridge Grundy.

27. Interview with Kevin Johnson, Indianapolis, June 24, 1993.

28. Interview with Erma Levin.

29. Feather, *From Pen to Screen*.

30. *Melody Maker*, May 2, 1970, 8.

31. *Ibid.*

32. Excerpted from an interview with Whitney Balliett, originally published in *The New Yorker*, March 19, 1972. It was subsequently reprinted in Whitney Balliett, *New York Notes: A Journal of Jazz, 1972–1975* (Boston: Houghton Mifflin, 1976), 11.

33. Interview with Chuck Berg "Dexter Gordon: Making His Great Leap Forward," reprinted in *Down Beat*, September 1989, 83.

34. David Baker, *J.J. Johnson, Trombone*. Jazz Monograph Series.(New York: Shattinger International Music, 1979), 11.

35. Interview with Kevin Johnson.

36. *Ibid.*

37. The tour that month also included Italian festival appearances, at Umbria Jazz (Perugia) and Pescara Jazz.

38. Interview with Kevin and Billy Johnson, Indianapolis, June 24, 1993.

39. Mike Hennessy,"The Return of J.J. Johnson," *Jazz Journal International,* vol. 30, no. 3, issue 5 (May 1980), 7.

40. Johnson pays tribute to George Tremblay in the course of a later composition, *Friendship Suite* (1992), the first movement of which is entitled "Ode to G.T."

Chapter 8

Why Indianapolis—Why Not Indianapolis?

How did J.J. Johnson come to resolve a personal dilemma? In the summer of 1988, following his return the previous fall to Indianapolis to settle permanently, Johnson premiered one of his most self-referential compositions, one bearing the same title as the present chapter.[1] Suffice it to say that the dilemma posed was very soon to be resolved most positively; ironically, it was a resolution achieved in the midst of the greatest personal grief. What is more, fortune was to smile upon Johnson as he overcame his mourning.

The first critical event in the process of post-Hollywood recovery came in the summer of 1987 when, on June 5, Johnson participated in the seventieth-birthday celebration of Dizzy Gillespie at Wolf Trap, outside Washington, D.C. Not only was he reconnecting with a seminal figure who had offered him the fateful endorsement "Man, you're elected" more than forty years earlier during the heyday of 52nd Street; he was also able on this occasion to have a man-to-man talk with Slide Hampton, a long-standing "Naptown"-born friend and fellow trombonist. Johnson was reportedly anxious about properly charting the future course of his career and making a comeback. Hampton's advice was soon to bear fruit in the person of Mary Ann Topper, whose artists' agency, The Jazz Tree, came to represent J.J. Johnson.

After his initial contact with Mary Ann Topper in early June 1987 Johnson gradually began putting back together the pieces of his career as a performing jazzman. An appearance on November 17, 1987, at the Village Vanguard signaled his formal return "back east," when forty musicians, most of them trombonists spanning at least two generations, made a presentation of a "welcome back" banner to J.J. Johnson—an event orchestrated largely by Slide Hampton.[2]

The strategic placement of Slide Hampton's name, serving in effect as a lintel holding together two vertical columns of names, signifies something more. Starting in the late 1970s, trombonists like Robin Eubanks, Curtis Fuller, Douglas Purviance, and Steve Turré were nurtured by their association with Hampton's World of Trombones. Eubanks has fondly recalled spending a good part of his formative years at Hampton's home in Brooklyn, where over the years it had been

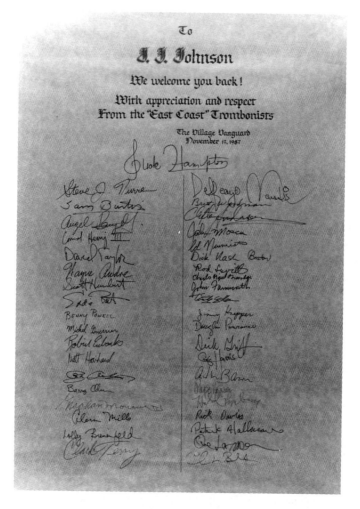

Fig. 8.1   "Welcome Back" banner presented to J.J. Johnson by Slide Hampton and the East Coast Trombones at the Village Vanguard, New York, November 17, 1987. Names appearing top to bottom are: *center-top,* Slide Hampton; *left column,* Steve Turré, Sam Burtis, Angel Rangeloff, Conrad Henry III, David Taylor, Wayne Andre, Scott Humbert, Eddie Bert, Benny Powell, Michel Guerrier, Robin Eubanks, Matt Haviland, Ray Anderson, Barry Allen, Gracian Moncur III, Glenn Mills, Lolly Bremenefeld, Clark Terry; *right column,* Delfeayo Marsalis, Britt Woodman, Clifton Anderson, John Mosca, Ed Neumeister, Dick Nash, Rod Levitt, Charles Najid Greenlee, John Farnsworth, Timothy Shea, Jimmy Knepper, Douglas Purviance, Dick Griffin, Craig Harris, Allen Blair, Papo Vasquez, Harold Mabry, Rick Davies, Patrick Hallaran, Ove Larsson, Clive Bulls. Courtesy of Mary Ann Topper and The Jazz Tree.

the usual thing for others like Wes Montgomery, Freddie Hubbard, John Coltrane, and Eric Dolphy to hang out. Eubanks has mentioned spending all day there listening to Johnson's album *First Place*, how scared he was upon first hearing "Turnpike," and having to put it away for a year.[3] As Hampton put it: "I was constantly trying to make all the younger guys . . . aware of J.J. at the time because J.J. had set the standard."[4]

When he made his celebrated comeback at the Village Vanguard in November 1987 Johnson was performing with a quintet of both tried and untried musicians. His front line included a relatively inexperienced tenor saxophone player fresh out of the Indiana University School of Music whose approach ultimately proved to be at odds with what Johnson had in mind.[5] However, members of the rhythm section were of a different order. Rufus Reid on bass and Victor Lewis on drums, who came with strong recommendations from Mary Ann Topper herself, remained with the quintet for several years. Cedar Walton, Johnson's personal choice, provided the sense of confidence and familiarity essential to Johnson's success. Besides, their warm association extended back to at least 1960 when Walton had been part of the J.J. Johnson Sextet, which had recently been revived during the summer 1984 tour that took them to France and Italy.

But by the summer of 1988 Johnson and his quintet were touring Canada with a different pianist and saxophonist. Because Walton had other commitments, Topper suggested replacing him with a "power player" in the person of Stanley Cowell, one who could rise to the challenge of Johnson's newest compositions.[6] By the same token, Topper's recommendation of Ralph Moore on tenor saxophone was dictated by a need for a consistent member of the group who could be counted on to produce a sound that Johnson would be happy with. In addition, what was required was a good reader who could master the charts of Johnson's latest compositions or arrangements, whether "Why Indianapolis—Why Not Indianapolis?," "Nefertiti," or "Quintergy."

By all accounts the reconstituted group was a dream come true. Less than a week before what proved to be a highly successful return engagement at the Village Vanguard (July 5–10, 1988), Johnson called Topper from Canada, where he was wrapping up a tour that had taken his group from Vancouver to Montreal, reportedly saying: "We have to record. This band is doing fabulous stuff."[7] Given less than a week's notice, Topper had to hire two top-flight recording engineers, one to monitor proceedings in the nightclub itself, the other to be in charge on the outside sound truck.[8] Even more daunting were the legal and financial arrangements. Leaving aside musical content for the moment, it is revealing to examine how the basic logistics of recording and producing jazz live in New York had changed since the time of Johnson's pre-Hollywood years. J.J. Johnson and Mary Ann Topper, listed as producer and executive producer, respectively, had major challenges on their hands. Both financed the recording project, and it would take close to three years before a satisfactory contract could be negotiated that provided for the release by Antilles of the two albums, *Quintergy* and *Standards*, in January and September 1991. In the interim various backers had come and gone, including Orrin Keepnews and sundry French (Verve-PolyGram) and Japanese players in the industry. In addition, there had been a certain skittishness on the part of the Japanese regarding the title *Quintergy*—it posed problems being printed in Japanese—and their insistence on replacing it with something more bland, like *Manhattan Skyline*. However, in the end both Johnson and Topper happily prevailed, firm in their conviction that *Quintergy* perfectly captured the quintet's energetic essence.

In his capacity as producer, Johnson showed a formidable command of recording detail, such as multitracking, and in notes jotted down for the engineers he is absolutely precise about how to best capture his sound. "3 tracks for trombone, desired overall effect is fat, dark, distinctive, but resonant timbre."[9] A fourth "quasi-sweetener track" is added in order to "enhance and reinforce the tromb./sax. interplay," while a fifth is left blank, "pending engineer's options," and the sixth is intended as an "overall" track for the quintet as a whole. Equalization—that is, the adjustment of various frequency areas within the total sound spectrum, decibel level, and hertz—specifying the number of vibrations per second—are precisely indicated by Johnson as follows:

> Track # 1, no EQ;
> Track # 2, EQ as follows: 3 db cut at 1000 Hz, 6 db cut at 2000 Hz,
>   12 db cut at 4000 Hz, Nothing above 8000 Hz
> Track # 3, sharp cut at 700 Hz, that is, no signal above 700 Hz.[10]

Ultimately, of course, it is the distinctive interpretive stamp of Johnson and his ensemble that counts the most in their traversal of jazz repertoire from New Orleans through Johnson's latest compositions. In the course of his commentary on Johnson's album Stanley Crouch observed:

> The result was a statement of perception so insightful that his five piece band was able to interpret the elements of jazz that had functioned from New Orleans through swing, bebop, and the reinterpretations of the tradition that had emerged during the sixties. As one would expect of him, Johnson did his work and used his band in a way that avoided pastiche or superficial emulation. It always sounded like his band, even when the composition wasn't his.[11]

Thus their treatment of even the traditional "When the Saints Go Marching In" has features of bebop harmony and rhythm that set it apart. Yet there will be other moments such as Sonny Stitt's piece "Bud's Blues," when, in a duo with Rufus Reid alone, Johnson will perfectly capture a funky, "down-home" sound. Other renditions are haunting in their power of understatement, particularly "It's All Right with Me," a Jay and Kai signature dating from 1955 and the context for their last public collaboration together at the 1982 Aurex Festival in Japan before

Winding's death the following year; and Johnson's unaccompanied solo meditation could not be more poignant.

Indeed, a recurring theme throughout the Village Vanguard appearance and the recording itself is the power of memory, not to mention the personification from time to time of the trombone as reflective protagonist. A case in point is "Coppin' the Bop," one of the early defining moments of Johnson's career when in 1946 he fronted his first identically constituted quintet, Jay Jay Johnson's Beboppers. However, the 1988 treatment here of Gershwin's "Rhythm" represents a virtually complete makeover of the 1946 version, with only the opening eight measures of the head and its incisive accents being recognizably the same. In the process of rearranging the piece Johnson expanded it to well over three times the original length—from 2:54 to 9:21—allowing for extended solos on piano, trombone, and saxophone as well as vividly contrasted breaks by each member of the ensemble. Other evocations of Johnson's memory are realized in Wayne Shorter's "Nefertiti," originally popularized in 1967 when Shorter and drummer Tony Williams were members of the Miles Davis Quintet. Johnson's treatment of the repetitious sixteen-bar tune shows tight voicing and an acute sense of harmonic color, all contributing to a laid-back impressionistic ambience. For sensuous, languorous playing, nothing here can surpass Johnson's performance on muted trombone of the ballad "You've Changed," evoking a 1958 recording he made as a sideman in the Ray Ellis Orchestra backing the vocal of Billie Holiday.

Arguably of the greatest interest are two of Johnson's latest compositions included on the album, "Why Indianapolis—Why Not Indianapolis?" and the title track, "Quintergy." The first of these, a hard-bop tour de force running to eight minutes, is based closely on Miles Davis's 1959 classic, "So What" and its dorian chord changes. There is an aggressive, competitive clambake quality as trombone and saxophone intrude on each other's musical space only to be topped by a climactic solo by Stanley Cowell. All of this is belied by an introduction given over entirely to a ruminative, unaccompanied trombone solo, almost two minutes in length and wide-ranging in every sense. Within the span of three octaves and a minor third (AA–c^2) Johnson's meditation is replete with growls, glissandos, blues touches, a bending of the flatted fifth, and a prefiguration of the riff that provides the basis for the composition as a whole. This turns out to be a quartal riff lifted largely intact from his 1984 work "Toots Suite," premiered that year at the JVC Grande Parade du Jazz Nice.

As for "Quintergy," characterized as "very high voltage" by Johnson in his recording notes, there is a provocative synthesis of elements from disparate sources. Much of that "very high voltage" is generated by the explosive drum breaks of Victor Lewis punctuating the quartal-sounding introduction—sonorities suggesting a generic, "modern" sound that some might associate with McCoy Tyner or Chick Corea but that for Johnson himself can also be traced back to his fascination with the pentatonicisms of Hindemith. The machine-gun rhythms that follow, with the entire ensemble in lockstep, further heighten the energy level. Once again, Johnson creatively borrows from himself, drawing generously upon the head of his "Why Not" as performed in Yokohama in April 1977. But even more masterful is the development of motives from this introduction in a polylinear texture that is built upon an ascending diminished whole-step scale on B-flat, first heard in the piano, which rises repeatedly to the flatted fifth. What is in fact embodied here is a remarkable case of stylistic affinity. The inclusion of this quintessentially bebop pitch set proves to be identical in virtually every respect to a unison passage from the first movement of Bartók's *Concerto for Orchestra,* and one of the scores in Johnson's personal library.[12]

Fig. 8.2   Bartók, *Concerto for Orchestra,* I, mm. 63–68.

Standards, the companion CD to *Quintergy,* is something of a revelation in its inclusion of two Johnson originals—"Sweet Georgia Gillespie" and "Shortcake"— and its recomposition of many repertoire staples. What shines through is Johnson's wonderful wit and sense of surprise, much of it achieved through understatement, fresh juxtaposition of instruments, and asymmetrical phrase structure. An especially telling example is his contrafact on "Sweet Georgia Brown" entitled "Sweet Georgia Gillespie"; it provides an occasion for a delicious pas de deux of trombone and tap-dancing drums. Johnson's allusions to Gillespie's "Salt Peanuts" and his quotation of "Joy to the World" only add to the sense of humor. Other selections such as "Autumn Leaves" are striking for their sense of abstraction—only the bridge is remotely recognizable—with chord extensions, the withholding of the saxophone until almost halfway through what is a rendition running to 9:21, a lengthy bass solo. Again, avoiding business as usual, Johnson offers a completely re-arranged version of Monk's "Misterioso," assigning the head to the piano alone and limiting the front line to intervallic fragments only. The piece thus receives a treatment here that is radically different from the version that Johnson had presented on his recent Japanese and European tours. In other instances the writing can be thick and dense, as in "What Is This Thing Called Love?," in which the piano styles of Horace Silver and Dave Brubeck are never far behind; nor can one ignore the many hints of Art Blakey. The polylinear layering of motives in the out chorus communicates a busy, sometimes urgent quality—a compelling embodiment of the question posed by the song itself.

The balance of 1988, continuing well into the fall, was devoted to touring, including appearances at the Mount Hood Festival near Portland and at the Monterey Jazz Festival, and performances in Holland and Spain, and at the Concord Jazz Festival in Japan. But by far the most memorable event during this period was the reunion with Stan Getz. On Wednesday, August 31, the opening night of the Tenth Annual Chicago Jazz Festival in Grant Park, Johnson and Getz were the headline attraction before a crowd of some fifty-thousand. Together on the same stage for the first time in more than thirty years and backed by the rhythm section of Kenny Barron, Rufus Reid, and Victor Lewis, they reprised various numbers from their historic joint appearance of September 29, 1957, at Chicago's Civic Opera. These included "Billie's Bounce," "Yesterdays," and "My Funny Valentine."

Johnson's touring activity continued more or less unabated until December 1988 when misfortune suddenly struck at the very core of his personal life. That month, during a tour of Japan, Vivian, Johnson's beloved wife, suffered a stroke that left her largely incapacitated for her remaining three years. That period was to claim the life of his mother as well. Johnson himself was profoundly shaken and on March 9, 1989, sent Mary Ann Topper a telegram asking her to cancel all engagements and to close his file permanently. What followed for some three and half years was at best a fitful career, one marked by deep gloom and only occasional flashes of hope.[13] Mary Ann Topper has speculated that Johnson's plunging into the extensive remodeling of his Indianapolis home very shortly after his March telegram was his way of coping with a period darkened by illness and impending death—a means of trying to maintain his sanity.[14] J.J. Johnson had lost

Fig. 8.3 *Left to right,* James Horace and Nina Geiger Johnson, J.J.
Johnson, and Rosemary Johnson Belcher, May 1973. Photograph
courtesy of J.J. Johnson.

his father, James Horace Johnson, on June 3, 1988. But there is no indication that the
event disrupted his career or caused him to stop in his tracks for very long. It was,
however, an event that coincided with the elaborate planning for the move back to
Indianapolis and provided a very valuable lesson in how close family and friends can
rally together in times of need. But, in the cases of his mother and wife, the emotional
attachment was infinitely greater. He was about to lose two women who had been
integral to his whole life—his mother, Nina Geiger Johnson (d. December 25, 1989) and
his wife of forty-four years, Vivian Elora Johnson (d. November 27, 1991), the very core
of his extended family. As Kevin Johnson put it: "His mom and his wife, that's all in the
same breath."[15]

The circumstances of Nina Johnson's passing held a uniquely intense
poignancy for J.J. Johnson. Arriving from Indianapolis at her bedside in a Chicago
nursing home, trombone in hand and all set to play her some Christmas carols, he
learned the painful truth that he was too late; she had already breathed her last.
Overcome by grief, it was some time before he could tear himself away. Once back
on the road to Indianapolis, tearful and alone, he conceived of a musical tribute,
"Mom, Are You Listening?," which, as he has said, "came to me in its entirety, title
and all."[16] Johnson played the piece at his mother's funeral and has since recorded
it in an arrangement for trombone, harp, celesta, and piano.[17]

The harrowing experience of dealing with Vivian's stroke took its toll as well.
Simply arranging for her return from Japan to the United States involved

emotionally draining negotiations with the American embassy and American Red Cross, for commercial airlines were very reluctant to transport her in her fragile condition. Once back in Indianapolis, Vivian was able to make only a halting and partial recovery, and matters were exacerbated by evidence of physical abuse at a local nursing home in the form of a broken nose. The greatest consolation for J.J. Johnson was at her funeral and in the turn of events that followed. The service on December 3, 1991, at Witherspoon United Presbyterian Church represented an outpouring of love and sympathy that only Johnson's nearest and dearest in Indianapolis could provide. The centerpiece of the service was the family tribute offered by Vivian's double cousin, Joy Gaddie. There was also the participation as pallbearers or honorary pallbearers by Johnson's two sons, Kevin and Billy, and other long-standing local musician friends such as Jimmy Coe and David Baker, not to mention close relatives.

The personal grief that Johnson suffered during this general period was to some extent mitigated by events in his public life that attested to his stature as composer, performer, and teacher. On May 7, 1988, slightly less than a month prior to his father's death, Johnson was awarded an honorary doctor of music degree by Indiana University, which was accompanied by a citation reading in part:

> J.J. Johnson is considered the founder of the modern generation of jazz trombonists. Through the exploration of virtually every aspect of trombone playing, he freed the instrument from the restrictions of tradition and restructured its harmonic vocabulary to be consistent with the demands of modern music. The sound that he evolved has set the standard for the modern trombone.

The International Trombone Association (ITA) issued him a Certificate of Life Membership (dated October 31, 1989), which was presented the following January, close to the time of his birthday. The letter of ITA president John Marcellus reads in part:

January 26, 1990

Dear J.J.,

> It gives me great pleasure to present you with this Life Membership Certificate in recognition of your contributions to the artistic advancement of trombone performance, pedagogy, and literature.

> The Officers and Board of the ITA recently approved the granting of life membership to those special people that have received the prestigious ITA Award, the highest honor that the Association can bestow upon an individual.

> You have been an idol to many trombonists in your career and this is just a small token in appreciation of your artistic achievements in the world of trombone.

In closing, I would like to invite you to visit future International Trombone Workshops so our members will have a chance to meet and talk with you—one of the most outstanding members of the trombone profession.

Slidingly yours,
John Marcellus, President

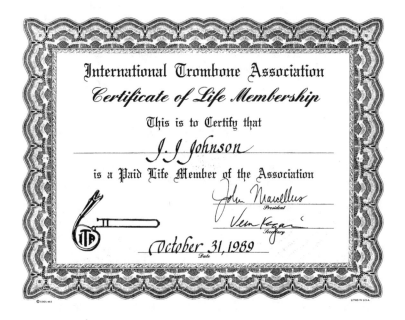

Fig. 8.4   J.J. Johnson's Certificate of Life Membership in the International Trombone Association, dated October 31, 1989, and signed by John Marcellus, president, and Vern Kagarice, secretary.

Between February and May 1991, during the period when his engagements were canceled and his file with Mary Ann Topper was "permanently closed," Johnson did serve as clinician and performer at Kentucky State University and also conducted a series of five master classes at Oberlin under the aegis of the Emil Danenburg Distinguished Artist Residence Fund. Furthermore, his performances abroad were not suspended completely. In fact, a little more than a fortnight before Vivian's death (November 27, 1991) Johnson appeared (November 8 and 10) at the Concord Jazz Festival in Osaka and Tokyo. His performances there provided the genesis for an album on Concord Records entitled *Vivian,* a project that had originally been sparked by a suggestion from producer Carl Jefferson and proved to be a loving tribute to his wife. "I was playing 'My Funny Valentine' and 'Misty' one night. Slow and moody. In

Fig. 8.5   J.J. Johnson on the occasion of being awarded an honorary doctor of music degree by Indiana University, May 7, 1988.

Fig. 8.6   J.J. Johnson and David N. Baker at the Baker residence in Bloomington, Indiana, May 7, 1988.

the wings, Carl Jefferson, when we got off, asked me if I'd like to do a ballad album for Concord Records. I thought about it, and I liked the idea."[18]

Widespread praise greeted *Vivian* following its release in September 1992. Johnson had risen magnificently to the challenge of writing exquisite arrangements for a series of ballads in slow or medium tempo performed by him fronting an ensemble consisting of Rob Schneiderman on piano, Ted Dunbar on guitar, Rufus Reid on bass, and Akira Tana on drums. Johnson can readily be heard as the pensive protagonist pondering his personal loss. An especially telling example is his long-breathed solo in the opening Dietz/Schwartz classic, "Alone Together," in which he is superbly complemented by Rob Schneiderman. Elsewhere there are moments of relief provided by, for example, the funky treatment of the blues "Frankie and Johnny" and its more equitable sharing of breaks and solos. Other numbers, such as "I Thought about You," are richly evocative in their power of muted understatement. By the same token, Johnson is indeed faithful to the dictum "What you don't play is as important as what you play." He is always keenly attuned to the need for silences, for variety in timbre and texture. The gentle call and response between guitar and trombone in the head of Gershwin's "But Not for Me" is a case in point. In "Azure Té" there is a subtle tension generated as guitar, bass, piano, and drums begin the piece without Johnson. In his review of *Vivian,* to which he gave a five-star rating, Thomas Conrad offered the following eloquent summation:

> Sadness and loss are transcended through the catharsis of art. Johnson's style, once famous for its speed, is now centered on his deep, dark tone, and he lingers over every scalar variation until its specific feeling is defined.[19]

Johnson's sense of transcendence was carried over into his personal life, when, in that same month—September 11 to be exact—he married Carolyn Reid. What follows is her account of how she and J.J. Johnson met:

> When I first met Jay Johnson (as I have always called him) I must admist that I really did not know a lot about jazz trombonist J.J. Johnson, alhtough I had heard of him. I was Branch Office Administrator at Bankers Life and Casualty Insurance Company's branch office here in Indianapolis. J.J. was one of our clients. For obvious reasons he had interaction with our office more so than the norm during the cycle that we are dealing with here. During one of his many visits to our office, I was personally introduced to J.J. by one of my coworkers at the office. After that, he called fairly frequently not only about business but also just to sometimes have a friendly chit-chat. That led to J.J. inviting me to have dinner with him. Then we began to date. Our friendship finally intensified to the point where J.J. asked me would I consider becoming his second wife. When I questioned J.J. about the haste of his decision to want to remarry, he told me that the emptiness and the loneliness of his life had started with Vivian's devastating stroke, and after her death had become so unbearable that he had

begun to mentally flirt with thoughts of the unthinkable and the unspeakable. He showed to me rough drafts, on scraps of paper, of notes to his family members that caused me to shudder in horror. We were married on September 11, 1992.[20]

Fig. 8.7 Carolyn and J.J. Johnson at the Jazz Kitchen, Indianapolis, March 2, 1995. Photograph courtesy of Carolyn Johnson.

By mid-September 1992, his juices clearly flowing once again, Johnson was talking with Mary Ann Topper about reactivating his file. This she eventually did in June 1993. Resuming her role as his manager, she organized a series of appearances promoting his latest Verve album, *Let's Hang Out,* that was released in August 1993. Coproduced by J.J. Johnson and Jean-Philippe Allard, the original session had taken place in New York on December 7, 8, and 9, 1992. The album's title, not to mention the new four-movement composition *Friendship Suite,* coupled with five other originals, signified a dramatically regenerated J.J. Johnson. Something of this new found energy was communicated in the few public appearances that Johnson made during 1993. These included his performances at Holland's North Sea Jazz Festival in July as well as at the Blue Note clubs in Osaka and Tokyo (November 8–14) and in New York (December 14–19).

A sense of awe and wonder greeted Johnson and his brand of music-making. Gary Giddins likened going to the Blue Note to taking "a trip to bop heaven" and spoke of Johnson's "superb new album" as sustaining "his claim as the greatest trombonist of our time."[21] Peter Watrous wrote: "Mr. Johnson's rare engagements in New York are a marvel, partly because his sound, with its warmth and flawless intonation, has such an emotional effect in concert, and partly because he has become such a classicist."[22]

Classicism, identified here with a consummate self-control and avoidance of excess, finds eloquent expression in *Let's Hang Out* as a whole and in the selection entitled "Syntax" in particular. Johnson has in fact expounded at some length on this word, one that he associates with his earliest bebop involvement.

> The first challenge for me was to become familiar with that jazz language. That was a specific language of jazz, a syntax, if you will. So the first order of business had nothing to do with the trombone; the first order of business was to become familiar with the syntax of that genre. That's what it's all about; it's all about syntax. It's not about the difficulty of the trombone, or a guy playing this fast, that fast. Syntax is the key word here . . . always has been, always will be!

> I have problem with that word "bebop." We all know that Dizzy Gillespie created that word himself. But in my opinion Dizzy Gillespie was much bigger . . . I can only hope that I, too, am bigger than the label.

> Dickie Wells was not known to play a lot of notes . . . but they were a wonderful few notes! Very well selected, very well chosen. One of my favorite jazz solos is Miles Davis's wonderful solo on "So What." In my opinion, it's the perfect example of that word that I call the key word, syntax. . . . He never comes out of the mid-to-upper register, never is he screaming in the upper register, he never plays a lot of high notes, he never plays a lot of fast notes. All he plays [are] lyric lines that seem to go well together and form a certain syntax that appeals to me very much.[23]

Yet Johnson's "Syntax" does not remotely sound like the 1959 classic of the Miles Davis sextet. Based on the changes of Gershwin's "Rhythm," it has a conventional unison head and out chorus on trombone and tenor saxophone, but, consistent with the general aesthetic ideal he has articulated, his work is limited to solos in medium tempo that avoid any sense of speed or extremes of register, and contain their few, well-chosen notes.

In surveying the other selections on the album *Let's Hang Out*, it is possible to misinterpret it as an occasion for easy informality, of hanging out with the guys; and in a sense there is admittedly a game of musical chairs that is played. Johnson's bassist, Rufus Reid, is in fact the only constant. For the rest, Victor Lewis and Lewis Nash alternate at the drum set, while Renee Rosnes and Stanley Cowell share the honors at the piano. Then again, in his front line Johnson will draw upon the talents of either Jimmy Heath or Ralph Moore, both on tenor saxophone, as well as Terence Blanchard on trumpet.

But what perhaps best capture the essence of the message behind the album's title are the first two movements of "Friendship Suite," in which Johnson flaunts a certain musical modernity, letting it all hang out as it were. "Ode to G.T." is a rather acerbic opening movement, two-thirds of it an unaccompanied trombone solo built in part on two twelve-tone rows. True to its name, this movement honors the memory of George Tremblay, the Los Angeles composer and pianist with whom Johnson briefly studied twelve-tone theory.[24] Shortly after the bass enters, in free imitation, the music lapses into a plaintive, bluesy sound drawing upon the circle of fifths. A dramatic "cadenza espagnole"—built on the Spanish Phrygian on d—brings in other members of the ensemble—Jimmy Heath, Renee Rosnes, and Lewis Nash.

The eponymous "Let's Hang Out" movement that follows offers some of Johnson's most astringent, angular writing. The ensemble performs homorhythmically in tight unisons and chords, while Lewis Nash's drums provide "heavy filler throughout," as specified in Johnson's chart. At the same time, Johnson's pitch syntax owes its origins to Bartók and Stravinsky, filtered through the likes of McCoy Tyner, Wayne Shorter, and Geri Allen, not to mention his own "Aquarius" from his 1960 album *J.J. Inc.* What he does here is to use the octatonic scale on d, or more specifically, the d-diminished scale in both its whole-step and half-step forms.

The remaining two movements of "Friendship Suite" suggest a kinship with John Coltrane. A brief ballad (0:56) entitled "Love You Nana" is affecting for its lyrical quartal melody for saxophone, juxtaposed with the touching Phrygian response by the trombone. "Reunion," the concluding fourth movement, is an uptempo number reminiscent of Coltrane's early 1960s brand of modal jazz. Jimmy Heath's solo and the interplay with others in the ensemble achieves a balance between freedom and control in what is essentially a one-chord Dorian-mode piece without a bridge. The effect that Johnson was seeking here is indicated by one of his rare, unbuttoned comments that appears on the title page to this movement: "Chaos and insanity is very desirable, not to mention—needed!"

"Stir Fry," based on a thirty-two-bar chorus, is a piece with a strong mix of funk and gospel. At the same time, its head and out chorus vividly evoke the sound of Coltrane's "Giant Steps." "Kenya," Johnson's most extended work included here (12:24), is a passionate tribute to the hard-bop spirit of Horace Silver and Art Blakey. The driving intensity of his front line—Terence Blanchard and Ralph Moore join Johnson on trumpet and tenor saxophone, respectively—immediately sets the appropriate tone. At the other extreme, Johnson's unaccompanied solo rendition of Victor Young's "Beautiful Love," represents a masterpiece of haunting understatement.

"May I Have Dis Dance," essentially a twenty-four-bar blues, finds Johnson in a funky, down-home frame of mind. The spirit of gospel blues hovers over much

Fig. 8.8 *Let's Hang Out* session, December 8, 1992. *Left to right,*
Rufus Reid, Renee Rosnes (piano), Jimmy Heath (tenor sax), J.J.
Johnson. Photograph courtesy of Cheung Ching Ming.

of the solo work of Johnson and Renee Rosnes. There is also a delightfully playful
spirit, readily apparent in the head and out chorus as well as in the exchanges
among trombone, drums, and soprano saxophone within the body of the piece.

Let's Hang Out was the first in a series of three, that Johnson undertook to
record for Verve starting in December 1992. But there was also a more public
aspect to his association with the label and its parent company, Polygram. On
April 6, 1994, Johnson appeared in Carnegie Hall on the occasion of Verve's
fiftieth anniversary. The pivotal role of Norman Granz, Verve's founder, was
highlighted through the interspersion at the concert of well-chosen video clips,
showing how he helped immortalize the priceless legacy of Art Tatum, Count
Basie, Lester Young, Stan Getz, Dizzy Gillespie, Miles Davis, Ella Fitzgerald, and
Billie Holiday, to mention a few. The live segments of the concert brought Johnson
on stage four times. He was part of the curtain-raising rendition of "Tea for Two,"
with Joe Henderson on tenor saxophone, Kenny Burrell on guitar, and Herbie
Hancock on piano (who was also cohosting the event with Vanessa Williams).
Johnson's other contributions included: playing in the Frank Foster 1955 hit
"Shiny Stockings," in which he, Kenny Burrell, and Renee Rosnes, together with
the Carnegie Hall Jazz Band, backed vocalist Dee Dee Bridgewater; joining Hank
Jones on piano, Charlie Haden on bass, and Al Foster on drums to back Abbey
Lincoln in her Billie Holiday tribute, "I Must Have That Man"; and finally
performing in the all-star "blowout" wrapping up the concert that featured
Parker's "Now's the Time," with Betty Carter providing an inimitable scat vocal.

More than a celebration of Verve's past achievements, the concert was also a benefit, the proceeds of which went to Carnegie Hall's JAZZED program, a form of outreach bringing area high school students a series of one-act musical plays based on the lives and times of famous jazz musicians. The concert was not only taped by Thirteen/WNET and subsequently aired in their *Great Performances* series; Polygram also made an audio and video recording. Johnson, like all other participating artists, was therefore asked to offer his services "for the applicable minimum scale payments based on public television's existing agreements" with the American Federation of Television and Radio Artists as well as the American Federation of Musicians.[25]

July 13–15, 1994, brought Johnson to London for the second of his Verve recording sessions, this one with the Robert Farnon Orchestra.[26] Also on hand for three cuts on the resulting album was Wynton Marsalis. The production of *Tangence,* released in March 1995, followed a rather painstaking two years' planning that had its episodes of gentlemanly miscommunication and frustration. As Johnson once remarked of Robert Farnon: "He is the supreme, quintessential diplomat . . . it's so gentlemanly that it's almost like you're not disagreeing at all."[27] At the same time, it was a project that realized a long-cherished dream of working with a man he held in awe. Farnon's sound had captivated him many years before with his distinctive sensuous string writing, particularly in his score to the 1951 movie epic *Captain Horatio Hornblower.* One special portion had bowled him over. "From that masterful score, the music that really blew me away was the majestic, lush, elegant tone poem, 'Lady Barbara.'"[28] Farnon is identified by Johnson as one of his "composer/orchestrator heroes" to be spoken of in the same breath as Ravel. As he puts it: "[Igor Stravinsky] once said of Maurice Ravel, that 'he orchestrates with the meticulous precision of a fine Swiss watchmaker.' In my humble opinion, the same can be said of Robert Farnon."[29]

The *Tangence* album, consisting mostly of ballads, provides a feast of Farnon orchestration, with such touches as celesta accents, octave doublings in strings, unison French horn/cello writing, and obbligato solo passages for oboe and saxophone in a low register. Among the ballads featured are Johnson's haunting "Lament," Michael Carr's "Dinner for One, Please James," and Ray Noble's "The Very Thought of You." But being the consummate musician that he is, Johnson is keenly attuned to the need for contrast. This is provided by two refreshingly quirky unaccompanied duos. In the first he is joined by Wynton Marsalis for an off-the-wall version of "For Dancers Only," as configured from the original 1937 Sy Oliver arrangement for the Jimmie Lunceford Orchestra, with Johnson and Marsalis standing in for the trombone and trumpet sections, respectively. Very much a tongue-in-cheek affair, filled with Oliver/Lunceford licks, it was a piece where Marsalis quickly got into the spirit of things, plunger mute and all. In the other duo Johnson is joined by bassist Chris Laurence for the funky blues "Opus De Focus." For the rest, the album is true to its name—a play on the geometric term and one incorporating multiple stylistic tangents in a trajectory that curves through many points in Johnson's career. Some fifty years of Johnson's life are represented, from Benny Carter's "People Time," to his own beloved ballad "Lament," to "Malaga Moon," a very recent composition by Renee Rosnes, the pianist in his quintet since 1992. Then again, categories become blurred in such cases as the traditional gospel hymn "Amazing Grace," not to mention the rendition of Cuban composer Ernesto Lecuona's "Malagueña."

"Amazing Grace" and "Malagueña" each help shed light on different facets of the Johnson/Farnon relationship. It appears that Johnson had some preconceived, if conflicted, ideas about the treatment of the hymn.

> It may or may not work. It is either a very good idea, or a very, very bad idea. In hindsight I'm not really sure of what I actually had in mind other than the transition from quasi-religioso to medium slow 9/8 meter with jazz undercurrents behind trombone improvisation. It may still be a good idea.[30]

Farnon reportedly found himself in an awkward position and strongly suggested that, with his preconceived ideas, Johnson was the better person to write the arrangement. But Johnson simply did not want to do this because Farnon had agreed to write the arrangements and conduct the orchestra for the album. Nothing was definitively settled and Johnson arrived at the London session not sure that "Amazing Grace" would even be on the music stands. Yet, there it was, and Farnon had come around almost full circle, very close to the original Johnson conception. "Malagueña," by comparison, was a simple matter to prepare, even though the resulting cut is arguably the most controversial on the album. Neither jazz nor pop, it sounds more like a classical orchestral piece with minimal, low-profile solos by Johnson and Marsalis.

What emerges too from the Johnson/Farnon correspondence is the delicate matter of key choice, its significance for trombone intonation and sonority, and the implications for sustaining low notes. Farnon's own piece, "Two's Company," was initially sent to Johnson in a "nice and comfortable" key of C. Yet when mailed the final version some time later, Johnson discovered that the key had been changed to F, a key more consistent with Farnon's overall "orchestral concept." Johnson became somewhat apprehensive about the initial low C and its not-always-predictable intonation. But he was relieved that other seemingly troublesome solo passages had been assigned to Wynton Marsalis.

In other respects Johnson was not one to be daunted. He has claimed to have been "so terribly intimidated" by the Gil Evans/Miles Davis traversal of "The Meaning of the Blues"—a performance in which Davis "never played with more expression, authority, and passion . . . one that sends shudders and shivers down J.J.'s spine."[31] Yet, he proceeded to add an introduction to the Bobby Troup score and structured a sketch that was detailed to the point of making Farnon feel that he was being left little space in which to maneuver. Once again, nothing more was said between them and Johnson was sure that Farnon would have nothing more of it. Yet again there it was at the recording session, and the resulting version is more than double the length of the Gil Evans/Miles Davis original.

Other titles on the *Tangence* album encompass other points in Johnson's career. Most compelling here are the ballads "People Time" (words and music by Benny Carter), Ray Noble's "The Very Thought of You"—a love note to Johnson's second wife, Carolyn Reid, and a piece played at their wedding—and Renee Rosnes's atmospheric, "Malaga Moon," originally heard quite by accident as part of a sound check on his quintet's tour.

The Johnson/Farnon collaboration signifies something more for both Johnson's own career and jazz history. Talking about his latter-day recording projects with Verve-Polygram, Johnson has explained:

> I am going through a cycle that I would like to call a creative or a conceptualizing cycle, where I'm looking for ways to do recording projects that are not just another day at the office. We . . . know that the market is flooded . . . with performances by fantastic musicians, beautiful albums, beautiful productions, fantastic jazz improvisations that really fall into the category of another day at the office.[32]

For Johnson, the undertaking of recording projects "that are not just another day at the office" has meant not only working with Robert Farnon but also recording with a Caribbean steel drum ensemble featuring Steve Turré playing conch shells. He has also at various times floated ideas for a rap album and an album with B.B. King. But what is special about the collaboration with Farnon is not simply that it represents the fulfillment of a long-cherished dream of Johnson's dating back to the *Captain Horatio Hornblower* soundtrack.

The Johnson/Farnon collaboration, it can well be argued, belongs to a tradition that includes jazzmen such as Charlie Parker, Coleman Hawkins, Warren Vaché, Ornette Coleman, and Ben Webster, all of whom made their share of successful recordings with strings. One could add to the list the name of Louis Armstrong, whose renditions of pop songs and joint appearances with Bing Crosby would typically have the backing of a large string section. Wynton Marsalis, aside from his recordings of Haydn and Hummel trumpet concertos and baroque repertoire with Kathleen Battle, has also recorded a jazz album with strings entitled *Hot House Flowers*. Then again, jazz guitarists from Wes Montgomery to Earl Klugh have been heard on string-backed albums, as have pianists from Oscar Peterson to Keith Jarrett, either in fresh arrangements or in new compositions.

In this general regard, strings have often been thought of as "sweetening" jazz, even making it more legitimate by associating it with European high culture— a phenomenon that has precedents in the work of Paul Whiteman and has provocative latter-day manifestations, notably in the performances of such crossover string quartets—the quintessential classical ensemble—as the Brodsky Quartet, the Kronos Quartet, or the Uptown String Quartet. Finally, it is revealing that Johnson, as noted earlier, has seen fit to characterize Robert Farnon in the same terms that Igor Stravinsky invoked when describing Maurice Ravel.

The release of Johnson's *Tangence* album—in March 1995 in the United States and a few months earlier in Europe—served as the primary impetus for a series of tours on both sides of the Atlantic. During the second half of November 1994 Johnson and his quintet were at the Hotel Meridien Etoile in Paris performing in the hotel's highly popular jazz venue, the Lionel Hampton Room, where, among other things, a tradition has developed of having big-band jazz brunches on Sundays. However, Johnson's French stint that November was complicated by personnel problems, particularly in the drum chair. Billy Drummond, Johnson's regular drummer (also the husband of his pianist Renee Rosnes) was unable to make the first few gigs because of the death of his father, and what transpired caused some turmoil. Instead of giving Drummond the option of rejoining the quintet after taking care of family matters, Johnson hired an expatriate living in Paris in the person of George Brown, a Rastafarian characterized as "a relatively unruly guy."[33] Brown accompanied the group to New York for appearances the following month at the Blue Note and at a Polygram recording session on December 20, 1994 (with Jamaican steel drums, conch shells, and the participation of Steve Turré). But his abrasive personal style took a heavy psychological toll on other members of the quintet, especially Renee Rosnes, who had seen her husband let go. Johnson was hardly oblivious to all of this, yet there was something in Brown's sound, a driving power reminiscent of Art Blakey and Elvin Jones, that energized Johnson in a critical way.

> It was a hard time. J.J. recognized this, even as it was going on in Paris. But again, his musical instinct told him this was what he wanted. And the personality conflicts that were occurring . . . as aware of them as he was, it was not going to in any way overcome his need for the drummer that he wanted. And so that was made perfectly clear.[34]

Don Sickler has put it even more pointedly.[35] Called in to conduct sections of the Polygram session, Sickler claims to have found Brown in an agitated state and in need of being calmed down. Even though Brown had already been fired from the band, Johnson so relished his reckless abandon, his ability to throw those "bombs," that he decided to retain him for this final date. By the same token Brown, "a rough kind of drummer, not a polished player," and essentially an "ear" musician, was reportedly flustered by the elaborate cues in the music, particularly Johnson's "Caravan" score. Heightening the tension was Johnson's stern written warning to Brown to the effect that he was to do exactly as Sickler asked because he was in charge of conducting "Caravan"; and if Brown gave any problems he was going to have to answer to J.J. Johnson.[36]

Personnel changes were hardly confined to the Brown episode, however hot that moment was. Already in early November 1994, at the San Francisco Jazz Festival, Johnson had had to find substitutes for Renee Rosnes and Billy Drummond in the persons of Geoff Keezer and Marvin "Smitty" Smith. By February, saxophonist Ralph Moore left to join the band on Jay Leno's *Tonight Show* and was replaced by Dan Faulk. A modicum of stability came at the end of February as the group, now with Bruce Cox in the drum chair, began rehearsing in Indianapolis in preparation for some extensive touring in the month of March that was timed to coincide with the release of the *Tangence* album. Indianapolis, Santa Cruz, Oakland, Seattle, Burghausen and Neuberg in Germany, and Forli, Ancona, and Bologna in Italy were among their stops. May 1995 saw the quintet in Chicago at the Jazz Showcase with Geoff Keezer as pianist. This was followed in June by a tour of six Canadian cities, a double bill with the Christian McBride Quartet and part of a Verve "package"; and Billy Childs, a vital presence at the 1977 Yokohama concert, was once again pressed into service at the keyboard.

Talking about these personnel changes, Johnson has minimized the issue of interpersonal turmoil to adopt a thoroughly pragmatic attitude.

> Ralph Moore got an offer that no one could refuse. He got an offer to go with the Jay Leno [band]. Lord knows, we should have such predictability, we should all have such security as a weekly paycheck. So I don't want to go further than that. The drummer situation is a little more complex and I would not care to articulate it. We needed a change of drummers. It's nothing really out of the ordinary . . . there's nothing unusual about [all of] this . . . the reasons are manifold, but mundane. [37]

In the discussion earlier in this chapter of the Johnson/Farnon collaboration on the *Tangence* album, we spoke about the practice of jazzmen performing with strings, and of the associated idea of imparting to jazz a certain legitimacy; what is compelling about the most recent phase of Johnson's career is how it has been marked by connections with institutions not immediately identified with jazz.

For some two years, from about 1993 to 1995, planning was under way for a high-profile concert at Lincoln Center's Alice Tully Hall featuring *Poem for Brass* and *Perceptions,* with the participation of Wynton Marsalis and Gunther Schuller. Plans for the event, originally scheduled for April 14, 1995 and subsequently re-scheduled for November 18 of that year, had to eventually be completely scrapped. A hoped-for tie-in with the March 1995 U.S. release of the Verve-Polygram *Tangence* album was not to be. As Mary Ann Topper put it: "J.J.'s penchant for extreme detail was overwhelming to the folks at Lincoln Center."[38] The realization of Johnson's dream would have meant a concert too costly for Jazz at Lincoln Center, what with the constraints of rehearsal time, unions, and general budget. Compounding the problem in the case of the November 18 date was the conflict with a Sonny Rollins concert during the week of the *Jazz Times* convention. And perhaps the ultimate irony was that exactly a month later the Lincoln Center Board "awarded the institution's jazz department, Jazz at Lincoln Center, equal status with the New York Philharmonic, the Metropolitan Opera, the New York City Ballet and the other so-called constituents of the Center."[39] That same December *Down Beat* published its 60th Annual Readers Poll announcing that Johnson had been voted into the *Down Beat* Hall of Fame and elected Trombone of the Year.

However, the following month, specifically, Friday evening, January 12, 1996, proved to be one of the defining moments marking the culmination of Johnson's career. The occasion was the 1996 Awards Concert of the National Endowment for the Arts (NEA) American Jazz Masters Fellowship Program. On hand at the Marriott Marquis in Atlanta, Georgia, were the 1996 recipients, Tommy Flanagan, Benny Golson, and J.J. Johnson, each of whom received a onetime fellowship of $20,000. Dr. Billy Taylor served as master of ceremonies, and musical guests were the   Clark Atlanta University Jazz Orchestra performing Lalo Schifrin's *Gillespiana,* with the composer himself included in the ensemble as well as Jon Faddis, Paquito D'Rivera, Rufus Reid, and Ignacio Berroa. Also on stage in other segments of the concert were other groups—Kurt Elling with Trio New and the Joe Lovano Symbiosis Quintet.

Initiated in 1982, the NEA "American Jazz Masters" Fellowship Program honored forty-three legendary jazz musicians through 1995, on an average three per year, among them Dizzy Gillespie, Count Basie, Miles Davis, Max Roach, Kenny Clarke, Art Blakey, Cecil Taylor, Ella Fitzgerald, George Russell, and Benny Carter. Nominations have typically been submitted by the public and members of the jazz community to the NEA in the form of a one-page letter stating why the candidate is thought to be worthy of the honor. The award has never been open to application. Nominees have then been reviewed by the Jazz Fellowships panel which has then proceeded to make its selection. For the first nine years, until 1991, the awards were mailed to the recipients without much publicity. However, that year D. Antoinette Handy, former director of the music program, realized that awards conveyed in this manner did little to raise public awareness of America's jazz heritage. Working with the Charlin Jazz Society and the International Association of Jazz Educators (IAJE), she established a tradition of having the awards presented at a special concert ceremony coinciding with the IAJE's annual conference.

There were greetings from both President Bill Clinton and Jane Alexander, the NEA chair. Jane Alexander offered these words of congratulation:

> An American Jazz Masters Fellowship is the most prestigious award our Federal government can bestow upon a jazz artist. Like the 43 legendary jazz musicians who precede them, these 1996 recipients are truly masters in every sense of the word. There is indeed cause for celebration. If it were not for the incredible creative energy, force of conviction, and fidelity to the form by a

handful of guiding spirits, such as Tommy Flanagan, Benny Golson, and J.J. Johnson, jazz might not have flourished. These three individuals have forged long and respected careers and made enduring contributions to the evolution of jazz in this country. For many years, each has been passing along his knowledge and passion for jazz so that new generations of jazz masters may carry on this American-born musical tradition.[40]

One other occasion representing a compelling institutional legitimacy for J.J. Johnson came on April 18–20, 1996, when he visited Harvard University as Kayden Artist in Residence, following a tradition that has similarly honored such Johnson colleagues as Benny Carter, Slide Hampton, Gerry Mulligan, John Lewis, Carla Bley, Buck Clayton, and Illinois Jacquet. Some three years in the planning, the residency was cosponsored by the Office for the Arts at Harvard and Radcliffe as well as the Harvard Jazz Band. The event was very much a tribute to the initiative and perseverance of Thomas Everett, former president of the International Trombone Association, founder of Harvard's jazz program in 1971, and director of Harvard University Bands. J.J. Johnson, who at times needs to be coaxed and cajoled more than most, only gradually warmed up to the idea of the residency. In the process it was also the persuasive powers of Mary Ann Topper, Johnson's artistic agent for some ten years, that prevailed. But there were apparently those moments when her patience was wearing rather thin, even while recognizing that her client almost invariably trusts her judgment implicitly.

> He knows what I feel is good for him, but we really have diehards [here], believe me! There are moments when I have to reach way back inside myself to say to Jay, "Look, there are a lot of young people out there who don't know who you are and what you were responsible for!" And as an educator I continually bring this up to him because I feel . . . one of the greatest things that he could be doing right now is touching other people.[41]

Thus it was that Johnson sat in on rehearsals and appeared as special soloist on selected numbers with the Harvard University Jazz Band at its concert in a packed Sanders Theater on Saturday, April 20, 1996—a retrospective rich in memory. The first half highlighted Johnson's career through the Jay and Kai years with such numbers as Wes Montgomery's "Four on Six," Charlie Parker's "Quasimodo," Oscar Pettiford's "Tricotism," and the signature piece of Cole Porter, "It's All Right With Me." Also included were arrangements by Johnson dating from his association with Benny Carter ("SPLO") and Count Basie ("Rambo"). "SPLO" was something of a novelty that, though a fairly conventional piece, was retrieved by Carter from his basement for the concert and heard for the first time in some fifty years. Finally, there were such features as a new brass orchestration of "Why Indianapolis—Why Not Indianapolis?," a revised version of *El Camino Real*, and "Mom, Are You Listening?"

A SALUTE TO **J.J. JOHNSON**

with Trombonist and Composer **J.J. Johnson**
special guest Saxophonist Dan Faulk
and the Harvard Jazz Band

1940's Johnson score re-discovered by **Benny Carter** to be performed

Saturday, April 20, 1996 8 PM
Sanders Theatre, Cambridge
Tickets: $ 8 General admission
$ 6 Students & Seniors
Sanders Theatre Box Office 496-2222
and Holyoke Center Ticket Office 495-2663

**for more information
call 495-8676**

OFA approved 4/21/96
Poster design: Terri Sanders

Fig. 8.9   Poster for Harvard University Jazz Band's "A Salute to J.J. Johnson" concert, April 20, 1996. Courtesy of the Harvard University Office for the Arts.

Fig. 8.10   Thomas Everett, *left*, and J.J. Johnson, *right*, Harvard University's Kayden Artist in Residence, during a rehearsal for the "Salute to J.J. Johnson" concert with the Harvard Jazz Band. Photograph courtesy of Kris Snibbe, Harvard News Office.

Two years past the biblically resonant age of three-score years and ten, Johnson was having his own Ivy League "love-in." It was a time of joyous affirmation when he was able to share with a younger generation something of the richness of his legacy—spiritual father of modern trombone, consummate arranger and composer pushing the boundaries of jazz, and one who has embodied in his own life many of the phases of its history from the latter days of the swing era, to the various styles of bebop and beyond. There, before a cheering crowd, stood a man, tall and proud, whose creative imagination has encompassed musical worlds from blues, Basie, Gillespie, Parker, Monk, and Davis, to Britten, Bartók, Hindemith, Ravel, and Stravinsky.

Johnson's creative imagination, his abiding passion for composition and arranging, has burned with ever greater intensity since the time of his Harvard appearance in April 1996. There have certainly been the tours, the travel to Turkey, to Hollywood, the Ravinia Festival in Chicago, and the Litchfield Jazz Festival in Connecticut—the last-mentioned venue marking an occasion of transcendent playing with his quintet.[42] But ever mindful of how precious time is, Johnson has recently dramatically reordered his priorities to retire from active touring with his quintet so as to better serve his creative muse. The decision-making process has admittedly been a slow and agonizing one, even predating his Harvard appearance. Writing in the late summer of 1996, Johnson confessed:

> For the past few years, two or three times a week, I wake up at 3 A.M., go sit quietly in the dark . . . and ask myself this burning question: "J.J., are you absolutely and positively sure that you are ready for total retirement?" The answer has been 100 percent "yes." I am absolutely and positively sure that I am ready for total retirement. But I must do it in a way that is pragmatic and comfortable.[43]

Johnson proceeds to outline his agenda: a final performance by his quintet on November 10, 1996, a few high-profile concerts in 1997, new recordings, and a "very quiet, unheralded exit from the arena of live performing; no farewell concerts or farewell performances whatsoever." Essentially the same information is contained in a round-robin "open letter/memorandum" dispatched in the late summer of 1996 to *Down Beat, The Instrumentalist,* and the *ITA Journal.*

His letter alludes to "a most exciting, satisfying career as a jazz performer" and proceeds to touch on how he will sorely miss his quintet, the jazz audience, and so on. But after acknowledging his debt of gratitude to Mary Ann Topper, The Jazz Tree, *Down Beat,* and "its legion of readers," his letter gets to the nub of the matter—what he hopes to do after retiring from active performing. "I hope to continue to compose, arrange, and orchestrate. More importantly, I will hopefully continue to study and develop as a composer, arranger, and orchestrator." Perhaps most revealing of all is his very human sign-off: "Mostly, I really hope to get re-acquainted with life."

But primarily through the prompt intervention of Mary Ann Topper in late August 1996—she had not been consulted first—publication of this letter was withheld by *Down Beat.* Commitments had already been made, and some serious issues of professional credibility were at stake. Accordingly, a *Down Beat* article announcing Johnson's "farewell to the road" scheduled for the November issue was postponed with the proviso that *Down Beat* would be the first to "go public" with Johnson's retirement.[44] An explosive situation was gradually defused, and apologies were made by Johnson to Mary Ann Topper and The Jazz Tree as he came crawling back.

By the time of Johnson's actual farewell quintet performance, Sunday, November 10, 1996, at William Paterson College, Wayne, New Jersey, the whole matter of publicly announcing his retirement had been reduced to a nonevent. No announcements, no intimations of any kind were made. By all appearances this was purely and simply another fine concert in the Jazz Room Series as produced by David Demsey, with Rufus Reid serving as artistic adviser.

In fact, Rufus Reid, long-standing bassist in Johnson's quintet as well as a member of the teaching faculty at William Paterson College, was instrumental in arranging this concert in the first place, an event that was not part of any regular tour. He has associated Johnson's retirement decision with his obsession with perfection—that "he would like to leave playing strong" and that "he was pretty paranoid about keeping his chops up and being able to produce. He knew people had expectations, but he had his own expectations about what he wanted to be able to do." Above all, it would now be "finis" to the quintet, to appearances with pick-up bands and "college situations" every week. His consuming interest was leaving an enduring legacy as a composer and arranger.[45]

Nothing more vividly captures Johnson's current state of mind than the *Brass Orchestra* recording sessions for Polygram of September 24–27, 1996. The selections are revealing for their range of music, the inclusiveness and stature of the musicians involved, and an exemplary collaborative spirit, all serving the higher goal of achieving a grand summation of Johnson's creative achievements as well as those of some close colleagues. For example, Jimmy Heath's "Gingerbread Boy" was recorded in an arrangement by Johnson, while Johnson's own "Enigma" was trotted out in an orchestration by Slide Hampton. Also featured were works by Robin Eubanks and Robert Farnon, not to mention Johnson's homage to Bela Bartók entitled "Canonn for Bela." Finally, there were his new arrangements of such works as "El Camino Real" and "Why Indianapolis—Why Not Indianapolis?" as previously heard at Harvard under Thomas Everett. Indeed, Thomas Everett was a vital presence in the recording studio, sharing conducting responsibilities with Slide Hampton; and it was Everett who conducted a blazing new performance of two movements from *Perceptions*, with Jon Faddis "playing his brains out" in the solo part.[46]

A unique part of a separate project recorded the following week by Johnson's quintet—released by Verve on the compact disc *Heroes*—involved writing a new piece, "In Walked Wayne," for Wayne Shorter, underscored by palpable angst about his being able to participate at all. In a communication of July 25, 1996, Johnson voiced his deep concern about whether the very idea of Shorter's participation represented a case of horrendous timing or the reverse. For it was only eight days earlier that the crash of TWA Flight 800 off Long Island had claimed the life of Shorter's beloved wife and personal manager, Ana Maria Shorter, as well as that of her seventeen-year-old niece, Dalila Lucien, as they were flying to meet Shorter on a European tour.

Although Johnson had adored Shorter's work for many years and was intimately familiar with his collaborations with Art Blakey and Miles Davis, he himself had actually never played with him. In fact, it was thanks to Mary Ann Topper that they met for the first time at the Blue Note on November 12, 1996, where Shorter was performing. The response of each to the other was reportedly magical, born of mutual respect and deep admiration.[47]

It was on the following Monday, November 18, 1996, that Shorter (also a Verve artist) laid down his solo track in what proved to be a transcendent performance of the Johnson work. Shorter's playing of "In Walked Wayne" spoke to something profoundly moving and eternally beautiful, attaining a level of performance that captured the eloquence of Johnson's own deeply felt assessment of the saxophonist: "He is on that very, very special plateau that includes only saxophonists Charlie Parker, Sonny Rollins, John Coltrane, Lester Young, Coleman Hawkins, and Wayne Shorter. After that the Bible is closed."[48]

Masterminding the production of all these astonishing Polygram sessions was Don Sickler. Their historic significance and compelling intensity occupied a "very, very special plateau" of their own—qualities that were cogently communicated by Maureen Sickler:

> Don wanted to tell you that he's now in the studio with J.J., recording an immense project which is envisioned by J.J. as the culmination of his life's energies. Don says J.J. is awesome in the studio, his "chops" are in incredible shape, and the force of his personality has to be experienced to be believed.[49]

Yet as of 1997 J.J. Johnson no longer thinks of himself as a jazz performer; after fify-four years he is "just weary of just being a slave to that trombone." Interviewed by Ed Enright, he said:

> In order to keep my chops in shape, in order to keep my game at its peak, my volley and my serve at its peak, man, it takes *daily* long tones before breakfast, *daily* scales and arpeggios, *daily* working with Jamey Aebersold's play-along tapes, a daily regimen that is almost militaristic.

No more of that. Johnson is now as committed as ever to composing, arranging, and orchestrating, not necessarily for recording purposes, but also "just for fun." And his fascination with MIDI (music instrument digital interface), electronic gadgetry, and the Internet continues apace. He is now a man at peace with himself, with what he has achieved, and with the legacy he is leaving.

> I try to keep a positive outlook. I feel good about things in general. I have no axes to grind about anybody. I don't know anybody I want to put down. Man, I love Slide Hampton, I love Robin Eubanks, Steve Turré. Man, those guys have their finger right on the pulse of the trombone panorama. I know that I'm leaving things in good hands.[50]

Notes

1.   The title of "Why Indianapolis—Why Not Indianapolis?" harks back to Johnson's 1977 composition "Why Not."

2. The name of trumpeter Clark Terry is a clear stand-out in this group of trombonists. Then again, at least two of the signatories, Angel Rangeloff and Ove Larsson, who hail from Bulgaria and Sweden, respectively, are not exactly "East coast trombonists."

3. Interview with Robin Eubanks, Brooklyn, New York, June 23, 1992.

4. Interview with Slide Hampton, New York, June 29, 1993.

5. Saxophonist Tom Gullion had been recommended by David Baker. He toured with the quintet in the fall of 1987, starting at the Jazz Showcase in Chicago and ending, November 17, 1987, at the Village Vanguard in New York.

6. Interview with Mary Ann Topper, New York, November 29, 1993.

7. *Ibid.*

8. The live recording took place on the last two nights of the quintet's run at the Village Vanguard—Saturday and Sunday, July 9 and 10, 1988.

9. Johnson's recording notes were kindly provided by Mary Ann Topper.

10. Johnson is meticulous in his attention to other details of the recording, writing in his notes, "CD to clearly indicate DDD in bold print." In other words, he wanted the finished product to be fully appreciated for what it represented in terms of recording sophistication—digital processing throughout, in the taping of the initial session, in the mixing and/or editing, and in the final mastering. Johnson's general fascination with electronic equipment and hi-fi systems dates back to at least the 1950s, when he began dabbling with Heathkit components and such.

11. Liner notes to *Quintergy,* Antilles 422-848 214-2.

12. The affinity with Bartók suggests a certain reformulation of standard bebop harmonic thinking harking back to the seminal ideas of Dizzy Gillespie in the early 1940s. It was then that Gillespie found new "pretty notes" such as the raised eleventh in extended chords and incorporated them to great effect as part of the flatted fifth relationship in such pieces as "A Night in Tunisia."

13. The burden of negotiating the contract with Antilles for the production of the two CDs, *Quintergy* and *Standards*, fell largely on Mary Ann Topper's shoulders during this trying time.

14. Interview with Mary Ann Topper.

15. Interview with Kevin Johnson, Indianapolis, June 24, 1993.

16. Interview with J.J. Johnson, New York, December 21, 1994.

17. It is included in a Polygram album, recorded in New York, December 20, 1994, and features Johnson's quintet performing with an ensemble of Jamaican steel drums, conch shells, and the like. The title remains unreleased.

18. Liner notes by Nat Hentoff to *Vivian*, Concord Jazz, CCD-4523.

19. Thomas Conrad in *CD Review*, April 1993.

20. Personal communication of Carolyn Reid Johnson, September 25, 1998.

21. *The Village Voice*, December 21, 1993.

22. *The New York Times*, December 18, 1993.

23. Interview with David Whiteis, *Down Beat* (April 1995), 25.

24. George Tremblay, to whom Johnson was introduced by Earle Hagen, is mentioned in the preceding chapter with regard to the "Pinnacles" recording session.

25. Fax from Catherine Gevers, Music Administrator, Carnegie Hall, to J.J. Johnson, January 27, 1994.

26. The name of the group is misleading in that the ensemble was essentially a pick-up orchestra assembled from members of the London Philharmonic Orchestra.

27. Interview with J.J. Johnson.

28. Liner notes to *Tangence*, Verve CD 314 526 588-2.

29. *Ibid.*

30. Fax from J.J. Johnson to Robert Farnon, October 1993.

31. Interview with J.J. Johnson.

32. *Ibid.*

33. Interview with Mary Ann Topper.

34. *Ibid.*

35. Trumpeter, conductor, and jazz publisher Don Sickler has been intimately involved in Johnson copyright renewals since around the mid-1980s. He now holds the rights to some seventeen Johnson titles that have been published by one of his companies, Second Floor Music.

36. Interview with Don Sickler, New York, July 7, 1996.

37. Interview with J.J. Johnson, Indianapolis, February 15, 1995.

38. Interview with Mary Ann Topper.

39. *The New York Times*, December 19, 1995, C15.

40. Program booklet, National Endowment for the Arts Sixth Annual American Jazz Masters Fellowships Awards Concert, January 12, 1996.

41. Interview with Mary Ann Topper. Her use of the phrase " as an educator" alludes to an earlier phase of her career when she taught at both the preschool and university levels.

42. Johnson, forever the perfectionist, reportedly gave his playing at Litchfield the rating of a "9." Interview with Mary Ann Topper and Anna Marta Sala, New York, January 7, 1997.

43. Undated communication from the late summer of 1996 addressed to Anna Marta Sala, personal assistant to Mary Ann Topper at The Jazz Tree.

44. In its issue of June 1997, *Down Beat* eventually published "J.J. Johnson's Changing Perspectives," an interview with Ed Enright.

45. Interview with Rufus Reid, Teaneck, New Jersey, December 4, 1996.

46. Interview with Mary Ann Topper and Anna Marta Sala, New York, January 7, 1997.

47. *Ibid.*

48. J.J. Johnson communication to Mary Ann Topper, July 25, 1996. According to the June 1997 *Down Beat* article by Ed Enright, the Wayne Shorter performance is part of a quintet album that also includes Marus Belgrave and Jimmy Heath as special guests. It is one of three albums "still on the shelf." The other two are *Nina May*, named after Johnson's late mother, and one of unreleased material from the *Brass Orchestra* sessions.

49. Personal letter of October 3, 1996, to Joshua Berrett.

50. Ed Enright, "J.J. Johnson's Changing Perspectives," *Down Beat* (June 1997), 33.

Appendix

On Peeking into J.J.'s Studio

J.J. Johnson's present home studio reveals a great deal about who he is and the values and priorities that define his world. It is a special private place where he can best ply his trade, and to a very large extent it is a space that determined the choice of house within the Indianapolis area where he now lives. Once the Johnson's decided to leave California, Vivian, working in tandem with Joy Gaddie, spent close to a year trying to find a house meeting J.J.'s requirements—many of them driven by his Tomita-inspired passion for electronic gadgetry.

> When we moved from California to Indianapolis there was over 20,000 pounds on the moving van. 10,000 pounds was J.J.'s "stuff" mostly related to my activity as a musician. At present I have 2 complete home music studios, each 20 by 20 feet, in the same household, that sits on a 4 acre lot. Vivian "searched and searched and searched" to find such a layout for my needs. That was her highest priority.[1]

Johnson has provided the following "partial list" of what is in his "primary studio":[2]

Apple Macintosh Quadra 650 computer
Apple 13-inch color monitor
Apple 21-inch two page color monitor
2 removable-cartridge hard drives
Apple Laserwriter printer
Videocassette recorder with black & white monitor for tutorial videos
Kurzweil K1000 keyboard MIDI controller
2 MIDI interfaces by Mark of the Unicorn
Proteus 1XR sound module
Proteus 2 orchestra sound module
Yamaha TG77 tone generator
Korg M1R rack-mount synthesizer
3 Kurzweil vintage expander modules
Kurzweil K2000-R rack-mounted synthesizer
Proteus Vintage Keys sound module

2 Roland D110 sound modules
2 ART reverb units
2 Alesis 1622 mixers in tandem
JBL stereo monitor speakers powered by vintage bi-amplifier, 120 watts per channel
Rane active electronic crossover
18-inch ElectroVoice subwoofer, powered by Carver 400 watt mono amplifier
Complete secondary playback-only system

But despite any appearances to the contrary, Johnson's general mode of arranging and composing continues to mix the old with the new, the acoustic with the electronic. He has consistently espoused this approach in a number of interviews, having never found anything electronic "to take the place of warm-blooded guys who know their craft and who are on the bandstand fired up—no way."[3] Similarly, nowhere in his entire discography can one find an instance of a completely synthesized album. On the contrary, he has found his own middle ground between the acoustic and electronic—something achieved in, for example, the *Pinnacles* album dating from his California years. At the same time he is quick to insist that "I know no reason why jazz . . . should sit in a little corner and behave itself, and never venture out in any direction, and never be 'bad,' and never be 'annoying,' and 'Mind your manners'!"[4] What is, however, an integral part of his creative process is the computerized preparation of charts for his quintet using both Macintosh/MIDI and Coda Music Technology's "Finale," a music notation software program.[5] This is how virtually all the material for the *Let's Hang Out* album was prepared, using also a laser printer. Johnson has credited Jimmy Heath with prompting him to try a variety of music notation and sequencer programs, MIDI, and more since about 1990; and he has come to relish every chance he has of playing back what he has just written, "experimenting" with twenty-four-stave or eighteen-stave scores, and the like.[6]

Johnson's trombone preferences over the years represent a separate story, one that has been treated with special sensitivity by Tom Everett.[7] Like many of his colleagues, Johnson has experimented with a rather broad range of horns, mouthpieces, and different configurations of bore sizes. His clearest and earliest recollection is of visiting the King factory where "a wonderful old dude" by the name of Clem Flak gave both him and Kai Winding virtually complete run of the place. "He was marvelous, and we did a lot of experimenting with horns. Both Kai and I ended up on the 3B. The 3B of course is a .508 bore, and it felt comfortable to me at that time. I stayed with it for a long time."[8]

A chance meeting with Bill Harris—introduced to him by Kai Winding—helped change some of Johnson's thoughts about trombone configuration. What he discovered was that a larger-bore bell with a smaller-bore slide worked better for him. So it was that he began playing on a King trombone with a 2B slide coupled to a 3B bell.

In fact, a lot of my recordings are with that combination. It's not a big deal; it's just that the factory has to make that coupler so that the 2B slide will couple with the larger bell. I stayed with that for quite a long time. In the interim I dabbled with just playing the straight 2B and just the straight 3B. The 2B felt a little confining. Somehow, it kicked back and didn't give me the freedom that the 3B gave me as far as projection is concerned.[9]

The choice of mouthpiece proved to be a far simpler matter in that Johnson used the stock King M-21 that came with the horn. But in due course he was to make other changes, and sometime during his last years in Hollywood, around 1985, he shifted to another brand of instrument, the Yamaha. This change is something he has attributed in part to the "leadpipe syndrome" and the fact that he was having a problem on the King instrument. "When you pulled out the mouthpiece, the leadpipe came out because the mouthpiece was stuck in so tight."[10] He had heard through the "trombone grapevine" about the instrument that Yamaha was producing and a few days later received two of their Model 691 trombones with a normal tenor bore. Johnson had been working at a club in the Santa Monica area with the Ray Brown Trio and one night had a chance to put the instrument to the test.

For the first time in my life as a trombonist, playing on that Yamaha 691, I hit the loudest high F. You wouldn't believe it. You could hear it a mile away, it was so loud, so strong. It was the first time I ever hit a high F in a live performance before a live audience. Of course I hit high F's at home, eked them out, and just squeaky, little pinny high F's while practicing; but this sucker was loud, fat, and round. And ever since then, I kinda stuck with Yamaha, and I still hit that high F on occasion.[11]

In addition, about the same time Johnson began playing a custom-made trombone. It is based on a prototype of his own design and was executed by Larry Minnick in California, a master brass instrument repairman to many prominent players.

Everyone thinks it's a bass trombone; it is a tenor trombone. It has a conical bore; where the mouthpiece is inserted into the slide it's the same as a normal tenor trombone; then as it rounds the bend past the "spit valve," it gets into a little larger-sized bore; then, past the coupler, it starts to expand even more; then, around the bend past the tuning slide, it flares out into this 12-and-a-half-inch bell. This trombone is to a trombone as a flugelhorn is to a trumpet; it's a little darker, a little mellower.[12]

Given his acute awareness of subtleties of timbre, Johnson has paid close attention to the different effects of mutes, both the Denis Wick cup and straight mutes. He has experimented with the straight mute, in particular, by drilling a half-inch hole in the center of the butt end. Unfortunately this has caused intonation problems in the lower register—a problem only partially solved by taping up the hole in varying degrees.[13]

Since the spring of 1996, around the time of his appearance at Harvard, Johnson has included another piece of equipment in his arsenal, something that affords him maximum mobility onstage in live performance much in the Miles Davis mode. It is a Sony WRT–820A synthesized transmitter that works in tandem with a UHF synthesized wireless microphone attached to the bell of his instrument. The microphone itself is connected to an input level attenuator that is adjustable in three-decibel steps within the range of zero to twenty-one decibels so as to minimize signal distortion. It affords him maximum mobility on stage, something he was able to use to advantage at his appearances at Harvard and at the Blue Note in New York.

Most elusive of all is the essential nature of Johnson's musical thinking, and the extent to which it has been shaped by his rather far-ranging interest in late nineteenth- and twentieth-century composers not immediately associated with jazz. The impact on his writing of such composers as Strauss, Stravinsky, Schoenberg, Hindemith, Bartók, Ravel, Britten, and Bloch has been addressed in some detail in previous chapters. There has also been some discussion of how this development came about once his career path crossed with those of Gunther Schuller, John Lewis, Gil Evans, John Carisi, Oliver Nelson, Earle Hagen, and George Tremblay. But what helps dramatize the importance of these composers to Johnson's creative process, and how they continue to engage his attention when he listens to music for pure enjoyment, are the contents of his collection of recordings, scores, and books.

> One of my favorite pieces—God, I never tire of it; I have about three versions of it, including the one I have in my car all the time, the one I keep in my luggage all the time for the road, and one I keep for the airport, sitting all the time—it's Ravel's *Daphnis and Chloé*. It's mind-blowing. I was just reading . . . all these years that I've loved this piece, I didn't know . . . it took him three years to compose that piece. Can you imagine, three years on a work![14]

Responding to a comment about Ravel's penchant for meticulous detail and Stravinsky's characterization of him as a Swiss clockmaker, Johnson continued:

> His scores! I have his scores. "Meticulous" is an understatement. But you hear that in his music. All that beautiful detail . . . I'm a Stravinsky nut. Also in my automobile and all over the house are versions of *Petrouchka,* a little known work, *The Song of the Nightingale*—wonderful piece, obviously *Le Sacré* and *The Firebird . . . L'Histoire du Soldat . . .* I'm a big freak on all that stuff. That's my composer–arranger mentality. I'm a jazz musician, but I have this crazy streak going that I love this Stravinsky business, and Bartók and Ravel. That's what I mostly listen to. I listen to jazz, but I'd say, when I have time—who has time to really listen these days in this crazy world we live in?—But when I do have the time I'd split it about 60 percent classical, the people we talked about, and about 40 percent jazz.[15]

Turning to some of his more extended works, such as *El Camino Real, Poem for Brass,* and *Perceptions,* and how they have been influenced by his favorite twentieth-century composers, Johnson added:

> I have been greatly influenced by Ravel, by Stravinsky, by Bartók, by Hindemith . . . I've had people tell me. "J.J., I can hear Hindemith in just about all of your brass stuff." I understand that because I'm big on Hindemith's brass stuff. I'm big on Hindemith's music, period. I particularly like his *Kammermusik,* his *Mathis der Maler* . . . I went through a cycle of *Mathis der Maler* where I just played it to death. I'm big on Richard Strauss's stuff like *Ein Heldenleben* . . . he was a guy with a heavy hand as an orchestrator . . . but it's beautiful stuff. These are some of my influences as a composer, as a jazz composer even. I hear those harmonies that I love in Stravinsky and Ravel, and I incorporate them. I studied a little bit during my years as a Hollywood film composer . . . got a bit of a handle on serial composition in the twelve-tone. . . . I'm by no means experienced, by no means do I have it under my thumb. I dabbled in it enough so that I'm experimenting with it now in my jazz compositions.[16]

What follows is not a formal and complete catalog of Johnson's personal collection of books, scores, and records. It is rather the result of some browsing, a summer afternoon of serendipity, undertaken in an area of his home to which he was kind enough to provide access.[17]

Books

I. Bazelon, *Knowing the Score*
R.E. Dolan, *Music in Modern Media*
H. Eisler and T.W. Adorno, *Composing for the Films*
C. Forsyth, *Orchestration*
E. Hagen, *Scoring for Films*
P. Hindemith, *The Craft of Musical Composition*
K.W. Kennan, *Technique of Orchestration*
W. Piston, *Orchestration*
G. Read, *Thesaurus of Orchestral Devices*

Scores

Bartók, *Concerto for Orchestra*
Bartók, *Concerto for Two Pianos and Percussion*
Bartók, *Music for Strings, Percussion, and Celesta*
Bartók, *Six String Quartets*
Britten, "Four Sea Interludes" from *Peter Grimes*
Britten, *Young Person's Guide to the Orchestra*
Debussy, *Prelude to the Afternoon of a Faun*
Hindemith, *Mathis der Maler*
The New Henry Mancini Songbook
The Johnny Mandel Songbook
The Music and Lyrics of Cole Porter

Prokofiev, *Peter and the Wolf*
Prokofiev, *Scythian Suite*
Ravel, *Daphnis and Chloé*
Ravel, *Ma Mere l'Oye*
Ravel, *Rhapsodie Espagnole*
The Rodgers and Hart Songbook
Stravinsky, *Chant du Rossignol*
Stravinsky, *Firebird* (1919 version)
Stravinsky, *Fireworks*
Stravinsky, *Les Noces*
Stravinsky, *Petrouchka* (1947 version)
Stravinsky, *Le Sacré du Printemps*
The Best of Jule Styne

Records
The Cannonball Adderley Quintet and Orchestra (Capitol)
Anthology of Music of Black Africa (Everest)
Bartók, *Mikrokosmos* (Vol. I)
Bartók, *The Miraculous Mandarin*
Bartók, *Piano Concerto no. 2* and Prokofiev, *Piano Concerto no. 5*
Bartók, *Six String Quartets*
Blues by Basie
Brookmeyer, *Gloomy Sunday*
String Quartets of Debussy and Ravel
The Sensuous Strings of Robert Farnon (Philips)
Gulda, *Music for Four Soloists and Band*
Hindemith, *Mathis der Maler* and *Concert Music for Strings and Brass*
Holst, *The Planets*
J.J. Johnson and Nat Adderley: The Yokohama Concert
Kronos Quartet, *Pieces of Africa*
Mussorgsky–Ravel, *Pictures at an Exhibition*
Ravel, *Daphnis and Chloé*
Ravel, *Valses Nobles et Sentimentales*
Respighi, *The Pines of Rome*
Arnold Schoenberg, Vol. II (Columbia boxed set)
Shostakovich, *Symphony no. 5*
Stravinsky, recordings of *Le Sacré du printemps* (both orchestral and two-piano versions); *Mavra*; *Les Noces*; *Firebird*; *Petrouchka*
Strauss, *Ein Heldenleben*
Vaughan Williams, *Symphony no. 2*
Winds in Hi-Fi (Mercury); selections by Grainger, Milhaud, Richard Strauss, and others
Miscellaneous albums featuring pieces by Quincy Jones, Antonio Carlos Jobim, Dave Grusin, Freddie Hubbard, Steve Turré, Marcel Grandjany, Grover Washington, and Johnson himself.

Notes

1.   Communication, presumably from January 1994, addressed by J.J. Johnson to Mary Ann Topper. The underlining of the thrice-stated word "searched" follows exactly what appears in the original.

2.   *Ibid.*

3.   David Whiteis, "At Home with J.J.," *Down Beat* (April 1995), 26–27.

4.   *Ibid.*

5.   Mark of the Unicorn's "Composers Mosaic" is another music notation software program that Johnson has used.

6.   Interview with J.J. Johnson, Indianapolis, July 28, 1992.

7.   See, for example, Tom Everett, "J.J. Johnson: On the Road Again," *Journal of the International Trombone Association* (Summer 1988), 23–27.

8.   *Ibid.,* 23.

9.   *Ibid.,* 24.

10.   *Ibid.*

11.   *Trombone Sounds* (Grand Rapids, Mich.: Yamaha Corporation of America Band and Orchestral Division, 1995).

12.   Whiteis, "At Home with J.J." In addition, Johnson has tried a Selmer 16M. In his fax of thanks to Selmer's Mark L. Swenson (February 2, 1994) Johnson says: "I received the 16M trombone. It is truly a beauty. Slide feels good. Response has positive promise. I will play it at [Verve] Carnegie Hall special event on April 6th . . . But as we know, the *true test* will be to play it concert after concert, on tour. That will happen soon."

13.   Everett, "J.J. Johnson: On the Road Again," 27.

14.   Interview with J.J. Johnson, Indianapolis, July 24, 1992.

15.   *Ibid.*

16.   *Ibid.* Johnson is presumably referring to the first movement of his *Friendship Suite* ("Ode to G.T.") when talking about his study of the twelve-tone method.

17.   Visit of June 24, 1993, to J.J. Johnson's home in Indianapolis.

Bibliography

What follows is a selective bibliography consisting primarily of books and periodicals. Primary sources, archival materials, interviews undertaken specifically for this book, and specialized references are cited elsewhere—in the preface, endnotes, and the introductions to the filmography, catalog of compositions, and discography.

Allen, Bonnie. "The Macho Men, What Ever Happened to Them?" *Essence* 9 (January 1979): 90.

Allsop, Kenneth. "Jazz and Narcotics." *Encounter* 12 (June 1961): 54–57.

Baker, David N. *J.J. Johnson: Jazz Monograph Series.* New York: Shattinger International Music, 1979.

Baker, Lida B. "J.J. Johnson—Expanding the Envelope." *The Instrumentalist* (April 1990): 17–21, 80–81.

Balliett, Whitney. *New York Notes: A Journal of Jazz, 1972–75.* Boston: Houghton Mifflin, 1976.

Bauer, Paul. "J.J. Johnson: Back on Track." *Jazz Educators Journal* (October 1994): 21–24.

Berger, Morroe, Edward Berger, and James Patrick. *Benny Carter: A Life in American Music,* 2 vols. Metuchen, N.J.: Scarecrow Press and Institute of Jazz Studies, 1982.

Berrett, Joshua. "The Golden Anniversary of the Emancipation Proclamation." *Black Perspective in Music,* vol. 16, no. 1 (Spring 1988): 63–80.

———. "Louis Armstrong and Opera." *Musical Quarterly,* vol. 76, no. 2 (Summer 1992): 216–241.

Bourgois III, Louis G. *Jazz Trombonist J.J. Johnson: A Comprehensive Discography and Study of the Early Evolution of his Style.* D.M.A. dissertation. The Ohio State University, 1986.

Burns, Jim. "J.J. Johnson: The Formative Years." *Jazz Journal,* vol. 28, no. 8 (August 1975): 4–7.

————. "Lesser Known Bands of the Forties, No. 6: Illinois Jacquet, Roy Porter, Machito." *Jazz Monthly* 164 (October 1968): 7.

Carr, Ian. *Miles Davis: A Biography.* New York: William Morrow, 1982.

Chambers, Jack. *Milestones: The Music and Times of Miles Davis,* 2 vols. Toronto: University of Toronto Press, 1983.

Chevigny, Paul. *Gigs: Jazz and the Cabaret Laws in New York City.* New York: Routledge, Chapman, and Hall, 1991.

Cohen, Maxwell T. *The Police Card Discord.* Metuchen, N.J.: Scarecrow Press and Institute of Jazz Studies, 1993.

Coss, Bill. "J.J. Johnson and Kai Winding." *Metronome* (April 1955): 24.

Crawford, Richard. *The American Musical Landscape.* Berkeley: University of California Press, 1993.

Cripps, Thomas. *Slow Fade to Black: The Negro in American Film, 1900–1942.* New York: Oxford University Press, 1977.

Davis, Mike. *City of Quartz.* New York: Vintage Books, 1990.

Davis, Miles, with Quincy Troupe. *Miles, The Autobiography.* New York: Simon and Schuster, 1989.

Deffaa, Chip. "J.J. Johnson: Reflections and Reemergence." *Jazz Times* (December 1993): 41–42.

Everett, Thomas. "J.J. Johnson—The Architect of the Modern Trombone." *Journal of the International Trombone Association,* vol. 16, no. 2 (Spring 1988): 31–33.

————. "J.J. Johnson on Record: An Overview." *Journal of the International Trombone Association,* vol. 16, no. 2 (Spring 1988): 34–35.

————. "J.J. Johnson: On the Road Again." *Journal of the International Trombone Association,* vol. 16, no. 3 (Summer 1988): 22–29.

Faulkner, Robert R. *Music on Demand: Composers and Careers in the Hollywood Film Industry.* New Brunswick, N.J.: Transaction Books, 1983.

Feather, Leonard. "J.J. Johnson: Blindfold Test." *Down Beat* (January 30, 1964): 30.

————. "From Pen to Screen." *International Musician,* 71 (July 1972): 9, 26.

Franklin, David. "J.J.—It's Back to Playing." *JazzTimes* (May 1988): 10–11.

Gabbard, Krin. "The Quoter and His Culture," in *Jazz in Mind,* edited by Reginald T. Buckner and Steven Weiland, eds. (Detroit: Wayne State University Press, 1991): 92–111.

————. *Jammin' at the Margins: Jazz and the American Cinema.* Chicago: University of Chicago Press, 1996.

Getz, Stan, featured letter in Jack Tracy column, "Narcotics and Music." *Down Beat* (April 21, 1954): 3.

Gianolio, Aldo, and Daniele Benati. "J.J. Johnson, il patriarca del trombone." *Musica Jazz* (January 1995): 24–26.

Gillespie, Dizzy, and Al Fraser. *To Be or Not to Bop: Memoirs of Dizzy Gillespie.* Garden City, N.Y.: Doubleday, 1979.

Gioia, Ted. *West Coast Jazz.* New York: Oxford University Press, 1992.

Gitler, Ira. *Jazz Masters of the Forties.* New York: Collier Macmillan, 1966.

———. "The Remarkable J.J. Johnson." *Down Beat* (May 11, 1961): 17–18.

———. *Swing to Bop.* New York: Oxford University Press, 1985.

Gottlieb, Louis. "Brandeis Festival Album, An Unsolicited Endorsement." *Jazz: A Quarterly of American Music* 2 (1959): 151–160.

Gourse, Leslie. *Louis' Children: American Jazz Singers.* New York: Morrow, 1984.

Guerrero, Ed. *Framing Blackness: The African-American Image in Film.* Philadelphia: Temple University Press, 1993.

Hagen, Earle. *Scoring for Films.* New York: Criterion Music, 1971.

Harrison, Max. "*Perceptions* and a Question of Unity." *Jazz Monthly* (July 1962): 25.

Heckman, Don. "Jazz Trombone—Five Views." *Down Beat* (January 28, 1965): 17–19.

Hennessey, Mike. "The Return of J.J. Johnson." *Jazz Journal International* (May 1980): 6–7.

Hentoff, Nat. "J.J., Kai Find Trombone Team Is OK with Fans." *Down Beat* (January 12, 1955): 7.

Hentoff, Nat, and Albert J. McCarthy, eds. *Jazz: New Perspectives on the History of Jazz by Twelve of the World's Foremost Jazz Critics and Scholars.* New York: Rinehart, 1959.

Hoefer, George. "Early J.J." *Down Beat* (January 28, 1965): 16, 33.

Raymond Horricks, "J.J. Johnson, Trombone Ultimate," in *These Jazzmen of Our Time* (London: The Jazz Book Club by arrangement with Victor Gollancz, 1959), 52–67.

Karlin, Fred, and Rayburn Wright. *On the Track: A Guide to Contemporary Film Scoring.* New York: Schirmer Books, 1990.

Kirk, Elise K. *Music at the White House.* Urbana and Chicago: University of Illinois Press, 1986.

Klotman, Phyllis R. *Frame by Frame: A Black Filmography.* Bloomington: Indiana University Press, 1979.

Leab, Daniel J. *From Sambo to Superspade.* Boston: Houghton Mifflin, 1976.

Leonard, Neil. *Jazz: Myth and Religion.* New York: Oxford University Press, 1987.

Lotz, Rainer E., and Ulrich Neuert. *The AFRS "Jubilee" Transcription Programs: An Exploratory Discography.* Frankfurt: Norbert Ruecker, 1985.

Marill, Alvin H. *Movies Made for Television: The Telefeature and the Mini-Series, 1964–1986.* New York: Zoetrope, 1987.

Martin, Henry. *Enjoying Jazz.* New York: Schirmer Books, 1986.

Mason, B.J. "The New Films: Culture or Con Game?" *Ebony* 28 (December 1972): 62.

McClellan, Lawrence, Jr. "The Eminent J.J. Johnson." *Jazz Educators Journal* (Winter 1989): 36–37.

McDonough, John. "Norman Granz: JATP Pilot Driving Pablo Home." *Down Beat* (October 1979): 30–32.

———. "Pablo Patriarch." *Down Beat* (November 1979): 35–36, 76.

Mickey, Rosie Cheatham. *Russell Adrian Lane: Biography of an Urban Negro School Administrator.* Ph.D. dissertation, University of Akron, 1983.

Morgan, Alun. "Illinois Jacquet." *Jazz Monthly* (September 1963): 8–10.

Nadeau, Remi. *Los Angeles: From Mission to Modern City.* New York and London: Longmans, Green, 1960.

Parish, James R., and George H. Hill. *Black Action Films.* Jefferson, N.C.: McFarland, 1989.

Peace and War: United States Foreign Policy, 1931–1941. Washington, D.C., 1943.

Porter, Lewis, and Michael Ullman, with Edward Hazell. *Jazz: From its Origins to the Present.* Englewood Cliffs, N.J.: Prentice-Hall, 1993.

Reeves, Scott D. *Creative Jazz Improvisation.* Englewood Cliffs, N.J.:Prentice-Hall, 1989.

Reig, Teddy, with Edward Berger. *Reminiscing in Tempo: The Life and Times of a Jazz Hustler.* Metuchen, N. J.: Scarecrow Press and Institute of Jazz Studies, 1990.

Russell, Ross. *Bird Lives! The High Life and Hard Times of Charlie (Yardbird) Parker.* New York: Charterhouse, 1973.

Shapiro, Nat, and Nat Hentoff. *Hear Me Talkin' to Ya.* New York: Dover Publications, 1966.

Shaw, Arnold. *52nd Street: The Street of Jazz.* New York: Da Capo, 1977.

The Sperry Corporation Twenty-first Annual Report (for the year ended December 31, 1953).

Stowe, David W. *Swing Changes: Big-Band Jazz in New Deal America.* Cambridge, Mass.: Harvard University Press, 1994.

Terrace, Vincent. *Fifty Years of Television: A Guide to Series and Pilots, 1937–1988.* New York: Cornwall Books, 1991.

Tirro, Frank. "The Silent Theme Tradition in Jazz." *Musical Quarterly* (July 1967): 313–334.

Ullman, Michael. *Jazz Lives.* Washington, D.C.: New Republic, 1980.

United States States Statutes at Large, vol. LV. Washington, D.C., 1943.

Valburn, Jerry. "Armed Forces Transcriptions as Source Materials." *Studies in Jazz Discography* (1971): 47–52.

Wakefield, Dan. *New York in the Fifties.* Boston: Houghton Mifflin, 1992.

Whiteis, David. "J.J. Johnson: At Home with J.J." *Down Beat* (April 1995): 24–27.

Williams, Martin. "Thoughts on Jazz Trombone." *Down Beat* (January 18, 1962): 25–27.

Winick, Charles. "The Use of Drugs by Jazz Musicians." *Social Problems,* 7, no. 3 (Winter 1959–60): 240–253.

Filmography

This filmography is a comprehensive, chronological listing of films, made-for-television films and miniseries, television series themes, and television series episodes for which J.J. Johnson was the sole or principal composer, a contributing composer in which previously composed materials were included in the soundtrack, or orchestrator for another composer.

Musical scores and cue sheets for Johnson's film and television compositional output are generally nonexistent. Throughout the film and television industry studios and production companies do not maintain music libraries; they prefer to destroy scores instead of storing them for future use. In most cases, the composer's work exists only in the soundtrack of the final cut of a film or videotape, and the only accessible written records are maintained by performance rights societies (in Johnson's case, Broadcast Music Inc.) and artist management agencies.

For this filmography, film and television credits were obtained from Michael McGehee and David Sanjek of Broadcast Music Inc. (BMI–Los Angeles and BMI–New York, respectively); Stan Millander of Bart, Millander, and Associates (Los Angeles); Erma Levin, music editor for Columbia Pictures/Television, Inc.; and Mary Ann Topper of The Jazz Tree (New York).

Within each category, motion picture or television titles and the dates (years) or range of dates of composition are listed. In a few cases, however, some titles were listed in documents obtained from Bart, Millander, and Associates, or The Jazz Tree, but no dates were given and could not be corroborated through other sources. These titles are listed with the notation, "n.d."

Just as there is a lack of written music and cue sheets in the film and television industry, there is also a lack of accurate cataloging information—at least for historical purposes—for specific television shows or series episodes. BMI records contain only information essential to the computation of royalties for the composer and the publisher: title of musical cue (usually listed without its associated television series title), clearance date (when the production company submitted the information, not when the cue was actually composed or the show broadcast), length of cue in minutes, royalty shares of the writer and publisher, payment account numbers, and amounts to be paid. As such, the composer is the only one who possibly could provide more specific documentation about his or her compositional output. In J.J. Johnson's case—as in the case of many film and television composers—such documentation has not been kept. Therefore, for the purposes of this filmography, only the year or range of years during which Johnson composed music for a television series, episode, special, or television movie is listed.

Categories of Musical Scores for Films and Television

Original Film Scores
Motion pictures for which J.J. Johnson composed the original musical score.

Films as a Contributing Composer of Source Music
Motion pictures for which previously composed works by J.J. Johnson are used on the soundtrack (for example, "Lament" is heard in the film *Sea of Love*).

Film Orchestrations
Musical scores in which J.J. Johnson orchestrated the musical sketches of the principal composer for the film.

Television Movies and Miniseries
Made-for-television movies that are aired in a single broadcast or in multiple broadcasts (miniseries).

Television Series Themes
Main title music (theme music) for a television series.

Television Series Pilots
Pilot episodes of a television series.

Television Specials
Special, single-broadcast shows.

Television Episodes
Regular season episodes of a television show series.

Television Serials as a Contributing Composer of Source Music
Daytime television shows with continuously running plots (soap operas) or themes (e.g., *Newton's Apple*) for which previously composed works by J.J. Johnson are used on the soundtrack.

Original Film Scores
1971   *Man and Boy* (released in 1972)
1972   *Across 110th Street*
1972   *Top of the Heap*
1973   *Willie Dynamite*
1973   *Cleopatra Jones*

Films as a Contributing Composer of Source Music
1983   *Scarface*
1989   *Angels*
1989   *Nasty Boys*
1989   *Sea of Love*

Film Orchestrations
1971   *Shaft* (musical score by Isaac Hayes)
1972   *Trouble Man* (musical score by Marvin Gaye)

Television Movies and Miniseries
1976   *Street Killing*
1977   *Future Cop: The Mad Bomber Mystery*
1983   *Mickey Spillane's Mike Hammer: Murder Me, Murder You*
        (Earle Hagen, cowriter)
n.d.   *D.A. for the People*

Television Series Themes
1977   *Lucan*
1977   *Future Cop*
1979   *Harris and Co.*

Television Series Pilots
1973   *The Fuzz Brothers*
1976   *Crunch*
1980   *Stone*

Television Specials
n.d.   *Muhammad Ali*
n.d.   *Travels with Flip*

Television Episodes
1970–71   *Barefoot in the Park*
1970–71   *Mayberry R.F.D.*
1970–71   *That Girl*
1970–73   *The Bold Ones*

1970–73	*Mod Squad*
1972–76	*Rookies*
1973–74	*Chase*
1973–74	*Roll Out!*
1973–78	*The Six Million Dollar Man*
1974–75	*Get Christie Love!*
1974–76	*Harry O*
1975	*Bronk*
1975–79	*Starsky and Hutch*
1976	*Jigsaw John*
1976–78	*Bionic Woman*
1977	*Future Cop*
1977–78	*Lucan*
1977–83	*CHIPS*
1978–81	*Vegas*
1979	*Harris and Company*
1979–81	*Buck Rogers in the 25th Century*
1980	*B.A.D. Cats*
1981	*Concrete Cowboys*
1981–82	*Cassie and Company*
1984–85	*Mickey Spillane's Mike Hammer*
1986	*The New Mike Hammer*

Television Serials as a Contributing Composer of Source Music

n.d.	*Name Your Adventure*
n.d.	*Newton's Apple*
n.d.	*One Life to Live*
n.d.	*The Young and the Restless*

Catalog of Compositions

This catalog of compositions is a comprehensive alphabetical listing of original works by J.J. Johnson and works coauthored by him with other writers. Each listing includes the year composed; title; and discography reference number and/or source; and, if known, any cowriters and publisher; in the following format:

Year	Title	[Disc. ref. no.]
	Cowriter(s)	Source
	Publisher	

1972	*Across 110th Street*	[254]
	Bobby Womack, cowriter	From the film *Across 110th Street*

1960	*Aquarius*	[179][180]
	MJQ Music	

1980	*Azure*	[272]
	Two Jays Publishing Co.	

1996	*Ballad for Joe*	[308]
	MJQ Music	

| 1979 | *Ballad from Tremblay* | [266] |

1960	*Ballade*	[181][234]
	MJQ Music; Second Floor Music	

1949	*Bee Jay*	[71]
	Screen Gems–EMI Music, Inc.	

| 1971 | *Better Days* | [253][266][310] |

1984	*Black Pianist*	From the television series *Mike Hammer*
	Screen Gems–EMI Music, Inc.	

1960   *Bloozineff*   [187]
Two Jays Publishing Co.

1966   *Blue*   [235]
Second Floor Music

1979   *Blue David*   BMI Archive
MCA Duchess Music Corporation

1949   *Blue Mode*   [76]
Prestige Music Co.

1980   *Blue Nun*   [273]
Two Jays Publishing Co.

1957   *Blue Trombone*   [157]
Second Floor Music

1954   *Blues for Trombones*   [104]
Screen Gems–EMI Music, Inc.

1949   *Blues in F*   BMI Archive
Fort Knox Music, Inc.; Trio Music, Inc.

1954   *Bone of Contention*   [108]
Windswept Pacific Songs

1946   *Boneology*   [62]
Screen Gems–EMI Music, Inc.

1996   *Brass TMX Suite*   [307]

1949   *B Yot*   BMI Archive
Illinois Jacquet, cowriter
Gilbert Music Publishers

1996   *Cadenza* (for *Why Indianapolis—Why Not Indianpolis?*)   [308]

1979   *Cannonball Junction*   [266]
Two Jays Publishing Co.

1996   *Canonn for Bela*   [309]
Second Floor Music

1996   *Carolyn*   [310]

1982   *Cassie and Co.*   From the television series *Cassie and Co.*
Intercept Music

1985	*Cheer Lieder* EMI Gold Horizon Music Corp.	From the television series *Mike Hammer*
1973	*Cleo and Reuben* Warner–Tamerlane Publishing Corp.	From the film *Cleopatra Jones*
1954	*Coffee Pot* Two Jays Publishing Co.	[107]
1957	*Commutation* Second Floor Music	[154][289][291]
1980	*Concepts In Blue* Two Jays Publishing Co.	[270]
1946	*Coppin' the Bop* Second Floor Music	[45][289]
1971	*Country Soul* Interior Music Corp.	From the film *Man and Boy*
1956	*Cube Steak* Second Floor Music	[142]
1984	*Dance Girl* EMI Gold Horizon Music Corp.	From the television series *Mike Hammer*
1955	*"Daylie" Double* Folkways Music Publishers, Inc.	[117]
1984	*Dead on a Dime* EMI Gold Horizon Music Corp.	From the television series *Mike Hammer*
1979	*Deak* Two Jays Publishing Co.	[266]
1973	*Desert Sunrise* Joe Simon, cowriter Warner–Tamerlane	From the film *Cleopatra Jones*
1947	*Diggin' the Count* Illinois Jacquet, cowriter Gilbert Music Publishers	[54]
1979	*Disco Again* MCA Duchess Music Corp.	BMI Archive
1979	*Disco David* MCA Duchess Music Corp.	BMI Archive

1969	*Diversions* C.F. Peters Corp.	American Wind Symphony Orchestra library
1988	*Doc Was Here* Second Floor Music	[289][291]
1979	*Don't Buzz Me, I'll Buzz You*	[265]
1967	*Downshift* Second Floor Music	BMI Archive
1946	*Down Vernon's Alley* Screen Gems–EMI Music, Inc.	[62]
1961	*Dues Blues* MJQ Music	BMI Archive
1959	*El Camino Real* MJQ Music	[208][308]
1949	*Elora* Prestige Music Co.	[76]
1971	*Emancipation Procrastination* Interior Music Corp.	BMI Archive
1947	*Embryo* Illinois Jacquet, cowriter Gilbert Music Publishers	[59]
1973	*Emdee* Bo Kay Music; Warner–Tamerlane	From the film *Cleopatra Jones*
1953	*Enigma* Second Floor Music	[97][306]
1979	*Etheros*	[266]
1965	*Eurosuite* Second Floor Music	[236]

Note: *Eurosuite* excerpts recorded in session [236] were issued as *Euro 1* and *Euro 2*.

1960	*Fatback* Two Jays Publishing Co.	[180]
1960	*Flat Black* Two Jays Publishing Co.	[187]

1946   *Fly Jay (Jay Bird)*   [45]
         Screen Gems–EMI Music, Inc.

1956   *Four Plus Four*   [136][307]
         Second Floor Music

1949   *Fox Hunt*   [72]
         Prestige Music Co.

1992   *Friendship Suite*   [296][301]
         Two Jays Publishing Co.

         Note: Individual movements of *Friendship Suite* are "Ode to
         G.T.," "Let's Hang Out," "Love You Nana," and "Reunion."

1973   *Gate 21*   BMI Archive

1984   *Ghetto Garotte*   From the television series *Mike Hammer*
         EMI Gold Horizon Music Corp.

1973   *Go Chase Cleo*   From the film *Cleopatra Jones*
         Warner–Tamerlane

1973   *Goin' to the Chase*   From the film *Cleopatra Jones*
         Warner–Tamerlane

1955   *Groovin'*   [117]
         Folkways Music Publishers, Inc.

1984   *Hammer, That Is*   From the television series *Mike Hammer*
         EMI Gold Horizon Music Corp.

1972   *Harlem Clavinette*   [254]
         EMI UnArt Catalog, Inc.   From the film *Across 110th Street*

1972   *Harlem Love Theme*   [254]
         EMI UnArt Catalog, Inc.   From the film *Across 110th Street*

1957   *Harvey's House*   [153]
         Second Floor Music

1992   *Hasten Jason*   [295][304]
         Two Jays Publishing Co.

1977   *Haven*   BMI Archive
         Bruin Music Co.

1967   *Hawk*   BMI Archive
         Second Floor Music

1997 *Helixx*   BMI Archive
      Second Floor Music

1946 *Hey Jay Jay (Jay Jay)*   [45]
      Screen Gems–EMI Music, Inc.

1954 *Hip Bones*   [109]
      Prestige Music Co.

1977 *Horace*   [263]
      Two Jays Publishing Co.

1984 *Hot Ice*   From the television series *Mike Hammer*
      EMI Gold Horizon Music Corp.

1996 *If I Hit the Lottery*   [307]

1960 *In Walked Horace*   [180]
      Second Floor Music

1996 *In Walked Wayne*   [311]

1965 *Incidental Blues*   [221]

1966 *J1*   BMI Archive
      Shirangie Music

1982 *Jake's Rhapsody*   From the television film *The Big Easy*
      Bruin Music Co.

1954 *Jay*   [107]

1946 *Jay Bird (Fly Jay)*   [45]
      Screen Gems–EMI Music, Inc.

1954 *Jay Jay's Blues*   [101]

1944 *Jay Jay's Jump (Polishin' Brass)*   [12]

1955 *Jay's Way*   BMI Archive
      Screen Gems–EMI Music, Inc.

1977 *Jevin*   [263]
      Two Jays Publishing Co.

1985 *Jolly's Blues*   BMI Archive
      EMI Gold Horizon Music Corp.

| 1961 | *Judy* | [185] |
| | MJQ Music, Inc. | |

| 1953 | *Kelo* | [97] |
| | Second Floor Music | |

| 1945 | *Kemptone* | Lavon Kemp personal library (Indianapolis) |

| 1992 | *Kenya* | [295][301] |
| | Two Jays Publishing Co. | |

| 1957 | *Kev* | [157] |
| | Second Floor Music | |

| 1967 | *KWOK* | BMI Archive |
| | Second Floor Music | |

| 1954 | *Lament* | [104][263][278][289][300][302] |
| | Screen Gems–EMI Music, Inc. | |

| 1986 | *Limo Blues* | From the television series *Mike Hammer* |
| | EMI Gold Horizon Music Corp. | |

| 1983 | *Little Brown Jug* | From the television movie |
| | EMI Gold Horizon Music Corp. | *Murder Me, Murder You* |

| 1966 | *Little Dave* | [234][235] |
| | Second Floor Music | |

| 1955 | *Lope City* | [111] |
| | Fort Knox Music; Trio Music Co. | |

| 1946 | *Mad Bebop* | [45] |
| | Screen Gems–EMI Music, Inc. | |

| 1973 | *Make It Right* | From the film *Willie Dynamite* |
| | MCA Duchess Music Corp. | |

| 1971 | *Man and Boy* | From the film *Man and Boy* |
| | Interior Music Corp. | |

| 1992 | *May I Have Dis Dance?* | [297] |
| | Two Jays Publishing Co. | |

| 1959 | *Me Too* | [172] |
| | Two Jays Publishing Co. | |

| 1977 | *Melodee* | [263] |
| | Two Jays Publishing Co. | |

1964   *Minor Blues*   [199]
        Two Jays Publishing Co.

1960   *Minor Mist*   [180]
        MJQ Music, Inc.

1960   *Mohawk*   [179][180][271]
        MJQ Music, Inc.

1991   *Mom, Are You Listening?*   [303]

1984   *Motorbikes*   From the television series *Mike Hammer*
        EMI Gold Horizon Music Corp.

1983   *Naked As a Jaybird*   [280]
        Two Jays Publishing Co.

1956   *Naptown, U.S.A.*   [143]
        Second Floor Music

1961   *Neckbones*   [171]
        MJQ Music, Inc.

1980   *Nermus*   [272]
        Two Jays Publishing Co.

1957   *Nickles and Dimes*   [153]
        Second Floor Music

1979   *Night Flight*   [265][306]
        Two Jays Publishing Co.

1994   *Nina Mae*   [303]

1984   *Not Very*   From the television series *Mike Hammer*
        EMI Gold Horizon Music Corp.

1960   *Number 8*   [181][221]
        Two Jays Publishing Co.

        Note: This title appears as "008" in [221].

1956   *NWPT (Newport)*   [139]
        Second Floor Music

1985   *Old Time Source*   From the television series *Mike Hammer*
        Earle Hagen, cowriter
        EMI Gold Horizon Music Corp.

1957   *Opus V*   [72]
Prestige Music Co.

1994   *Opus de Focus*   [300]
Two Jays Publishing Co.

1956   *Overdrive*   [141][150]
Second Floor Music

1973   *Parade Strut*   From the film *Willie Dynamite*
MCA Duchess Music Corp.

1973   *Passion's Dilemma*   From the film *Willie Dynamite*
MCA Duchess Music Corp.

1961   *Perceptions*   [190]
MJQ Music, Inc.

Note: Individual movements of *Perceptions* are "The Sword of
Orion," "Jubelo," "Blue Mist," "Fantasia," " Horn of Plenty," and
"Ballade." The movements "Horn of Plenty" and "Ballade" also
recorded in session [309].

1984   *Perfect Twenty*   From the television series *Mike Hammer*
EMI Gold Horizon Music Corp.

1979   *Pinnacles*   [265]
Two Jays Publishing Co.

1967   *Poem for Alto Sax*   BMI Archive
Second Floor Music

1956   *Poem for Brass*   [145]
MJQ Music, Inc.

Note: This title appears in the BMI song title database also as *Jazz
Suite for Brass*.

1971   *Pull Jubal Pull*   From the film *Man and Boy*
Interior Music Corp.

1988   *Quintergy*   [289][290][291][304]
Second Floor Music

1945   *Rambo*   [33][44]

1947   *Riffette*   [62]

1954   *Riviera*   [109]
Prestige Music Co.

1969   *Rondeau for Quartet and Orchestra*   BMI Archive
        MJQ Music, Inc.

1971   *Rosita*   From the film *Man and Boy*
        Interior Music Corp.

1984   *Satan, Cyanide and Murder*   From the television series *Mike Hammer*
        EMI Gold Horizon Music Corp.

1966   *Say When*   [234]
        Second Floor Music

1966   *Scenario for Trombone and Orchestra*   BMI Archive
        MJQ Music, Inc.

1984   *Seven Dead Eyes*   From the television series *Mike Hammer*
        EMI Gold Horizon Music Corp.

1966   *Short Cake (Shortcake)*   [236][288][291][302]
        Second Floor Music

        Note: This title is listed on RCA LPM3833 (1966 LP recording)
        and Bluebird 6277-2-RB (CD reissue) as "Short Cake"; on Antilles
        314-510 059-2 (1988 CD recording) it is listed as "Shortcake."

1984   *Shots in the Dark*   From the television series *Mike Hammer*
        EMI Gold Horizon Music Corp.

1960   *Shutterbug*   [179]
        Two Jays Publishing Co.

1959   *Sidewinder*   [169][173][174]
        Two Jays Publishing Co.

1961   *Sketch*   BMI Archive
        MJQ Music, Inc.

1973   *Sketch for Trombone and Orchestra*   BMI Archive
        MJQ Music, Inc.

1984   *Skid the Record*   From the television series *Mike Hammer*
        EMI Gold Horizon Music Corp.

1971   *Slo Mo*   BMI Archive
        Interior Music Corp.

1969   *Smoky*   BMI Archive
        Two Jays Publishing Co.

1969	*Sonny* Windswept Pacific Songs	BMI Archive
1966	*Space Walk* Second Floor Music	[235]
1972	*Speak Out* Craig Bradford, cowriter	From the film *Top of the Heap*
1977	*Splashes* Two Jays Publishing Co.	[263]
1943	*SPLO*	Benny Carter personal library
1992	*Stir Fry* Two Jays Publishing Co.	[295]
1955	*Stolen Bass* Fort Knox Music	[112]
1988	*Sweet Georgia Gillespie* Two Jays Publishing Co.	[288]
1992	*Syntax (Bebop Song)* Two Jays Publishing Co.	[297]
1949	*Teapot* Prestige Music Co.	[76][158]
1961	*Tee Jay* MJQ Music, Inc.	BMI Archive
1996	*Ten-85*	[310]
1996	*Thelonious the Onliest*	[310]
1984	*Toots Suite*	[283][285]
1972	*Top of the Heap* Craig Bradford, cowriter Top of the Heap Music (Valley Meadow Music)	From the film *Top of the Heap*
1984	*Torch Song* Earle Hagen, cowriter EMI Gold Horizon Music Corp.	From the television series *Mike Hammer*
1971	*Trekkin'* Interior Music Corp.	BMI Archive

1960	*Trixie* MJQ Music Inc.	[185]
1956	*Tromboniums in Motion* Second Floor Music	[140]
1956	*True Blue Tromboniums*	[139]
1955	*Turnabout* Folkways Music Publishers, Inc.	[119]
1953	*Turnpike* MJQ Music, Inc.	[98][114][180]
1984	*Vickie's Song* EMI Gold Horizon Music Corp.	From the television series, *Mike Hammer*
1955	*Viscosity* Folkways Music Publishers, Inc.	[117]
1954	*Vista* Windswept Pacific Songs	[108]
1955	*We Two* Folkways Music Publishers, Inc.	[118]
1947	*Wee Dot* Screen Gems–EMI Music, Inc.	[61][99]
1988	*When the Saints Go Marching In* Second Floor Music	[289][290]
1988	*Why Indianapolis—Why Not Indianapolis?* Second Floor Music	[288][290][301][308]
1977	*Why Not* Two Jays Publishing Co.	[263]
1973	*Willie Chase* Moses Gilbert, cowriter MCA Duchess Music Corp.	From the film, *Willie Dynamite*
1973	*Willie Dynamite* MCA Duchess Music Corp.	From the film, *Willie Dynamite*
1973	*Willie Escapes* MCA Duchess Music Corp.	From the film, *Willie Dynamite*

1984 *24 Karats Dead*   From the television series *Mike Hammer*
      EMI Gold Horizon Music Corp.

1957 *100 Proof*   [156]
      Second Floor Music

Discography

This discography is a comprehensive chronological listing of issued and unissued recorded performances by J.J. Johnson as a group leader or section musician. Each listing appears in the following format:

[Number] Date of recording　　　　　　　　　　Location of recording
　　　　Leader and group　　　　　　　　　　　Type of recording

　　　　Personnel and instrumentation

　　　　Matrix number—Song title and release data
　　　　Annotation

The assigned discography reference number appears in brackets. The date of recording, when available, is listed in full. The recording location indicates the city in which the session took place and, when available, its type—studio, radio broadcast, television broadcast, etc. The leader and group are listed in italics. When a leader name appears in the heading, it is listed first in the personnel roster. The instrumentation is abbreviated and enclosed in parentheses after each name or group of names. The abbreviations used in the discography appear on pages 260–261. When available for issued items, the matrix number, or code number assigned to each recording, is listed. When multiple song titles occur, the principal title is listed first, followed by the alternate title enclosed in parentheses. Domestic release information is then given by disc format—ET (electrical transcription of a radio broadcast for distribution to network radio stations), 78 (78 rpm), EP (extended play record), 45 (45 rpm single), LP (includes seven-inch, ten-inch, and twelve-inch long-playing records), and CD (compact disc). Cassette tape and tape cartridge listings are not included. Compact disc reissues of previously released recordings (or new releases of previously unissued recordings) have been noted where possible; however, reissue listings are not exhaustive—current information on compact disc reissues may be obtained from various resources on the Internet, including World Wide Web pages of record companies, commercial vendors, and collectors. The source of the listing and any additional information appears in the annotation. Foreign issues and any unauthorized issues may be found by cross-checking listings in other available sources.

Sources of listings include Jamey Aebersold; David N. Baker; Morroe Berger, Edward Berger, and James Patrick, *Benny Carter: A Life in American Music,* vol. 2; Louis G. Bourgois III; Walter Bruyninckx, *Sixty Years of Recorded Jazz: 1917–1977*; CBS Records, Inc. archive; Fantasy-Milestone Records, Inc.; Francesco Fini, *The Complete J.J. Johnson Discography* (1962); Yasuhiro Fujioka, with Lewis Porter and Yoh-ichi Hamada, *John Coltrane: A Discography and Musical Biography*; Institute of Jazz Studies; Jorgen Grunnet Jepsen, *Jazz Records 1942–1962/69,* 8 vols.; J.J. Johnson (personal documents and production notes for the compact discs *Quintergy: Live at the Village Vanguard, Standards, Let's Hang Out, Tangence,* and *The Brass Orchestra*); Jack Litchfield, *A Canadian Jazz Discography*; Edward Michel (Edward Michel Productions, engineering notes for the album, *Pinnacles*); Mosaic Records, Inc.; Music Corporation of America, Inc.; Jay Newland (Hipshake Productions, engineering notes for the compact disc *Let's Hang Out*); Thomas Owens, *Charlie Parker: Techniques of Improvisation,* 2 vols. (Ph.D. dissertation); Lewis Porter; RCA Records, Inc.; Michel Ruppli, *The Prestige Label: A Discography*; Michel Ruppli, *The Savoy Label: A Discography*; Richard Sears, *V-Discs: A History and Discography*; Chris Sheridan, *Count Basie: A Bio-Discography*; Benjamin Young (Verve Records research coordinator); and Christopher Smith.

Abbreviations

alto flute	af	guitar	g
arranger	arr	harmonica	h
alto saxophone	as	French horn	hn
acoustic bass	b	harp	hp
bass clarinet	bc	harpsichord	hs
bass flute	bf	keyboards	kb
baritone horn	bh	mellophone	ml
baritone saxophone	bs	organ	o
bassoon	bsn	oboe	ob
bass trombone	bt	piano	p
contrabassoon	cbsn	piccolo	pc
celesta	cel	percussion	per
clarinet	cl	multiple reeds	reeds
cornet	cn	soprano saxophone	ss
composer	comp	synthesizer	syn
conductor	cond	trombone	tb
drums	d	trumpet	tp
electric bass	eb	tenor saxophone	ts
electric guitar	eg	tuba	tu
electric harpsichord	ehs	vibraphone	v
electric piano	ep	viola	va
euphonium	eu	violoncello	vc
flugelhorn	fg	violin	vn
flute	fl	vocals	voc

[1] December 18, 1942   Los Angeles, California
    Benny Carter and His Orchestra   AFRS broadcast

Benny Carter (as, arr), George Treadwell, Hal Mitchell, Chiefie Scott (tp), Earl Hardy, J.J. Johnson, John Haughton, Alton Moore (tb), Ted Barnett, Stretch Ridley, Gene Porter, Eddie DeVerteuil (reeds), Ted Brannon (p), Johnny Smith (g), Curly Russell (b), Alvin Burroughs (d), Savannah Churchill (voc).

        Stompin' at the Savoy
        ET: Armed Forces Radio Service (AFRS) Jubilee 4
        CD: Jazz Hour JH1005

        All I Need Is You
        ET: AFRS Jubilee 4

        I Can't Get Started
        ET: AFRS Jubilee 4

        Ol' Man River
        ET: AFRS Jubilee 4
        CD: Jazz Hour JH1005

[2]   Late 1942   Los Angeles, California
     Benny Carter and His Orchestra   AFRS broadcast

Personnel unknown, but may be similar to [1].

        Why Don't You Do Right
        ET: AFRS Basic Library of Popular Music 8

        Ill Wind
        ET: AFRS Basic Library of Popular Music 8

[3]   March 24, 1943   Los Angeles, California
     Benny Carter and His Orchestra   Radio broadcast

Benny Carter (tp, as, arr), Gerald Wilson, Snooky Young, Walter Williams, Fred Trainer (tp), John Haughton, J.J. Johnson, Alton Moore (tb), Kirt Bradford, Willard Brown, Gene Porter, Eddie Davis (reeds), Ted Brannon (p), Curly Russell (b), Oscar Bradley (d), the Charioteers (voc).

Fish Fry
LP: International Association of Jazz Record Collectors 17
CD: Jazz Hour JH1005

I Can't Get Started
Joshua Fit De Battle of Jericho
Ain't That Somethin'

Note: "Fish Fry" is announced as "Blueberry Hill Fish Fry" and listed on IAJRC 17
as "Blueberry Hill Jamboree." "Ain't That Somethin'" is incomplete. This show was
the pilot for what was to be the civilian version of the AFRS Jubilee series, aired over
the CBS radio network.

[4]   April 10, 1943   Los Angeles, California
      Benny Carter and His Orchestra   Hollywood Club aircheck

Benny Carter (as, tp, voc, arr), Gerald Wilson, Snooky Young, Walter
Williams, Fred Trainer (tp), Alton Moore, John Haughton, J.J.
Johnson (tb), Kirt Bradford, Willard Brown, Gene Porter, Eddie
Davis (reeds), Ted Brannon (p), Curly Russell (b), Oscar Bradley (d),
Savannah Churchill (voc).

        Melancholy Lullaby
        I've Heard That Song Before
        Without a Song
        One o'Clock Jump
        Ill Wind
        Back Bay Boogie

Note: According to Morroe Berger, Edward Berger, and James Patrick, *Benny
Carter: A Life in American Music,* vol. 2, discography reference number [123], 108–
109, the titles "Without a Song" and "One o'Clock Jump" were probably arranged by
J.J. Johnson.

[5]   May or later in 1943   Los Angeles, California
      Benny Carter and His Orchestra   AFRS broadcast

Benny Carter (as, arr), Claude Dunson, Vernon Porter, Teddy Buckner,
Freddie Webster (tp), Alton Moore, J.J. Johnson, John Haughton (tb),
Porter Kilbert (as), Willard Brown (as, bs), Gene Porter, Bumps Myers
(ts), Ted Brannon (p), Ulysses Livingston (g), Curly Russell (b), Oscar
Bradley (d), Savannah Churchill (voc), Frank Comstock (arr).

Sleep
ET: AFRS Basic Library of Popular Music P-33
LP: Alamac QSR2449
CD: Drive Archive 80674-42449-2, 80674-42449-2

I Used to Love You
ET: AFRS Basic Library of Popular Music P-33
LP: Alamac QSR2449
CD: Drive Archive 80674-42449-2, 80674-42449-2

Ill Wind
ET: AFRS Basic Library of Popular Music P-33
LP: Alamac QSR2449, Palm Club 12, Swing Treasury ST109
CD: Drive Archive 80674-42449-2, 80674-42449-2

Fish Fry
ET: AFRS Basic Library of Popular Music P-33
LP: Alamac QSR2449, Palm Club 12
CD: Drive Archive 80674-42449-2, 80674-42449-2

[6] October 25, 1943   San Francisco, California
     Benny Carter and His Orchestra   Studio performance

Benny Carter (as, arr), Claude Dunson, Vernon Porter, Teddy
Buckner, Freddie Webster (tp), Alton Moore, J.J. Johnson, John
Haughton (tb), Porter Kilbert (as), Willard Brown (as, bs), Gene
Porter, Bumps Myers (ts), Ted Brannon (p), Ulysses Livingston (g),
Curly Russell (b), Oscar Bradley (d), Savannah Churchill (voc),
Frank Comstock (arr).

93   Poinciana
          78: Capitol 144
          LP: Mosaic MQ19-170
          CD: Mosaic MD12-170

94   Just a Baby's Prayer at Twilight
          78: Capitol 165
          LP: Mosaic MQ19-170
          CD: Mosaic MD12-170

95   Hurry Hurry
          78: Capitol 144
          LP: Mosaic MQ19-170
          CD: Mosaic MD12-170

96   Love for Sale
              78:   Capitol 100
              LP: Capitol M11057, Mosaic MQ19-170
              CD: Mosaic MD12-170

Note: J.J. Johnson's first recorded solo—essentially a melodic restatement of the
tune's bridge—occurs on the title "Love For Sale."

[7]   1943   Hollywood, California
       Lena Horne with   Film soundtrack, *Thousands Cheer*
       Benny Carter and His Orchestra

Lena Horne (voc), Benny Carter (as, arr), remainder of personnel
unknown but may be similar to [5].

              Honeysuckle Rose
              LP: MCA 2-11002, Hollywood Soundstage SS409

[8]   1943   Los Angeles, California
       Benny Carter and His Orchestra   AFRS broadcast

Personnel unknown, but may be similar to [5].

              Swanee River
              ET: AFRS Basic Library of Popular Music P-3480674-42449-2
              LP: Alamac QSR2449, Palm Club 12
              CD: Drive Archive 80674-42449-2, 80674-42449-2

              All of Me
              ET: AFRS Basic Library of Popular Music P-34
              LP: Alamac QSR2449, Palm Club 12
              CD: Drive Archive 80674-42449-2, 80674-42449-2

              Honeysuckle Rose
              ET: AFRS Basic Library of Popular Music P-34
              LP: Alamac QSR2449, Palm Club 12
              CD: Drive Archive 80674-42449-2, 80674-42449-2

              Midnight
              ET: AFRS Basic Library of Popular Music P-34
              LP: Alamac QSR2449
              CD: Drive Archive 80674-42449-2, 80674-42449-2

[9]   1943   Los Angeles, California
       Benny Carter and His Orchestra   AFRS broadcast

Personnel unknown, but may be similar to [5].

> ### Prelude to a Kiss
> ET: AFRS Basic Library of Popular Music P-40
> LP: Alamac QSR2449
> CD: Drive Archive 80674-42449-2, 80674-42449-2
>
> ### I Heard You Cried Last Night
> ET: AFRS Basic Library of Popular Music P-40
> LP: Alamac QSR2449
> CD: Drive Archive 80674-42449-2, 80674-42449-2
>
> ### On the Alamo
> ET: AFRS Basic Library of Popular Music P-40
> LP: Alamac QSR2449
> CD: Drive Archive 80674-42449-2, 80674-42449-2

[10] 1943   Los Angeles, California
    Benny Carter and His Orchestra   AFRS broadcast

Benny Carter (as, arr), Rex Stewart (cn), remainder of personnel unknown but may be similar to [5].

> ### Boy Meets Horn
> ET: AFRS Basic Library of Popular Music P-86, AFRS Downbeat 218
> LP: Black Jack LP3010, Spotlite SPJ147
> CD: Jazz Door 1206

[11] May 21, 1944   Los Angeles, California
    Benny Carter and His Orchestra   Studio performance

Benny Carter (as, tp, arr), John Carroll, Karl George, Edwin Davis, Milton Fletcher (tp), Alton Moore, J.J. Johnson, John Haughton, Bart Varsalone (tb), Porter Kilbert (as), Willard Brown (as, bs), Gene Porter, Bumps Myers (ts), Gerald Wiggins (p), Jimmy Edwards (g), Charles Drayton (b), Max Roach (d), Dick Gray (voc).

> 254   ### I Can't Escape from You
> 78: Capitol 40048
> LP: Capitol M11057, Mosaic MQ19-170
> CD: Mosaic MD12-170
>
> 255   ### I'm Lost
> 78: Capitol 165
> LP: Mosaic MQ19-170
> CD: Mosaic MD12-170

256   I Can't Get Started
           78:   Capitol 48015
           LP: Capitol M11057, Mosaic MQ19-170
           CD: Mosaic MD12-170

257   I Surrender Dear
           78:   Capitol 200
           LP: Capitol H235, M11057, Time-Life STL-J10, Mosaic MQ19-170
           CD: Mosaic MD12-170

[12]   June 12, 1944   Los Angeles, California
       Benny Carter and His Orchestra   AFRS broadcast

Benny Carter (as, tp, arr), Milton Fletcher, Sleepy Grider, Fatso Ford,
Edwin Davis (tp), John Haughton, Alton Moore, J.J. Johnson (tb),
Porter Kilbert, Bumps Myers, Gene Porter, Willard Brown (reeds),
Gerald Wiggins (p), Jimmy Edwards (g), Charles Drayton (b), Max
Roach (d), Savannah Churchill (voc).

           Jay Jay's Jump (Polishin' Brass; No Title Jump)
           ET: AFRS Jubilee 83
           LP: Hindsight HSR-218

           Then You've Never Been Blue
           ET: AFRS Jubilee 83

           I Surrender Dear
           ET: AFRS Jubilee 83
           LP: Hindsight HSR-218

           Ol' Man River
           ET: AFRS Jubilee 83

[13]   July 2, 1944   Los Angeles, California
       Jazz at the Philharmonic   Embassy Theater
                                                     Concert performance

Illinois Jacquet, Jack McVea (ts), J.J. Johnson (tb), Nat King Cole (p),
Les Paul (g), Johnny Miller (b), Lee Young (d).

455V17   Blues (part 1)
           78:   Mercury 11053, Disc 6024, Arco 1231
           LP: Mercury MG35005, Clef MG-4, Verve MG-3, VSP-14
           CD: Verve 314-521-646-2

456V18   Blues (part 2)
                    78:   Disc 6024, Arco 1232, Mercury 11053
                    LP: Mercury MG35005, Clef MG-4, Verve MG-3, VSP-14
                    CD: Verve 314-521-646-2

457V19   Blues (part 3)
                    78:   Disc 6025, Arco 1233
                    LP: Mercury MG35005, Clef MG-4, Verve MG-3, VSP-14
                    CD: Verve 314-521-646-2

458V22   Lester Leaps In (part 1)
                    78:   Disc 6025, Arco 1231
                    LP: Mercury MG35005, Clef MG-4, Verve MG-3, VSP-25
                    CD: Verve 314-521-646-2

459V23   Lester Leaps In (part 2)
                    78:   Disc 6026, Arco 1232
                    LP: Mercury MG35005, Clef MG-4, Verve MG-3, VSP-25,
                    CD: Verve 314-521-646-2

460V24   Lester Leaps In (part 3)
                    78:   Disc 6026, Arco 1233
                    LP: Mercury MG35005, Clef MG-4, Verve MG-3, VSP-25,
                    CD: Verve 314-521-646-2

D725   Body and Soul (part 1)
                    78:   Disc 6028
                    LP: Mercury MG35006, Clef MG-5, Verve MG-3, VSP-25
                    CD: Verve 314-521-646-2

D726   Body and Soul (part 2)
                    78:   Disc 6028
                    LP: Mercury MG35006, Clef MG-5, Verve MG-3, VSP-25
                    CD: Verve 314-521-646-2

D727   Body and Soul (part 3)
                    78:   Disc 6029
                    LP: Mercury MG35006, Clef MG-5, Verve MG-3, VSP-25
                    CD: Verve 314-521-646-2

D728   Body and Soul (part 4)
                    78:   Disc 6029
                    LP: Mercury MG35006, Clef MG-5, Verve MG-3, VSP-25
                    CD: Verve 314-521-646-2

123-1935   Tea for Two (part 1)
                    78:   Mercury 11006, Clef 104
                    LP: Mercury MG35008, Clef MG-7, Verve MG-5, VSP-14
                    CD: Verve 314-521-646-2

124-1936   Tea for Two (part 2)
                78: Mercury 11006, Clef 104
                LP: Mercury MG35008, Clef MG-7, Verve MG-5, VSP-14
                CD: Verve 314-521-646-2

125-1937   Tea for Two (part 3)
                78: Mercury 11007, Clef 105
                LP: Mercury MG35008, Clef MG-7, Verve MG-5, VSP-14
                CD: Verve 314-521-646-2

126-1938   Tea for Two (part 4)
                78: Mercury 11007, Clef 105
                LP: Mercury MG35008, Clef MG-7, Verve MG-5, VSP-14
                CD: Verve 314-521-646-2

Note: Three additional titles recorded omit Johnson: "I've Found A New Baby,"
"Rosetta," and "Bugle Call Rag."   Each title—a continuous performance—was
edited into multiple parts in order to fit onto 78 rpm records.

[14]   July 11, 1944   Los Angeles, California
       Benny Carter and His Orchestra   AFRS broadcast

Personnel unknown, but may be similar to [11].

                Sweet Georgia Brown
                ET: AFRS Jubilee 87

                I Lost My Sugar in Salt Lake City
                ET: AFRS Jubilee 87

                Stardust
                ET: AFRS Jubilee 87
                LP: Hindsight HSR-218
                CD: Jazz Door 1206

                Rose Room
                ET: AFRS Jubilee 87
                LP: Jazz Society AA502, Jazz Anthology JA5123, KayDee KD2,
                      Hindsight HSR-218

[15]   September 11, 1944?   New York, New York
       Benny Carter and His Orchestra   Studio performance

Personnel unknown, but probably includes J.J. Johnson (tb).

32633   Among My Souvenirs

Note: This unissued title was recorded for the V-Disc series. According to Morroe Berger, Edward Berger, and James Patrick, *Benny Carter: A Life in American Music,* vol. 2, discography reference number [133], 113, the date that appears on the sleeve of the acetate disc is only approximate since the orchestra was on tour at this time, but probably not in New York.

[16]   1944   New York, New York
       Benny Carter and His Orchestra   Apollo Theater aircheck

Personnel unknown, but probably includes J.J. Johnson (tb).

Back Bay Boogie

[17]   1944   Los Angeles, California
       Benny Carter and His Orchestra   AFRS broadcast

Personnel unknown, but may be similar to [11].

Two Again
ET: AFRS Downbeat 218, AFRS Basic Library of Popular Music P-238

I Never Mention Your Name
ET: AFRS Downbeat 218, AFRS Basic Library of Popular Music P-238

I Lost My Sugar in Salt Lake City
ET: AFRS Downbeat 215, AFRS Basic Library of Popular Music P-238

[18]   Early 1945   Los Angeles, California
       Benny Carter and His Orchestra   AFRS broadcast

Personnel unknown, but probably includes Benny Carter (as, tp, arr), Frank Comstock (ts), and J.J. Johnson (tb).

Somebody Loves Me
ET: AFRS Downbeat (?)

Moon Glow
ET: AFRS Downbeat (?)

Rose Room
ET: AFRS Downbeat 215

Stardust
ET: AFRS Downbeat 97, AFRS Downbeat 215
LP: Spotlite SPJ147

After You've Gone
ET: AFRS Downbeat (?)

Note: AFRS Downbeat issue numbers are unknown for the titles, "Somebody Loves Me,"
"Moon Glow," and "After You've Gone." Johnson is the soloist on "Stardust."

[19]   February 26, 1945   New York, New York
       Timmie Rogers and His Orchestra   Studio performance

Timmie Rogers (voc), William Johnson, Talib Dawud, Felix Barboza,
Loyal Walker (tp), Alton Moore, John Haughton, George Washington,
J.J. Johnson (tb), Benny Carter, Porter Kilbert, Jewell Grant (as), Harold
Clark, Don Byas (ts), Willard Brown (bs), Rufus Webster (p), Herman
Mitchell (g), Charles Drayton (b), Max Roach (d).

W1256   Daddy-O
               78:   Regis 7001

W1258   Good Deal
               78:   Regis 7001

               Capacity (unissued)

               If You Can't Smile and Say Yes, Don't Cry and Say
               No (unissued)

[20]   February 27, 1945   New York, New York
       Savannah Churchill and Her All-Star Orchestra   Studio performance

Savannah Churchill (voc), Benny Carter (as, tp, arr), William Johnson,
Talib Dawud, Felix Barboza, Loyal Walker (tp), Alton Moore, John
Haughton, George Washington, J.J. Johnson (tb), Porter Kilbert, Jewell
Grant, Harold Clark, Don Byas, Willard Brown (reeds), Rufus Webster
(p), Herman Mitchell (g), Charles Drayton (b), Max Roach (d).

W1261   All Alone
               78:   Manor 1004

W1262   Daddy Daddy
               78:   Manor 1004

Note: The two-line note "Trombone Solo" (line above) and "Jay Jay" (line below)
appears on the Manor 1004 center label for the title "Daddy Daddy."

[21] March 19, 1945   Los Angeles, California
       Benny Carter and His Orchestra   AFRS broadcast

Benny Carter (as, tp, arr), Irving Lewis, Fred Trainer, Gerald
Wilson, Emmett Berry, Paul Cohen (tp), J.J. Johnson, George
Washington, Louis Taylor (tb), Porter Kilbert, Jewell Grant (as),
Bumps Myers, Harold Clark (ts), John Taylor (bs), Rufus Webster
(p), Herman Mitchell (g), Charles Drayton (b), Max Roach (d),
Timmie Rogers (voc).

> Sweet Georgia Brown
> ET: AFRS Jubilee 125, AFRS Jubilee 219, AFRS Downbeat (?)
> LP: Palm Club 12, Jazz Society AA502, Joyce LP5007, Jazz Anthology
>   JA5123, Golden Era LP15058
>
> Daddy-O
> ET: AFRS Jubilee 125, AFRS Jubilee 219
> LP: Joyce LP5007
>
> Just You, Just Me
> ET: AFRS Jubilee 125, AFRS Jubilee 219
> LP: Palm Club 12

Note: The AFRS Downbeat issue number is unknown for the title "Sweet Georgia Brown."
Carter announces Bumps Myers and J.J. Johnson as soloists on *Sweet Georgia Brown,* on
the AFRS Downbeat show. The announcement is not present on the Jubilee show.

[22] March 26, 1945   Los Angeles, California
       Benny Carter and His Orchestra   AFRS broadcast

Benny Carter (as, tp, arr), Barney Bigard (cl), Irving Lewis, Fred
Trainer, Gerald Wilson, Emmett Berry, Paul Cohen (tp), George
Washington, J.J. Johnson, Louis Taylor (tb), Porter Kilbert, Jewell
Grant (as), Bumps Myers, Harold Clark (ts), John Taylor (bs), Rufus
Webster (p), Herman Mitchell (g), Charles Drayton (b), Max Roach
(d), Timmie Rogers, Betty Roche (voc), Arthur Treacher, Nat
"King" Cole (spoken voc).

> Jubilee Jump
> ET: AFRS Jubilee 126, AFRS Jubilee 131, AFRS Jubilee 207
> LP: Extreme Rarities 1007, Jazz Society AA502, Jazz Anthology
>   JA5123, Joyce LP5007
>
> Trouble Trouble
> ET: AFRS Jubilee 126, AFRS Jubilee 207
> LP: Joyce LP5007

Good Deal
ET: AFRS Jubilee 126
LP: Joyce LP5007

Tea for Two
ET: AFRS Jubilee 126, AFRS Jubilee 207, AFRS Jubilee 292
LP: Sunbeam SB214, Black Jack LP3003, Joyce LP5007, Spotlite
     SPJ147
CD: Jazz Door 1206

Back Bay Boogie
ET: AFRS Jubilee 126, AFRS Jubilee 207
LP: Sunbeam SB214, Joyce LP5007

[23] April 2, 1945   Los Angeles, California
      Benny Carter and His Orchestra   AFRS broadcast

Personnel unknown, but may be similar to [21].

Rosita (Slick Mix)
ET: AFRS Jubilee 127
LP: Jazz Society AA502, Jazz Anthology JA5123, KayDee KD2

If You Can't Smile and Say Yes, Don't Cry and Say No
ET: AFRS Jubilee 127

[24] May 14, 1945   New York, New York
      Count Basie and His Orchestra   NBC Studio 8H, Radio City
                                                   Studio performance

Count Basie (p), Buck Clayton, Harry Edison, Karl George, Ed Lewis,
Al Killian (tp), Ted Donnelly, J.J. Johnson, Eli Robinson, Dickie Wells
(tb), Jimmie Powell, Earl Warren (as), Buddy Tate, Lucky Thompson
(ts), Rudy Rutherford (bs), Freddie Green (g), Rodney Richardson (b),
Shadow Wilson (d), Jimmy Rushing, Taps Miller (voc).

VP1356   High Tide (I Ain't Mad at You)
             ET: AFRS Basic Library of Popular Music P-574, AFRS Downbeat 284
             78: V-Disc 483B
             LP: Palm Club 3, Alto 702, Caracol CAR427, Festival ALB147, Jazz
                  Society AA506, Joker SM3968, SM3970/2, Swing House SWH29,
                  Sarabandas LPJT4
             CD: Classics 934

VP1357   Sent for You Yesterday
             ET: AFRS Basic Library of Popular Music P-574, AFRS Downbeat 284

           78: V-Disc 534B
           LP: Palm Club 3, Jazz Society AA506, Joker SM3968, SM3970/2, Swing
                House SWH29, For Discriminating Collectors 502
           CD: Classics 934

VP1358   Jimmy's Boogie Woogie (I May Be Wrong)
           78: V-Disc-534A
           LP: Palm Club 15, Caracol CAR427, For Discriminating Collectors 502,
                Festival ALB147, Jazz Society AA506, Joker SM3969, SM3970/2,
                SM4085, Sarabandas LPJT4
           CD: Classics 934

VP1686   Tippin' on the Q.T.
           78: V-Disc 627
           LP: Caracol CAR427, For Discriminating Collectors 502, Jazz Society
                AA506
           CD: Classics 934

JBB296   San Jose
           78: V-Disc 744A
           LP: Palm Club 4, Festival ALB147, Jazz Society AA506
           CD: Classics 934

JBB296   B-flat Blues
           78: V-Disc 744A
           LP: Palm Club 4, Festival ALB147, Jazz Society AA506
           CD: Classics 934

JBB297   Sweet Lorraine
           78: V-Disc 802A
           LP: Jazz Society AA506
           CD: Classics 934

Note: Johnson is a soloist on "Tippin' on the Q.T."

[25] June 5, 1945   New York, New York
      Count Basie and His Orchestra   Paramount Theater
              WNEW "Tribute to Glenn Miller" radio broadcast

Count Basie (p), Harry Edison, Karl George, Ed Lewis, Al Killian (tp),
Ted Donnelly, J.J. Johnson, Eli Robinson, Dickie Wells (tb), Preston
Love, Jimmie Powell, Earl Warren (as), Buddy Tate, Lucky Thompson
(ts), Rudy Rutherford (cl, bs), Freddie Green (g), Rodney Richardson
(b), Shadow Wilson (d), Pearl Bailey, Maxine Johnson (voc).

           One o'Clock Jump
           LP: Metronome MNR-1213

B-flat Blues
LP: Metronome MNR-1213

I'm Gonna See My Baby
LP: Metronome MNR-1213

The Jumpin' Jive (unissued)

Duration Blues
LP: Metronome MNR-1213

Red Bank Boogie (incomplete, program closer)

Note: The program also featured a performance by Cab Calloway singing a medley of "Minnie the Moocher," "Kickin' the Gong Around," and "St. James Infirmary" accompanied by a rhythm section.

[26]   July 2, 1945   Los Angeles, California
       Count Basie and His Orchestra   Starlight Grove
                                                          AFRS broadcast

Count Basie (p), Harry Edison, Karl George, Ed Lewis, Snooky Young (tp), Ted Donnelly, J.J. Johnson, Eli Robinson, Dickie Wells (tb), George Dorsey, Preston Love (as), Buddy Tate, Lucky Thompson (ts), Rudy Rutherford (cl, bs), Freddie Green (g), Rodney Richardson (b), Shadow Wilson (d), Lena Horne, Timmie Rogers, Jimmy Rushing (voc).

5699-1   One o'Clock Jump
            ET: AFRS Jubilee 140

            B-flat Blues
            ET: AFRS Jubilee 140

            Sent for You Yesterday
            ET: AFRS Jubilee 140

7870-1   Honeysuckle Rose
            ET: AFRS Jubilee 140

            Daddy-O
            ET: AFRS Jubilee 140

            Jumpin' at the Woodside
            ET: AFRS Jubilee 140

[27] July 2, 1945   Hollywood, California
      Count Basie and His Orchestra   NBC Studio D
                                                               AFRS broadcast

Count Basie (p), Harry Edison, Karl George, Ed Lewis, Snooky
Young (tp), Ted Donnelly, J.J. Johnson, Eli Robinson, Dickie Wells
(tb), George Dorsey, Preston Love (as), Buddy Tate, Lucky
Thompson (ts), Rudy Rutherford (cl, bs), Freddie Green (g), Rodney
Richardson (b), Shadow Wilson (d), Ann Moore, the King Sisters
(Alyce, Donna, Louise, and Yvonne King), Jimmy Rushing (voc).

7895-1   One o'Clock Jump (incomplete, program opener)
             ET: AFRS Jubilee 141

7895-1   Basie Boogie
             ET: AFRS Jubilee 141
             LP: Joyce LP5002

             What Can I Say, Dear?
             ET: AFRS Jubilee 141
             LP: Joyce LP5002

7896-1   Gotta Be This or That
             ET: AFRS Jubilee 141
             LP: Joyce LP5002

             Andy's Blues
             ET: AFRS Jubilee 141
             LP: Joyce LP5002, KayDee KD-2

             One o'Clock Jump (incomplete, program closer)

[28] July 16, 1945   Hollywood, California
      Count Basie and His Orchestra   NBC Studio D
                                                               AFRS broadcast

Count Basie (p), Harry Edison, Karl George, Ed Lewis, Snooky Young
(tp), Ted Donnelly, J.J. Johnson, Eli Robinson, Dickie Wells (tb),
George Dorsey, Preston Love (as), Buddy Tate, Lucky Thompson (ts),
Rudy Rutherford (cl, bs), Freddie Green (g), Rodney Richardson (b),
Shadow Wilson (d), Martha Lewis (voc).

7970-1   One o'Clock Jump (incomplete, program opener)
             ET: AFRS Jubilee 142

Avenue C
ET: AFRS Jubilee 142
LP: Flutegrove FL-7

I Never Knew (I Could Love Anybody)
ET: AFRS Jubilee 142

7971-1   Hey! Rube
ET: AFRS Jubilee 142

I Should Care
ET: AFRS Jubilee 142

My, What a Fry!
ET: AFRS Jubilee 142

One o'Clock Jump (incomplete, program opener)

[29]   July 23, 1945   Hollywood, California
        Count Basie and His Orchestra   NBC Studio D
                                                        AFRS broadcast

Count Basie (p), Harry Edison, Karl George, Ed Lewis, Snooky Young
(tp), Ted Donnelly, J.J. Johnson, Eli Robinson, Dickie Wells (tb),
George Dorsey, Preston Love (as), Buddy Tate, Lucky Thompson (ts),
Rudy Rutherford (cl, bs), Freddie Green (g), Rodney Richardson (b),
Shadow Wilson (d), June Richmond, the Delta Rhythm Boys (voc).

5554-1   One o'Clock Jump (incomplete, program opener)
ET: AFRS Jubilee 143

Queer Street
ET: AFRS Jubilee 143
LP: Joyce LP5001

Are You Living, Old Man?
ET: AFRS Jubilee 143
LP: Joyce LP5001, KayDee KD-2

Ol' Man River
ET: AFRS Jubilee 143
LP: Joyce LP5001

I'm Beginning to See the Light
ET: AFRS Jubilee 143
LP: Joyce LP5001

Hey! John
ET: AFRS Jubilee 143
LP: Joyce LP5002

High Tide
ET: AFRS Jubilee 143
LP: Joyce LP5002, KayDee KD-2

Note: The program also featured performances by Alvino Rey and the AFRS Orchestra, and comedian Victor Borge.

[30] July 1945   Culver City, California
       Count Basie and His Orchestra   Casa Mañana
                                                      AFRS broadcast

Count Basie (p), Harry Edison, Karl George, Ed Lewis, Snooky Young (tp), Ted Donnelly, J.J. Johnson, Eli Robinson, Dickie Wells (tb), George Dorsey, Preston Love (as), Buddy Tate, Lucky Thompson (ts), Rudy Rutherford (cl, bs), Freddie Green (g), Rodney Richardson (b), Shadow Wilson (d), Lena Horne, Timmie Rogers, Jimmy Rushing (voc).

SUR-8-8   Gotta Be This or That
             ET: AFRS Magic Carpet 39

             Swing Shift
             ET: AFRS Magic Carpet 39

             I Want a Little Girl
             ET: AFRS Magic Carpet 39

             Exactly Like You
             ET: AFRS Magic Carpet 39

[31] August 2, 1945   Los Angeles, California
       Karl George Octet   Studio performance

Karl George (tp), J.J. Johnson (tb), Rudy Rutherford (cl), Buddy Tate (ts), Bill Doggett (p), Freddie Green (g), John Simmons (b), Shadow Wilson (d).

KM1314   Grand Slam
             78: Melodisc 111

KM1315   Baby It's Up to You
              78: Melodisc 111

KM1316   Peekaboo
              78: Melodisc 112

KM1317   How Am I to Know
              78: Melodisc 112

[32] August 8, 1945   Hollywood, California
      Count Basie and His Orchestra   NBC Studio D
                                               AFRS Christmas broadcast

Count Basie (p), Harry Edison, Karl George, Ed Lewis, Snooky Young
(tp), Ted Donnelly, J.J. Johnson, Eli Robinson, Dickie Wells (tb),
George Dorsey, Preston Love (as), Buddy Tate, Lucky Thompson (ts),
Rudy Rutherford (cl, bs), Freddie Green (g), Rodney Richardson (b),
Shadow Wilson (d), Bing Crosby, the Delta Rhythm Boys, Lena Horne
(voc).

5554-1   One o'Clock Jump (incomplete, program opener)
              ET: AFRS Jubilee Christmas

SOF1522   Jumping at Ten
              ET: AFRS Jubilee Christmas
              78: Jazz Society AA555
              LP: Caracol CAR-427, First Heard FH–22, FH–55

5713-1   Just a Settin' And a Rockin'
              ET: AFRS Jubilee Christmas
              LP: Swing House SWH-29

              Gotta Be This or That
              ET: AFRS Jubilee Christmas
              LP: Swing House SWH-29

              Jumpin' at the Woodside
              ET: AFRS Jubilee Christmas
              LP: First Heard FH–22, Swing House SWH-29

[33] September 10, 1945   Hollywood, California
      Count Basie and His Orchestra   NBC Studio D
                                                        AFRS broadcast

Count Basie (p), Harry Edison, Karl George, Ed Lewis, Snooky Young (tp), Ted Donnelly, J.J. Johnson, Eli Robinson, Dickie Wells (tb), George Dorsey, Preston Love (as), Buddy Tate, Lucky Thompson (ts), Rudy Rutherford (cl, bs), Freddie Green (g), Rodney Richardson (b), Shadow Wilson (d), Ann Moore, Jimmy Rushing (voc).

12530-1   One o'Clock Jump (incomplete, program opener)

           Rambo
           ET: AFRS Jubilee 147
           LP: Joyce LP5001

           Mean to Me
           ET: AFRS Jubilee 147
           LP: Joyce LP5001

12531-1   Boogie Woogie (I May Be Wrong)
           ET: AFRS Jubilee 147
           LP: Joyce LP5001

           Astructed (Andy's Blues)
           ET: AFRS Jubilee 147
           LP: Joyce LP5001

           One o'Clock Jump (incomplete; program closer)

Note: J.J. Johnson is the trombone soloist on "Rambo." The program also featured performances by Bob Crosby and Sam Donahue and His Orchestra.

[34]   September 1945   Los Angeles, California
       Lucky Thompson All-Stars   Studio performance

Lucky Thompson (ts), Karl George (tp), J.J. Johnson (tb), Rudy Rutherford (cl), Bill Doggett (p), Freddie Green (g), Rodney Richardson (b), Shadow Wilson (d), Thelma Love (voc).

           Short Day
           78:    Excelsior 144

           You're in My Heart
           78:    Excelsior 144

           Why Not
           78:    Excelsior 145

           No Good Man Blues
           78:    Excelsior 145

Irresistible You
78: Excelsior 146

Phace
78: Excelsior 146

[35] September 17, 1945   Hollywood, California
      Count Basie and His Orchestra   NBC Studio D
                                                        AFRS broadcast

Count Basie (p), Harry Edison, Karl George, Ed Lewis, Snooky Young
(tp), Ted Donnelly, J.J. Johnson, Eli Robinson, Dickie Wells (tb),
George Dorsey, Preston Love (as), Buddy Tate, Lucky Thompson (ts),
Rudy Rutherford (cl, bs), Freddie Green (g), Rodney Richardson (b),
Shadow Wilson (d), Ann Moore, Jimmy Rushing (voc).

12555-1   One o'Clock Jump (incomplete, program opener)
             ET: AFRS Jubilee 148

             I've Found a New Baby
             ET: AFRS Jubilee 148
             LP: Flutegrove FL–7

             Blue Skies
             ET: AFRS Jubilee 148
             LP: Flutegrove FL–7

12556-1   Jivin' Joe Jackson
             ET: AFRS Jubilee 148
             LP: Flutegrove FL–7

             Taps Miller
             ET: AFRS Jubilee 148
             LP: Flutegrove FL–7

             One o'Clock Jump (incomplete, program closer)

Note: The program also featured performances by Mel Tormé and the Mel-
Tones, Sam Donahue and His Orchestra, and Bob Crosby.

[36] September 24, 1945   Hollywood, California
      Count Basie and His Orchestra   NBC Studio D
                                                        AFRS broadcast

Count Basie (p), Harry Edison, Karl George, Ed Lewis, Snooky Young (tp), Ted Donnelly, J.J. Johnson, Eli Robinson, Dickie Wells (tb), George Dorsey, Preston Love (as), Buddy Tate, Lucky Thompson (ts), Rudy Rutherford (cl, bs), Freddie Green (g), Rodney Richardson (b), Shadow Wilson (d), Jimmy Rushing, the Delta Rhythm Boys (voc).

12627-1   One o'Clock Jump (incomplete, program opener)
ET: AFRS Jubilee 149, AFRS Jubilee 223

Rhythm Man
ET: AFRS Jubilee 149, AFRS Jubilee 223

Gotta Be This or That
ET: AFRS Jubilee 149, AFRS Jubilee 223

Jazz Me Blues
ET: AFRS Jubilee 149, AFRS Jubilee 223

12628-1   Please Don't Talk about Me When I'm Gone
ET: AFRS Jubilee 149, AFRS Jubilee 223
LP: First Heard FH22, Flutegrove FL7

It's Sand, Man
ET: AFRS Jubilee 149, AFRS Jubilee 223
LP: Bandstand BS7128, First Heard FH22, Flutegrove FL7

Note: Johnson is the trombone soloist on "Please Don't Talk about Me When I'm Gone." The program also features performances by Dick Haymes, Jeri Sullivan, and Alvino Rey and the AFRS Orchestra.

[37]   Late 1945   Los Angeles, California
Russell Jacquet and His All-Stars   Studio performance

Russell Jacquet (tp, voc), Snooky Young, Harry Edison, Gerald Wilson, Paul Jones (tp), Eli Robinson, Ted Donelly, J.J. Johnson (tb), Rudy Rutherford, Willie Smith, Preston Love (as), Illinois Jacquet, Lucky Thompson (ts), Bill Doggett (p), Freddie Green (g), Billy Hadnott (b), Al Wichard (d).

Blues
78:   Modern Music 129, Jazz Selection 595

Mean and Evil Old World
78:   Modern Music 129, Jazz Selection 595

Note: The personnel and location of the session suggest that it occurred between
September 5 and October 1, 1945, when the Count Basie Orchestra was in the Los
Angeles area, prior to traveling to New York City. See Chris Sheridan, *Count Basie: A
Bio-Discography*, Appendix 2, 1118.

[38]   October 1945   Los Angeles, California
        Count Basie and His Orchestra   AFRS broadcast

Count Basie (p), Emmett Berry, Harry Edison, Ed Lewis, Snooky
Young (tp), Ted Donelly, J.J. Johnson, Eli Robinson, Dickie Wells (tb),
Preston Love, George Dorsey (as), Buddy Tate, Illinois Jacquet (ts),
Rudy Rutherford (bs), Freddie Green (g), Rodney Richardson (b),
Shadow Wilson (d), Jimmy Rushing, Ann Moore (voc).

> Let's Jump
> ET: AFRS Basic Library of Popular Music P-481
>
> One o'Clock Jump
> ET: AFRS Basic Library of Popular Music P-481
>
> Jazz Me Blues
> ET: AFRS Basic Library of Popular Music P-481
>
> Basie Boogie
> ET: AFRS Basic Library of Popular Music P-481
>
> Jumpin' at the Woodside
> ET: AFRS Basic Library of Popular Music P-482
>
> Basie Blues
> ET: AFRS Basic Library of Popular Music P-482
>
> Blue Lou
> ET: AFRS Basic Library of Popular Music P-482
>
> Dance of the Gremlins
> ET: AFRS Basic Library of Popular Music P-482

[39]   October 1, 1945   Hollywood, California
        Count Basie and His Orchestra   NBC Studio D
                                                               AFRS broadcast

Count Basie (p), Harry Edison, Karl George, Ed Lewis, Snooky Young
(tp), Ted Donnelly, J.J. Johnson, Eli Robinson, Dickie Wells (tb),
George Dorsey, Preston Love (as), Buddy Tate, Lucky Thompson (ts),

Rudy Rutherford (cl, bs), Freddie Green (g), Rodney Richardson (b), Shadow Wilson (d), Lena Horne (voc).

12688-1 One o'Clock Jump (incomplete, program opener)
ET: AFRS Jubilee 150, AFRS Jubilee 224

San Jose
ET: AFRS Jubilee 150, AFRS Jubilee 224
LP: First Heard FH22, Flutegrove FL7

One for My Baby and One More for the Road
ET: AFRS Jubilee 150, AFRS Jubilee 224

Good for Nothin' Joe
ET: AFRS Jubilee 150, AFRS Jubilee 224

Tush
ET: AFRS Jubilee 150, AFRS Jubilee 224
LP: First Heard FH22, Flutegrove FL7

One o'Clock Jump (incomplete, program closer)

Note: Comedian and singer Harry "The Hipster" Gibson, the Slim Gaillard Trio, and Alvino Rey and the AFRS Orchestra also perform on this session.

[40] October 9, 1945 Hollywood, California
Count Basie and His Orchestra Studio performance

Count Basie (p), Emmett Berry, Harry Edison, Ed Lewis, Snooky Young (tp), Ted Donnelly, J.J. Johnson, Eli Robinson, Dickie Wells (tb), George Dorsey, Preston Love (as), Illinois Jacquet, Buddy Tate (ts), Rudy Rutherford (cl, bs), Freddie Green (g), Rodney Richardson (b), Shadow Wilson (d), Ann Moore, Jimmy Rushing (voc).

HC01563-1 Blue Skies
78: Columbia 37070
LP: Fontana 662020TR, Ajaz LP256, CBS 66102 (54163), CBS 88674, Franklin Mint 19 (Jazz 073), Queen Q035
CD: Classics 934

HC01564-1 Jivin' Joe Jackson
ET: AFRS Basic Library of Popular Music P-582
78: Columbia 36899
LP: Fontana 662020TR, Ajaz LP256, CBS 66102 (54163), CBS 88674, Queen Q035
CD: Classics 934

HC01565-1   High Tide
        78: Columbia 36990, DB2288
        EP: Columbia ESRF-1018
        LP: Fontana 662020TR, Ajaz LP256, CBS 66102 (54163),
              CBS 88674, Queen Q035
        CD: Classics 934

HC01565-2   High Tide
        LP: Columbia 66102

HC01565-3   High Tide
        LP: Columbia 66102

HC01566-1   Queer Street
        ET: AFRS Basic Library of Popular Music P-582
        78: Columbia 36889, DF-3480
        EP: Columbia B2555, Fontana TFE17015
        LP: Columbia FP1021, FP1026, Fontana 662020TR,
              Ajaz LP256, CBS 66102, 88674, Franklin Mint 34-15,
              Queen Q035
        CD: Classics 934

HC01566-2   Queer Street
        LP: CBS 66102

HC01566-3   Queer Street
        LP: CBS 66102

One o'Clock Jump (incomplete, program closer)

[41]   October 1945   Los Angeles, California?
     Count Basie and His Orchestra   Radio broadcast

Count Basie (p), Emmett Berry, Harry Edison, Ed Lewis, Snooky
Young (tp), Ted Donnelly, J.J. Johnson, Eli Robinson, Dickie Wells
(tb), George Dorsey, Preston Love (as), Illinois Jacquet, Buddy Tate
(ts), Rudy Rutherford (cl, bs), Freddie Green (g), Rodney Richardson
(b), Shadow Wilson (d), Jimmy Rushing (voc).

               Wild Bill's Boogie
               ET: U.S. State Department DSP D31649, Voice of America
                     VOA 35

               Baby, Don't You Cry
               ET: U.S. State Department DSP D31649, Voice of America
                     VOA 35
               LP: Palm Club 3, Caracol CAR427

Sent for You Yesterday
ET: U.S. State Department DSP D31649, Voice of America VOA 35
LP: Palm Club 3, Caracol CAR427, Festival ALB147,
        Joker SM3109, Pentagon U50046

That's All She Wrote
ET: U.S. State Department DSP D31649, Voice of America VOA 35
LP: Palm Club 3, Caracol CAR427

Queer Street
ET: U.S. State Department DSP D31649, Voice of America VOA 35
LP: Palm Club 4

[42]   December 31, 1945   New York, New York
        Count Basie and His Orchestra   AFRS Broadcast–
                                                            AFRS Parade of Bands

Count Basie (p), Emmett Berry, Harry Edison, Ed Lewis, Joe Newman (tp), Ted Donelly, J.J. Johnson, Eli Robinson, George Matthews (tb), Preston Love, Jimmy Powell (as), Buddy Tate, Illinois Jacquet (ts), Rudy Rutherford (bs), Freddie Green (g), Rodney Richardson (b), Shadow Wilson (d).

One o'Clock Jump

Note: According to Chris Sheridan, *Count Basie: A Bio-Discography*, discography reference number 45-1231, 256, the AFRS *Parade of Bands* probably was broadcast from the Apollo Theater in Harlem.

[43]   January 9, 1946   New York, New York
        Count Basie and His Orchestra   Liederkranz Hall
                                                            Concert performance

Count Basie (p), Emmett Berry, Harry Edison, Ed Lewis, Joe Newman (tp), Ted Donelly, J.J. Johnson, Eli Robinson, George Matthews (tb), Preston Love, Jimmy Powell (as), Buddy Tate, Illinois Jacquet (ts), Rudy Rutherford (bs), Freddie Green (g), Rodney Richardson (b), Shadow Wilson (d), Jimmy Rushing (voc).

C035602-1   Patience and Fortitude
        78:   Columbia 36946
        EP: Fontana TFE17115
        LP: Columbia CL997, CBS 66102, 88674, Ajaz LP256
        CD: Classics 934

C035602-2   Patience and Fortitude
LP: CBS 66102

C035602-3   Patience and Fortitude
LP: CBS 66102

C035603-1   The Mad Boogie
78: Columbia 36946, BF115, DC370, DY136, DZ425,
GNS5078, M321, Parlophone R3012
EP: Columbia ESRF1010
LP: Columbia FP1026, Fontana 662020TR, Ajaz LP256,
CBS 66102, 68254, 21063, 88675, CSP173, CL754,
Fontana TFL5077, Harmony HL7229
CD: Classics 934

C035603-2   The Mad Boogie
LP: CBS 66102

C035603-3   The Mad Boogie
LP: CBS 66102

C035603-4   The Mad Boogie
LP: CBS 66102

[44] February 4, 1946   New York, New York
Count Basie and His Orchestra   Liederkranz Hall
Concert performance

Count Basie (p), Emmett Berry, Harry Edison, Ed Lewis, Joe Newman
(tp), Ted Donelly, J.J. Johnson, Eli Robinson, George Matthews (tb),
Earl Warren (as, voc), Jimmy Powell (as), Buddy Tate, Illinois Jacquet
(ts), Rudy Rutherford (bs), Freddie Green (g), Rodney Richardson (b),
Jo Jones (d), Jimmy Rushing (voc).

C035730-1   Lazy Lady Blues
78: Columbia 36990, CB368, DC368, DF3174, DZ415,
Parlophone R3009
LP: Fontana 662020TR, Ajaz LP256, CBS 66102, 88675,
Queen Q035
CD: Classics 934

C035730-2   Lazy Lady Blues
LP: CBS 66102

C035730-3   Lazy Lady Blues
LP: Columbia 36990

C035731-1   Rambo
ET: AFRS SY–82
78: Columbia BF115, DC370, DYC136, DZ425, GNS5078,
       Parlophone R3012, R3014
EP: Columbia B2100, ESDF1010
LP: Columbia 31421, CL2560, CL6079, KL5142, CL754,
       Fontana 662020TR,TFL5077, Ajaz LP256, CBS 66102,
       88675, SONP-50437, Harmony HL7229
CD: Smithsonian 3325-108-2, Classics 934

C035731-1A Rambo
LP: CBS 66102

C035731-2   Rambo
LP: CBS 66102

C035731-3   Rambo
LP: CBS 66102

C035731-4   Rambo (unissued)

C035732-1   Stay Cool
78: Columbia CB368, DC368, DF3480, DZ415,
       Parlophone R3009
EP: Columbia ESRF1009, Fontana TFE17115
LP: Columbia CL6079, FP1026, CL997, Fontana
       662020TR, Ajaz LP256, CBS, 66102, 88675,
       SONP-50437
CD: Classics 934

C035732-2   Stay Cool
LP: CBS 66102

C035732-3   Stay Cool
LP: CBS 66102

C035733-1   The King
78: Columbia 37070, BF636
EP: Columbia B2555, ESRF1018
LP: Columbia FP1026, CL754, Fontana 662020TR, Ajaz
       LP256,CBS 68254, 21063, 26033, 88675, CSP173,
       SONP50437, Fontana TFL5077, Franklin Mint
       FM-71, Harmony HL7229, Record Bazarre RB9,
       Time-Life STL-J22
CD: Classics 934

C037533-2   The King
LP: CBS 66102

C037533-3   The King
              LP: CBS 66102

Note: Johnson is a soloist on all takes of "Rambo," and takes 1 and 3 of "The King."
On some 78 RPM issues, "Rambo," take 1 also appears as "Bambo."

[45]   June 26, 1946   New York, New York
       Jay Jay Johnson's Beboppers   Studio performance

J.J. Johnson (tb), Cecil Payne (as), Bud Powell (p), Leonard
Gaskin (b), Max Roach (d).

S3309-1   Jay Bird (Fly Jay)
              LP: Savoy SJL2232

S3309-9   Jay Bird
              LP: Savoy SJL2232

S3309-11   Jay Bird
              78:   Savoy 975
              EP: Savoy XP8047
              LP: Savoy SJL2232, MG9022, MG12106
              CD: Savoy SV-0151

S3310-1   Coppin' the Bop
              78:   Savoy 615, 926
              EP: Savoy XP8047
              LP: Savoy SJL2232, MG9025, MG12106
              CD: Savoy SV-0151

S3311-1   Jay Jay (Hey Jay Jay)
              LP: Savoy SJL2232

S3311-2   Jay Jay
              78:   Savoy 615, 926
              EP: Savoy XP8047
              LP: Savoy SJL2232, MG9025, MG12106
              CD: Savoy SV-0151

S3311-4   Jay Jay
              LP: Savoy SJL2232

S3312-1   Mad Bebop
              78:   Savoy 930
              EP: Savoy XP8047
              LP: Savoy MG9024, SJL2232
              CD: Savoy SV-0151

[46]   July 26, 1946   New York, New York
       Count Basie and His Orchestra   Aquarium Restaurant
                                                    AFRS *One Night Stand* broadcast

Count Basie (p), Emmett Berry, Harry Edison, Ed Lewis, Joe
Newman, Snooky Young (tp), Ted Donnelly, J.J. Johnson, George
Matthews, Eli Robinson (tb), Rudy Rutherford (cl, as), Preston Love
(as), Illinois Jacquet, Buddy Tate (ts), Jack Washington (bs), Freddie
Green (g), Walter Page (b), Jo Jones (d), Bob Bailey, Ann Moore,
Jimmy Rushing (voc).

SSC9273   One o'Clock Jump (incomplete, program opener)
               ET: AFRS ONS1111

               Jazz Me Blues
               ET: AFRS ONS1111

               I'm Just a Lucky So and So
               ET: AFRS ONS1111, ONS1142

               San Jose
               ET: AFRS ONS1111

               Adventure
               ET: AFRS ONS1111, ONS1142, ONS1220

               Red Bank Boogie
               ET: AFRS ONS1111

SSC9274   Take Me Back, Baby
               ET: AFRS ONS1111

               Queer Street
               ET: AFRS ONS1111

               Mean to Me
               ET: AFRS ONS1111

               Every Tub (incomplete, program closer)
               ET: AFRS ONS1111

[47]   July 28, 1946   New York, New York
       Count Basie and His Orchestra   Aquarium Restaurant
                                                    CBS Radio Network broadcast

Count Basie (p), Emmett Berry, Harry Edison, Ed Lewis, Joe Newman, Snooky Young (tp), Ted Donnelly, J.J. Johnson, George Matthews, Eli Robinson (tb), Rudy Rutherford (cl, as), Preston Love (as), Illinois Jacquet, Buddy Tate (ts), Jack Washington (bs), Freddie Green (g), Walter Page (b), Jo Jones (d), Bob Bailey, Ann Moore, Jimmy Rushing (voc).

High Tide/I Ain't Mad at You
LP: Everybodys EV3004

One o'Clock Jump (incomplete, program closer)

[48]   July 30, 1946   New York, New York
       Count Basie and His Orchestra   Aquarium Restaurant
                                              CBS Radio Network broadcast

Count Basie (p), Emmett Berry, Harry Edison, Ed Lewis, Joe Newman, Snooky Young (tp), Ted Donnelly, J.J. Johnson, George Matthews, Eli Robinson (tb), Rudy Rutherford (cl, as), Preston Love (as), Illinois Jacquet, Buddy Tate (ts), Jack Washington (bs), Freddie Green (g), Walter Page (b), Jo Jones (d), Bob Bailey, Ann Moore, Jimmy Rushing (voc).

Blue House

No Name

[49]   July 31, 1946   New York, New York
       Count Basie and His Orchestra   Liederkranz Hall
                                              Concert performance

Count Basie (p), Emmett Berry, Harry Edison, Ed Lewis, Joe Newman, Snooky Young (tp), Ted Donnelly, J.J. Johnson, George Matthews, Eli Robinson (tb), Rudy Rutherford (cl, as), Preston Love (as), Illinois Jacquet, Buddy Tate (ts), Jack Washington (bs), Freddie Green (g), Walter Page (b), Jo Jones (d), Bob Bailey, Ann Moore, Jimmy Rushing (voc).

C036702-1   Hob Nail Boogie
             78:   Columbia DF3468, DZ368
             EP: Columbia ESRF1009;
             LP: Columbia 31421, CL6079, CL2560, FP1026, Ajaz
                   LP256, CBS 66102, 21063, 88675, Queen Q035

C036702-2　　Hob Nail Boogie
　　　　　　　LP:　CBS 66102

C036702-3　　Hob Nail Boogie
　　　　　　　LP:　CBS 66102

C036702-4　　Hob Nail Boogie
　　　　　　　LP:　CBS 66102

C036703-1　　Danny Boy
　　　　　　　ET:　AFRS Basic Library of Popular Music P-1929
　　　　　　　78:　Columbia 39075, DZ368
　　　　　　　EP:　Columbia B2100
　　　　　　　45:　Columbia 3-39075, 1-930
　　　　　　　LP:　Columbia CL6079, CL2560, Ajaz LP256, CBS 66102,
　　　　　　　　　　88675, Queen Q035, Juke Box USA 48

C036704-1　　Mutton Leg
　　　　　　　ET:　AFRS SD–12
　　　　　　　78:　Columbia 37093, BF636, DZ710, B9971,
　　　　　　　EP:　Columbia ESRF1018, Fontana TFE17015
　　　　　　　LP:　Columbia FP1026, CL997, AFRS SD12, , Ajaz LP269,
　　　　　　　　　　CBS 66102, 88675

C036704-2　　Mutton Leg
　　　　　　　LP:　CBS 66102

C036704-3　　Mutton Leg
　　　　　　　LP:　CBS 66102

C036704-4　　Mutton Leg
　　　　　　　LP:　CBS 66102

　　　　　　　Stay on It
　　　　　　　LP:　CBS 66102, 88675

[50]　December 4, 1946　　　　　　　　　　　New York, New York
　　　Esquire All-American Award Winners　　　Studio performance

Charlie Shavers, Buck Clayton (tp), J.J. Johnson (tb), Coleman Hawkins
(ts), Harry Carney (bs), Teddy Wilson (p), John Collins (g), Chubby
Jackson (b), Shadow Wilson (d).

D6VB3369　　Indiana Winter
　　　　　　　78:　Victor 40-0137
　　　　　　　LP:　Victor LPV544
　　　　　　　CD:　RCA/Bluebird 6757

D6VB3371   Blow Me Down
              78: Victor 40-0134
              CD: RCA/Bluebird 6757

D6VB3372   Buckin' the Blues
              78: Victor 40-0135
              LP: Victor LPV544, Camden CAL383
              CD: RCA/Bluebird 6757

Omit Buck Clayton (tp):

D6VB3370   Indian Summer
              78: Victor 40-0136
              LP: Victor LPV544
              CD: RCA/Bluebird 6757

[51]   December 4, 1946   New York, New York
       Chubby Jackson and His Jacksonville Seven   Studio performance

Chubby Jackson (b), Charlie Shavers (tp), J.J. Johnson (tb), Coleman
Hawkins (ts), Harry Carney (bs), Teddy Wilson (p), John Collins (g),
Shadow Wilson (d).

D6VB3373   Dixieland Stomp
              LP: Camden CAL446

Note: The date listed in Jorgen Grunnet Jepsen, *Jazz Records*, vol. 4C, 6, is incorrect
(December 12), indicated by the consecutive matrix numbers for [50].

[52]   December 1946   New York, New York
       Coleman Hawkins and His Orchestra   Studio performance

Coleman Hawkins (ts), Fats Navarro (tp), J.J. Johnson (tb), Porter
Kilbert (as), Hank Jones (p), Curly Russell (b), Max Roach (d).

SR1857   I Mean You
              78: Sonora 3027
              LP: Prestige PR7824
              CD: Prestige PRCD 2532-24124-2

Add Milt Jackson (v):

SR1858-1   Bean and the Boys
              78: Sonora 3024
              LP: Prestige PR7824
              CD: Prestige PRCD 2532-24124-2

SR1858-2   Bean and the Boys
LP: Prestige PR7824
CD: Prestige PRCD 2532-24124-2

[53] April 1, 1947   New York, New York
Illinois Jacquet and His Orchestra   Studio performance

Illinois Jacquet (ts), Russell Jacquet, Fats Navarro, Joe Newman (tp),
J.J. Johnson (tb), Jimmy Powell (as), Leo Parker (bs), Sir Charles
Thompson (p), Freddie Green (g), Al Lucas (b), Shadow Wilson (d).

137AL   Blow, Illinois, Blow
78: Aladdin 3001
EP: Aladdin EP501
LP: Aladdin LP701, LP803, Mosaic MQ6-165
CD: Mosaic MD4-165

Note: An additional title, "Illinois Blows the Blues," features Illinois Jacquet
only with the rhythm section.

[54] May 21, 1947   New York, New York
Illinois Jacquet and His Orchestra   Studio performance

Illinois Jacquet (ts), Joe Newman (tp), J.J. Johnson (tb), Leo Parker
(bs), Sir Charles Thompson (p), Al Lucas (b), Shadow Wilson (d).

R1214-1   South Street Special
LP: Mosaic MQ6-165
CD: Mosaic MD4-165

R1214-2   South Street Special
78: Apollo 785
LP: Apollo LP477, Mosaic MQ6-165
CD: Mosaic MD4-165

R1215-2   Diggin' the Count
78: Apollo 769
LP: Apollo LP477, Grand Award LP33-315, Jazztone
     J1250, Mosaic MQ6-165
CD: Mosaic MD4-165

R1216-2   Robbins Nest
78: Apollo 769
EP: Apollo EP602
LP: Apollo LP104, Grand Award LP33-315, Jazztone
     J125C, Mosaic MQ6-165
CD: Mosaic MD4-165

R1217   Music Hall Beat
             78: Apollo 777
             LP: Mosaic MQ6-165
             CD: Mosaic MD4-165

R1218   Jumpin' at the Woodside
             78: Apollo 777
             LP: Grand Award LP33-315, Mosaic MQ6-165
             CD: Mosaic MD4-165

R1218-4   Jumpin' at the Woodside
             LP: Mosaic MQ6-165
             CD: Mosaic MD4-165

[55] September 10, 1947   New York, New York
      Illinois Jacquet and His Orchestra   Studio performance

Illinois Jacquet (ts), Russell Jacquet (tp, voc), Joe Newman (tp), J.J.
Johnson (tb), Leo Parker (bs), Sir Charles Thompson (p), John
Collins (g), Al Lucas (b), Shadow Wilson (d).

WOR260-1   Goofin' Off
             LP: Mosaic MQ6-165
             CD: Mosaic MD4-165

WOR261-2   Riffin' with Jacquet
             LP: Mosaic MQ6-165
             CD: Mosaic MD4-165

WOR262-1   Don't Push Daddy
             78: Aladdin 3260

WOR263-2   Sahara Heat
             78: Aladdin 3260

WOR263-3   Sahara Heat
             LP: Mosaic MQ6-165
             CD: Mosaic MD4-165

[56] November 7, 1947   Chicago, Illinois
      Illinois Jacquet and His Orchestra   Studio performance

Illinois Jacquet (ts), Russell Jacquet (tp, voc), Joe Newman (tp), J.J.
Johnson (tb), Leo Parker (bs), Sir Charles Thompson (p), John
Collins (g), Al Lucas (b), Shadow Wilson (d).

480   Destination Moon
         78:   Aladdin 3180
         EP: Aladdin EP504
         LP: Aladdin LP708, LP803, Mosaic MQ6-165
         CD: Mosaic MD4-165

481   For Truly
         78:   Aladdin 3180
         EP: Aladdin EP511
         LP: Aladdin LP708, LP803, Mosaic MQ6-165
         CD: Mosaic MD4-165

482-1   I Surrender Dear
         LP: Mosaic MQ6-165
         CD: Mosaic MD4-165

482-2   I Surrender Dear (unissued)

Note: The November 7, 1947, session date appears in the Aladdin master book although the original discs (78, EP, and Aladdin LP) are dated November 28, 1947.

[57]   December 11, 1947   New York, New York
      Coleman Hawkins and His Orchestra   Studio performance

Coleman Hawkins (ts), Fats Navarro (tp), J.J. Johnson (tb), Budd Johnson (as), Marion DiVeta (bs), Hank Jones (p), Chuck Wayne (g), Jack Lesberg (b), Max Roach (d).

D7VB2659   April in Paris
            78:   Victor 20-3057
            CD: RCA 7863-66617-2, 09026-68515-2

D7VB2660   How Strange
            78:   Victor 20-3057
            CD: RCA 7863-66617-2, 09026-68515-2

D7VB2661   Half Step Down, Please
            78:   Victor 20-3143
            CD: RCA 7863-66617-2, 09026-68515-2

D7VB2662   Angel Face
            LP: Victor LPV-544
            CD: RCA 7863-66617-2, 09026-68515-2

D7VB2663-1   Jumpin' for Jane
            78:   Victor 20-3143

[58]   December 17, 1947   New York, New York
        Charlie Parker Sextet   Studio performance

Charlie Parker (as), Miles Davis (tp), J.J. Johnson (tb), Duke
Jordan (p), Tommy Potter (b), Max Roach (d).

D1151-1   Drifting on a Reed (unissued)

D1151-2   Drifting on a Reed (Big Foot, Giant Swing)
               78:   Dial 1056
               LP: Spotlite 106, Dial LP905
               CD: Stash ST-CD-567-70

D1151-3   Drifting on a Reed (unissued)

D1151-4   Drifting on a Reed
               LP: Spotlite 106, Dial LP904
               CD: Stash ST-CD-567-70

D1151-5   Drifting on a Reed (Air Conditioning)
               78:   Dial 1043
               LP: Spotlite 106, LP207
               CD: Stash ST-CD-567-70

D1152-1   Quasimodo
               LP: Dial LP203, Spotlite 106, Roost RLP2210
               CD: Stash ST-CD-567-70

D1152-2   Quasimodo (Trade Winds)
               78:   Dial 1015
               LP: Spotlite 106, LP904
               CD: Stash ST-CD-567-70

D1153-1   Charlie's Wig (unissued)

D1153-2   Charlie's Wig (Bongo Bop, Crazeology)
               LP: Dial LP905, Spotlite 106
               CD: Stash ST-CD-567-70

D1153-3   Charlie's Wig (unissued)

D1153-4   Charlie's Wig (Drifting on a Road)
               LP: Dial LP203, Spotlite 106
               CD: Stash ST-CD-567-70

D1153-5   Charlie's Wig
               78:   Dial 1040
               LP: Dial LP904, Spotlite 106
               CD: Stash ST-CD-567-70

D1154-1   Bird Feathers (unissued)

D1154-2   Bird Feathers (Bongo Beep, Dexterity)
LP: Dial LP904, Spotlite 106
CD: Stash ST-CD-567-70

D1154-3   Bird Feathers (Bongo Beep)
LP: Dial LP207, Spotlite 106
CD: Stash ST-CD-567-70

D1155-1   Crazeology (Little Benny)/incomplete take
CD: Stash ST-CD-567-70

D1155-2   Crazeology (Little Benny)/incomplete take
78: Dial 1034
LP: Dial LP207, Spotlite 106
CD: Stash ST-CD-567-70

D1155-3   Crazeology (Little Benny)
78: Dial 1034
LP: Dial LP207, Spotlite 106
CD: Stash ST-CD-567-70

D1155-4   Crazeology
78: Dial 1034
LP: Dial LP207, Spotlite 106
CD: Stash ST-CD-567-70

D1156-1   How Deep Is the Ocean
78: Dial 1055
LP: Dial LP904, Spotlite 106
CD: Stash ST-CD-567-70

D1156-2   How Deep Is the Ocean
LP: Dial LP211, Spotlite 106
CD: Stash ST-CD-567-70

Note: D1151-5, "Drifting on a Reed," issued as "Air Conditioning" on Dial LP207 and Roost RLP2210; D1152-2, "Quasimodo," issued as "Trade Winds" on Jazztone J1004; D1153-B, "Charlie's Wig," issued as "Crazeology" on Jazztone J1004, J1214, and as "Bongo Bop" on Jazztone J1240; D1154-B, "Bird Feathers," issued as "Dexterity" on Dial LP904; and D1154-3, "Bird Feathers," issued as "Bongo Bop" on Jazztone J1214.

[59] December 18, 1947   New York, New York
      Illinois Jacquet and His Orchestra   Studio performance

Illinois Jacquet (ts), Leo Parker (bs), Joe Newman, Russell Jacquet

(tp), J.J. Johnson (tb), Sir Charles Thompson (p), Al Lucas (b),
Shadow Wilson (d).

D7VB2854   Jet Propulsion
            78:   Victor 20-2892, 547-0514
            LP: Victor LPT3236, RCA/Bluebird 6571-1-RB, Mosaic MQ6-165
            CD: Mosaic MD4-165, RCA 7863-61123-2

D7VB2855   King Jacquet
            78:   Victor 20-2702, 547-0514
            LP: Victor LPT3236, RCA/Bluebird 6571-1-RB, Mosaic MQ6-165
            CD: Mosaic MD4-165

D7VB2856   Try Me One More Time
            78:   Victor 20-2892
            LP: RCA/Bluebird 6571-1-RB, Mosaic MQ6-165
            CD: Mosaic MD4-165, RCA 7863-61123-2

D7VB2857   Embryo
            78:   Victor 20-3278
            LP: RCA/Bluebird 6571-1-RB, Mosaic MQ6-165
            CD: Mosaic MD4-165

[60] December 19, 1947   New York, New York
      Illinois Jacquet and His Orchestra   Studio performance

Illinois Jacquet (ts), Joe Newman (tp), Russell Jacquet (tp, voc), J.J.
Johnson (tb), Leo Parker (bs), Sir Charles Thompson (p), John
Collins (g), Al Lucas (b), Shadow Wilson (d).

D7VB2889   Riffin' at 24th Street
            78:   Victor 20-2702, 547-0514
            LP: Victor LPM3236, RCA/Bluebird 6571-1-RB, Mosaic MQ6-165
            CD: Mosaic MD4-165, RCA 7863-61123-2

D7VB2890   Mutton Leg
            78:   Victor 20-3060, 547-0513
            LP: RCA/Bluebird 6571-1-RB, Mosaic MQ6-165
            CD: Mosaic MD4-165

D7VB2891   Symphony in Sid
            78:   Victor 20-3060
            LP: RCA/Bluebird 6571-1-RB, Mosaic MQ6-165
            CD: Mosaic MD4-165, RCA 7863-61123-2

Note: An additional title, "A Jacquet for Jack the Bellboy," features Illinois Jacquet only with the rhythm section.

[61]   December 19, 1947   New York, New York
        Leo Parker's All-Stars   Studio performance

Leo Parker (bs), Joe Newman (tp), J.J. Johnson (tb), Dexter Gordon (as, ts), Hank Jones (p), Curly Russell (b), Shadow Wilson (d).

S3495-1   Wee Dot
           LP: Savoy SJL2211

S3495-2   Wee Dot
           LP: Savoy SJL2225

S3495-3   Wee Dot
           78:   Savoy 950
           LP: Savoy SJL2211, XP8060, MG9009

S3495-4   Wee Dot
           LP: Savoy SJL2225

S3496   Solitude
           78:   Savoy 929
           EP: Savoy XP8060
           LP: Savoy MG9024, SJL2225

S3497-1   The Lion Roars
           LP: Savoy SJL2211

S3497-2   The Lion Roars
           LP: Savoy SJL2225

S3497-3   The Lion Roars
           78:   Savoy 929
           EP: Savoy XP8060
           LP: Savoy SJL2211, MG9026

S3497-4   The Lion Roars
           LP: Savoy SJL2225

S3498   Mad Lad Boogie
           78:   Savoy 929
           EP: Savoy XP8060

S3499   (untitled, unissued)

Note: Matrix number S3497-3, "The Lion Roars," issued as "The Lion's Roar" on Savoy XP8060 and MG9026.

[62]   December 24, 1947   New York, New York
        Jay Jay Johnson's Bop Quintet   Studio performance

J.J. Johnson (tb), Leo Parker (bs), Hank Jones (p), Al Lucas (b),
Shadow Wilson (d).

S3519   Boneology
                78:   Savoy 942
                EP: Savoy XP8086
                LP: Savoy MG12106, SJL2232, MG15048
                CD: Savoy SV-0151, 4053-276-2

S3520   Down Vernon's Alley
                78:   Savoy 942
                EP: Savoy XP8086
                LP: Savoy MG12106, SJL2232, MG15048
                CD: Savoy SV-0151, 4053-276-2, SV-0163

S3521   Yesterdays
                EP: Savoy XP8086
                LP: Savoy MG12106, SJL2232, MG15048, MG12010
                CD: Savoy SV-0151, 4053-276-2

S3522   Riffette
                EP: Savoy XP8086
                LP: Savoy MG12106, SJL2232, MG15048
                CD: Savoy SV-0151, 4053-276-2

[63]   December 19, 1948   New York, New York
        Royal Roost Jam Session   Royal Roost club date
                                                         Audience tape

Benny Harris (tp), Bud Johnson (ts), Lee Konitz (as), Cecil Payne
(bs), Buddy DeFranco (cl), J.J. Johnson (tb), Bud Powell (p), Chuck
Wayne (g), Nelson Boyd (b), Max Roach (d).

                Jumpin' with Symphony Sid
                I'll Be Seeing You
                2nd Street Theme
                Ornithology

Note: All titles issued on the LP, Beppo 503, *Royal Roost Jam.*

[64]   April 1948   Detroit, Michigan
        Russell Jacquet and His All-Stars   Studio performance

Russell Jacquet (tp, voc), J.J.Johnson (tb), Sonny Stitt (as), Maurice Simon (ts), Leo Parker (bs), Sir Charles Thompson (p), Al Lucas (b), Shadow Wilson (d).

4009   Relaxin' with Randle
        78: Sensation 12, King 4259
        EP: King EP309
        LP: King LP295-30

4010   Lion's Roar
        78: Sensation 8, King 2242
        LP: King LP295-30
        CD: Galaxy OJCCD-1771-2

4011-1   Suede Jacquet
        78: Sensation 8, King 2242
        LP: King LP295-30
        CD: Galaxy OJCCD-1771-2

4011-2   Suede Jacquet
        CD: Galaxy OJCCD-1771-2

4012   Scamparoo
        78: Sensation 12, King 4259
        EP: King EP309
        LP: King LP295-30
        CD: Galaxy OJCCD-1771-2

[65] January 3, 1949   New York, New York
     Metronome All-Stars   Studio performance

Dizzy Gillespie, Fats Navarro, Miles Davis (tp), Kai Winding, J.J. Johnson (tb), Buddy DeFranco (cl), Charlie Parker (as), Charlie Ventura (ts), Ernie Caceres (bs), Lennie Tristano (p), Billy Bauer (g), Eddie Safranski (b), Shelly Manne (d).

D9VB-0021-1   Overtime
        78: Victor 20-3361
        LP: Camden CAL426
        CD: RCA/Bluebird 07863-66528-2, 7636-1-RB

D9VC-1000-1   Overtime
        LP: Victor LPT3046, Camden CAL426
        CD: RCA/Bluebird 07863-66528-2, 7636-1-RB

D9VC-1001-1   Victory Ball
        LP: Victor LPT3046, Camden CAL339
        CD: RCA/Bluebird 07863-66528-2, 7636-1-RB

Omit Navarro, Davis, Johnson, and Caceres:

D9VB-0022-1   Victory Ball
              78:   Victor 20-3361
              CD: RCA/Bluebird 07863-66528-2, 7636-1-RB

D9VB-0022-2   Victory Ball
              LP: Victor LPT3046, Camden CAL426

[66]   January 20, 1949   New York, New York
       Babs Gonzales and His Orchestra   Studio performance

Babs Gonzales (voc), Jordan Fordin (as), Sonny Rollins (ts), Bennie
Green, J.J. Johnson (tb), Julius Watkins (hn), Linton Garner (p), Art
Phipps (b), Jack Parker (d).

3393   Capitolizing
              78:   Capitol 57-60000
              LP: Capitol M-11059
              CD: Blue Note BN84464

3394   Professor Bop
              78:   Capitol 57-60000
              LP: M-11059
              CD: Blue Note BN84464

[67]   March 20, 1949   Los Angeles, California
       Babs Gonzales and His Orchestra   Studio performance

Babs Gonzales (voc), Art Pepper (as), Herbie Steward (ts), J.J.
Johnson (tb), Wynton Kelly (p), Bill Tinney (g,voc), Bruce
Lawrence (b), Roy Haynes (d).

4100   Prelude to a Nightmare
              78:   Capitol 57-60012
              LP: Capitol M-11059
              CD: Blue Note BN84464

[68]   April 21, 1949   New York, New York
       Tadd Dameron and His Orchestra   Studio performance

Tadd Dameron (p), Miles Davis (tp), J.J. Johnson (tb), Sahib Shihab
(as), Benjamin Lundy (ts), Cecil Payne (bs), John Collins (g), Curly
Russell (b), Kenny Clarke (d), Kay Penton (voc).

3760 John's Delight
78: Capitol 60015
LP: Capitol M-11059
CD: Blue Note 72437-33373-2

3761 What's New
LP: Capitol M-11059
CD: Blue Note 72437-33373-2

3762 Heaven's Doors Are Open Wide
LP: Capitol M-11059
CD: Blue Note 72437-33373-2

3763 Focus
78: Capitol 60015
LP: Capitol M-11059
CD: Blue Note 72437-33373-2

[69] April 22, 1949   New York, New York
Miles Davis Nonet   Studio performance

Miles Davis (tp), J.J. Johnson (tb), Sandy Siegelstein (hn), Bill Barber
(tu), Lee Konitz (as), Gerry Mulligan (bs), John Lewis (p), Nelson
Boyd (b), Kenny Clarke (d).

3764 Venus De Milo
78: Capitol 1221
LP: Capitol M-11026
CD: Capitol CDP7-92862-2

3765 Rouge
LP: Capitol M-11026
CD: Capitol CDP7-92862-2

3766 Boplicity
78: Capitol 60011
LP: Capitol M-11026
CD: Capitol CDP7-92862-2

3767 Israel
78: Capitol 60011
LP: M-11026
CD: Capitol CDP7-92862-2

[70] April 27, 1949   New York, New York
Babs Gonzales and His Orchestra   Studio performance

Babs Gonzales (voc), J.J. Johnson (tb), Tony Scott (fl), Sonny
Rollins (ts), Don Redman (ss), Wynton Kelly (p), Bruce Lawrence
(b), Roy Haynes (d).

3779   St. Louis Blues
              78:   Capitol 57-60012
              LP: Capitol M-11059
              CD: Blue Note BN84464

3780   Real Crazy
              LP: Capitol M-11059
              CD: Blue Note BN84464

              Then You'll Be Boppin' Too
              CD: Blue Note BN84464

              When Lovers They Loose
              CD: Blue Note BN84464

[71]   May 11, 1949   Hackensack, New Jersey
       Jay Jay Johnson's Boppers   Studio performance

J.J. Johnson (tb), Sonny Rollins (ts), John Lewis (p), Gene Ramey (b),
Shadow Wilson (d).

S36-130-1   Audobon
              LP: Savoy SJL2232

S36-130-3   Audobon
              78:   Savoy 947
              LP: Savoy MG12106, SJL2232
              CD: Savoy SV-0151

S36-131   Don't Blame Me
              78:   Savoy 949
              LP: Savoy MG15049, SJL2232
              CD: Savoy SV-0151

S36-132-2   Goof Square
              LP: Savoy SJL2232

S36-132-4   Goof Square
              LP: Savoy SJL2232

S36-132-8   Goof Square
  78: Savoy 944
  LP: Savoy MG15049, MG12106, SJL2232
  CD: Savoy SV-0151

S36-133-3   Bee Jay
  LP: Savoy SJL2232

S36-133-5   Bee Jay
  78: Savoy 949
  LP: Savoy MG12106, SJL2232
  CD: Savoy SV-0151

Note: Francesco Fini, *The Complete J.J. Johnson Discography*, 9, incorrectly dates this session as February 1949.

[72] May 26, 1949   New York, New York
      Jay Jay Johnson's Boppers   Studio performance

J.J. Johnson (tb), Kenny Dorham (tp), Sonny Rollins (ts), John Lewis (p), Leonard Gaskin (b), Max Roach (d).

JRC20B   Elysees
  78: New Jazz 803, 810, Prestige 810
  EP: Prestige EP1330
  LP: Prestige LP109, LP7023, LP7253, LP16-4, P-24067
  CD: Fantasy 2531-91-2

JRC21C   Opus V
  78: New Jazz 806, Prestige 806
  EP: Prestige EP1330
  LP: Prestige LP109, LP7023, LP7253, LP16-4, P-24067
  CD: Fantasy 2531-91-2

JRC22C   Hilo
  78: New Jazz 806, Prestige 806
  EP: Prestige EP1330
  LP: Prestige LP109, LP7023, LP7253, LP16-4, P-24067
  CD: Fantasy 2531-91-2

JRC23D   Fox Hunt
  78: Prestige 810
  EP: Prestige EP1330
  LP: Prestige LP109, LP7023, LP7253, LP16-4, P-24067
  CD: Fantasy 2531-91-2

[73]   July 6, 1949   New York, New York
       Dizzy Gillespie and His Orchestra   Studio performance

Dizzy Gillespie, Benny Harris, Willie Cook, Elmon Wright (tp), J.J.
Johnson, Charles Greenlea, Andy Duryea (tb), John Brown, Ernie Henry
(as), Yusef Lateef, Joe Gayles (ts), Al Gibson (bs), James Foreman (p),
Al McKibbon (b), Teddy Stewart (d), Joe Carroll (voc).

D9VB-1793-1 Hey Pete! Le's Eat Mo' Meat
             78: Victor LJM1009
             LP: Victor LPV530
             CD: RCA/Bluebird 07863-66528-2

Omit Joe Carroll (voc):

D9VB-1794-1 Jumpin' with Symphony Sid
             78: Victor LJM1009
             LP: Victor LPV530
             CD: RCA/Bluebird 07863-66528-2

Add Johnny Hartman (voc):

D9VB-1795-1 If Love Is Trouble
             78: Victor 20-3538
             CD: RCA/Bluebird 07863-66528-2

Omit Johnny Hartman (voc); add Joe Carroll, Dizzy Gillespie (voc):

D9VB-1796-1 In the Land Of Oo-Bla-Dee
             78: Victor 20-3538
             LP: Victor LPV530
             CD: RCA/Bluebird 07863-66528-2, RCA Victor 9027-68499-2

[74]   August 23, 1949   New York, New York
       Howard McGhee All-Stars   Studio performance

Howard McGhee (tp), J.J. Johnson (tb), Brew Moore (ts), Kenny
Drew (p), Curly Russell (b), Max Roach (d).

BN370-2   Lo Flame
             78: Blue Note 1574
             LP: Blue Note BLP5012

BN371-1   Fuguetta
             78: Blue Note 1572
             LP: Blue Note BLP5012

BN372   Fluid Drive
78:   Blue Note 1573
LP: Blue Note BLP5012

BN373   Meciendo
78:   Blue Note 1574
LP: Blue Note BLP5012

BN374   Donello Square
78:   Blue Note 1573
LP: Blue Note BLP5012

BN375   I'll Remember April
78:   Blue Note 1572
LP: Blue Note BLP5012

[75]   August 29, 1949   New York, New York
Coleman Hawkins and His All-Stars   Studio performance

Coleman Hawkins (ts), J.J. Johnson (tb), Cecil Payne (bs), Al Haig (p), John Collins (g), Nelson Boyd (b), Shadow Wilson (d).

276-5   The Big Head
78:   Clef 8909
45:   Clef EPC114

277-7   Skippy
78:   Clef 8912
45:   Clef EPC114

Note: Bennie Green (tb) replaces Johnson for two additional titles from this session—"Platinum Love" and "Small Hotel." Alternate takes of "The Big Head" and "Skippy" were probably incomplete and could not be issued. Francesco Fini, *The Jay Jay Johnson Complete Discography*, 11, does not include the personnel change for this session.

[76]   October 17, 1949   New York, New York
Jay Jay Johnson's Boppers   Studio performance

J.J. Johnson (tb), Sonny Stitt (ts), John Lewis (p), Nelson Boyd (b), Max Roach (d).

JRC600A   Afternoon in Paris
LP: Prestige PR7839
CD: Fantasy 2531-9-1, Fantasy/Original Jazz Classics OJC CD009-2

JRC600B		Afternoon in Paris
			78:	New Jazz 820, Prestige 820
			EP:	Prestige EP1332
			LP:	Prestige LP123, LP7024, PR7248, P24044, P24081, PR7839
			CD:	Fantasy 2531-9-1, Fantasy/Original Jazz Classics OJC CD009-2

JRC601A		Elora
			78:	New Jazz 814
			LP:	Prestige PR7839
			CD:	Fantasy 2531-9-1, Fantasy/Original Jazz Classics OJC CD009-2

JRC601B		Elora
			78:	New Jazz 814, Prestige 814
			EP:	Prestige EP1332
			LP:	Prestige LP123, LP7024, PR7248, P24044, P24081, PR7839
			CD:	Fantasy 2531-9-1, Fantasy/Original Jazz Classics OJC CD009-2

JRC602A		Teapot
			LP:	Prestige PR7839
			CD:	Fantasy 2531-9-1, Fantasy/Original Jazz Classics OJC CD009-2

JRC602B		Teapot
			78:	New Jazz 820, Prestige 820
			EP:	Prestige EP1332
			LP:	Prestige LP123, LP7024, PR7248, P24044, P24081, PR7839
			CD:	Fantasy 2531-9-1, Fantasy/Original Jazz Classics OJC CD009-2

JRC603B		Blue Mode
			78:	New Jazz 814
			LP:	Prestige PR7839
			CD:	Fantasy 2531-9-1, Fantasy/Original Jazz Classics OJC CD009-2

JRC603C		Blue Mode
			78:	New Jazz 814, Prestige 814
			EP:	Prestige EP1332
			LP:	Prestige LP123, LP7024, PR7248, P24044, P24081, PR7839
			CD:	Fantasy 2531-9-1, Fantasy/Original Jazz Classics OJC CD009-2

Note:	Matrix number JRC601A, "Elora," appears as JRC601B in the wax of New
Jazz 814—an issue that pairs the titles, "Elora" and "Blue Mode." Two versions of the
disc were issued—one with matrix numbers JRC601A and JRC603B paired, and one
with JRC601B and JRC603C paired.

[77]	November 4, 1949							New York, New York
		Betty Mays and Her Swingtet					Studio performance

Betty Mays (voc), Bernie Glow (tp), Kai Winding, J.J. Johnson (tb),
Percy France (cl, ts), Cecil Payne (bs), Gil Coggins (p), Arthur
Phipps (b), George James (d).

1110   May's Haze
         78: Regal 3243

1111   Slow Rock
         78: Regal 3243

         Old Mill Stream (unissued)

         Why Fool Yourself (unissued)

         Gimme a Pound (unissued)

[78]   February 10, 1950   New York, New York
       Miles Davis Sextet   Radio broadcast from Birdland

Miles Davis (tp), J.J. Johnson (tb), Stan Getz (ts), Tadd Dameron (p),
Gene Ramey (b), Art Blakey (d).

                 Conception
                 Ray's Idea
                 Max Is Making Wax
                 Woody'n You

Note: An additional title, "That Old Black Magic," features Stan Getz only with the
rhythm section. All titles are issued on the LP Ozone 1.

[79]   February 14, 1950   New York, New York
       Charlie Parker Quintet with J.J. Johnson   Audience tape, Birdland

Charlie Parker (as), Red Rodney (tp), J.J. Johnson (tb), Al Haig (p),
Tommy Potter (b), Roy Haynes (d).

                 Hot House
                 Out of Nowhere
                 Visa
                 52nd Street Theme
                 Anthropology
                 Allen's Alley
                 What's New
                 Half Nelson (Little Willie Leaps)
                 Yesterdays
                 52nd Street Theme
                 52nd Street Theme
                 Dizzy Atmosphere
                 Perdido (Wahoo)

                    I Can't Get Started
                    Allen's Alley
                    52nd Street Theme
                    Slow Boat to China
                    Night in Tunisia
                    52nd Street Theme

Note: All titles are issued on the compact discs Philology CDW19/29-2 and EPM
FDC 5710.

[80]   March 9, 1950   New York, New York
        Miles Davis Nonet   Studio performance

Miles Davis (tp), J.J. Johnson (tb), Gunther Schuller (hn), Bill
Barber (tu), Lee Konitz (as), Gerry Mulligan (bs), John Lewis (p),
Al McKibbon (b), Max Roach (d).

        4346   Deception
                        LP: Capitol M-11026
                        CD: Capitol CDP7-92862-2

        4347   Rocker
                        LP: Capitol M-11026
                        CD: Capitol CDP7-92862-2

        4348   Moon Dreams
                        LP: Capitol M-11026
                        CD: Capitol CDP7-92862-2

Add Kenny Hagood (voc):

        4349   Darn That Dream
                        78:   Capitol 1221
                        LP: Capitol M-11026
                        CD: Capitol CDP7-92862-2

[81]   March 15, 1950   New York, New York
        Chubby Jackson and His Orchestra   Studio performance

Chubby Jackson (b), Howard McGhee, Al Porcino, Don Ferrara
(tp), Kai Winding, J.J. Johnson (tb), Charlie Kennedy (as), Zoot
Sims, Georgie Auld (ts), Gerry Mulligan (bs), Tony Aless (p), Don
Lamond (d).

JRC63   Flying the Coop
         78: New Jazz 825, Presitge 825
         EP: Prestige EP1323
         LP: Prestige LP8280, LP105, PR7641
         CD: Fantasy/Original Jazz Classics 2531-711-2

JRC64   I May Be Wrong
         78: New Jazz 825, Prestige 825
         EP: Prestige EP1318
         LP: LP8280, LP7013, LP105, PR7641
         CD: Fantasy/Original Jazz Classics 2531-711-2

JRC65   New York
         78: New Jazz 836, Prestige 836
         EP: Prestige EP1323
         LP: Prestige LP105, PR7641
         CD: Fantasy/Original Jazz Classics 2531-711-2

JRC66   Sax Appeal
         78: New Jazz 839, Prestige 830
         EP: Prestige LP105, PR7641
         CD: Fantasy/Original Jazz Classics 2531-711-2

JRC67   Hot Dog
         78: New Jazz LP8280, Prestige 745
         EP: Prestige EP1323
         LP: PrestigeLP105, PR7641
         CD: Fantasy/Original Jazz Classics 2531-711-2

JRC68   Why Not?
         78: New Jazz 836, Prestige 836
         EP: Prestige EP1323
         LP: Prestige LP105, PR7641
         CD: Fantasy/Original Jazz Classics 2531-711-2

JRC69   Leavin' Town
         78: New Jazz 830, Prestige 830
         LP: Prestige LP105, PR7641
         CD: Fantasy/Original Jazz Classics 2531-711-2

Omit Howard McGhee, Al Porcino, Don Ferrara (tp), Georgie Auld (ts):

JRC70   So What
         78: Prestige 745, 842
         EP: Prestige EP1318
         LP: New Jazz LP8280, Prestige LP7013, LP105, PR7641
         CD: Fantasy/Original Jazz Classics 2531-711-2

[82]   May 17–30, 1950   New York, New York
       Miles Davis and His Birdland All-Stars   Audience tapes, Birdland

Miles Davis, Fats Navarro (tp), J.J. Johnson (tb), Brew Moore (ts),
Tadd Dameron (p), Curly Russell (b), Art Blakey (d).

> ### Wee
> LP: Alto 701
> CD: Jazz Music Yesterday JMY ME-6401
>
> ### Deception
> LP: Alto 701
> CD: Jazz Music Yesterday JMY ME-6401
>
> ### Hot House
> LP: Session 101
> CD: Jazz Music Yesterday JMY ME-6401
>
> ### Eronel
> LP: Session 102
> CD: Jazz Music Yesterday JMY ME-6401
>
> ### Slow Broadway Theme
> LP: Session 102
> CD: Jazz Music Yesterday JMY ME-6401

Note: Charlie Parker (as) added on "Deception." Alternate titles were assigned for
the Alto and Session releases for "Wee" (Rambunctious Rambling), "Deception"
(Poohbah), "Hot House" (Miles' Midnight Breakaway), and "Eronel" (Overturia).

[83]   February 3, 1951   New York, New York
       Dizzy Gillespie Septet   Radio broadcast from Birdland

Dizzy Gillespie (tp), John Coltrane (ts), J.J. Johnson (tb), Milt
Jackson (v), Billy Taylor (p), Percy Heath (b), Art Blakey (d).

> ### Birk's Works
> LP: Oberon 5100
>
> ### I Can't Get Started
> LP: Oberon 5100
>
> ### Jumpin' with Symphony Sid
> LP: Oberon 5100
>
> ### Good Bait
> LP: Oberon BT009

Note: An additional, unissued title from this broadcast, "Lady Be Good," is a feature for vocalist Joe Carroll.

[84]   February 17, 1951   New York, New York
       Miles Davis All-Stars   WJZ Radio broadcast from Birdland

Miles Davis (tp), J.J. Johnson (tb), Sonny Rollins (ts), Kenny Drew (p), Tommy Potter (b), Art Blakey (d).

        Jumpin' with Symphony Sid
        Evance (Out of the Blue)
        Half Nelson
        Tempus Fugit
        Move
        Jumpin' with Symphony Sid (incomplete)

Note: "Symphony" Sid Torin is the emcee for this program.

[85]   March 17, 1951   New York, New York
       Dizzy Gillespie Septet   Radio broadcast from Birdland

Dizzy Gillespie (tp, voc), John Coltrane (as, ts), J.J. Johnson (tb), Milt Jackson (v), John Lewis (p), Percy Heath (b), Carl Fields (d).

        Birk's Works
        LP: Oberon 5100
        CD: Savoy SV-0170

        Tin Tin Daeo
        LP: Oberon BT009
        CD: Savoy SV-0170

        I Can't Get Started (unissued)

        The Champ
        LP: Oberon BT009
        CD: Savoy SV-0170

        Jumpin' with Symphony Sid
        LP: Oberon BT009

Note: An additional, unissued title from this broadcast, "Lady Be Good," is a feature for vocalist Joe Carroll.

[86]   April 14, 1951   New York, New York
        Dizzy Gillespie All-Stars   Birdland club date
                                                           Audience tape

Dizzy Gillespie (tp), Budd Johnson (ts), J.J. Johnson (tb), Percy
Heath (b), John Lewis (p), Milt Jackson (v), Art Blakey (d), Joe
Carroll (per).

                    Good Bait
                    Night in Tunisia
                    Birk's Works
                    Tin Tin Deo
                    Theme (Jumpin' with Symphony Sid)

Note: "Symphony" Sid Torin announces at the end that Joe Carroll was playing
maracas and did not sing on this set.

[87]   April 16, 1951   New York, New York
        Dizzy Gillespie Septet   Studio performance

Dizzy Gillespie (tp), J.J. Johnson (tb), Budd Johnson (ts), Milt Jackson
(v, p), Percy Heath (b), Art Blakey (d), Melvin Moore (voc).

3637   Love Me Pretty Baby
                EP: DeeGee XP4004
                LP: Regent MG6043, Savoy SJL2209, MG12204
                CD: Savoy SV-0157

Omit Melvin Moore (voc):

3638   The Champ
                EP: DeeGee XP4000
                LP: Dee Gee MG1000, Savoy MG12047, SJL2209
                CD: Savoy SV-0170

Note: In Michel Ruppli, *The Savoy Label: A Discography*, 240, an additional title
from this session, "Lady Be Good," is listed with personnel that omits J.J. Johnson
(tb) and Budd Johnson (ts), and adds vocalist Joe Carroll. However, Savoy compact
disc SV-0157 does not omit the two Johnsons from the personnel roster.
Additionally, J.J. Johnson can be heard playing background figures with the
ensemble.

[88]   April 21, 1951   New York, New York
        Dizzy Gillespie All-Stars   Birdland club date
                                                           Audience tape

Dizzy Gillespie (tp), Budd Johnson (ts), J.J. Johnson (tb), Percy Heath (b), John Lewis (p), Milt Jackson (v), Art Blakey (d).

Klook (The Champ, dedicated to Kenny Clarke)

Add Chano Pozo (per):

Tin Tin Deo

Omit Chano Pozo (per):

Love Me

Add Joe Carroll (voc):

Lady Be Good

Omit Joe Carroll (voc):

Birk's Works

Note: "Symphony" Sid Torin is the announcer for this set.

[89] April 21, 1951   New York, New York
      Dizzy Gillespie All-Stars   Birdland club date
                                                                  Audience tape

Dizzy Gillespie (tp), Budd Johnson (ts), J.J. Johnson (tb), Percy Heath (b), John Lewis (p), Milt Jackson (v), Art Blakey (d).

Klook
Birk's Works
Congo Blues

Note: "Symphony" Sid Torin is the announcer for this set.

[90] June 2, 1951   New York, New York
      Miles Davis All-Stars   Birdland club date
                                                                  Audience tape

Miles Davis (tp), J.J. Johnson (tb), Sonny Rollins (ts), Kenny Drew (p), Tommy Potter (b), Art Blakey (d).

Move
LP: Session 102, Ozone 7, Beppo 501

Half Nelson
LP: Session 102, Ozone 7, Beppo 501

Down
LP: Session 102, Ozone 7, Beppo 501

Note: On some LPs, "Move" appears as "Moo," "Half Nelson" appears as "Two,"
and "Down" appears as "The Blues" and "Mick's Blues."

[91]   November 3, 1951   New York, New York
       Jesse Powell Octet   Studio performance

Jesse Powell (ts), Buck Clayton (tp), J.J. Johnson (tb), Cecil Payne
(bs), Bill Doggett (p), Johnny Jones (g), Jam Smith (b), Herb Lovelle
(d), Fluffy Hunter (voc).

F190   My Natch'l Man
              78:   Federal 12060

F191   Love Is a Fortune
              78:   Federal 12056

F192   As Long As You're Satisfied
              78:   Federal 12060

F193   The Walkin' Blues
              78:   Federal 12056

[92]   1951   New York, New York
       Budd Johnson All-Stars   Studio performance

Budd Johnson (ts), Howard McGhee (tp), J.J. Johnson (tb), Charlie
Singleton (ts, voc), Cecil Payne (bs), Kenny Drew (p), Oscar
Pettiford (b), Carl Fields (d), Freddie Jackson (voc).

107A   Sometimes I Feel Like Going Home
              78:   Faith 315

107B   Grooving in Birdland
              78:   Faith 315

108A   I'm All Alone
              78:   Faith 314

108B   Talk of the Town
            78:   Faith 314

Note: The title "Sometimes I Feel Like Going Home" is a vocal feature for Freddie
Jackson; the title "I'm All Alone" is a vocal feature for Charlie Singleton.

[93]   Late 1951   South Pacific Tour
        Howard McGhee All-Stars   Location unknown

Howard McGhee (tp), J.J. Johnson (tb), Rudy Williams (ts), Clifton
Best (g), Oscar Pettiford (b), Charlie Rice (d).

            Royal Garden Blues
            LP: Regent MG6001, Savoy MG12205, SJL2219
            CD: Savoy 4053-219-2

            St. Louis Blues
            LP: Regent MG6001, Savoy MG12205, SJL2219
            CD: Savoy 4053-219-2

            Mood Indigo
            LP: Regent MG6001, Savoy MG12205, SJL2219
            CD: Savoy 4053-219-2

            Harvest Time
            LP: Regent MG6001, Savoy MG12205, SJL2219
            CD: Savoy 4053-219-2

            Lady Be Good
            LP: Regent MG6001, Savoy MG12205, SJL2219, HiLo LP6001
            CD: Savoy 4053-219-2

Note: The title, "Lady Be Good" was issued as "Guamania" on HiLo LP6001.

[94]   January 17, 1952   South Pacific Tour
        Howard McGhee All-Stars   Guam Island concert performance

Howard McGhee (tp), J.J. Johnson (tb), Rudy Williams (ts), Clifton
Best (g), Charlie Rice (d), unknown (b).

HL401   How High the Moon (part 1)
            78:   HiLo 1409
            LP: HiLo LP6001, Savoy SJL2219

HL402   How High the Moon (part 2)
            78:   HiLo 1409
            LP: HiLo LP6001, Savoy SJL2219

HL403   Stardust
               78:   HiLo 1410
               LP: HiLo LP6001 Savoy SJL2219

HL404   Body and Soul
               78:   HiLo 1410
               LP: HiLo LP6002, Regent MG6001, Savoy SJL2219, MG12205
               CD: Savoy 4053-219-2

HL405   Twelfth Street Rag
               78:   HiLo 1414
               LP: HiLo LP6001, Savoy SJL2219

HL406   Man with a Horn
               78:   HiLo 1414
               LP: HiLo LP6002, Regent MG6001, Savoy SJL2219, MG12205
               CD: Savoy 4053-219-2

               Perdido
               LP: HiLo LP6002, Regent MG6001, Savoy SJL2219, MG12205
               CD: Savoy 4053-219-2

               Stormy Weather
               LP: HiLo LP6002, Regent MG6001, Savoy SJL2219, MG12205
               CD: Savoy 4053-219-2

               Stompin' at the Savoy
               LP: HiLo LP6002, Regent MG6001, Savoy SJL2219, MG12205
               CD: Savoy 4053-219-2

               One o'Clock Jump
               LP: HiLo LP6002, Regent MG6001, MG12205
               CD: Savoy 4053-219-2

               Don't Blame Me
               LP: HiLo LP6001, Regent MG6001, Savoy SJL2219, MG12205
               CD: Savoy 4053-219-2

Note: Matrix number HL405, "Twelfth Street Rag," was issued as "12th Street Bop" on the HiLo label. Michel Ruppli, *The Savoy Label: A Discography*, 269, points out that the titles of [93] and [94] could have been recorded in one session in Guam without Pettiford, who had to leave the band in late 1951 and was replaced by an unnamed player.

[95]   March 24, 1952   New York, New York
       Gene Ammons Octet   Studio performance

Bill Massey (tp), J.J. Johnson (tb), Gene Ammons (ts), Sonny Stitt (bs), John Houston (p), unknown (g), Benny Stuberville (b), George Brown (d).

I'll Walk Alone
78: Decca 28094

Old Folks
78: Decca 28094

Beezy
78: Decca 28222

Somewhere Along the Way
78: Decca 28222

[96] May 9, 1952   New York, New York
      Miles Davis All-Stars   Studio performance

Miles Davis (tp), J.J. Johnson (tb), Jackie McLean (as), Gil Coggins
(p), Oscar Pettiford (b), Kenny Clarke (d).

428   Dear Old Stockholm
               78: Blue Note 1595
               LP: Blue Note BLP5013, BLP1501
               CD: EMD/Capitol 7777-81501-2, Blue Note CDP7-81512-2

429A   Chance It (Max Is Making Wax)
               78: Blue Note 1596
               LP: Blue Note BLP5013, BLP1501
               CD: EMD/Capitol 7777-81501-2, Blue Note CDP7-81512-2

429B   Chance It
               CD: EMD/Capitol 7777-81501-2, Blue Note CDP7-81512-2

430A   Donna
               78: Blue Note 1595
               LP: Blue Note BLP5013, BLP1502
               CD: EMD/Capitol 7777-81501-2, Blue Note CDP7-81512-2

430B   Donna
               45: Blue Note 45-1633
               LP: Blue Note BLP1501
               CD: EMD/Capitol 7777-81501-2, Blue Note CDP7-81512-2

431A   Woody'n You
               78: Blue Note 1596
               EP: Blue Note EP204
               LP: Blue Note BLP5013, BLP1502
               CD: EMD/Capitol 7777-81501-2, Blue Note CDP7-81512-2

431B   Woody'n You
                LP: Blue Note BLP1514, BLP1502
                CD: EMD/Capitol 7777-81501-2, Blue Note CDP7-81512-2

[97] April 20, 1953   New York, New York
      Miles Davis All-Stars   Studio performance

Miles Davis (tp), J.J. Johnson (tb), Jimmy Heath (ts), Gil Coggins
(p), Percy Heath (b), Art Blakey (d).

                Tempus Fugit
                78: Blue Note 1618
                45: Blue Note 45-1649
                LP: Blue Note BLP5022, BLP1501, BLP1001
                CD: Blue Note CDP7-81502-2

                Tempus Fugit (alternate take)
                LP: Blue Note BLP1502
                CD: Blue Note CDP7-81502-2

                Enigma (alternate take)
                78: Blue Note 1618
                LP: Blue Note BLP5022, BLP1501
                CD: Blue Note CDP7-81502-2

                Enigma
                CD: Blue Note CDP7-81502-2

                Ray's Idea
                78: Blue Note 1619
                LP: Blue Note BLP5022, BLP1501
                CD: Blue Note CDP7-81502-2

                Ray's Idea (alternate take)
                LP: Blue Note BLP1502
                CD: Blue Note CDP7-81502-2

                Kelo (alternate take)
                78: Blue Note 1620
                LP: Blue Note BLP5022, BLP1501
                CD: Blue Note CDP7-81502-2

                Kelo
                CD: Blue Note CDP7-81502-2

                C.T.A. (alternate take)
                78: Blue Note 1620
                LP: Blue Note BLP5022, BLP1501
                CD: Blue Note CDP7-81502-2

C.T.A.
LP: Blue Note BLP1501
CD: Blue Note CDP7-81502-2

Note: An additional title from this session, issued on LP and reissued on CD, "I Waited for You," omits Johnson and Heath.

[98]   June 22, 1953   New York. New York
       J.J. Johnson Sextet   WOR studio performance

J.J. Johnson (tb), Clifford Brown (tp), Jimmy Heath (ts,bs), John Lewis (p), Percy Heath (b), Kenny Clarke (d).

BN503-2   Capri (take 3)
           45: Blue Note 1621
           LP: Blue Note BLP5028, BLP1505
           CD: Blue Note CDP7-81505-2

BN503-3   Capri (take 4)
           LP: Blue Note BLP1506
           CD: Blue Note CDP7-81505-2

BN504-0   Lover Man (take 6)
           LP: Blue Note BLP5028, BLP1505
           CD: Blue Note CDP7-81505-2

BN505-0   Turnpike (take 6)
           45: Blue Note 1621
           LP: Blue Note BLP5028, BLP1505
           CD: Blue Note CDP7-81505-2

BN505-2   Turnpike (take 8)
           LP: Blue Note BLP1506
           CD: Blue Note CDP7-81505-2

BN506-2   Sketch One (take 11)
           LP: Blue Note BLP5028, BLP1505
           CD: Blue Note CDP7-81505-2

Omit Clifford Brown (tp), Jimmy Heath (ts, bs):

BN507-0   It Could Happen to You (take 12)
           LP: Blue Note BLP5028, BLP1505
           CD: Blue Note CDP7-81505-2

Add Clifford Brown (tp), Jimmy Heath (ts):

BN508-0   Get Happy (take 14)
                 LP: Blue Note BLP5028, BLP1505
                 CD: Blue Note CDP7-81505-2

BN508-1   Get Happy (take 15)
                 LP: Blue Note BN-LA267G
                 CD: Blue Note CDP7-81505-2

[99] September 18, 1953   New York, New York
      Jazz Workshop/Trombone Rapport   Club date performance
                                                   Putnam Central Club

J.J. Johnson, Kai Winding, Bennie Green, Willie Dennis (tb), John
Lewis (p), Charles Mingus (b), Arthur Taylor (d).

Move
LP: Debut 5, 6005, 6008
CD: Fantasy/Prestige 2532-24097-2

Yesterdays
LP: Debut 5

I'll Remember April
LP: Debut 14, 6005, 6008
CD: Fantasy/Prestige 2532-24097-2

Blues for Some Bones (Wee Dot)
LP: Debut 14, 6005, 6008
CD: Fantasy/Prestige 2532-24097-2

Ow!
LP: Debut 126, 6005, 6008
CD: Fantasy/Prestige 2532-24097-2

Now's the Time
LP: Debut 126, 6005, 6008
CD: Fantasy/Prestige 2532-24097-2

Trombosphere
LP: Debut 126, 6005, 6008
CD: Fantasy/Prestige 2532-24097-2

Chazzanova
LP: Debut 126, 6005, 6008
CD: Fantasy/Prestige 2532-24097-2

Kai's Day
LP: Debut 198, Design LP29

Omit Bennie Green, Willie Dennis (tb):

> Conversation
> LP: Roost OJ-1

Note: An additional title from this club date, "Stardust," features Bennie Green only with the rhythm section, issued on Debut LP 5.

[100] February 28, 1954   New York, New York
Henri Renaud Septet   Studio performance

Henri Renaud (p), Jerry Hurwitz (tp), J.J. Johnson (tb), Al Cohn (ts), Gigi Gryce (bs), Curly Russell (b), Walter Bolden (d).

> Wallington Special
> LP: Swing M33327, Period LP1213
> CD: Fresh Sound FSR-CD-170

> Lisa
> LP: Swing M33327, Period LP1213
> CD: Fresh Sound FSR-CD-170

> Boo Wah
> LP: Swing M33327, Period LP1213
> CD: Fresh Sound FSR-CD-170

> Something for Lili
> LP: Swing M33327, Period LP1213
> CD: Fresh Sound FSR-CD-170

Note: The liner notes to Fresh Sound compact disc FSR-CD-170 reverse the date of this session with [101].

[101] March 7, 1954   New York, New York
Henri Renaud All–Stars   Studio performance

Henri Renaud (p), J.J. Johnson (tb), Al Cohn (ts), Milt Jackson (v), Percy Heath (b), Charlie Smith (d).

> I'll Remember April
> LP: Swing M33320, LDM30050, Period SPL1211
> CD: Fresh Sound FSR-CD-170

> Jay Jay's Blues
> LP: Swing M33320, LDM30050, Period SPL1211
> CD: Fresh Sound FSR-CD-170

Out of Nowhere
LP: Swing M33320, LDM30050, Period SPL1211
CD: Fresh Sound FSR-CD-170

If I Had You (1)
LP: Swing M33321, LDM30050, Period SPL1212
CD: Fresh Sound FSR-CD-170

If I Had You (2)
LP: Swing M33327

Omit Al Cohn (ts):

Jerry Old Man
LP: Swing M33320, LDM30050, Period SPL304, SPL1212
CD: Fresh Sound FSR-CD-170

There's No You
LP: Swing M33320, LDM30050, Period SPL1211
CD: Fresh Sound FSR-CD-170

Omit Henri Renaud (p), add Milt Jackson (p):

Indiana
LP: Swing M33321, LDM30050, Period SPL1212
CD: Fresh Sound FSR-CD-170

The More I See You
LP: Swing M33321, Period SPL1211

Note: Milt Jackson also sings vocals on the title, "The More I See You." An additional title, "Lullaby Of The Leaves," is performed only by Jackson, Heath, and Smith.

[102] April 29, 1954   New York, New York
Miles Davis All-Star Sextet   Studio performance

Miles Davis (tp), J.J. Johnson (tb), Lucky Thompson (ts), Horace Silver (p), Percy Heath (b), Kenny Clarke (d).

568   Blue 'N' Boogie
             EP: Prestige EP1358
             LP: Prestige LP182, LP7076
             CD: Prestige/Original Jazz Classics OJCCD-213-2

569   Walkin'
             45: Prestige 45-157
             EP: Prestige EP1357
             LP: Prestige LP182, LP7076, PR7457
             CD: Prestige/Original Jazz Classics OJCCD-213-2

[103] May 24, 1954   New York, New York
Dizzy Gillespie and His Orchestra   Studio performance

Dizzy Gillespie, Quincy Jones, Ernie Royal, Jimmy Nottingham (tp),
J.J. Johnson, Leon Comegys, George Matthews (tb), Hilton Jefferson,
George Dorsey (as), Hank Mobley, Lucky Thompson (ts), Danny Bank
(bs), Wade Legge (p), Lou Hackney, Robert Rodriguez (b), Charlie
Persip (d), Jose Mangual, Ubaldo Nieto, Candido Camero, Ramon
"Mongo" Santamaria (per).

1711	Manteca Theme
	LP: Norgran MGN1003, Verve MGV8208, MGV8191
1712	Contrasts
	LP: Norgran MGN1003, Verve MGV8208, MGV8191
1713	Jungla
	LP: Norgran MGN1003, Verve MGV8208, MGV8191
1714	Rhumba Finale
	LP: Norgran MGN1003, Verve MGV8208, MGV8191
1715	6/8 (unissued)

[104] August 24, 1954   Hackensack, New Jersey
J.J. Johnson/Kai Winding Quintet   Studio performance

J.J. Johnson, Kai Winding (tb), Billy Bauer (g), Charles Mingus (b),
Kenny Clarke (d).

Blues for Trombones
78: Savoy 4506
EP: Savoy XP8140
LP: Savoy MG15038, MG12125, MG12010, SJL2232
CD: Savoy SV-0163

What Is This Thing Called Love
EP: Savoy XP8140
LP: Savoy MG15048, MG12010, SJL2232
CD: Savoy SV-0163

Lament
EP: Savoy XP8142
LP: Savoy MG15038, MG12010, SJL2232
CD: Savoy SV-0163

The Major
EP: Savoy XP8141
LP: Savoy MG15048, MG12010, SJL2232
CD: Savoy SV-0163

[105] August 26, 1954   New York, New York
       J.J. Johnson/Kai Winding Quintet   Studio performance

J.J. Johnson, Kai Winding (tb), Wally Cirillo (p), Charles Mingus
(b), Kenny Clarke (d).

Bernie's Tune
78:   Savoy 4506
EP: Savoy XP8141
LP: Savoy MG15038, MG12010, SJL2232
CD: Savoy SV-0163

Reflections
EP: Savoy XP8141
LP: Savoy MG15038, MG12010, SJL2232
CD: Savoy SV-0163

Co-Op
EP: Savoy XP8140
LP: Savoy MG15038, MG12010, SJL2232
CD: Savoy SV-0163

Blues in Twos
EP: Savoy XP8142
LP: MG15038, MG12010, SJL2232
CD: Savoy SV-0163

[106] September 15, 1954   New York, New York
       Dizzy Gillespie and His Orchestra   Studio performance

Dizzy Gillespie, Quincy Jones, Ernie Royal, Jimmy Nottingham (tp),
J.J. Johnson, Leon Comegys, George Matthews (tb), Hilton Jefferson,
George Dorsey (as), Hank Mobley, Lucky Thompson (ts), Danny
Bank (bs), Wade Legge (p), Lou Hackney (b), Charlie Persip (d).

1980   Cool Eyes
              EP: Norgran EPN114
              LP: Norgran MGN1023, MGN1090, Verve MGV8178

1981   Confusion
            EP: Norgran EPN114
            LP: Norgran MGN1023, MGN1090, Verve MGV8178

1982   Pile Driver
            EP: Norgran EPN114
            LP: Norgran MGN1023, MGN1090, Verve MGV8178

1983   Hob Nail Special
            EP: Norgran EPN114
            LP: Norgran MGN1023, MGN1090, Verve MGV8178

[107] September 24, 1954   Hackensack, New Jersey
      J.J. Johnson Quintet   Studio performance

J.J. Johnson (tb), Wynton Kelly (p), Charles Mingus (b), Kenny
Clarke (d), Sabu Martinez (per).

            Too Marvelous for Words (take 2)
            LP: Blue Note BLP5057, BLP1505
            CD: Blue Note CDP7-81506-2

            Jay (take 4)
            45: Blue Note 45-1651
            LP: Blue Note BLP5057, BLP1505
            CD: Blue Note CDP7-81506-2

            Old Devil Moon (take 5)
            45: Blue Note 45-1651
            LP: Blue Note BLP5057, BLP1505
            CD: Blue Note CDP7-81506-2

Omit Sabu Martinez (per):

            It's You or No One (take 7)
            LP: Blue Note BLP5057, BLP1505
            CD: Blue Note CDP7-81506-2

            Time after Time (take 10)
            LP: Blue Note BLP5057, BLP1506
            CD: Blue Note CDP7-81506-2

Add Sabu Martinez (per):

            Coffee Pot (take 11)
            LP: Blue Note BLP5057, BLP1505
            CD: Blue Note CDP7-81506-2

[108] October 17, 1954   New York, New York
J.J. Johnson/Kai Winding Quintet   Birdland club date performance

J.J. Johnson, Kai Winding (tb), Dick Katz (p), Peck Morrison (b),
Al Harewood (d).

    F4JB-0666   Funnybone
                    LP: RCA "X" LXA1040, RCA PL42069, Camden CAL385
                    CD: RCA M11053

    F4JB-0667   Cornerstone
                    LP: RCA "X" LXA1040, RCA PL42069, Camden CAL385
                    CD: RCA M11053

    F4JB-0668   Bone of Contention
                    LP: RCA "X" LXA1040, RCA PL42069, Camden CAL385
                    CD: RCA M11053

    F4JB-0669   Lullaby of Birdland
                    LP: RCA "X" LXA1040, RCA PL42069, Camden CAL385
                    CD: RCA M11053

    F4JB-0670   Birdland Festival
                    LP: RCA "X" LXA1040, RCA PL42069, Camden CAL385
                    CD: RCA M11053

    F4JB-0671   Vista
                    LP: RCA "X" LXA1040, RCA PL42069, Camden CAL385
                    CD: RCA M11053

Note: LP discographical data were obtained from the RCA archive.

[109] December 3, 1954   New York, New York
J.J. Johnson/Kai Winding Quintet   Studio performance

J.J. Johnson, Kai Winding (tb), Dick Katz (p), Peck Morrison (b),
Al Harewood (d).

    651   Riviera
                    EP: Prestige EP1362
                    LP: Prestige LP195, LP7030, PR7253, P24067, LP16-4
                    CD: Prestige/Original Jazz Classics OJCCD-1727-2

    652   Dinner for One Please, James
                    EP: Prestige EP1362
                    LP: Prestige LP195, LP7030, PR7253, P24067, LP16-4
                    CD: Prestige/Original Jazz Classics OJCCD-1727-2

653   **Hip Bones**
- EP: Prestige EP1362
- LP: Prestige LP195, LP7030, PR7253, P24067, LP16-4
- CD: Prestige/Original Jazz Classics OJCCD-1727-2

654   **Wind Bag**
- EP: Prestige EP1362
- LP: Prestige LP195, LP7030, PR7253, P24067, LP16-4
- CD: Prestige/Original Jazz Classics OJCCD-1727-2

655   **We'll Be Together Again**
- EP: Prestige EP1368
- LP: Prestige LP195, LP7030, PR7253, P24067, LP16-4
- CD: Prestige/Original Jazz Classics OJCCD-1727-2

656   **Don't Argue**
- 78: Prestige 919
- EP: Prestige EP1368
- LP: Prestige LP195, LP7030, PR7253, P24067, LP16-4
- CD: Prestige/Original Jazz Classics OJCCD-1727-2

657   **How Long Has This Been Going On?**
- EP: Prestige EP1368
- LP: Moodsville (Prestige) MV33, Prestige LP195, LP7030, PR7253, P24067, LP16-4
- CD: Prestige/Original Jazz Classics OJCCD-1727-2

658   **Bags' Groove**
- 78: Prestige 919
- EP: Prestige EP1368
- LP: Prestige LP195, LP7030, PR7253, P24067, LP16-4
- CD: Prestige/Original Jazz Classics OJCCD-1727-2

[110] December 7, 1954   New York, New York
King Pleasure with Quincy Jones   Studio performance
and His Orchestra

King Pleasure (voc), Quincy Jones (arr, cond), Lucky Thompson (ts), Danny Bank (bs), J.J. Johnson, Kai Winding (tb), Jimmy Jones (p), Paul Chambers (b), Joe Harris (d), John Hendricks, Eddie Jefferson, The Three Riffs (voc).

659   **Don't Get Scared**
- 78: Prestige 913
- 45: Prestige 45-124
- LP: Prestige LP208. LP7128, PR7586, PR24017
- CD: Fantasy/Original Jazz Classics OJCCD 2531-217-2

660   I'm Gone
               78: Prestige 908
               LP: Prestige LP208, LP7128, PR7586, PR24017
               CD: Fantasy/Original Jazz Classics OJCCD 2531-217-2

661   You're Crying
               78: Prestige 908
               LP: Prestige PR7586, PR24017

662   Funk Junction
               78: Prestige 913
               LP: Prestige PR7586, PR24017

[111] January 26, 1955   New York, New York
       J.J. Johnson/Kai Winding Quintet   Studio performance

J.J. Johnson, Kai Winding (tb), Dick Katz (p), Wendell Marshall
(b), Al Harewood (d).

               Thou Swell
               45: Bethlehem 45-11031
               EP: Bethlehem BEP116
               LP: Bethlehem BCP13, BCP6065, BCP6001
               CD: Bethlehem 20-40062

               It's All Right with Me
               EP: Bethlehem BEP116
               LP: Bethlehem BCP13, BCP6001
               CD: Bethlehem 20-40062

               It's All Right with Me (alternate take 2)
               CD: Bethlehem 20-40062

               It's All Right with Me (alternate take 15)
               CD: Bethlehem 20-40062

               Lope City
               EP: Bethlehem BEP116
               LP: Bethlehem BCP13, BCP6001
               CD: Bethlehem 20-40062

               Lope City (alternate take 2)
               CD: Bethlehem 20-40062

[112] January 27, 1955   New York, New York
       J.J. Johnson/Kai Winding Quintet   Studio performance

J.J. Johnson, Kai Winding (tb), Dick Katz (p), Milt Hinton (b), Al Harewood (d).

Stolen Bass
45: Bethlehem 45–11030
EP: Bethlehem BEP116
LP: Bethlehem BCP13, BCP6001
CD: Bethlehem 20-40062

Out of This World
45: Bethlehem 45–11030
LP: Bethlehem BCP13, BCP6001
CD: Bethlehem 20-40062

Out of This World (alternate take 8)
CD: Bethlehem 20-40062

Gong Rock
45: Bethlehem 45–11031
EP: Bethlehem BEP115
LP: Bethlehem BCP13, BCP83, BCP6036, BCP6001
CD: Bethlehem 20-40062

Gong Rock (alternate take 1)
CD: Bethlehem 20-40062

Yes Sir! That's My Baby
EP: Bethlehem BEP115
LP: Bethlehem BCP13, BCP6001
CD: Bethlehem 20-40062

Mad about the Boy
EP: Bethlehem BEP115
LP: Bethlehem BCP13, BCP6001
CD: Bethlehem 20-40062

Lover
EP: Bethlehem BEP115
LP: Bethlehem BCP13, BCP6001
CD: Bethlehem 20-40062

Lover (alternate take 13)
CD: Bethlehem 20-40062

That's How I Feel about You
LP: Bethlehem BCP6001
CD: Bethlehem 20-40062

That's How I Feel about You (alternate take 7)
CD: Bethlehem 20-40062

[113] February 25, 1955   New York, New York
Quincy Jones and His All-Stars   Studio performance

Quincy Jones (arr, cond), Ernie Royal, Bernie Glow, Al Porcino, Jimmy Nottingham (tp), J.J. Johnson, Kai Winding, Urbie Green, Jimmy Cleveland (tb), Herbie Mann (fl), Dave Schildkraut (as), Sonny Stitt, Al Cohn (ts), Jack Nimitz (bs), Horace Silver (p), Oscar Pettiford (b), Osie Johnson, Art Blakey (d).

14S   Grasshopper
            LP: Columbia CL1970, CS8770

Note: Discographical data were obtained from the CBS archive.

[114] March 14, 1955   New York, New York
Modern Jazz Society   Studio performance

James Politis (fl), Tony Scott (cl), Manuel Zegler (bsn), Stan Getz (ts), Gunther Schuller (hn), J.J. Johnson (tb), Janet Putnam (hp), John Lewis (p), Percy Heath (b), Connie Kay (d).

            Queen's Fancy (rehearsal take)
            CD: Verve 314 559 827-2

5000-6   Queen's Fancy
            EP: Norgran EPN140
            LP: Norgran MGN1040, Verve MGV8131
            CD: Verve 314 559 827-2

5001-4   Midsömmer
            LP: Norgran MGN1040, Verve MGV8131
            CD: Verve 314 559 827-2

Omit Tony Scott (cl), Stan Getz (ts);
Add Aaron Sachs (cl), Lucky Thompson (ts):

5002   Sun Dance
            LP: Norgran MGN1040, Verve MGV8131
            CD: Verve 314 559 827-2

5003   Django
            LP: Norgran MGN1040, Verve MGV8131
            CD: Verve 314 559 827-2

5004   Little David's Fugue
EP: Norgran EPN 140
LP: Norgran MGN1040, Verve MGV8131
CD: Verve 314 559 827-2

Turnpike (rehearsal take)
CD: Verve 314 559 827-2

Note: Discographical data were obtained from the Verve Group archive. Francesco Fini, *The Jay Jay Johnson Complete Discography* incorrectly dates the recording of the titles "Sun Dance," "Django," and "Little David's Fugue" as March 15, 1955. The original title of the LP Norgran MGN1040 is *The Modern Jazz Society Presents a Concert of Contemporary Music*.

[115] March 29, 1955   New York, New York
Kenny Dorham Octet   Studio performance

Kenny Dorham (tp), J.J. Johnson (tb), Hank Mobley (ts), Cecil Payne (bs), Horace Silver (p), Oscar Pettiford (b), Art Blakey (d), Carlos Valdez (per).

Afrodisia
LP: Blue Note BLP5065, BLP1535
CD: Blue Note CDP-7-46815-2

Basheer's Dream
LP: Blue Note BLP5065, BLP1535
CD: Blue Note CDP-7-46815-2

Lotus Flower
LP: Blue Note BLP5065, BLP1535
CD: Blue Note CDP-7-46815-2

Minor's Holiday
LP: Blue Note BLP5065, BLP1535
CD: Blue Note CDP-7-46815-2

Minor's Holiday (alternate take)
CD: Blue Note CDP-7-46815-2

[116] April 1955   New York, New York
Chris Connor   Studio performance

Chris Connor (voc), Herbie Mann (fl, ts), J.J. Johnson, Kai Winding (tb), Ralph Sharon (p), Joe Puma (g), Milt Hinton (b), Osie Johnson (d).

From This Moment On
EP: Bethlehem BEP126
LP: Bethlehem BCP20, BCP56

The Thrill Is Gone
EP: Bethlehem BEP126
LP: Bethlehem BCP20, BCP6006

Someone to Watch over Me
EP: Bethlehem BEP129
LP: Bethlehem BCP20

I Concentrate on You
EP: Bethlehem BEP129
LP: Bethlehem BCP20

Don't Wait Up for Me
EP: Bethlehem BEP127
LP: Bethlehem BCP56

A Good Man Is a Seldom Thing
EP: Bethlehem BEP127
LP: Bethlehem BCP56

In Other Words
EP: Bethlehem BEP127
LP: Bethlehem BCP56

[117] June 6, 1955   New York, New York
       Jay Jay Johnson Quintet   Studio performance

J.J. Johnson (tb), Hank Mobley (ts), Horace Silver (p), Paul
Chambers (b), Kenny Clarke (d).

Pennies from Heaven (alternate take)
45:   Blue Note 45–1632
LP: Blue Note BLP5070, BLP1506
CD: Blue Note CDP7-81506-2

Pennies from Heaven
CD: Blue Note CDP7-81506-2

Viscosity
LP: Blue Note BLP5070, BLP1506
CD: Blue Note CDP7-81506-2

Viscosity (alternate take)
CD: Blue Note CDP7-81506-2

You're Mine You
LP: Blue Note BLP5070, BLP1506
CD: Blue Note CDP7-81506-2

"Daylie" Double
LP: Blue Note BLP5070, BLP1506
CD: Blue Note CDP7-81506-2

Groovin'
45: Blue Note 45–1632
LP: Blue Note BLP5070, BLP1506
CD: Blue Note CDP7-81506-2

Portrait of Jennie
LP: Blue Note BLP5070. BLP1506
CD: Blue Note CDP7-81506-2

"Daylie" Double (alternate take)
CD: Blue Note CDP7-81506-2

[118] June 23, 1955   New York, New York
J.J. Johnson/Kai Winding Quintet   Studio performance

J.J. Johnson, Kai Winding (tb), Dick Katz (p), Paul Chambers (b),
Osie Johnson (d).

C053493   Give Me the Simple Life
               LP: Columbia CL742

C053494   This Can't Be Love
               LP: Columbia CL742

C053495   Trombone for Two
               LP: Columbia CL742

C053496   We Two
               LP: Columbia CL742

C053497   Let's Get Away from It All
               LP: Columbia CL742, CL777

Note: Discographical data were obtained from the CBS archive.

[119] June 24, 1955   New York, New York
       J.J. Johnson/Kai Winding Quintet   Studio performance

J.J. Johnson, Kai Winding (tb), Dick Katz (p, cel), Paul Chambers
(b), Osie Johnson (d).

C053503	Turnabout
	LP: Columbia CL742

C053504	It's Sand, Man
	LP: Columbia CL742

C053505	Close As the Pages in a Book
	LP: Columbia CL742

C053506	The Whiffenpoof Song
	LP: Columbia CL742

C053507	Goodbye
	LP: Columbia CL742

Note: Discographical data were obtained from the CBS archive.

[120] July 29, 1955   New York, New York
       Julian "Cannonball" Adderley and His Orchestra   Studio performance

Julian Adderley (as), Jerome Richardson (ts, fl), Cecil Payne (bs),
Nat Adderley (cn), J.J. Johnson (tb), John Williams (p), Paul
Chambers (b), Kenny Clarke (d).

YB11961	Cannonball
	EP: EmArcy EP1-6144
	LP: EmArcy MG36043

YB11962	Nat's Everglade
	LP: EmArcy MG36043

YB11963	You'd Be So Nice to Come Home To
	LP: EmArcy MG36043

[121] July 1955   New York, New York
       Tony Aless and His Orchestra   Studio performance

Tony Aless (p), Dave Schildkraut (as), Seldon Powell, Pete
Mondello (ts), Nick Travis (tp), J.J. Johnson, Kai Winding (tb),
Billy Bauer (g), Arnold Fishkin (b), Don Lamond (d).

Valley Stream
LP: Roost RLP2202

Greenport
LP: Roost RLP2202

Fire Island
LP: Roost RLP2202

Massapeque
LP: Roost RLP2202

Note: Four additional titles from this session, "Levittown," "Corona," "Aqueduct,"
and "Riverhead," omit Johnson. The liner notes list Winding and Johnson as "Moe"
and "Joe."

[122]   August 5, 1955   New York, New York
   Julian "Cannonball" Adderley and His Orchestra   Studio performance

Julian Adderley (as), Jerome Richardson (ts, fl), Cecil Payne (bs), Nat
Adderley (cn), J.J. Johnson (tb), John Williams (p), Paul Chambers
(b), Max Roach (d).

YB11994   Willows
                 LP: EmArcy MG36043

YB11995   Fallen Feathers
                 LP: EmArcy MG36043

YB11996   Rose Room
                 LP: EmArcy MG36043

[123]   September 30, 1955   New York, New York
   Sonny Stitt with Quincy Jones and His Orchestra   Studio performance

Sonny Stitt (as, ts), Quincy Jones (arr, cond), Anthony Ortega (fl, as),
Seldon Powell (ts), Cecil Payne (bs), Jimmy Nottingham, Ernie Royal
(tp), J.J. Johnson (tb), Hank Jones (p), Freddie Green (g), Oscar
Pettiford (b), Jo Jones (d).

Come Rain or Come Shine
LP: Roost RLP2204

Love Walked In
LP: Roost RLP2204

If You Could See Me Now
LP: Roost RLP2204

Lover
LP: Roost RLP2204

[124] October 25, 1955   New York, New York
       Frankie Laine with Buck Clayton and His Orchestra   Studio performance

Frankie Laine (voc), Buck Clayton, Ray Copeland (tp), Lawrence
Brown, J.J. Johnson, Kai Winding (tb), Hilton Jefferson (as), Budd
Johnson, Nick Nicholas (ts), Dave McRae (bs), Sir Charles Thompson
(p), Clifton Best (g), Milt Hinton (b), Bobby Donaldson (d).

ZEP37278   Roses of Picardy
              LP: Columbia CL808, B8081

Substitute Al Lerner (p):

C057126-1   You'd Be So Nice to Come Home To (unissued)

Note: Discographical data were obtained from the CBS archive.

[125] October 25, 1955   New York, New York
       Sarah Vaughan with Ernie Wilkins and His Orchestra   Studio performance

Sarah Vaughan (voc), Ernie Wilkins (cond, arr), Ernie Royal, Bernie
Glow (tp), J.J. Johnson, Kai Winding (tb), Julian Adderley, Sam
Marowitz (as), Jerome Richardson (fl, ts), Jimmy Jones (p), Turk Van
Lake (g), Joe Benjamin (b), Roy Haynes (d).

YB12266   Sometimes I'm Happy
              LP: EmArcy MG36058,Mercury MG20133
              CD: Verve 31451-26454-2

YB12267   I'll Never Smile Again
              LP: EmArcy MG36058
              CD: Verve 31451-26454-2

YB12268   Don't Be on the Outside
              LP: EmArcy MG36058
              CD: Verve 31451-26454-2

YB12269   It Shouldn't Happen to a Dream
              LP: EmArcy MG36058, MG36086, Mercury 70086
              CD: Verve 31451-26454-2

[126] October 26, 1955   New York, New York
      Frankie Laine with Buck Clayton and His Orchestra   Studio performance

Frankie Laine (voc), Buck Clayton, Ray Copeland (tp), Urbie Green,
J.J. Johnson, Kai Winding (tb), Hilton Jefferson (as), Budd Johnson,
Nick Nicholas (ts), Dave McRae (bs), Al Lerner (p), Clifton Best (g),
Milt Hinton (b), Bobby Donaldson (d).

    ZEP37277   Takin' a Chance on Love
                LP: Columbia CL808, B8081

Note: Discographical data were obtained from the CBS archive.

[127] October 26, 1955   New York, New York
      Sarah Vaughan with Ernie Wilkins and His Orchestra   Studio performance

Same personnel as [125].

    YB12270   An Occasional Man
                LP: EmArcy MG36058
                CD: Verve 31451-26454-2

    YB12271   Soon
                LP: EmArcy MG36058
                CD: Verve 31451-26454-2

    YB12272   Cherokee
                LP: EmArcy MG36058
                CD: Verve 31451-26454-2

    YB12273   Maybe
                LP: EmArcy MG36058
                CD: Verve 31451-26454-2

[128] October 27, 1955   New York, New York
      Sarah Vaughan with Ernie Wilkins and His Orchestra   Studio performance

Same personnel as [125].

    YB12278   Why Can't I?
                LP: EmArcy MG36058
                CD: Verve 31451-26454-2

    YB12279   How High the Moon
                LP: EmArcy MG36058
                CD: Verve 31451-26454-2

YB12280 Over the Rainbow
LP: EmArcy MG36058, MG36086, Mercury 70086
CD: Verve 31451-26454-2

YB12281 Oh My!
LP: EmArcy MG36058
CD: Verve 31451-26454-2

[129] November 17, 1955   New York, New York
J.J. Johnson/Kai Winding Quintet   Studio performance

J.J. Johnson, Kai Winding (tb), Dick Katz (p), Milt Hinton (b), Shadow Wilson (d).

C057126-2 You'd Be So Nice to Come Home To
LP: Columbia CL973, CL2573

Add Candido Camero (per):

C057127 Caribe
LP: Columbia CL973, CL2573

Omit Candido Camero (per):

C057128 Happiness Is a Thing Called Joe
LP: Columbia CL973, CL2573

C057129 The Song Is You
LP: Columbia CL973, CL2573

C057130 In the Wee Small Hours of the Morning
LP: Columbia CL973, CL2573

Note: Discographical data were obtained from the CBS archive.

[130] February 1956   New York, New York
Gene Krupa and His Orchestra   Studio performance

Gene Krupa (d), Roy Eldridge, Ernie Royal, Bernie Glow, Joe Ferrante, Nick Travis (tp), Jimmy Cleveland, J.J. Johnson, Kai Winding, Fred Ohms (tb), Sam Marowitz (as), Hal McKusick (as, cl), Aaron Sachs (ts, cl), Eddie Shu (ts), Danny Bank (bs), Dave McKenna (p), Barry Galbraith (g), John Drew (b), Anita O'Day (voc).

Let Me Off Uptown
LP: Verve MGV2008, MGV8087, 10008, MGV8571
CD: Verve 827-843-2

Opus 1
LP: Verve MGV2008, MGV8087, MGV8207
CD: Verve 827-843-2

Drummin' Man
LP: Verve MGV2008, MGV8087
CD: Verve 827-843-2

Boogie Blues
LP: Verve MGV2008, MGV8087
CD: Verve 827-843-2

Slow Down
LP: Verve MGV2008, MGV8087
CD: Verve 827-843-2

That's What You Think
LP: Verve MGV2008, MGV8087, MGV8207
CD: Verve 827-843-2

Omit Anita O'Day (voc):

Rockin' Chair
LP: Verve MGV2008, MGV8087
CD: Verve 827-843-2

Leave Us Leap
LP: Verve MGV2008, MGV8087
CD: Verve 827-843-2

Wire Brush Stomp
LP: Verve MGV2008, MGV8087
CD: Verve 827-843-2

After You've Gone
LP: Verve MGV2008, MGV8087
CD: Verve 827-843-2

Fish Fry
LP: Verve MGV2008, MGV8087
CD: Verve 827-843-2

Drum Boogie
LP: Verve MGV2008, MGV8087
CD: Verve 827-843-2

Note: Roy Eldridge also sings on "Let Me Off Uptown."

[131] March 21, 1956   New York, New York
      Johnny Mathis and His Orchestra   Studio performance

Johnny Mathis (voc), Gil Evans (arr, cond), John LaPorta (as),
George Barrow (bs), Jimmie Maxwell, Buck Clayton (tp),
J.J.Johnson (tb), Thomas Mitchell (bt), Hank Jones (p), Bill
Pemberton (b), Billy Exiner (d).

C055650   Love, Your Magic Spell Is Everywhere
             LP: Columbia CL887
             CD: Columbia CK64890

C055651   It Might As Well Be Spring
             LP: Columbia CL887
             CD: Columbia CK64890

C055652   Easy to Love
             LP: Columbia CL887
             CD: Columbia CK64890

C055653   Spring Is Everywhere (unissued)

Note: Discographical data were obtained from the CBS archive.

[132] April 2, 1956   New York, New York
      J.J. Johnson/Kai Winding: Jay & Kai + 6   Studio performance

J.J. Johnson, Kai Winding, Eddie Bert, Urbie Green, Jimmy
Cleveland, Bob Alexander (tb), Bart Varsalone, Tom Mitchell (bt),
Hank Jones (p), Milt Hinton (b), Osie Johnson (d).

C055723   No Moon at All
             LP: Columbia CL892
             CD: Collectables Records 1421-5677-2

C055724   You're My Thrill
             LP: Columbia CL892
             CD: Collectables Records 1421-5677-2

C055725   Jeanne
             LP: Columbia CL892
             CD: Collectables Records 1421-5677-2

C055726-1   The Surrey with the Fringe on Top (unissued)

Note: LP discographical data were obtained from the CBS archive.

[133] April 3, 1956   New York, New York
     J.J. Johnson/Kai Winding Quintet   Basin Street Club
                                                   Audience tape

J.J. Johnson, Kai Winding (tb), remainder of personnel unknown but may be Ray Bowle (p), Al Cobb (d), Al Harewood (d).

        Give Me That Simple Life
        Close As the Pages in a Book
        Yes Sir! That's My Baby
        Theme

[134] April 4, 1956   New York, New York
     J.J. Johnson/Kai Winding: Jay & Kai + 6   Studio performance

Same personnel as [132].

    C055736   You Don't Know What Love Is
                     LP: Columbia CL892
                     CD: Collectables Records 1421-5677-2

    C055737-1   The Continental (unissued)

    C055738   Piece for Two Tromboniums
                     LP: Columbia CL892
                     CD: Collectables Records 1421-5677-2

    C055739-1   Rise 'N' Shine (unissued)

Note: LP discographical data were obtained from the CBS archive.

[135] April 5, 1956   New York, New York
     J.J. Johnson/Kai Winding: Jay & Kai + 6   Studio performance

J.J. Johnson, Kai Winding, Eddie Bert, Urbie Green, Jimmy Cleveland, Bob Alexander (tb), Bart Varsalona, Tom Mitchell (bt), Hank Jones (p), Ray Brown (b), Osie Johnson (d), Candido Camero (per).

    C055739-2   Rise 'N' Shine
                     LP: Columbia CL892
                     CD: Collectables Records 1421-5677-2

Note: LP discographical data were obtained from the CBS archive.

[136] April 6, 1956   New York, New York
      J.J. Johnson/Kai Winding: Jay & Kai + 6   Studio performance

Same personnel as [132].

C055737-2   The Continental
              LP: Columbia CL892
              CD: Collectables Records 1421-5677-2

C055726-2   The Surrey with the Fringe on Top
              LP: Columbia CL892
              CD: Collectables Records 1421-5677-2

Omit Milt Hinton (b); add Ray Brown (b), Candido Camero (per):

C055754   Night in Tunisia
              LP: Columbia CL892
              CD: Collectables Records 1421-5677-2

C055755   All At Once You Love Her
              LP: Columbia CL892
              CD: Collectables Records 1421-5677-2

C055756   The Peanut Vendor
              LP: Columbia CL892
              CD: Collectables Records 1421-5677-2

C055757   Four Plus Four
              LP: Columbia CL892
              CD: Collectables Records 1421-5677-2

Note: LP discographical data were obtained from the CBS archive.

[137] July 4, 1956   New York, New York
      J.J. Johnson/Kai Winding Quintet with Sonny Stitt   Basin Street Club
                                                         Audience tape

J.J. Johnson, Kai Winding (tb), Sonny Stitt (ts), remainder of
personnel unknown but may be Ray Bowle (p), Al Cobb (d), Al
Harewood (d).

              Thou Swell
              Happiness Is a Thing Called Joe
              Blues for 'Bones
              Theme

[138] July 6, 1956   Newport, Rhode Island
Buck Clayton's All-Stars   Newport Jazz Festival
                                  Concert performance

Buck Clayton (tp), J.J. Johnson (tb), Coleman Hawkins (ts), Dick Katz (p), Benny Moten (b), Gus Johnson (d).

C056793   You Can Depend on Me
                  LP: Columbia CL933

C056794   In a Mellotone
                  LP: Columbia CL933

C056795   Newport Jump
                  LP: Columbia CL933

Note: Discographical data were obtained from the CBS archive.

[139] July 6, 1956   Newport, Rhode Island
J.J. Johnson/Kai Winding Quintet   Newport Jazz Festival
                                  Concert performance

J.J. Johnson, Kai Winding (tb), Dick Katz (p), Bill Crow (b), Rudy Collins (d).

C056796   Lover Come Back to Me
                  LP: Columbia CL932

C056797   True Blue Tromboniums
                  LP: Columbia CL932

C056798   NWPT (Newport)
                  LP: Columbia CL932

Note: These titles appear on side 2 of the LP, *Dave Brubeck and Jay & Kai at Newport.* Discographical data were obtained from the CBS archive.

[140] July 13, 1956   New York, New York
J.J. Johnson/Kai Winding Quintet   Studio performance

J.J. Johnson, Kai Winding (tb), Dick Katz (p), Bill Brown (b), Kenny Clarke (d).

C056493   Too Close for Comfort
                  LP: Columbia CL973

C056494   'S Wonderful
               LP: Columbia CL973

C056495   Tromboniums in Motion
               LP: Columbia CL973

C056496   How High the Moon
               LP: Columbia CL973

C056497   Violets for Your Furs
               LP: Columbia CL973

Note: Discographical data were obtained from the CBS archive.

[141] July 24, 1956   New York, New York
      J.J. Johnson Quintet   Studio performance

J.J. Johnson (tb), Bobby Jaspar (ts,fl), Hank Jones (p), Percy Heath
(b), Elvin Jones (d).

C056830-1   I Should Care
               LP: Mosaic MQ11-169
               CD: Mosaic MD7-169

C056831   Overdrive
               LP: Columbia CL935, Mosaic MQ11-169
               CD: Mosaic MD7-169

C056832   Undecided
               LP: Columbia CL935, Mosaic MQ11-169
               CD: Mosaic MD7-169

C056833-1   Joey Joey Joey
               LP: Mosaic MQ11-169
               CD: Mosaic MD7-169

C056834   Angel Eyes
               LP: Columbia CL935, Mosaic MQ11-169
               CD: Mosaic MD7-169

Note: Columbia LP discographical data were obtained from the CBS archive.

[142] July 25, 1956   New York, New York
      J.J. Johnson Quintet   Studio performance

J.J. Johnson (tb), Bobby Jaspar (ts), Hank Jones (p), Wilbur Little
(b), Elvin Jones (d).

C056835 Tumbling Tumbleweeds
     LP: Columbia CL935, Mosaic MQ11-169
     CD: Mosaic MD7-169

C056836 Cube Steak
     LP: Columbia CL935, Mosaic MQ11-169
     CD: Mosaic MD7-169

C056837 Never Let Me Go
     LP: Columbia CL935, Mosaic MQ11-169
     CD: Mosaic MD7-169

C056838 Solar
     LP: Columbia CL935, Mosaic MQ11-169
     CD: Mosaic MD7-169

Note: Columbia LP discographical data were obtained from the CBS archive.

[143] July 27, 1956   New York, New York
J.J. Johnson Quintet   Studio performance

J.J. Johnson (tb), Bobby Jaspar (ts), Tommy Flanagan (p), Wilbur
Little (b), Elvin Jones (d).

C056315 Chasing the Bird
     LP: Columbia CL935, Mosaic MQ11-169
     CD: Mosaic MD7-169

C056316 Naptown, U.S.A.
     LP: Columbia CL935, Mosaic MQ11-169
     CD: Mosaic MD7-169

C056317 It Might As Well Be Spring
     LP: Columbia CL935, Mosaic MQ11-169
     CD: Mosaic MD7-169

Note: Columbia LP discographical data were obtained from the CBS archive.

[144] October 20, 1956   New York, New York
The Jazz and Classical Music Society Brass Ensemble Studio performance

Gunther Schuller (cond), Miles Davis, Bernie Glow, Arthur Statter,
Joe Wilder, John Ware, Melvin Broiles, Carmine Fornarotto (tp),
Arthur Sussman, Ray Alonge, James Buffington, Joseph Singer (hn),
J.J. Johnson, Urbie Green, John Clark (tb), Ronald Richetts, John

Swallow (bh), John Barber (tu), Richard Horowitz (per), John Lewis (p), Milt Hinton (b), Osie Johnson (d).

> ### Three Little Feelings (John Lewis, comp)
> LP: Columbia CL941
> CD: Columbia/Legacy 7464-64929-2

Note: LP discographical data were obtained from the CBS archive. The matrix number for this title was unavailable.

[145] October 23, 1956   New York, New York
       The Jazz and Classical Music Society Brass Ensemble   Studio performance

Same personnel as [144].

> ### Poem for Brass (J.J. Johnson, comp)
> LP: Columbia CL941
> CD: Columbia/Legacy 7464-64929-2

Omit Richard Horowitz (per), Miles Davis (tp);

> ### Pharaoh (Jimmy Giuffre, comp)
> LP: Columbia CL941
> CD: Columbia/Legacy 7464-64929-2

Note: LP discographical data were obtained from the CBS archive. The matrix numbers for these titles were unavailable.

[146] January 26, 1957   Pensauken, New Jersey
       J.J. Johnson Quintet   Red Hill Inn

Personnel probably same as [143].

> ### It's All Right with Me
> ### Undecided
> ### Jay's Original (Thad's Been Wess)

Note: All titles issued on the LP, Queen Disc Q-046, which incorrectly lists Thad Jones's "Thad's Been Wess" as "Jay's Original."

[147] January 27, 1957   New York, New York
       J.J. Johnson Quintet   Studio performance

Same personnel as [143].

C056830-2   I Should Care
              LP: Columbia CL973, Mosaic MQ11-169
              CD: Mosaic MD7-169

Note: Columbia LP discographical data were obtained from the CBS archive.
Francesco Fini, *The Jay Jay Johnson Complete Discography*, 21, incorrectly dates
this session as July 24, 1956. Jorgen Grunnet Jepsen, *Jazz Records,* vol. 4C, 173,
incorrectly places the title "I Should Care" on a January 31, 1957, session.

[148] January 29, 1957   New York, New York
      J.J. Johnson Quintet   Studio performance

      Same personnel as [143].

      C057273   Bird Song
                  LP: Columbia CL1084, Mosaic MQ11-169
                  CD: Sony XJAK-027130, Mosaic MD7-169

      C057274   It Could Happen to You
                  LP: Columbia CL1084, Mosaic MQ11-169
                  CD: Sony XJAK-027130, Mosaic MD7-169

      C057275   Our Love Is Here to Stay
                  LP: Columbia CL1084, Mosaic MQ11-169
                  CD: Sony XJAK-027130, Mosaic MD7-169

      C057276   Blue Haze
                  LP: Columbia CL1084, Mosaic MQ11-169
                  CD: Sony XJAK-027130, Mosaic MD7-169

Note: The title "It Could Happen to You" is a feature for flutist Bobby Jaspar;
Johnson is heard only in the closing bars of the tune playing long tones. Columbia
LP discographical data were obtained from the CBS archive.

[149] January 31, 1957   New York, New York
      J.J. Johnson Quintet   Studio performance

      Same personnel as [143].

      C057277   Barbados
                  LP: Columbia CL1084, Mosaic MQ11-169
                  CD: Sony XJAK-027130, Mosaic MD7-169

      C057278   In a Little Provincial Town
                  LP: Columbia CL1084, Mosaic MQ11-169
                  CD: Sony XJAK-027130, Mosaic MD7-169

C057279   Cette Chose
                 LP: Columbia CL1084, Mosaic MQ11-169
                 CD: Sony XJAK-027130, Mosaic MD7-169

C056833-2   Joey Joey Joey
                 LP: Playboy 1529/30, Mosaic MQ11-169
                 CD: Sony XJAK-027130, Mosaic MD7-169

Note: Columbia LP discographical data were obtained from the CBS archive.

[150] February 2, 1957   New York, New York
      J.J. Johnson Quintet   Cafe Bohemia

Personnel probably same as [143].

                 Overdrive
                 Angel Eyes
                 Bags' Groove

Note: All titles issued on the LP, Queen Disc Q-046.

[151] February 1957   New York, New York
      J.J. Johnson Quintet   Cafe Bohemia

Personnel probably same as [143].

                 Bernie's Tune
                 In a Little Provincial Town
                 I Should Care
                 Angel Eyes
                 Old Devil Moon
                 "Daylie" Double
                 Solar

Note: All titles issued on the compact disc Fresh Sound FSR CD-143

[152] March 12–15, 1957   New York, New York
      Coleman Hawkins All-Stars   Studio performance

Coleman Hawkins (ts), Idrees Sulieman (tp), J.J. Johnson (tb), Hank
Jones (p), Barry Galbraith (g), Oscar Pettiford (b), Jo Jones (d).

                 Chant
                 LP: Riverside RLP12-233
                 CD: Riverside/Original Jazz Classics OJCCD-027-2

Juicy Fruit
LP: Riverside RLP12-233
CD: Riverside/Original Jazz Classics OJCCD-027-2

Think Deep
LP: Riverside RLP12-233, RLP12-284
CD: Riverside/Original Jazz Classics OJCCD-027-2

Laura
LP: Riverside RLP12-233, RLP12-284
CD: Riverside/Original Jazz Classics OJCCD-027-2

Blue Lights
LP: Riverside RLP12-233
CD: Riverside/Original Jazz Classics OJCCD-027-2

Sancticity
LP: Riverside RLP12-233
CD: Riverside/Original Jazz Classics OJCCD-027-2

[153] April 11, 1957   New York, New York
J.J. Johnson Quartet   Studio performance

J.J. Johnson (tb), Tommy Flanagan (p), Paul Chambers (b), Max
Roach (d).

C057801   I've Got You Under My Skin
               LP: Columbia CL1020, Mosaic MQ11-169
               CD: Mosaic MD7-169

C057802   Harvey's House
               LP: Columbia CL1030, Mosaic MQ11-169
               CD: Mosaic MD7-169

C057803   Nickles and Dimes
               LP: Columbia CL1030, Mosaic MQ11-169
               CD: Mosaic MD7-169

C057804   That Tired Routine Called Love
               LP: Columbia CL1030, Mosaic MQ11-169
               CD: Mosaic MD7-169

C057805   For Heaven's Sake
               LP: Columbia CL1030, Mosaic MQ11-169
               CD: Mosaic MD7-169

C057806   Paul's Pal
                 LP: Columbia CL1030, Mosaic MQ11-169
                 CD: Mosaic MD7-169

Note: Columbia LP discographical data were obtained from the CBS archive.

[154] April 12, 1957   New York, New York
      J.J. Johnson Quartet   Studio performance

Same personnel as [148].

C057807-4   It's Only a Paper Moon
                 LP: Columbia CL1030, Mosaic MQ11-169
                 CD: Mosaic MD7-169

C057808-1   Out of My Dreams
                 LP: Mosaic MQ11-169
                 CD: Mosaic MD7-169

C057809-1   Commutation
                 LP: Columbia CL1030, Mosaic MQ11-169
                 CD: Mosaic MD7-169

C057810-2   God Bless' the Child
                 LP: Mosaic MQ11-169
                 CD: Mosaic MD7-169

C057811-5   Be My Love
                 LP: Columbia CL1030, Mosaic MQ11-169
                 CD: Mosaic MD7-169

Note: Columbia LP discographical data were obtained from the CBS archive.

[155] April 14, 1957   New York, New York
      Sonny Rollins Quintet   Studio performance

Sonny Rollins (ts), J.J. Johnson (tb), Horace Silver (p), Paul
Chambers (b), Art Blakey (d).

                 Why Don't I?
                 45: Blue Note 45-1687
                 LP: Blue Note BLP1558
                 CD: Blue Note 72437-81558-1, 72437-93203-2, 72437-21371-2

                 Wail March
                 LP: Blue Note BLP1558
                 CD: Blue Note 72437-81558-1, 72437-21371-2

You Stepped out of a Dream
45: Blue Note 45-1687
LP: Blue Note BLP1558
CD: Blue Note 72437-81558-1, 72437-21371-2

Poor Butterfly
LP: Blue Note BLP1558
CD: Blue Note 72437-81558-1, 72437-93203-2, 72437-21371-2

Omit Horace Silver (p); add Thelonious Monk (p):

Misterioso
LP: Blue Note BLP1558
CD: Blue Note 72437-81558-1, 72437-93203-2, 72437-21371-2

Note: An additional title, "Reflections," omits Johnson and Silver and adds Thelonious Monk (p).

[156] April 26, 1957   New York, New York
J.J. Johnson Quartet   Studio performance

Same personnel as [153].

C057724-1   Cry Me a River
             LP: Columbia CL1030, Mosaic MQ11-169
             CD: Columbia CK44443, Mosaic MD7-169

C057725-4   Hello, Young Lovers
             LP: Columbia CL1303, CS8009, Sony XJAK027131,
                 Mosaic MQ11-169
             CD: Mosaic MD7-169

C057726-5   100 Proof
             LP: Columbia CL1303, CS8009, Mosaic MQ11-169
             CD: Sony XJAK027131, Mosaic MD7-169

C057727-2   What's New?
             LP: Columbia CL1303, CS8009, Mosaic MQ11-169
             CD: Columbia CK44443, Sony XJAK027131, Mosaic MD7-169

Note: Columbia LP discographical data were obtained from the CBS archive.

[157] May 3, 1957   New York, New York
J.J. Johnson Quartet   Studio performance

Same personnel as [153].

C057909   Kev
               LP: Columbia CL1303, CS8009, Mosaic MQ11-169
               CD: Sony XJAK027131

C057910   Gone with the Wind
               LP: Columbia CL1303, CS8009, Mosaic MQ11-169
               CD: Sony XJAK027131

C057911-1   Blue Trombone (part 1)
               LP: Columbia CL1303, CS8009, Mosaic MQ11-169
               CD: Columbia CK44443, Sony XJAK027131, Mosaic MD7-169

C057911-2   Blue Trombone (part 2)
               LP: Columbia CL1303, CS8009, Mosaic MQ11-169
               CD: Columbia CK44443, Sony XJAK027131, Mosaic MD7-169

Note: "Blue Trombone" was issued in two parts on sides A and B of CL1303 and CS8009 because the tape ran out during the bass solo causing the break in the tune. The Mosaic LP and CD reissues contain "Blue Trombone" as one uninterrupted track. Columbia LP discographical data were obtained from the CBS archive.

[158] May 14, 1957   New York, New York
      J.J. Johnson Quintet   Studio performance

Same personnel as [143].

C057944-1   Come Rain or Come Shine
               LP: Mosaic MQ11-169
               CD: Mosaic MD7-169

C057945-6   Teapot
               LP: Columbia CL1084, Mosaic MQ11-169
               CD: Sony XJAK-027130, Mosaic MD7-169

C057947-3   Old Devil Moon
               LP: Columbia CL1084, Mosaic MQ11-169
               CD: Sony XJAK-027130, Mosaic MD7-169

Note: An additional title, "So Sorry Please," matrix number C057946-2, is a feature for the rhythm section and omits Johnson and Jaspar. Columbia LP discographical data were obtained from the CBS archive.

[159] September 29, 1957   Chicago, Illinois
      Stan Getz/J.J. Johnson Sextet   Civic Opera House
                                                       Concert performance

Stan Getz (ts), J.J. Johnson (tb), Oscar Peterson (p), Herb Ellis (g), Ray Brown (b), Connie Kay (d).

Billie's Bounce
LP: Verve MGVS6027, MGV6-8450
CD: Verve 831272-2

My Funny Valentine
LP: Verve MGVS6027, MGV6-8450
CD: Verve 831272-2

Crazy Rhythm
LP: Verve MGVS6027, MGV6-8450
CD: Verve 831272-2

Blues in the Closet
LP: Verve MGVS6027, MGV6-8450
CD: Verve 831272-2

Note: The liner notes to the compact disc reissue of these titles, *Stan Getz and J.J. Johnson at the Opera House* (Verve 831-272-2), by jazz historian Phil Schaap corrects the date and location of this concert recording as listed in the Jepsen, Bruyninckx, and Fini discographies.

[160] October 7, 1957   Los Angeles, California
       Stan Getz/J.J. Johnson Sextet   Shrine Auditorium
                                                             Concert performance

Stan Getz (ts), J.J. Johnson (tb), Oscar Peterson (p), Herb Ellis (g), Ray Brown (b), Connie Kay (d).

Billie's Bounce
LP: Verve MGV8265
CD: Verve 831272-2

My Funny Valentine
LP: Verve MGV8265
CD: Verve 831272-2

Crazy Rhythm
LP: Verve MGV8265
CD: Verve 831272-2

Omit Stan Getz (ts):

Yesterdays
LP: Verve MGV8265
CD: Verve 831272-2

Add Stan Getz (ts):

> Blues in the Closet
> LP: Verve MGV8265
> CD: Verve 831272-2

Note: An additional title, "It Never Entered My Mind," omits Johnson. See also the note
to [159].

[161] October 19, 1957   Chicago, Illinois
       Jazz at the Philharmonic All-Stars   Civic Opera House
                                                           Concert performance

Stan Getz, Coleman Hawkins (ts), Roy Eldridge (tp), J.J. Johnson
(tb), John Lewis (p), Percy Heath (b), Connie Kay (d).

> Stuffy
> LP: Verve MGV8267, MGV6-8489, MGVS-6029

[162] October 25, 1957   Los Angeles, California
       Ella Fitzgerald with the   Philharmonic Hall
       Jazz at the Philharmonic All-Stars   Concert performance

Ella Fitzgerald (voc), Roy Eldridge (tp), Sonny Stitt (as), Lester
Young, Illinois Jacquet, Coleman Hawkins, Stan Getz, Flip Phillips
(ts), J.J. Johnson (tb), Oscar Peterson (p), Herb Ellis (g), Ray Brown
(b), Connie Kay (d).

> Stompin' at the Savoy
> LP: Verve 89187, MGV8264
> CD: Verve 31451-31269-2

> Lady Be Good
> LP: Verve 89187, MGV8264
> CD: Verve 31451-31269-2

Note: Francesco Fini, *The Jay Jay Johnson Complete Discography*, 23, incorrectly places
this concert at the Opera House in Chicago.

[163] December 19, 1957   New York, New York
       Benny Golson Sextet   Studio performance

Benny Golson (ts), Kenny Dorham (tp), J.J. Johnson (tb), Wynton
Kelly (p), Paul Chambers (b), Charlie Persip (d).

Hymn to the Orient
LP: Riverside RLP12-256, RLP12-284
CD: Riverside OJCCD-1797-2

Blues on Down
LP: Riverside RLP12-256, RLP12-284
CD: Riverside OJCCD-1797-2

Namely You
LP: Riverside RLP12-256, RLP12-284
CD: Riverside OJCCD-1797-2

[164] December 23, 1957   New York, New York
Benny Golson Sextet   Studio performance

Same personnel as [163].

Reunion
LP: Riverside RLP12-256, RS1124
CD: Riverside OJCCD-1797-2

Venetian Breeze
LP: Riverside RLP12-256
CD: Riverside OJCCD-1797-2

Out of the Past
LP: Riverside RLP12-256, RS1124, RLP3505
CD: Riverside OJCCD-1797-2

[165] Early 1958   Washington, D.C.
J.J. Johnson Quintet   Spotlite Club

J.J. Johnson (tb), Nat Adderley (cn), Tommy Flanagan (p), Wilbur
Little (b), Albert Heath (d).

Decision
Overdrive

Note: Both titles issued on the LP Queen Disc Q-046.

[166] February 19, 1958   New York, New York
J.J. Johnson Quintet   Studio performance

Same personnel as [165].

Tune Up
LP: Columbia CL1161, CS8009, Mosaic MQ11-169
CD: Mosaic MD7-169

Laura
LP: Columbia CL1161, CS8009, Mosaic MQ11-169
CD: Columbia CK44443, Mosaic MD7-169

Walkin'
LP: Columbia CL1161, CS8009, Mosaic MQ11-169
CD: Mosaic MD7-169

What Is This Thing Called Love?
LP: Columbia CL1161, CS8009, Mosaic MQ11-169
CD: Columbia CK44443, Mosaic MD7-169

Misterioso
LP: Columbia CL1161, CS8009, Mosaic MQ11-169
CD: Columbia CK44443, Mosaic MD7-169

My Old Flame
LP: Columbia CL1161, CS8009, Mosaic MQ11-169
CD: Columbia CK44443, Mosaic MD7-169

Now's the Time
LP: Columbia CL1161, CS8009, Mosaic MQ11-169
CD: Mosaic MD7-169

Note:　Columbia LP discographical data were obtained from the CBS archive. Charles Edward Smith's liner notes for the Columbia LP *J.J.! In Person* states that the titles are "recordings of an actual concert" although its location is never mentioned. On the contrary, the album was actually a studio performance with Johnson's introductions and "canned" audience noise and applause dubbed in. The Mosaic LP and CD reissues omit the dubbed effects.

[167] February 20, 1958　　　　　　　　　　　　　New York, New York
　　　Billie Holiday with Ray Ellis and His Orchestra　　　Studio performance

Billie Holiday (voc), Ray Ellis (cond), George Ochner, Milt Lomask, Leo Kruczek, Max Cahn, Harry Katzman, Samuel Rand, David Sarcer, Harry Hoffman, Felix Giglio, David Newman (vn), Sid Brecher, David Dickler (va), David Soyer, Maurice Brown (vc), Janet Putnam (hp), Urbie Green, J.J. Johnson, Tom Mitchell (tb), Ed Powell, Tom Pashley, Romeo Penque, Phil Bodner (reeds), Mal Waldron (p), Barry Galbraith (g), Milt Hinton (b), Don Lamond (d), Bradley Spinney (per), unknown vocal ensemble.

C060467-1   I Get Along without You Very Well
              LP: Columbia CL1157, CS8048
              CD: Columbia CK40247

C060468-1   Glad to Be Unhappy
              LP: Columbia CL1157, CS8048
              CD: Columbia CK40247

C060469-1   You've Changed
              LP: Columbia CL1157, CS8048
              CD: Columbia CK40247

C060470-21   The End of a Love Affair
              CD: Columbia CK40247

C060471-1   Violets for Your Furs
              LP: Columbia CL1157, CS8048
              CD: Columbia CK40247

Note: LP discographical data were obtained from the CBS archive. The original stereo LP, CS8048, omitted the title, "The End of a Love Affair" due to technical and musical difficulties that warranted only a monaural version of the tune to be recorded. The track that appears on the CD reissue is a digitally edited version that combines an unmixed music track and a vocal tape of Holiday and the rhythm section.

[168] May 26, 1958   New York, New York
     J.J. Johnson Quintet   Studio performance

Same personnel as [165].

C061161-5   Darling, je vous aime beaucoup
              LP: Mosaic MQ11-169
              CD: Mosaic MD7-169

C061162-2   Almost Like Being in Love
              LP: Mosaic MQ11-169
              CD: Mosaic MD7-169

C061163-3   Love Letters
              LP: Mosaic MQ11-169
              CD: Mosaic MD7-169

C061164-2   Decision
              LP: Mosaic MQ11-169
              CD: Mosaic MD7-169

Note: Discographical data obtained from the CBS archive indicates that these titles were originally unissued.

[169] August 29, 1958   New York, New York
       J.J. Johnson Quintet   Studio performance

Same personnel as [165].

   C061444-2   Stardust
                LP: Mosaic MQ11-169
                CD: Mosaic MD7-169

   C061445-2   Sidewinder
                LP: Mosaic MQ11-169
                CD: Mosaic MD7-169

   C061446-1   Bags' Groove
                LP: Columbia FC38509, Mosaic MQ11-169
                CD: Mosaic MD7-169

   C061447-2   Pennies from Heaven
                LP: Mosaic MQ11-169
                CD: Mosaic MD7-169

   C061448-3   Alone Together
                LP: Mosaic MQ11-169
                CD: Mosaic MD7-169

Note: Columbia LP discographical data were obtained from the CBS archive.

[170] September 29, 1958   Location unknown
       Lee Konitz All-Stars   European concert performance
                                                               Audience tape

Lee Konitz (as), Zoot Sims (ts), J.J.Johnson, Kai Winding (tb), Red
Garland (p), Oscar Pettiford (b), Kenny Clarke (d).

                Our Delight
                Yardbird Suite

Note: Both titles issued on the LP Unique UJ25, *The All Stars Live European Concert.*

[171] December 26, 29, 31, 1958   New York, New York
       The Trombones, Incorporated   Studio performance

J.J. Johnson (comp, arr), Frank Rehak, Jimmy Cleveland, Eddie Bert,
Benny Powell, Bob Brookmeyer, Melba Liston, Henry Coker, Bennie
Green (tb), Dick Hixson, Bart Varsalona (bt), Hank Jones (p), Wendell
Marshall (b), Osie Johnson (d).

Neckbones (J.J. Johnson, comp)

Omit Henry Coker (tb), Wendell Marshall (b); add Bob Alexander (tb), Milt Hinton (b):

Dues Blues (J.J. Johnson, comp)
Soft Winds

Omit Bennie Green, Bob Alexander (tb), Milt Hinton (b); add Henry Coker (tb), Wendell Marshall (b):

Long Before I Knew You
Tee Jay (J.J. Johnson, comp)

[172] March 18, 1959   New York, New York
J.J. Johnson Sextet   Studio performance

J.J. Johnson (tb), Nat Adderley (cn), Bobby Jaspar (ts,fl), Cedar Walton (p), James DeBrest (b), Albert Heath (d).

C062425-6   Me Too
               LP: Columbia CL1383, CS8178, CL1610, CS8410, Mosaic MQ11-169
               CD: Mosaic MD7-169

C062426-3   Alone Together
               LP: Mosaic MQ11-169
               CD: Mosaic MD7-169

C062427-5   Speak Low
               LP: Columbia CL1383, CS8178, Mosaic MQ11-169
               CD: Mosaic MD7-169

Note: The Mosaic reissue of this session incorrectly lists the title "Me Too" as "Really Livin'," the title of the original LP issue. Columbia LP discographical data were obtained from the CBS archive.

[173] March 19, 1959   New York, New York
J.J. Johnson Sextet   Studio performance

Same personnel as [172].

C062433   Decision
               LP: Columbia CL1383, CS8178, Mosaic MQ11-169
               CD: Mosaic MD7-169

C062434   Sidewinder
           LP: Mosaic MQ11-169
           CD: Mosaic MD7-169

C062435   God Bless' the Child
           LP: Columbia CL1383, CS8178, Mosaic MQ11-169
           CD: Mosaic MD7-169

Note: An additional title, "Red Cross," matrix number C062436-5, is a feature for piano and rhythm section, omitting Johnson, Adderley, and Jaspar. Columbia LP discographical data were obtained from the CBS archive.

[174] March 24, 1959   New York, New York
       J.J. Johnson Sextet   Studio performance

Same personnel as [172].

C062437-7   Nearness of You
           LP: Mosaic MQ11-169
           CD: Mosaic MD7-169

C062438-6   Almost Like Being in Love
           LP: Columbia CL1383, CS8178, Mosaic MQ11-169
           CD: Mosaic MD7-169

Omit Bobby Jaspar (ts) and Nat Adderley (cn):

C062439-3   Stardust
           LP: Columbia CL1383, CS8178, Mosaic MQ11-169
           CD: Mosaic MD7-169

Add Nat Adderley (cn):

C062442-5   I Got It Bad
           LP: Columbia CL1383, CS8178, Mosaic MQ11-169
           CD: Mosaic MD7-169

Add Bobby Jaspar (ts):

C062434-11   Sidewinder
           LP: Columbia CL1383, CS8178, Mosaic MQ11-169
           CD: Mosaic MD7-169

Note: Columbia LP discographical data were obtained from the CBS archive.

[175] May 19, 1959   New York, New York
     One World Jazz   Multiple studio performances

Roy East (as), Ben Webster (ts), Clark Terry (tp), J.J. Johnson, George Chisholm (tb), Hank Jones (p), Kenny Burrell (g), George Duvivier (b), Jo Jones (d), Stephane Grappelli (vn):

C063351   Misty
                 LP: Columbia WL162, WS314

Roy East (as), Ben Webster, Bob Garcia (ts), Clark Terry, Roger Guerin (tp), J.J. Johnson, George Chisholm (tb), Hank Jones, Martial Solal (p), Kenny Burrell (g), George Duvivier (b), Jo Jones (d), Stephane Grappelli (vn):

C063352   International Blues
                 LP: Columbia WL162, WS314

Roy East (as), Ben Webster, Bob Garcia (ts), Clark Terry, Roger Guerin (tp), J.J. Johnson, George Chisholm (tb), Hank Jones (p), Kenny Burrell (g), George Duvivier (b), Jo Jones (d):

C063353   Cotton Tail
                 LP: Columbia WL162, WS314

Ben Webster (ts), Clark Terry (tp), J.J. Johnson (tb), Hank Jones (p), Kenny Burrell (g), George Duvivier (b), Jo Jones (d), Stephane Grappelli (vn):

C063354   Nuages
                 LP: Columbia WL162, WS314

Roy East (as), Ben Webster (ts), Ronnie Ross (bs), Clark Terry (tp), J.J. Johnson, George Chisholm, Ake Persson (tb), Hank Jones (p), Kenny Burrell (g), George Duvivier (b), Jo Jones (d):

C063355   In a Mellotone
                 LP: Columbia WL162, WS314

Roy East (as), Ben Webster (ts), Ronnie Ross (bs), Clark Terry (tp), J.J. Johnson, George Chisholm (tb), Hank Jones, Martial Solal (p), Kenny Burrell (g), George Duvivier (b), Jo Jones (d):

C063356   Big Ben Blues
                 LP: Columbia WL162, WS314

Note: Discographical data were obtained from the CBS archive. The original New York studio master tape contained tracks of all titles recorded by Ben Webster, Clark Terry, J.J. Johnson, Hank Jones, Kenny Burrell, George Duvivier, and Jo Jones. Additional tracks were dubbed onto the master recording by musicians in London (Roy East, George Chisholm, Ronnie Ross) on June 22, 1959, Stockholm (Ake Persson) on June 30, 1959, and Paris (Roger Guerin, Bob Garcia, Stephane Grappelli, Martial Solal) on July 3, 1959.

[176] June 23, 1960   New York, New York
       J.J. Johnson: Trombone and Voices   Studio performance

J.J. Johnson (tb), Frank DeVol (arr,cond), Hank Jones (p), Wendell Marshall (b), Charlie Persip (d), unknown vocal sextet.

    C054964   Lazy Bones
                 LP: Columbia CL1547, CS8347

    C054965   Sometimes I Feel Like a Motherless Child
                 LP: Columbia CL1547, CS8347

    C054966   Jennie's Song
                 LP: Columbia CL1547, CS8347

    Note: Discographical data were obtained from the CBS archive.

[177] June 24, 1960   New York, New York
       J.J. Johnson: Trombone and Voices   Studio performance

J.J. Johnson (tb), Frank DeVol (arr,cond), Hank Jones (p), Wendell Marshall (b), Osie Johnson (d), unknown vocal sextet.

    C054971   I'm Glad There Is You
                 LP: Columbia CL1547, CS8347

    C054972   Get Out of Town
                 LP: Columbia CL1547, CS8347, 4-42071

    C054973   You're My Girl
                 LP: Columbia CL1547, CS8347, 4-42071

    Note: Discographical data were obtained from the CBS archive.

[178] June 28, 1960   New York, New York
       J.J. Johnson: Trombone and Voices   Studio performance

Same personnel as [176].

C054990   What Is There to Say
               LP: Columbia CL1547, CS8347

C054991   Hymn (unissued)

C054992   To the Ends of the Earth
               LP: Columbia CL1547, CS8347

C054993   In a Sentimental Mood
               LP: Columbia CL1547, CS8347

C054994   Only the Lonely
               LP: Columbia CL1547, CS8347

Note: Discographical data were obtained from the CBS archive.

[179] August 1, 1960   New York, New York
       J.J. Johnson Sextet   Studio performance

J.J. Johnson (tb), Freddie Hubbard (tp), Clifford Jordan (ts), Cedar
Walton (p), Arthur Harper (b), Albert Heath (d).

C065102-L4   Mohawk (long version)
               LP: Columbia CL1606, CS8406, Mosaic MQ11-169
               CD: Columbia CK65296, Mosaic MD7-169

C065103-3   Shutterbug
               LP: Columbia CL1606, CS8406, Mosaic MQ11-169
               CD: Columbia CK65296, Mosaic MD7-169

C065104-L2   Aquarius (long version)
               LP: Mosaic MQ11-169
               CD: Mosaic MD7-169

C065105-2   Blue 'N' Boogie
               CD: Columbia CK65296, Mosaic MD7-169

Note: Columbia LP discographical data were obtained from the CBS archive.

[180] August 3, 1960   New York, New York
       J.J. Johnson Sextet   Studio performance

Same personnel as [179].

C065116-L4   Fatback (long version)
              LP: Columbia CL1970, CS8770, BPG62141, Mosaic MQ11-169
              CD: Columbia CK65296, Mosaic MD7-169

C065116-S2   Fatback (short version)
              LP: Columbia CL 1606, CS8406, Mosaic MQ11-169
              CD: Columbia CK65296, Mosaic MD7-169

C065117-3   In Walked Horace
              LP: Columbia CL1606, CS8406, Mosaic MQ11-169
              CD: Columbia CK65296, Mosaic MD7-169

C065118-3   Minor Mist
              LP: Columbia CL1606, CS8406, Mosaic MQ11-169
              CD: Columbia CK65296, Mosaic MD7-169

C055119-1   Turnpike
              CD: Columbia CK65296, Mosaic MD7-169

C065102-S2   Mohawk (short version)
              LP: Mosaic MQ11-169
              CD: Mosaic MD7-169

C065104-S6   Aquarius (short version)
              LP: Columbia CL1606, CS8406, Mosaic MQ11-169
              CD: Columbia CK65296, Mosaic MD7-169

Note: The piano introduction was edited out of the short version of "Fatback"
issued on CS8406 (*J.J., Inc.*). The long version issued on CS8770 (*The Giants of
Jazz*) is shortened by nearly four minutes. The Mosaic LP and CD reissues present the
unedited short version (6:35) and long version (11:42) intact. Columbia LP
discographical data were obtained from the CBS archive.

[181] September 1, 1960   Lenox, Massachusetts
      Lenox School of Jazz Benefit Concert   Berkshire Music Barn
                                                              Audience tape

J.J. Johnson (cond), Don Ellis (tp), J. R. Monterose (ts), Vera Auer
(v), Harold McKinney (p), Sue Freeman (b), Earl Zindars (d).

                    Another Blues
                    Short Bridge
                    Homeless
                    Ballade (J.J. Johnson, comp)
                    Number 8 (J.J. Johnson, comp)

John Garvey (cond), J.J. Johnson (tb), Peter Brown, Melissa Brown (cl), Peggy Andrix, Derry Deane, Alan Grishman (vn), John Garvey, George Andrix (va), John Lewis (p), Bill Takas (b), Earl Zindars (d).

Champagne Blues

J.J. Johnson (tb), Alan Grishman, Peggy Andrix, Derry Deane (vn), John Garvey, George Andrix (va), Peter Brown, Melissa Brown (cl), Bill Takas (b), Earl Zindars (d), Gary McFarland (comp).

Piece for Strings

[182] October 3, 1960 New York, New York
J.J. Johnson/Kai Winding Quintet Studio performance

J.J. Johnson, Kai Winding (tb), Bill Evans (p), Paul Chambers (b), Roy Haynes (d).

This Could Be the Start of Something
LP: Impulse 201, A-lS
CD: Impulse MCAD-42012

Note: LP discographical data were obtained from the MCA Records, Inc. archive.

[183] November 2, 1960 New York, New York
J.J. Johnson/Kai Winding Quintet Studio performance

Same personnel as [182].

I Concentrate on You
LP: Impulse 201, A-lS
CD: Impulse MCAD-42012

Blue Monk
LP: Impulse 201, A-lS
CD: Impulse MCAD-42012

Side by Side
LP: Impulse 201, A-lS
CD: Impulse MCAD-42012

Note: LP discographical data were obtained from the MCA Records, Inc. archive.

[184] November 4, 1960   New York, New York
    J.J. Johnson/Kai Winding Quintet   Studio performance

J.J. Johnson, Kai Winding (tb), Bill Evans (p), Tommy Williams
(b), Art Taylor (d).

        Alone Together
        LP: Impulse A-lS
        CD: Impulse MCAD-42012

        Theme from "Picnic"
        LP: Impulse A-lS
        CD: Impulse MCAD-42012

        Going, Going, Gong!
        LP: Impulse A-lS
        CD: Impulse MCAD-42012

        Just for a Thrill
        LP: Impulse A-lS
        CD: Impulse MCAD-42012

Note: LP discographical data were obtained from the MCA Records, Inc. archive.

[185] November 9, 1960   New York, New York
    J.J. Johnson/Kai Winding Quintet

Same personnel as [184].

        Judy
        LP: Impulse A-lS
        CD: Impulse MCAD-42012

        Georgia on My Mind
        LP: Impulse A-lS
        CD: Impulse MCAD-42012

        Trixie
        LP: Impulse A-lS
        CD: Impulse MCAD-42012

Note: LP discographical data were obtained from the MCA Records, Inc. archive.

[186] November 21, 1960   Stockholm, Sweden
    Jazz at the Philharmonic   Konserthuset
                                                         Concert performance

Benny Carter, Julian Adderley (as), Dizzy Gillespie (tp), J.J.
Johnson (tb), Lalo Schifrin (p), Art Davis (b), Chuck Lampkin (d).

> Bernie's Tune
> LP: Verve MGV6-8539, 2V6S-8823

> Swedish Jam
> LP: Verve MGV6-8539, 2V6S-8823

Leo Wright (as), Stan Getz (ts), Dizzy Gillespie (tp), J.J. Johnson
(tb), Lalo Schifrin (p), Art Davis (b), Chuck Lampkin (d), Candido
Camero (d).

> Kush
> LP: Verve MGV6-8542

> The Mooch
> LP: Verve MGV6-8542

> Wheatleigh Hall
> LP: Verve MGV6-8542

Stan Getz (ts), Dizzy Gillespie (tp), J.J. Johnson (tb), Vic Feldman
(p, v), Sam Jones (b), Louis Hayes (d).

> Bop 'N' Boogie
> LP: Verve MGV6-8540

Stan Getz (ts), J.J. Johnson (tb), Vic Feldman (p, v), Sam Jones (b),
Louis Hayes (d).

> Yesterdays
> LP: Verve MGV6-8540

> Sweet Georgia Brown
> LP: Verve MGV6-8540

> I Waited for You
> LP: Verve MGV6-8540

> Trotting
> LP: Verve MGV6-8540

Note: Jorgen Grunnet Jepsen, *Jazz Records 1942–1962/69,* incorrectly dates the
concert on November 22, 1960. Morroe Berger, Edward Berger, and James Patrick,
Benny Carter: A Life in American Music, vol. 2, discography reference number
[269],182, indicates that Carter's passport shows that he left Sweden on November
21; also, a concert poster reproduced on the cover of Verve MGV6-8541 shows the
date as November 21.

[187] December 14, 1960   New York, New York
      J.J. Johnson Quartet: A Touch of Satin   Studio performance

J.J. Johnson (tb), Vic Feldman (p, cel, o), Sam Jones (b), Louis Hayes (d).

C065714-2   Satin Doll
             LP: Columbia CL1737, CS8537, Mosaic MQ11-169
             CD: Columbia CK44443, Mosaic MD7-169

C065715-3   Flat Black
             LP: Columbia CL1737, CS8537, Mosaic MQ11-169
             CD: Mosaic MD7-169

C065716-8   Gigi
             LP: Columbia CL1737, CS8537, Mosaic MQ11-169
             CD: Mosaic MD7-169

C065717-2   Bloozineff
             LP: Columbia CL1737, CS8537, Mosaic MQ11-169
             CD: Mosaic MD7-169

C065717-3   Bloozineff (alternate version)
             LP: Columbia CS8565, Mosaic MQ11-169
             CD: Mosaic MD7-169

Note: The Mosaic LP and CD reissues incorrectly list the title "Flat Black" as
"Flat Rock." On the title "Gigi," Vic Feldman plays celesta; on the alternate version
of the title, "Bloozineff," matrix number C065717-3, he plays organ instead of
piano. Columbia LP discographical data were obtained from the CBS archive.

[188] December 21, 1960   New York, New York
      J.J. Johnson Quartet   Studio performance

J.J. Johnson (tb), Vic Feldman (p, v), Sam Jones (b), Louis Hayes (d).

C065745-5   Goodbye
             LP: Columbia CL1737, CS8537, Mosaic MQ11-169
             CD: Columbia CK44443, Mosaic MD7-169

C065746-2   When the Saints Go Marching In
             LP: Columbia CL1737, CS8537, Mosaic MQ11-169
             CD: Mosaic MD7-169

C065747-4   I Waited for You
             LP: Mosaic MQ11-169
             CD: Mosaic MD7-169

C065867-8   How Long Has This Been Going On?
LP: Mosaic MQ11-169
CD: Mosaic MD7-169

Note: Vic Feldman plays vibraphone on the titles "Goodbye" and "How Long Has This Been Going On" and piano on the remaining titles. Columbia LP discographical data were obtained from the CBS archive.

[189] January 12, 1961   New York, New York
J.J. Johnson Quartet   Studio performance

J.J. Johnson (tb), Vic Feldman (p), Sam Jones (b), Louis Hayes (d).

C065798-2   Jackie-ing
LP: Columbia CL1737, CS8537, Mosaic MQ11-169
CD: Mosaic MD7-169

C065799-3   Sophisticated Lady
LP: Columbia CL1737, CS8537, Mosaic MQ11-169
CD: Mosaic MD7-169

C065345-12   Full Moon and Empty Arms
LP: Columbia CL1737, CS8537, Mosaic MQ11-169
CD: Mosaic MD7-169

Note: Columbia LP discographical data were obtained from the CBS archive.

[190] May 18 & 22, 1961   Englewood Cliffs, New Jersey
Dizzy Gillespie: Perceptions   Van Gelder Recording Studio
                                                                       Studio performance

J.J. Johnson (comp, arr), Dizzy Gillespie (tp), Gunther Schuller (cond), Bernie Glow, Robert Nagel, Ernie Royal, Doc Severinsen, Nick Travis, Joe Wilder (tp), Urbie Green, Jimmy Knepper (tb), Paul Faulise, Dick Hixson (bt), John Barrows, James Buffington, Paul Ingraham, Robert Northern (hn), Harvey Phillips, Bill Stanley (tu), Gloria Agostini, Laura Newell (hp), George Duvivier (b), Charlie Persip (d), Michael Colgrass (per).

61VK261   The Sword Of Orion
61VK262   Jubelo
61VK263   Blue Mist
61VK264   Fantasia
61VK265   Horn of Plenty

61VK266   Ballade

Note: All tracks issued on Verve LP V6-8411, and reissued on Verve CD 314-537-748-2.

[191] December 1961   New York, New York
      André Previn Quartet   Studio performance

André Previn (p), J.J. Johnson (tb), Red Mitchell (b), Frank Capp (d).

>   Bilbao Song
>   LP: Columbia CL1741, CS8541
>   CD: Columbia/Legacy CK57637

>   Barbara Song
>   LP: Columbia CL1741, CS8541

>   Overture
>   LP: Columbia CL1741, CS8541

>   Seeräuber Jenny
>   LP: Columbia CL1741, CS8541

>   Mack the Knife
>   LP: Columbia CL1741, CS8541
>   CD: Columbia/Legacy CK57637

>   Surabaya-Johnny
>   LP: Columbia CL1741, CS8541

>   Wie man sich bettet
>   LP: Columbia CL1741, CS8541

>   Unzulänglichkeit
>   LP: Columbia CL1741, CS8541

Note: LP discographical data were obtained from the CBS archive.

[192] July 27, 1962   New York, New York
      Miles Davis with Gil Evans and His Orchestra: Studio performance
      Quiet Nights

Miles Davis (tp), Gil Evans (arr, cond), Steve Lacy (ss), Jerome
Richardson, Al Block (fl), Ray Beckenstein (fl, reeds), Bob Triscario
(bsn), Garvin Bushell (bsn, cbsn), Ernie Royal, Bernie Glow, Louis
Mucci, Harold "Shorty" Baker (tp), J.J. Johnson, Frank Rehak (tb),

Julius Watkins, Ray Alonge, Don Corrado (hn), Bill Barber (tu), Janet Putnam (hp), Paul Chambers (b), Jimmy Cobb (d), William Correa (Willie Bobo) bongos, Elvin Jones (per).

Aos Pes Da Cruz
LP: Columbia CL2106, CS8906, CBS/Sony SONP-50163, Mosaic MQ11-164
CD: CBS/Sony SRCS-5703, SRCS-9318, Columbia CK65293, CXK-67397

Corcovado
LP: Columbia CL2106, CS8906, CBS/Sony SONP-50163, Mosaic MQ11-164
CD: CBS/Sony SRCS-5703, SRCS-9318, Columbia CK65293, CXK-67397

Note: Columbia LP discographical data were obtained from the CBS archive.

[193] August 13, 1962   New York, New York
Miles Davis with Gil Evans and His Orchestra: Studio performance
Quiet Nights

Same personnel as [192].

Song #1
LP: Columbia CL2106, CS8906, CBS/Sony SONP-50163, Mosaic MQ11-164
CD: CBS/Sony SRCS-5703, SRCS-9318, Columbia CK65293, CXK-67397

Wait Till You See Her
LP: Columbia CL2106, CS8906, CBS/Sony SONP-50163, Mosaic MQ11-164
CD: CBS/Sony SRCS-5703, SRCS-9318, Columbia CK65293, CXK-67397

Note: Columbia LP discographical data were obtained from the CBS archive.

[194] November 6, 1962   New York, New York
Miles Davis with Gil Evans and His Orchestra: Studio performance
Quiet Nights

Same personnel as [192].

Song #2
LP: Columbia CL2106, CS8906, CBS/Sony SONP-50163,
     Mosaic MQ11-164
CD: CBS/Sony SRCS-5703, SRCS-9318, Columbia CK65293,
     CXK-67397

Once Upon a Summertime
LP: Columbia CL2106, CS8906, CBS/Sony SONP-50163,
     Mosaic MQ11-164
CD: CBS/Sony SRCS-5703, SRCS-9318, Columbia CK65293,
     CXK-67397

Note: Columbia LP discographical data were obtained from the CBS archive.

[195] March 12, 1963   New York, New York
      J.J. Johnson: J.J.'s Broadway   Studio performance

J.J. Johnson, Urbie Green, Lou McGarity, Tom Mitchell, Paul
Faulise (tb), Hank Jones (p), Chuck Israels (b), Walter Perkins (d).

63VK313   Nobody's Heart
            LP: Verve MGV6-8530

63VK314   Who Will Buy?
            LP: Verve MGV6-8530

Omit Hank Jones (p):

63VK315   Lovely
            LP: Verve MGV6-8530

63VK316   Mira
            LP: Verve MGV6-8530

63VK317   The Sweetest Sounds
            LP: Verve MGV6-8530

63VK318   Small World (unissued)

63VK319   Sleeping Bee
            LP: Verve MGV6-8530

[196] April 6, 1963   New York, New York
      J.J. Johnson: J.J.'s Broadway   Studio performance

J.J. Johnson (tb), Hank Jones (p), Richard Davis (b), Walter Perkins (d).

63VK358   Put on a Happy Face
               LP: Verve MGV6-8530

63VK359   Make Someone Happy
               LP: Verve MGV6-8530

63VK360   My Favorite Things
               LP: Verve MGV6-8530, MGV6-8579

63VK361   A Second Chance
               LP: Verve MGV6-8530

[197] August 15, 1963   Montreal, Quebec, Canada
      J.J. Johnson Quartet   Loew's Theater
                                             Montreal Jazz Festival radio broadcast

J.J. Johnson (tb), Bobby Timmons (p), Arthur Harper (b), Frank
Gant (d).

               Neo
               ET: Canadian Broadcasting Corporation (CBC) RM-101

               Misterioso
               ET: CBC RM-101

               Jackie-ing
               ET: CBC RM-101

Note: The "RM" designation stands for "relais musique"—radio broadcast
transcriptions selected from live programs of the Canadian Broadcasting
Corporation (CBC) network and distributed to radio stations abroad. The
transcriptions were intended to be played once and then returned to the CBC or
destroyed.

[198] August 1963   Vancouver, B.C., Canada
      J.J. Johnson with the Chris Gage Trio   Vancouver Jazz Festival
                                                                   Radio broadcast

J.J. Johnson (tb), Chris Gage (p), Paul Ruhland (b), Al Johnson (d).

               It's Almost Like Being in Love
               ET: CBC RM-111

               Autumn Leaves
               ET: CBC RM-111

Sometimes I Feel Like A Motherless Child
ET: CBC RM-111

It's Only a Paper Moon
ET: CBC RM-111

[199] May 1, 1964   New York, New York
       J.J. Johnson Quartet: Proof Positive   Studio performance

J.J. Johnson (tb), Harold Mabern (p), Arthur Harper (b), Frank
Gant (d).

Neo
LP: Impulse A-68, AS-68
CD: Impulse GRD-145

Stella by Starlight
LP: Impulse A-68, AS-68
CD: Impulse GRD-145

Minor Blues
LP: Impulse A-68, AS-68
CD: Impulse GRD-145

My Funny Valentine
LP: Impulse A-68, AS-68
CD: Impulse GRD-145

Blues Waltz
LP: Impulse A-68, AS-68
CD: Impulse GRD-145

Gloria
LP: Impulse AS-100
CD: Impulse GRD-145

[200] 1964   New York, New York
       J.J. Johnson Quintet   Studio performance

J.J. Johnson (tb), McCoy Tyner (p), Toots Thielemans (g, h),
Richard Davis (b), Elvin Jones (d).

Lullaby of Jazzland
LP: Impulse A-68, AS-68

Across the Karoo
LP: Impulse 227

Theme from "Lilies of the Field"
LP: Impulse 227

Note: The master tapes and pressings of "Across the Karoo" and "Theme from 'Lilies of the Field'" are missing from the MCA Records, Inc., archive and may have been lost or destroyed.

[201] June 10–11, 1964   Englewood Cliffs, New Jersey
Lalo Schifrin and His Orchestra   Studio performance

Lalo Schifrin (p, arr, cond), Jerome Richardson (ts, fl), Marky Markowitz, Ernie Royal, Clark Terry, Snooky Young (tp), Jimmy Cleveland, Kai Winding, J.J. Johnson, Urbie Green (tb), Tony Studd (bt), Bob Northern, Ray Alonge, Richard Berg, Earl Chapin (hn), Don Butterfield (tu), Mundell Lowe (g), George Duvivier (b), Grady Tate (d).

6VK400	Prelude No. 2
6VK401	Slaughter on Tenth Avenue
6VK402	Sabre Dance
6VK403	El Salon Mexico
6VK404	Bachianas Brasileiras No. 5
6VK405	The Blues
6VK406	The Peanut Vendor
6VK407	New Fantasy

Note: All titles issued on the LP Verve V/V6-8601.

[202] July 4, 1964   Newport, Rhode Island
Tribute to Charlie Parker   Newport Jazz Festival
                                                          Concert performance

Sonny Stitt (ts), Howard McGhee (tp), J.J. Johnson (tb), Harold Mabern (p), Arthur Harper (b), Max Roach (d).

UPAS3862   Buzzy
LP: RCA LPM3783

UPAS3863   Now's the Time
LP: RCA LPM3783

UPAS3864   Wee
LP: RCA LPM3873

Note: Reverend Norman O'Connor is the narrator for this performance.
Discographical data were obtained from the RCA archive.

[203] August 21, 1964   New York, New York
      J.J. Johnson and His Orchestra   Studio performance

J.J. Johnson (tb), Stan Applebaum (arr, cond), Ernie Royal (tp), Ray
Beckenstein (reeds), William Slapin (bs), Wayne Andre, Tom
Mitchell (tb), Richard Hyman (o), George Duvivier (b), Don
Arnone, Arthur Ryerson (eg), Bucky Pizzarelli (eb), Sol Gubin (d),
Arthur Marotti (per), Gene Orloff, Leo Kruczek, Harry Lookofsky,
Roaul Poliakin, Harry Zarief, Paul Winter, Harry Katzman (vn),
Joseph Tekula, Peter Makas, Edgardo Sodero (vc).

RPA16291-5   Nancy's Theme (unissued)

RPA16292-4   Bim-Bom (unissued)

RPA16293-5   Seven Days to Tahiti (unissued)

RPA16294-5   The Shark (unissued)

Note: These titles were to have been issued as pop singles. Discographical data
were obtained from the RCA archive.

[204] October 18, 1964   London, England
      J.J. Johnson All-Stars: Tribute to Charlie Parker   Television broadcast
                                                 British Broadcasting Corporation

J.J. Johnson (tb), Howard McGhee (tp), Sonny Stitt (as), Walter
Bishop (p), Tommy Potter (b), Kenny Clarke (d).

          Buzzy

Omit J.J. Johnson (tb), Howard McGhee (tp):

          Lover Man

Add J.J. Johnson (tb), Howard McGhee (tp):

          Now's the Time

Ornithology

Note: This session was broadcast by the BBC on a program entitled *Jazz 625.*

[205] November 17–18, 1964   Englewood Cliffs, New Jersey
Donald Byrd: Brass with Voices   Studio performance

Donald Byrd (tp, fg), Stanley Turrentine (ts), Herbie Hancock (p), Freddie Roach (o), Grant Green (g), Bob Cranshaw (b), Grady Tate (d), Ernie Royal, Snooky Young, Jimmy Owens, Clark Terry, Joe Ferrante (tp), J.J. Johnson, Jimmy Cleveland, Henry Coker, Benny Powell (tb), James Buffington, Bob Northern (hn), Don Butterfield (tu), unidentified vocal octet, Coleridge Perkinson (cond).

> Brother Isaac
> Noah
> I'm Tryin' to Get Home
> I've Longed and Searched for My Mother
> March Children
> Pearly Gates

Note: All titles issued on Blue Note LP, BST84188.

[206] December 7, 1964   New York, New York
J.J. Johnson and His Orchestra   Studio performance

J.J. Johnson (tb), Clark Terry (tp, fg), Ernie Royal (tp), Jerry Dodgion (as, fl), Oliver Nelson (as, ts), Jerome Richardson (ts, bs, fl), Jimmy Cleveland (tb), Tony Studd (bt), Hank Jones (p), Bob Cranshaw (b), Grady Tate (d).

RPA16874-11   My Little Suede Shoes
              LP: RCA LPM3350, LSP3350
              CD: RCA/Bluebird 6277-2-RB, RCA M11504

RPA16875-8   Stratusphunk
              LP: RCA LPM3350, LSP3350
              CD: RCA/Bluebird 6277-2-RB, RCA M11504

RPA16876-14   So What
              LP: RCA LPM3350, LSP3350
              CD: RCA/Bluebird 6277-2-RB, RCA M11504

RPA16877-2   Bemsha Swing
                  LP: RCA LPM3350, LSP3350
                  CD: RCA/Bluebird 6277-2-RB, RCA M11504

Note: LP discographical data were obtained from the RCA archive.

[207] December 8, 1964   New York, New York
      J.J. Johnson and His Orchestra   Studio performance

J.J. Johnson (tb), Ernie Royal, Thad Jones (tp, fg), Jerry Dodgion (as,
fl, af), Oliver Nelson (as, ts), Ray Beckenstein (bs, fl, bc), Jimmy
Cleveland (tb), Tony Studd (bt), Hank Jones (p), Bob Cranshaw (b),
Grady Tate (d).

RPA16878-1   Stolen Moments
                  LP: RCA LPM3350, LSP3350
                  CD: RCA/Bluebird 6277-2-RB, RCA M11504

RPA16879-12   Swing Spring
                  LP: RCA LPM3350, LSP3350
                  CD: RCA/Bluebird 6277-2-RB, RCA M11504

RPA16880-7   Supplication (unissued)

RPA16881-4   Ally (unissued)

Note: LP discographical data were obtained from the RCA archive.

[208] December 9, 1964   New York, New York
      J.J. Johnson and His Orchestra   Studio performance

J.J. Johnson (tb), James Maxwell, Joe Wilder (tp), Thad Jones, Ernie
Royal (tp, fg), William Stanley (tu), Jerry Dodgion (as, fl, af),
Harvey Estrin (ss, as, fl, af, cl), Oliver Nelson (as, ts, cl), Hank Jones
(p), Bob Cranshaw (b), Grady Tate (d).

RPA16882-7   Train Samba
             LP: RCA LPM3350, LSP3350
             CD: RCA M11504

RPA16883-1   Winter's Waif
             LP: RCA LPM3350, LSP3350
             CD: RCA M11504

RPA16884-3   El Camino Real
    LP: RCA LPM3350, LSP3350
    CD: Bluebird 6277-2-RB, RCA M11504

Note: LP discographical data were obtained from the RCA archive.

[209] December 20, 1964   New York, New York
Quincy Jones and His Orchestra   Studio performance

Quincy Jones (arr, cond), Dizzy Gillespie, Nat Adderley, Freddie Hubbard, Jimmy Maxwell, Jimmy Nottingham, Joe Newman (tp), Jerry Dodgion, Phil Woods (as), James Moody (fl, as ts), Rahsaan Roland Kirk, Benny Golson, Lucky Thompson (ts), Pepper Adams (bs), J.J. Johnson, Curtis Fuller, Kai Winding, Melba Liston (tb), Milt Jackson (v), Bobby Scott (p), Bob Cranshaw (b), Art Blakey (d), Billy Byers, Benny Golson (arr).

34247   I Had a Ball
               LP: Limelight LM86002
               CD: Mercury 846630-2, BMG/Razor & Tie 7999-82088-2

34248   Almost
               LP: Limelight LM82002

34249   Addie's At It Again
               LP: Limelight LM82002
               CD: Mercury 846630-2

[210] February 16, 1965   New York, New York
Elvin Jones Septet: And Then Again   Studio performance

Elvin Jones (d), Hunt Peters [J.J. Johnson] (tb), Frank Wess (ts, fl), Charles Davis (bs), Don Friedman (p), Paul Chambers (b), Melba Liston (arr, cond).

8631   Azan
8632   Len Sirrah
8633   Soon After

Note: This session is attributed by some discographers to J.J. Johnson on the basis of aural evidence although the name "Hunt Peters" appears on the album liner notes. All titles issued on the LP Atlantic LP1443.

[211] February 20, 1965   New York, New York
       Quincy Jones and His Orchestra   Studio performance
                                                   Film soundtrack, *The Pawnbroker*

Quincy Jones (comp, arr), Freddie Hubbard (tp), J.J. Johnson (tb), Anthony Ortega (ss), Jerry Dodgion (as), Oliver Nelson (as, ts), Don Elliot (v), Bobby Scott (p), Kenny Burrell (g), Tommy Williams (b), Elvin Jones (d), Ed Shaughnessy (per), Billy Byers, Dick Hazard (arr), Marc Allen (voc), remainder of personnel unknown.

35105   Theme from *The Pawnbroker*

Omit Marc Allen (voc):

35106   Main Title
35107   Harlem Drive
35108   The Naked Truth
35109   Otez's Night Off
35110   Theme from *The Pawnbroker* (instrumental version)
35111   How Come You People
35112   Rack 'Em Up
35113   Death Scene
35114   End Title

Note: Actor Rod Steiger and an unknown narrator dub a voiceover on the title, "How Come You People." All titles issued on LP (Mercury MG21011, SR61011) and CD (Verve 314-531-233-2).

[212] March 18, 1965   New York, New York
       Elvin Jones Septet: And Then Again   Studio performance

Elvin Jones (d), Hunt Peters [J.J. Johnson] (tb), Thad Jones (cn), Charles Davis (bs), Hank Jones (p), Art Davis (b).

               Elvin Elpus
               All Feliberate Speed
               Forever Summer

Note: See the note to [210].

[213] March 27, 1965   New York, New York
       Elvin Jones Septet: And Then Again   Carnegie Hall
                                                            Concert performance

Roy Eldridge (tp), Coleman Hawkins (ts), C.C. Siegel (bt) [J.J. Johnson (tb)], Billy Taylor (p), Tommy Potter (b), Roy Haynes (d).

Now's the Time

Kenny Dorham, Dizzy Gillespie, Howard McGhee (tp), Lee Konitz (as), C.C. Siegel (bt) [J.J. Johnson (tb)], Billy Taylor (p), Tommy Potter (b), Roy Haynes (d).

Bird Watcher/Disorder at the Border

Note: This session is attributed by some discographers to J.J. Johnson on the basis of aural and photographic evidence (liner photo) although the name "C.C. Siegel" appears on the album liner notes. All titles issued on the CD Limelight 826-985-2.

[214] April 14, 1965   Englewood Cliffs, New Jersey
Stanley Turrentine with Oliver Nelson   Van Gelder Studios
and His Orchestra   Studio performance

Oliver Nelson (arr, cond), Stanley Turrentine (ts), Ernie Royal, Snooky Young (tp), Clark Terry (tp, fg), J.J. Johnson, Jimmy Cleveland, Henry Coker (tb), Phil Woods, Jerry Dodgion, Budd Johnson, Robert Ashton, Danny Bank (reeds), Herbie Hancock (p), Kenny Burrell (g), Bob Cranshaw (b), Grady Tate (d).

River's Invitation
I Wonder Where Our Love Has Gone
Little Sheri
Mattie T
Bayou
A Taste of Honey

Note: All titles are issued on Blue Note LP, BLP4201

[215] April 15, 1965   Englewood Cliffs, New Jersey
Lionel Hampton's Jazz All-Stars   Van Gelder Studios
                                    Studio performance

Lionel Hampton (v, p), Clark Terry (tp), Thad Jones (tp, fg, arr), J.J. Johnson (tb), Lucky Thompson (ss), Coleman Hawkins (ts), Hank Jones (p), Arvell Shaw (b), Osie Johnson (d).

Stardust
LP: Who's Who WWLP 21010, Legends of Music RJL2650
CD: TelArchive CD-83318

Midnight Blues
LP: Who's Who WWLP 21010, Glad Hamp GHS 1027

As Long As We're Here
LP: Who's Who WWLP 21010

Note: LP discographical data in Lionel Hampton with James Haskins, *Hamp: An Autobiography* (New York: Warner Books, 1989), pp. 254–255, discography by Vincent Pelote.

[216] May 21, 1965   Los Angeles, California
      Lalo Schifrin and His Orchestra   Studio performance

Lalo Schifrin (p, cond), Jerome Richardson, James Moody, Phil Woods (reeds), Freddie Hubbard, Ernie Royal, Snooky Young, Clark Terry (tp), Jimmy Cleveland, J.J. Johnson, Bob Brookmeyer, Tony Studd (tb), James Buffington, Robert Northern, Willie Ruff (hn), Don Butterfield (tu), Margaret Ross (hp), Kenny Burrell (g), Bob Cranshaw (b), Grady Tate, Dave Bailey (d), unknown string section.

65VK314   Once a Thief

Add Irene Reed (voc):

65VK315   The Joint
65VK416   The Man from Thrush

Note: All titles issued on the LP Verve V/V6-8624.

[217] May 23, 1965   Los Angeles, California
      Lalo Schifrin and His Orchestra   Studio performance

Same personnel as [216].

65VK317   Insinuations
65VK318   Roulette Rhumba
65VK319   The Cat

Add Irene Reed (voc):

65VK320   Once a Thief

Omit Irene Reed (voc):

65VK321   Return to Trieste
65VK322   Blues a Go Go

Add Irene Reed (voc):

65VK323   The Right to Love

Note: All titles issued on the LP Verve V/V6-8624

[218] July 12, 1965   New York, New York
     J.J. Johnson and His Orchestra   Studio performance

J.J. Johnson (tb), Billy Byers (arr, cond), Clark Terry (fg), Jerome Richardson (as, ts, fl), Phil Bodner (reeds, fl), Romeo Penque (reeds, af), Ray Starling (ml), Alan Raph (tb), Bucky Pizzarelli (g), Richard Davis (b), Bobby Rosengarden (d), John Pacheco, Doug Allen (per), Marlene VerPlanck (voc).

SPA13554-9   Agua de beber
              LP: RCA LPM3458, LSP3458

SPA13555-12 Pense à moi
              LP: RCA LPM3458, LSP3458

Note: Discographical data were obtained from the RCA archive.

[219] July 13, 1965   New York, New York
     J.J. Johnson and His Orchestra   Studio performance

J.J. Johnson (tb), Richard Hyman (arr, cond), Clark Terry (tp, fg), Alan Raph (tb), Ray Starling (ml), Jerome Richardson (as, fl, ts), Phil Bodner (reeds, fl), Danny Bank (bs, fl, bc), Bucky Pizzarelli (g), Richard Davis (b), Bobby Rosengarden (d), Phil Kraus (per), unknown vocal ensemble.

SPA13556-10 How Insensitive
              LP: RCA LPM3458, LSP3458, P8S-5046

SPA13557-5   I'm All Smiles
              LP: RCA LPM3458, LSP3458

SPA13558-4   G'won Train
LP: RCA LPM3458, LSP3458

SPA13559-7   Feeling Good
LP: RCA LPM3458, LSP3458

Note: Discographical data were obtained from the RCA archive.

[220] July 19, 1965   New York, New York
J.J. Johnson and His Orchestra   Studio performance

J.J. Johnson (tb), Slide Hampton (arr, cond), Clark Terry (tp, fg), Ray
Starling (ml), Alan Raph (tb), Jerome Richardson (as, ts, fl), Phil
Bodner (reeds, fl), Barry Galbraith (g), Carl Lynch (eb), Richard
Davis (b), Sol Gubin (d), Warren Smith (per), Osie Johnson (voc).

SPA13560-8   The Seventh Son
LP: RCA LPM3458, LSP3458

SPA13561-12 In the Name of Love
LP: RCA LPM3458, LSP3458

SPA13562-6   No Particular Place to Go
LP: RCA LPM3458, LSP3458

Note: Discographical data were obtained from the RCA archive.

[221] July 20, 1965   New York, New York
J.J. Johnson and His Orchestra   Studio performance

J.J. Johnson (tb, arr, cond), Jerome Richardson (ss, as, fl), Phil
Bodner (reeds, fl), Clark Terry (tp, fg), Ray Starling (ml), Alan Raph
(tb), Richard Hyman (p), Richard Davis (b), Osie Johnson (voc).

SPA13563-7   008
LP: RCA LPM3458, LSP3458

SPA13564-12 Billy Boy
LP: RCA LPM3458, LSP3458

SPA13565-5   Incidental Blues
LP: RCA LPM3458, LSP3458

Note: Discographical data were obtained from the RCA archive.

[222] September 13–14, 1965   Vienna, Austria
Friedrich Gulda and His Euro-Orchestra   Studio performance

Friedrich Gulda (p), Freddie Hubbard, Stan Roderick (tp), Kenny Wheeler (tp, ml), Robert Politzer (fg), J.J. Johnson, Erich Kleinschuster, Harry Roche, Rudolf Josl (tb), Alfie Reece (tu), Herb Geller (as), Rolf Kuhn (ts, cl), Tubby Hayes (ts, fl), Sahib Shihab (bs, fl), Pierre Cavalli (g), Ron Carter (b), Mel Lewis (d).

Music for Four Soloists and Band
Minuet
The Excursion (unissued)

Note: "Music for Four Soloists and Band" and "Minuet" were issued in Europe.

[223] October 22, 1965   Englewood Cliffs, New Jersey
J.J. Johnson with the Horace Silver Quintet   Van Gelder Studios
                                       Studio performance

Horace Silver (p), J.J. Johnson (tb), Woody Shaw (tp), Joe Henderson (ts), Bob Cranshaw (b), Roger Humphries (d).

Nutville
LP: Blue Note BLP4220. BST84220
CD: Blue Note CDP7-84220-2

Bonita
LP: Blue Note BLP4220. BST84220
CD: Blue Note CDP7-84220-2

Mo' Joe
LP: Blue Note BLP4220. BST84220
CD: Blue Note CDP7-84220-2

[224] December 10, 1965   New York, New York
J.J. Johnson and His Orchestra   Studio performance

J.J. Johnson (tb), Richard Hyman (arr, cond), Jerome Richardson, Frank Wess (fl), Romeo Penque (fl, cl, ob), Emmanuel Vardi, Harold Coletta, Selwart Clarke (va), Harry Shapiro, George Ricci, Lucien Schmit (vc), Hank Jones (p), Richard Davis (b), Bucky Pizzarelli, Al Caiola (g), George Devens, Dom Um Romao, Halcio Milito (per).

SPA18877-6   The End (unissued)

SPA18878-13   Hot Afternoon (unissued)

SPA18879-10   Yeah! (unissued)

SPA18880-8   Five Four and Go (unissued)

Note: These titles were to have been issued as pop singles. Discographical data
were obtained from the RCA archive.

[225] December 13, 1965   New York, New York
      J.J. Johnson and His Orchestra   Studio performance

J.J. Johnson (tb), Mundell Lowe (arr, cond), Jerome Richardson (pc,
fl, af, cl), Phil Bodner (fl,ob, cl, bc), Frank Wess (fl, cl, bc), Danny
Bank (pc, fl, cl), Ernie Royal, Burt Collins (tp, fg), James Buffington,
Robert Northern (hn), Tony Studd, Richard Hixson (bt), Hank Jones
(p), Kenny Burrell, Carl Lynch (g), Richard Davis (b), Grady Tate
(d), Phil Kraus (per).

SPA18885-6   Once in a Lifetime
               LP: RCA LMP3544, LSP3544

SPA18886-9   Sunrise, Sunset
               LP: RCA LPM3544, LSP3544, P8S-1176

SPA18887-4   Sew the Buttons On
               LP: RCA LPM3544, LSP3544

SPA18888-3   More Than One Way
               LP: RCA LPM3544, LSP3544

Note: Discographical data were obtained from the RCA archive.

[226] December 16, 1965   New York, New York
      J.J. Johnson and His Orchestra   Studio performance

J.J. Johnson (tb), Mundell Lowe (arr, cond). Jerome Richardson (as,fl,
cl, bc), Frank Wess (ts, fl, cl, bc), Danny Bank (bs, fl, cl, bc), Phil Bodner
(ts, fl, ob, cl), Ernie Royal, Joe Newman, Burt Collins (tp, fg), James
Buffington, Robert Northern (hn), Wayne Andre (tb), Tony Studd,
Richard Hixson (bt), Hank Jones (p), Carl Lynch, Kenny Burrell (g),
Richard Davis (b), Grady Tate (d), Warren Smith (per).

SPA18889-8   Night Song
             LP: RCA LPM3544, LSP3544

SPA18890-6   Come Back to Me
             LP: RCA LPM3544, LSP3544

SPA18891-6   Something's Coming
             LP: RCA LPM3544, LSP3544

SPA18892-8   Why Did I Choose You
             LP: RCA LPM3544, LSP3544

Note: Discographical data were obtained from the RCA archive.

[227] December 17, 1965   New York, New York
      J.J. Johnson and His Orchestra   Studio performance

J.J. Johnson (tb), Mundell Lowe (arr, cond), Jerome Richardson (as, fl, af, cl), Phil Bodner (ts, fl, ob, cl), Frank Wess (ts, fl, cl, bc), Danny Bank (bs, fl, cl, bc), Ernie Royal, Burt Collins (tp, fg), Robert Northern, James Buffington (hn), Tony Studd, Richard Hixson (bt), Hank Jones (p), Carl Lynch, Everett Barksdale (g), Richard Davis (b), Grady Tate (d), Phil Kraus (per).

SPA18893-8   The Joker
             LP: RCA LPM3544, LSP3544

SPA18894-5   Goodbye, Old Girl
             LP: RCA LPM3544, LSP3544

SPA18895-7   I Believe in You
             LP: RCA LPM3544, LSP3544

SPA18896-7   Xanadu
             LP: RCA LPM3544, LSP3544

Note: Discographical data were obtained from the RCA archive.

[228] March 1966   New York, New York
      Sonny Stitt and His Orchestra   Studio performance

Sonny Stitt (as, ts), Eddie "Lockjaw" Davis (ts), George Berg (bs), Joe Newman, Clark Terry (tp), Urbie Green, J.J. Johnson (tb), Wild Bill Davis (o), Junior Mance, Billy Taylor (p), Les Spann, Barry Galbraith (g), Milt Hinton, Eddie Safranski (b), Walter Perkins (d), Ray Barreto, Tito Puente (per), Henry Glover (arr).

Duketation
T'wanna
Icy Stone
Pink Gloves
Let My People Split
Samba de Orfeo
Liberian Love Song
Handkerchief Head
Stitt's Song

Note: All titles issued on the LP Roulette R25339.

[229] April 28, 1966   Englewood Cliffs, New Jersey
       Lalo Schifrin and His Orchestra   Studio performance

Lalo Schifrin (comp, arr, cond, p), Jerome Richardson (f, af), Romeo
Penque (f, ts), Ernie Royal, Clark Terry, Snooky Young (tp), Ray
Alonge, Richard Berg, James Buffington (hn), Urbie Green, J.J.
Johnson, Kai Winding (tb), Thomas Mitchell (bt), Don Butterfield
(tu), Richard Davis (b), Grady Tate (d).

    100177   Blues for Johann Sebastian (Bach to the Blues)
                  LP: Verve V/V6-8654, MV2055
                  CD: Verve 314-537-751-2

    100178   Troubadour
                  LP: Verve V/V6-8654, MV2055
                  CD: Verve 314-537-751-2

    100179   The Wig
                  LP: Verve V/V6-8654, MV2055
                  CD: Verve 314-537-751-2

    100180   Bossa Antique
                  LP: Verve V/V6-8654, MV2055
                  CD: Verve 314-537-751-2

Note: The original LP album title is *The Dissection and Reconstruction of Music
from the Past as Performed by the Inmates of Lalo Schifrin's Demented Ensemble
as a Tribute to the Memory of Marquis de Sade.*

[230] July 28 & 30, 1966   New York, New York
       Sonny Stitt and His Orchestra   Studio performance

Sonny Stitt (as, ts), Illinois Jacquet (ts), George Berg (bs), Eddie

Preston, Joe Wilder (tp), J.J. Johnson (tb), Billy Taylor, Ellis Larkins
(p), Wild Bill Davis, Ernie Hayes (o), Mike Manieri (v), Les Spann
(g), Jan Arnet, George Dubibier (b), Walter Perkins (d).

> Jumpin' with Symphony Sid
> Stardust
> Cocktails For Two
> Georgia On My Mind
> Mame
> Morgan's Song
> Fever
> 'Round Midnight
> I've Got The World on a String
> If I Didn't Care
> The Beastly Blues

Note: All titles issued on the LP Roulette R25343.

[231] October 20, 1966   New York, New York
       Hank Jones with Oliver Nelson and His Orchestra   Studio performance

Hank Jones (ehs), Oliver Nelson (comp, arr), Bob Ashton, Jerry
Dodgion, Phil Woods, Jerome Richardson (reeds), Danny Bank (bs),
Ernie Royal, Snooky Young, Joe Newman, Clark Terry (tp), J.J.
Johnson, Jimmy Cleveland, Tommy Mitchell, Britt Woodman (tb),
George Duvivier (b), Grady Tate (d).

> Happenings
> Mas Que Nada
> Lou's Good Dues Blues
> Winchester Cathedral

Note: Clark Terry sings vocals on "Winchester Cathedral." All titles issued on the
LP Impulse A(S)9132.

[232] November 3, 1966   Englewood Cliffs, New Jersey
       Leonard Feather's   Studio performance
       Encyclopedia of Jazz All-Stars

Oliver Nelson (arr, cond), Phil Woods, Jerry Dodgion (as), Zoot
Sims, Jerome Richardson (ts), Danny Bank (bs), Ernie Royal, Burt
Collins, Joe Newman, Joe Wilder, Clark Terry, Snooky Young (tp, fg),

J.J. Johnson, Jimmy Cleveland, Bob Brookmeyer (tb), Tony Studd (bt), Al Dailey (p), Eric Gale (g), Ron Carter (b), Grady Tate (d), Phil Kraus (per).

101574	Ricardo's Dilemma
	LP: Verve V6-8743
	CD: Verve 314-527-654-2

101575	St. Louis Blues
	LP: Verve V6-8743
	CD: Verve 314-527-654-2, 314-553-246-2

101576	Patterns for Orchestra
	LP: Verve V6-8743
	CD: Verve 314-527-654-2

101577	I Remember Bird
	LP: Verve V6-8743
	CD: Verve 314-527-654-2

[233] November 4, 1966   Englewood Cliffs, New Jersey
       Leonard Feather's   Studio performance
       Encyclopedia of Jazz All-Stars

Oliver Nelson (arr, cond), Phil Woods, Jerry Dodgion (as), Zoot Sims, Jerome Richardson (ts), Danny Bank (bs), Ernie Royal, Nat Adderley, Joe Newman, Joe Wilder, Clark Terry, Snooky Young (tp, fg), J.J. Johnson, Jimmy Cleveland, Bob Brookmeyer (tb), Tony Studd (bt), Hank Jones (p), Eric Gale (g), Ron Carter (b), Grady Tate (d), Bobby Rosengarden (per).

101578	Twelve Tone Blues
	LP: Verve V6-8743
	CD: Verve 314-527-654-2

101579	Sidewalks of New York
	LP: Verve V6-8743
	CD: Verve 314-527-654-2

101580	Greensleeves
	LP: Verve V6-8743
	CD: Verve 314-527-654-2

101581	John Brown's Blues
	LP: Verve V6-8743
	CD: Verve 314-527-654-2

[234] November 30, 1966   New York, New York
     J.J. Johnson and His Big Bands: Say When   Studio performance

J.J. Johnson (comp, tb), Jerome Richardson, Phil Bodner, Tommy Newsom (reeds), Art Farmer, Snooky Young, Danny Stiles (tp), Benny Powell, Paul Faulise (tb), Hank Jones (p), Ron Carter (b), Grady Tate (d).

TPA15279-16 Say When
          LP: RCA LPM3833, LSP3833
          CD: RCA/Bluebird 6277-2-RB

TPA15280-5 Ballade
          LP: RCA LPM3833, LSP3833
          CD: RCA/Bluebird 6277-2-RB

TPA15281-11 Little Dave (unissued)

Note: LP discographical data were obtained from the RCA archive.

[235] December 2, 1966   New York, New York
     J.J. Johnson and His Orchestra   Studio performance

J.J. Johnson (comp, tb), Jerome Richardson (reeds, fl), Phil Bodner (reeds, af), Tommy Newsom (reeds, fl, cl), Art Farmer, Ernie Royal, Burt Collins (tp), Benny Powell, Paul Faulise (tb), Hank Jones (p), Ron Carter (b), Grady Tate (d), Bobby Rosengarden (per).

TPA15281-16 Little Dave
          LP: RCA LPM3833, LSP3833
          CD: RCA/Bluebird 6277-2-RB

TPA15282-6 Space Walk
          LP: RCA LPM3833, LSP3833
          CD: RCA/Bluebird 6277-2-RB

TPA15283-9 In Walked Horace
          LP: RCA LPM3833, LSP3833
          CD: RCA/Bluebird 6277-2-RB

TPA15284-6 Blue
          LP: RCA LPM3833, LSP3833

Note: Discographical data were obtained from the RCA archive.

[236] December 5, 1966   New York, New York
J. J. Johnson and His Orchestra   Studio performance

J.J. Johnson (comp, tb), Jerome Richardson, Frank Wess, Tommy Newsom (reeds, fl), Ray Alonge, James Buffington (hn), Art Farmer, Burt Collins (tp, fg), Snooky Young (tp), Benny Powell, Tony Studd (tb), Hank Jones (p), Ron Carter (b), Grady Tate (d).

TPA15285-11   Euro 1
               LP: RCA LPM3833, LSP3833
               CD: RCA/Bluebird 6277-2-RB

TPA15286-3   Euro 2
               LP: RCA LMP3833, LSP3833
               CD: RCA/Bluebird 6277-2-RB

TPA15287-2   Short Cake
               LP: RCA LPM3833, LSP3833
               CD: RCA/Bluebird 6277-2-RB

Note: LP discographical data were obtained from the RCA archive.

[237] 1966   New York, New York
Nat Adderley and His Orchestra: Sayin' Somethin'   Studio performance

Nat Adderley (cn), Seldon Powell (ts), Artie Kaplan (bs), Ernie Royal (tp), J.J. Johnson (tb), Paul Griffin (p), Al Gorgoni, Billy Suyker (g), George Duvivier (b), Herb Lovelle (d), George Devens (per), Jimmy Wisner (arr, cond).

                  Manchild
                  Call Me
                  Gospelette
                  Satin Doll

Note: All titles issued on the LP, Atlantic 1460.

[238] 1966   New York, New York
Manny Albam and His Orchestra: Soul of the City   Studio performance

Manny Albam (arr, cond), Jerome Richardson, Phil Woods, Don Ashworth, Chuck Russo, Frank Wess, Seldon Powell (reeds), Ernie Royal, Joe Newman, Burt Collins, Snooky Young, John Frosk, Freddie Hubbard (tp), J.J. Johnson, Eddie Bert, Wayne Andre, Tony Studd (tb), James Buffington, Earl Chapin, Howard Howard, Al

Richman (hn), Hank Jones (p), Mike Mainieri (v), unknown (g), Richard Davis, Ron Carter (b), Mel Lewis (d), Phil Kraus (per), unknown string section.

> Born on Arrival
> Children's Corner
> Museum Pieces
> Game of the Year
> View from the Outside
> Tired Faces, Going Places
> View from the Inside
> Ground Floor Rear (Next to the Synagogue)
> Riverview
> El Barrio Latino

Note: All titles issued on the LP Solid State 18009.

[239] January 23–24, 1967   New York, New York
      Sarah Vaughan: Sassy Swings Again   Studio performance

Sarah Vaughan (voc), Benny Golson, Phil Woods (reeds), Joe Newman, Charlie Shavers, Freddie Hubbard, Clark Terry (tp), J.J. Johnson, Kai Winding (tb), Bob James (p), remainder of personnel unknown.

> Sweet Georgia Brown
> Take the "A" Train
> I Left My Heart in San Francisco
> S'posin'
> Every Day I Have the Blues
> I Want to Be Happy
> All Alone
> Sweetest Sounds
> On the Other Side of the Tracks
> I Had a Ball

Note: All titles issued on the LP Mercury SR-61116 and the CDs Mercury 814587-2 and Polygram 814587.

[240] 1968   New York, New York
      Urbie Green: 21 Trombones   Studio performance

Urbie Green, Wayne Andre, Will Bradley, Bill Elton, Phil Giardina, Marvin Gold, Mickey Gravine, J.J. Johnson, Barry Maur, Lou McGarity, Johnny Messner, Buddy Morrow, Jack Rains, Sonny Russo, Charles Small, Chauncey Welsch, Kai Winding (tb), Paul Faulise, Dick Hixson, Thomas Mitchell, Alan Raph (bt), Tony Mottola, Barry Galbraith or Al Casamenti, Bucky Pizzarelli (g), George Duvivier (b), Grady Tate, Bobby Rosengarden, Phil Krause (per).

> Here's That Rainy Day
> The Look of Love
> What Now, My Love?
> If He Walked into My Life
> Because of You
> You Only Live Once
> Stardust
> Blue Again
> Watch What Happens
> Stars Fell on Alabama
> Without a Song
> Something You've Got

Note: All titles issued on the LP Project-3 PR5014SD.

[241] February 19, 1968   New York, New York
      J. J. Johnson/Kai Winding Sextet   Studio performance

J.J. Johnson, Kai Winding (tb), Herbie Hancock (p), Eric Gale (g), Ron Carter (b), Grady Tate (d).

> Never My Love
> Saturday Night Is the Loneliest Night of the Week

Note: All titles issued on the LP A&M SP3008.

[242] March 4, 1968   New York, New York
      J.J. Johnson/Kai Winding Sextet   Studio performance

Same personnel as [241].

> Israel

Note: Title issued on the LP A&M SP3008.

[243] March 12, 1968   New York, New York
      J.J. Johnson/Kai Winding Sextet   Studio performance

J.J. Johnson, Kai Winding (tb), Al Brown (va), Charles Libove,
David Nadien (vn), George Ricci (vc), unknown rhythm section.

St. James Infirmary
Catherine's Theme

Note: All titles issued on the LP, A&M SP3008.

[244] April 16, 1968   New York, New York
      J.J. Johnson/Kai Winding Orchestra   Studio performance

J.J. Johnson, Kai Winding (tb), Bernie Glow (tp, fg), Phil Bodner,
George Marge, Romeo Penque, Frank Schwartz (reeds, fl), Walter
Kane (fl, bsn), Lewis Eley, Leo Kruczek, Eugene Orloff, Tosha
Samarof (vn), Al Brown (va), George Ricci (vc), Ross Tompkins (p,
ep, hs), Bucky Pizzarelli (g), Richard Davis (b), Grady Tate (d),
Eugene Bianco (hp).

My Funny Valentine
Am I Blue
Django
Try to Remember

Note: All titles issued on the LP, A&M SP3008.

[245] May 21, 1968   New York, New York
      Urbie Green: 21 Trombones, Vol. 2   Studio performance

Urbie Green, Wayne Andre, Eddie Bert, Will Bradley, Jimmy
Cleveland, Harry DeVito, Bill Elton, Phil Giardina, Marvin Gold,
Mickey Gravine, J.J. Johnson, Barry Maur, Lou McGarity, Johnny
Messner, Buddy Morrow, Jack Rains, Sonny Russo, Charles Small,
Chauncey Welsch, Kai Winding (tb), Paul Faulise, Dick Hixson,
Thomas Mitchell, Tony Studd (bt), Dick Hyman (p), Tony Mottola,
Jay Jay Berliner (g), Bob Haggart (b), Grady Tate (d), Jack Arnold,
Phil Krause (per).

Blue Flame
Perdido

How Come You Do Me Like You Do?

Note: All titles issued on the LP Project-3 DR5025SD.

[246] May 28, 1968   New York, New York
       Urbie Green: 21 Trombones, Vol. 2   Studio performance

Personnel same as [245].

> Mood Indigo
> Sunny
> The Party
> Just Dropped In

Note: All titles issued on the LP Project-3 DR5025SD.

[247] June 4, 1968   New York, New York
       Urbie Green: 21 Trombones, Vol. 2   Studio performance

Personnel same as [245].

> Timbre
> I Get the Blues When It Rains
> The Green Bee
> I Gotta Right to Sing the Blues

Note: All titles issued on the LP Project-3 DR5025SD.

[248] October 22, 29; November 5, 1968   New York, New York
       J.J. Johnson/Kai Winding Orchestra   Studio performance

J.J. Johnson, Kal Winding (tb), Herbie Hancock (p), Roger Kellaway
(cl), Charles Covington (o), Joe Beck, Eric Gale (g), Ron Carter (b),
Charles Domanico, Russell George, Chuck Rainey (eb), Leo Morris,
Denny Seiwell (d), Airto Moreira, Warren Smith (per), unknown
string section.

> Casa Forte
> Betwixt and Between
> Little Drummer Boy
> Don't Go Love, Don't Go
> Mojave
> Stormy

Wichita Lineman
Just a Funky Old Vegetable Bin
Willie, Come Home

Note: All titles issued on the LP A&M SP3016.

[249] October, November 1968   New York, New York
Paul Desmond: Summertime   Studio performance

Paul Desmond (as), George Marge (fl, ob), Bob Tricarico (fl, bsn),
Burt Collins, Joe Shepley, Marvin Stamm, John Ekert (tp, fg), Ray
Alonge, James Buffington, Tony Miranda (hn), Urbie Green, J.J.
Johnson, Bill Watrous, Kai Winding, Wayne Andre, Paul Faulise
(tb), Herbie Hancock (p), Mike Manieri (v), Jay Berliner, Joe Beck,
Bucky Pizzarelli (g), Margaret Ross (hp), Ron Carter, Frank Bruno
(b), Leo Morris, Airto Moreira (d, per), Jack Jennings, Joe Venuto
(per).

Olvidar
Emily
Lady in Cement
Someday My Prince Will Come
Summertime
Where Is Love?
North by Northeast
Autumn Leaves
Samba with Some Barbeque
Ob-La-Di, Ob-La-Da

Note: All titles issued on the LP A&M SP3015.

[250] June 1969   New York, New York
Quincy Jones and His Orchestra   Studio performance

Quincy Jones (tp, arr, voc), Jerome Richardson (ss), Rahsaan Roland
Kirk (ts), Hubert Laws (fl, ts), Joel Kaye (fl, reeds), Freddie Hubbard
(tp), Marvin Stamm, John Frosk, Llowd Michels, Dick Williams,
Snooky Young (tp, fg), Jimmy Cleveland, George Jeffers, J.J.
Johnson, Norman Pride, Kai Winding (tb), Alan Raph, Tony Studd
(bt), Bob James, (p, kb), Paul Griffin (ep), Eric Gale (g), Toots
Thielmans (g, h), Chuck Rainey (b), Ray Brown (b, eb), Grady Tate,
Bernard Purdie (d), Hilda Harris, Marilyn Jackson, Jesse Kirkland,
Valerie Simpson, Maretha Stewart (voc).

Dead End
Walking in Space
Killer Joe
Love and Peace
I Never Told You
Oh Happy Day

Note: Personnel changes for each title are unknown. All titles issued on the LP A&M
93023, and the CD A&M 75021-0801-2.

[251] 1969   New York, New York
      J.J. Johnson/Kai Winding Orchestra   Studio performance

J.J. Johnson, Kai Winding (tb), Marvin Stamm (fg), Paul Ingraham
(hn), Tony Studd (bt), Stuart Scharf (g), remainder of personnel
unknown.

Bach Chorale 237
Plus Nine
Troika
Bach Chorale 241
Onion Rings Rondo
Bach Invention 4
Bach Invention 1

Note: All titles issued on the LP A&M SP3016.

[252] 1969   New York, New York
      J.J. Johnson/Kai Winding All-Stars: Stonebone   Studio performance

J.J. Johnson, Kai Winding (tb), George Benson (g), Herbie Hancock (p,
kb), Bob James, Ross Tompkins (kb), Ron Carter (b), Grady Tate (d).

Recollections
LP: A&M SP3027

Note: Remainder of tunes are unknown; album is unreleased in the United States.

[253] 1971?   Los Angeles, California
      Joe Pass: Better Days   Studio performance

Joe Pass (g), Tom Scott (ts, fl, af), Conte Candoli (tp, fg), J.J. Johnson
(tb), Carol Kaye (eb), Paul Humphrey (d).

Better Days
Burning Spear

Omit Carol Kaye (eb); add Ray Brown (b):

Free Sample
Head Start

Omit Paul Humphrey (d); add Earl Palmer (d):

After School
Balloons
We'll Be Together Again

Omit Ray Brown (b); add Carol Kaye (eb):

It's Too Late
Gotcha!

Omit Carol Kaye (eb); add Ray Brown (eb):

Alison

Note: Originally intended for issue as instructional materials, all titles now issued
on the CDs Hot 9014C, Hot Wire 12068, EFA 12068.

[254] 1972   Los Angeles, California
J.J. Johnson and His Orchestra   Studio performance
                                    Film soundtrack, *Across 110th Street*

J.J. Johnson (comp,[1] cond), Bobby Womack (comp,[2] voc[3]), *Peace*
ensemble,[3] remainder of personnel unknown.

Across 110th Street[1, 2, 3]
Harlem Clavinette[1]
If You Don't Want My Love[2, 3]
Hang on in There[2] (instrumental version)
Quicksand[2,3]
Harlem Love Theme[1]
Across 110th Street[1, 2] (instrumental version)
Do It Right[2, 3]
Hang on in There[2, 3]

If You Don't Want My Love[2]
Across 110th Street[1, 2, 3]

Note:　(i) All titles issued on the LP, United Artists UAS5225 and the CD
Rykodisc 10706. Additional titles appearing on the CD reissue—"We Thought We
Were OK," "Punk Errand Boy," "The Man," "150 Rounds," "Sick & Tired," "Take
The Money," "This Is the Police"—are dialogue-only tracks.

(ii) Johnson shares billing with gospel singer–songwriter Bobby Womack. The
main title credits state "score composed and conducted by J.J. Johnson"; "title song
composed by Bobby Womack and J.J. Johnson"; "additional songs composed by
Bobby Womack and performed by him." Writer credits were obtained from the
Broadcast Music Incorporated (BMI) Participant Catalog Listing provided by
David Sanjek (BMI Archivist–New York) and Michael McGehee (Film/TV
Relations–Los Angeles). Additional information appears in the liner notes of the
CD reissue.

[255]　December 10, 1973　　　　　　　　　　Los Angeles, California
　　　　Count Basie: Basie Jam　　　　　　　　　Studio performance

Count Basie (p, o), Harry Edison (tp), Eddie Davis, Zoot Sims (ts), J.J.
Johnson (tb), Ray Brown (b), Irving Ashby (g), Louis Bellson (d).

　　　　　　　　Doubling Blues
　　　　　　　　Hanging Out
　　　　　　　　Red Bank Blues
　　　　　　　　One-Nighter
　　　　　　　　Freeport Blues

Note:　All titles issued on the LP Pablo 2310-718, 2625-713 and the CD Pablo
PACD-2310-718-2, J33J-20017.

[256]　December 11, 1973　　　　　　　　　　Los Angeles, California
　　　　Count Basie with Joe Turner: The Bosses　　　Studio performance

Count Basie (p, o), Harry Edison (tp), J.J. Johnson (tb), Eddie
"Lockjaw" Davis, Zoot Sims (ts), Irving Ashby (g), Ray Brown (b),
Louis Bellson (d).

　　　　　　　　Honey Hush
　　　　　　　　Blues around the Clock
　　　　　　　　Flip, Flop and Fly
　　　　　　　　Good Morning Blues
　　　　　　　　Roll 'Em Pete

Note: All titles issued on the LP Pablo 2310-709 and the CD Pablo/Original Jazz Classics OJCCD-821-2; five additional titles from this session omit Johnson—"The Honeydripper," "Night Time Is Right Time," "Since I Fell for You," "Cherry Red," and "Wee Baby Blues."

[257] December 22, 1974   Los Angeles, California
Maria Muldaur   The Troubadour
with Benny Carter and His Orchestra   Radio broadcast

Maria Muldaur (voc), Benny Carter (as, comp, arr), Bud Shank (as, fl, cl), Plas Johnson (ts), Shahib Shihab (bs), Snooky Young, Harry Edison (tp), J.J. Johnson (tb), Marty Harris (p, ep), Mundell Lowe (g), John Williams (b), Earl Palmer (d).

> Squeeze Me
> Any Old Time
> Gee, Ain't I Good to You
> Sweetheart
> Doozy
> It Don't Mean a Thing If It Ain't Got That Swing
> Lover Man
> Walkin' One and Only
> Don't You Make Me High
> I'm a Woman
> It Ain't the Meat, It's the Motion

[258] March 17, 1975   Los Angeles, California
Moacir Santos: Carnival of the Spirits   Studio performance

Moacir Santos (as, bs, per, vcl), Gary Foster (as), Don Menza (fl, af, ts), Jerome Richardson (ss, af), Ray Pizzi (cl, bc, ss), Ernie Watts (bf), Oscar Brashear, Mike Price, Jerry Rusch (tp), David Duke (hn), J.J. Johnson, George Bohanon (tb), Larry Nash (ep, kb), Clare Fischer (p), Jerry Peters (o), Dennis Budimir, Dean Parks (g), Chuck Domanico (b), Harvey Mason (d), Roberto Silva, Paulinho Da Costa, Louis Alves (per), Lynda Lawrence (voc), Dale Oehler (arr).

> Tomorrow Is Mine
> Coisa No. 2

Note: All titles issued on the LP Blue Note BN-LA463-G

[259] March 18, 1975   Los Angeles, California
      Moacir Santos: Carnival of the Spirits   Studio performance

Personnel unknown, but may be same as [258].

> Route
> Kamba

Note: All titles issued on the LP Blue Note BN-LA463-G

[260] March 19, 1975   Los Angeles, California
      Moacir Santos: Carnival of the Spirits   Sudio performance

Personnel unknown, but may be same as [258]; add Moacir Santos (arr).

> Quiet Carnival
> Anon

Note: All titles issued on the LP Blue Note BN-LA463-G

[261] March 20, 1975   Los Angeles, California
      Moacir Santos: Carnival of the Spirits   Studio performance

Personnel unknown, but may be same as [258].

> Sampaguita
> Jaquine

Note: All titles issued on the LP, Blue Note BN-LA463-G

[262] 1976?   Hollywood, California
      Ray Charles/Cleo Laine: Porgy and Bess   Studio performance

Ray Charles, Cleo Laine (voc), Frank DeVol (arr, cond), Bill Berry, Buddy Childers, Harry "Sweets" Edison, Albert Aarons, Oscar Brashear, Ray Triscari (tp), Jimmy Cleveland, Britt Woodman, J.J. Johnson, Benny Powell, George Roberts (tb), William Green (as), Plas Johnson (ts), Sam Most, Bill Perkins, Jerome Richardson, Gary Herbig, Wilbur Schwartz, Bud Shank, Ernie Watts, William Hood (cl), Joe Pass, John Morell, Lee Ritenour (g), Victor Feldman, Paul Smith, Ralph Grierson (p), Joe Sample (o, p), Washington Rucker (d), Jerry Williams, Larry Bunker, Alan Estes, Emil Radocchia (per),

Tommy Morgan (h), Catherine Gotthoffer, Dorothy Remsen, Denizel
Gail Laughton (hp), Erno Neufeld, Gerald Vinci, Israel Baker,
Thelma Beach, Harry Bluestone, Charles Veal, Ronald Folsom,
Karen Jones, Anatol Kaminsky, Jacob Krachmalnick, Bernard
Kundell, Marvin Limonick, Nathan Ross, Ralph Schaeffer, Daniel
Shindaryov, Marshall Sosson, Spiro Stamos, Marcia Van Dyke,
George Kaufman, Paul Lowenkron, Ambrose Russo (vn), Meyer
Bello, Rollice Dale, Norman Forrest, Pamela Goldsmith, Allan
Harshman, Dan Neufeld (va), Ronald Cooper, Douglas Davis, Anne
Goodman, Ron Leonard, Harry Schlutz, David Speltz (vc), Max
Bennett, Chuck Berghofer, Chuck Domanico, Jim Hughart (b).

> Summertime
> My Man's Gone
> A Woman Is a Sometime Thing
> They Pass By Singin'
> What You Want Wid Bess?
> I Got Plenty O' Nuttin'
> Buzzard Song
> Bess, You Is My Woman
> Oh, Doctor Jesus
> Crab Man
> Here Come De Honey Man
> Strawberry Woman (shorter version)
> Strawberry Woman (longer version)
> It Ain't Necessarily So
> There's a Boat Dat's Leavin' Soon for New York
> I Loves You, Porgy
> Oh Bess, Oh Where's My Bess? (shorter version)
> Oh Bess, Oh Where's My Bess? (longer version)
> Oh Lord, I'm on My Way

Note: All titles issued on the LP RCA 1831-4-R and reissued on the CD RCA
1831-2-R.

[263] April 20, 1977   Yokohama, Japan
      J.J. Johnson Quintet   Kanagawa Kenritsu Ongakudo
                                                       Concert performance

J.J. Johnson (tb), Nat Adderley (tp), Billy Childs (kb), Tony Dumas
(b), Kevin Johnson (d).

6363	Horace
6364	Cyclops
6365	Why Not
6366	Splashes
6367	It Happens
6368	Work Song
6369	Walkin'
6370	Jevin
6371	Lament
6372	Hummin'
6373	Melodee

Note: All titles issued on the LP Pablo 2620-109 and the CD Pablo PACD 2620-109-2.

[264] August 14, 1979; December 10–11, 1979;
May 13, 1980   Hollywood, California
Zoot Sims: Black Butterfly   Studio performance

Zoot Sims (ts), Benny Carter (arr, cond), Marshall Royal (as), Frank
Wess (as, fl), Plas Johnson, Buddy Collete (ts), Bobby Bryant, Oscat
Brashear, Al Aarons, Earl Gardner (tp), J.J. Johnson, Britt Woodman,
Grover Mitchell, Benny Powell (tb), Jimmy Rowles (p), John Collins
(g), Andy Simpkins (b), Grady Tate (d).

In a Mellotone
I Got It Bad and That Ain't Good
It Don't Mean a Thing
I Let a Song Go out of My Heart
Black Butterfly

Note: All titles issued on the LP Pablo 2312-120. Chronology of titles recorded
was unavailable.

[265] September 17, 1979   Berkeley, California
J.J. Johnson: Pinnacles   Studio performance

J.J. Johnson (comp, tb, syn), Tommy Flanagan (p, ep, kb), Ron
Carter (eb), Billy Higgins (d), Ed Michel (syn).

It Was a Very Good Year (unissued)

Omit Ed Michel (syn); add Oscar Brashear (tp):

Don't Buzz Me, I'll Buzz You (unissued)

Omit Oscar Brashear (tp); add Joe Henderson (ts):

Pinnacles
LP: Milestone M9093

Night Flight
LP: Milestone M9093

Note: Discographical data were obtained from the producer, Ed Michel.

[266] September 18, 1979   Berkeley, California
J.J. Johnson: Pinnacles   Studio performance

J.J. Johnson (comp, tb, syn), Tommy Flanagan (p, ep, kb), Ron
Carter (eb), Billy Higgins (d).

Better Days (unissued)

Add Ed Michel (syn):

Ballad from Tremblay (unissued)

Omit Ed Michel (syn); Add Joe Henderson (ts), Oscar Brashear (tp):

Cannonball Junction
LP: Milestone M9093

Deak
LP: Milestone M9093

Etheros (unissued)

Note: Discographical data were obtained from the producer, Ed Michel.

[267] September 19, 1979   Berkeley, California
J.J. Johnson: Pinnacles   Studio performance

J.J. Johnson (comp, tb, syn), Oscar Brashear (tp), Tommy Flanagan
(p, ep, kb), Ron Carter (eb), Billy Higgins (d), Kenneth Nash (per).

See See Rider
LP: Milestone M9093

Mr. Clean
LP: Milestone M9093

Note: Discographical data were obtained from the producer, Ed Michel.

[268] December 1979   New York, New York
       Ron Carter: New York Slick   Studio performance

Ron Carter (b), Hubert Laws (fl), Art Farmer (fg), J.J. Johnson (tb),
Jay Berliner, Kenny Barron (p), Billy Cobham (d), Ralph McDonald
(per).

New York Slick
Slight Smile
Tierra Española
Aromatic
Alternate Route

Note: All titles issued on the LP Milestone M-9096 and reissued on the CD Fantasy/
Original Jazz Classics OJCCD 2531-916-2.

[269] April 10, 1980   Hollywood, California
       Count Basie: Kansas City 7   Cherokee Studios
                                                       Studio performance

Count Basie (p), Freddie Hubbard (tp, fg), Eddie "Lockjaw" Davis
(ts), J.J. Johnson (tb), Joe Pass (g), John Heard (b), Jake Hanna (d).

Jaylock
Exactly Like You
I'll Always Be in Love with You
If I Could Be with You One Hour Tonight
Honi Coles
Blues for Norman
Count Me In

Note: All titles except "Count Me In" issued on the LP Pablo 2310-908 and the CD
Pablo OJCCD-690-2; "Count Me In" only issued on the CD Pablo OJCCD-690-2.

[270] September 23, 1980   Hollywood, California
       J.J. Johnson: Concepts in Blue   Studio performance

J.J. Johnson (comp, tb), Clark Terry (tp, fg), Ernie Watts (as, ts), Billy Childs (kb), Ray Brown (b), Kevin Johnson (d).

7100   Freddie the Freeloader (unissued)

7101   Concepts in Blue
        LP: Pablo 2312-123
        CD: Pablo OJCCD-735-2

[271] September 24, 1980   Hollywood, California
    J.J. Johnson: Concepts in Blue   Studio performance

J.J. Johnson (comp, tb), Clark Terry (tp, fg), Ernie Watts (as, ts), Pete Jolly (kb), Ray Brown (b), Kevin Johnson (d).

7102   Village Blues
7103   Mohawk

Note: All titles issued on the LP Pablo 2312-123 and the CD Pablo OJCCD-735-2.

[272] September 25, 1980   Hollywood, California
    J.J. Johnson: Concepts in Blue   Studio performance

Same personnel as [271].

7104   Nermus
7105   Azure

Note: All titles issued on the LP Pablo 2312-123 and the CD Pablo OJCCD-735-2.

[273] September 26, 1980   Hollywood, California
    J.J. Johnson: Concepts in Blue   Studio performance

J.J. Johnson (comp, tb), Clark Terry (tp, fg), Ernie Watts (as, ts), Victor Feldman (kb, v), Tony Dumas (b), Kevin Johnson (comp, d).

7106   Blue Nun
7107   Coming Home

Note: All titles issued on the LP Pablo 2312-123 and the CD Pablo OJCCD-735-2.

[274] 1982   Hollywood, California
       Lalo Schifrin and His Orchestra   Studio performance
                                           Film soundtrack, *The Sting II*

Lalo Schifrin (arr, cond), Abe Most (cl), Snooky Young (tp), J.J.
Johnson (tb), Mike Lang (p), Ray Brown (b), remainder of personnel
unknown.

            Heliotrope Bouquet
            A Breeze from Alabama (The Setup)
            The Chrysanthemum
            Calliope March
            The Entertainer
            Heliotrope Bouquet (Main Title)
            Coney Island
            Scott Joplin Finale

Add Linda Hopkins (voc):

            Most Men

[275] September 1, 1982   Budokan, Tokyo, Japan
       All-Star Jam   Aurex Jazz Festival Concert
                                                    Audience tape

Clark Terry (tp, fg, voc), J.J. Johnson, Kai Winding (tb), Dexter
Gordon (ts), Tommy Flanagan (p), Kenny Burrell (g), Richard Davis
(b), Roy Haynes (d).

            The Snapper
            Blues for Squeaky
            Eclypso
            Autumn Leaves
            Milestones

Note: All titles issued in Japan.

[276] September 2, 1982   Osaka, Japan
       All-Star Jam   Aurex Jazz Festival Concert
                                                    Audience tape

Clark Terry (tp, fg, voc), J.J. Johnson, Kai Winding (tb), Dexter
Gordon (ts), Tommy Flanagan (p), Kenny Burrell (g), Richard Davis
(b), Roy Haynes (d).

I Want a Little Girl
It's All Right with Me
Soba Up
God Bless' the Child
Walkin'
Minor Mishap (unissued)
The Snapper
Milestones
Now's the Time

Note: All titles except for "Minor Mishap" issued in Japan.

[277] September 5, 1982   Yokohama, Japan
All-Star Jam   Aurex Jazz Festival Concert
                                                             Audience tape

Clark Terry (tp, fg, voc), J.J. Johnson, Kai Winding (tb), Dexter Gordon (ts), Tommy Flanagan (p), Kenny Burrell (g), Richard Davis (b), Roy Haynes (d).

Listen to the Dawn
Georgia on My Mind
Walkin' (unissued)
Minor Mishap
Milestones

Note: All titles except for "Walkin'" issued in Japan.

[278] May 25–26, 1983   Hollywood, California
Jackson, Johnson, Brown & Company   Studio performance

Milt Jackson (v), J.J. Johnson (tb), Ray Brown (b), Tom Ranier (p), John Collins (g), Roy McCurdy (d).

Jaybone
Lament
Our Delight
Bags' Groove
Watch What Happens
My One and Only Love
Jumpin' Blues

Note: All titles issued on the LP Pablo 2310-897 and the CD Fantasy 2531-907-2.

[279] 1983   Tokyo, Japan
Jazz at the Philharmonic: Return to Happiness   Yoyogi National Stadium
                                     Concert performance

J.A.T.P. All-Stars:
Zoot Sims, Eddie "Lockjaw" Davis (ts), Clark Terry, Harry "Sweets"
Edison (tp), J.J. Johnson, Al Grey (tb), Oscar Peterson (p), Joe Pass (g),
Niels-Henning Orsted Pedersen (b), Martin Drew (d).

            Sunday
            Undecided

Omit all personnel except J.J. Johnson (tb), Joe Pass (g):

            Misty

Add Oscar Peterson (p):

            What's New?

Add remainder of *J.A.T.P. All-Stars:*

            Spotlite

Add Ella Fitzgerald (voc):

            Flying Home

Note: All titles issued on the LP Pablo 2620-117 and the CD Fantasy 2523-2620117-2; the titles "Misty" and "What's New?" are solo features for Johnson.

[280] October 26, 1983   Hollywood, California
J.J. Johnson/Joe Pass Duo   Studio performance

J.J. Johnson (tb), Joe Pass (g).

            Wave
            We'll Be Together Again
            Naked As a Jaybird
            Blue Bossa
            Limehouse Blues
            How Long Has This Been Going On?
            Bud's Blues
            Nature Boy
            Solar
            When Lights Are Low

Note: All titles issued on the LP Pablo 2310-911 and reissued on the CD Fantasy/Original Jazz Classics OJCCD 2531-909-2.

[281] November 9, 1983   Portland, Oregon
      Don Manning Jazz Show: Interview   KBOO Radio broadcast

40 minutes in length; interspersed with recordings.

[282] November 28–29, 1983   New York, New York
      J.J. Johnson/Al Grey Sextet   Studio performance

J.J. Johnson, Al Grey (tb), Kenny Barron (p, kb), Ray Brown (b), Mickey Roker (d), Dave Carey (per).

> Soft Winds
> Let Me See
> Softly As in a Morning Sunrise
> It's Only A Paper Moon
> Boy Meets Horn
> Things Ain't What They Used to Be
> Things Are Getting Better All the Time
> Doncha Hear Me Callin' To Ya

Note: All titles issued on the LP Pablo 2312-141 and the CD Pablo OJCCD-745-2.

[283] July 6, 1984   Nice, France
      J.J. Johnson All-Stars   JVC Grande Parade du Jazz
                                        Audience tape

J.J. Johnson (tb), Harold Land (ts), Nat Adderley (cn), Cedar Walton (p), Richard Davis (b), Roy McCurdy (d).

> Toots Suite
> Misterioso
> What Is This Thing Called Love?
> Invitation
> The Blues Walk
> My Funny Valentine

Omit Harold Land (ts), Nat Adderley (cn);
add Al Grey, Slide Hampton, George Masso (tb):

> Milestones
> In a Mellotone
> Walkin'

Improvisation
Oleo

[284] July 10, 1984   Nice, France
    J.J. Johnson All-Stars   JVC Grande Parade du Jazz
                                                        Audience tape

J.J. Johnson (tb), Harold Land (ts), Nat Adderley (cn), Cedar Walton
(p), Richard Davis (b), Roy McCurdy (d).

Walkin'
Oleo
My Funny Valentine
The Blues Walk
Invitation
Milestones

[285] July 19, 1984   Vitoria, Spain
    J.J. Johnson All-Stars   Concert performance
                                                        Audience tape

J.J. Johnson (tb), Harold Land (ts), Nat Adderley (cn), Cedar Walton
(p), Richard Davis (b), Roy McCurdy (d).

Toots Suite
Misterioso
Without a Song
Blues Walk
My Funny Valentine
Milestones

[286] July 20, 1984   Pescara, Italy
    J.J. Johnson All-Stars   Pescara Jazz Festival Concert
                                                        Audience tape

J.J. Johnson (tb), Richard Davis (b).

Blues for Two

Note: "Blues For Two" issued on the LP Philology W100.

[287] July 1985   Nice, France
       All-Star Jam   JVC Grande Parade du Jazz
                                  Audience tape

J.J. Johnson, Al Grey (ts), Benny Carter (as), Harry "Sweets" Edison (tp), Johnny O'Neal (p), George Duvivier (b), Oliver Jackson (d).

            In a Mellotone
            Blue 'N' Boogie
            The Nearness of You
            Lover Man
            Summertime
            The Great Life
            Sweet Georgia Brown

[288] July 9, 1988   New York, New York
       J.J. Johnson Quintet   Village Vanguard
                           Club date performance

J.J. Johnson (tb), Ralph Moore (reeds), Stanley Cowell (p), Rufus Reid (b), Victor Lewis (d).

            Why Indianapolis—Why Not Indianapolis?
            CD: Antilles 422-848 214-2

            Shortcake
            CD: Antilles 314-510 059-2

            Sweet Georgia Gillespie
            CD: Antilles 314-510 059-2

            You've Changed
            CD: Antilles 422-848 214-2

            Just Friends
            CD: Antilles 314-510 059-2

            'Round Midnight (unissued)

            The Song Is You (unissued)

            My One and Only Love (unissued)

            Blues Walk (rejected)

Notes: (i) The titles on Antilles compact disc 422-848 214-2 (*The J.J. Johnson Quintet: Quintergy/Live at the Village Vanguard*, released in January 1991) and on Antilles compact disc 314-510 059-2 (*The J.J. Johnson Quintet: Standards— Live at the Village Vanguard,* released in September 1991) were recorded during a two-day engagement at the Village Vanguard in New York City.

(ii) Since the album focused either on the performance of the quintet as a whole or the solo trombone with the rhythm section, "'Round Midnight" (piano solo), "The Song Is You" (saxophone solo), and "My One and Only Love" (saxophone solo) were not released. "Blues Walk" was rejected. Discographical data were obtained from J.J. Johnson's production notes.

[289] July 10, 1988   New York, New York
       J.J. Johnson Quintet   Village Vanguard
                                                       Club date performance

J.J. Johnson (tb), Ralph Moore (reeds), Stanley Cowell (p), Rufus Reid (b), Victor Lewis (d).

> When the Saints Go Marching In
> Blue Bossa
> Doc Was Here
> Bud's Blues
> Quintergy
> Lament
> It's All Right with Me
> Coppin' the Bop
> Nefertiti
> Commutation (Confirmation)

Note: All of the above titles issued on the CD Antilles 422-848 214-2.

> You Stepped out of a Dream
> My Funny Valentine
> Misterioso
> See See Rider
> Misty
> Autumn Leaves (Les feuilles mortes)
> What Is This Thing Called Love?

Note: All of the above titles ("You Stepped Out Of A Dream" . . . "What Is This Thing Called Love?") issued on the CD Antilles 314-510 059-2.

> Siena (unissued)

> Night Flight (rejected)

Blues Walk (rejected)

Notes: (i) See [288], note (i).
(ii) Since the album focused either on the performance of the quintet as a whole or the solo trombone with the rhythm section, *Siena* (piano solo) was not released. *Night Flight* and *Blues Walk* were rejected.

[290] August 6, 1988   Portland, Oregon
      J.J. Johnson Quintet   Mt. Hood Jazz Festival
                                                Audience tape

J.J. Johnson (tb), Ralph Moore (ts, kb), Stanley Cowell (p), Rufus Reid (b), Victor Lewis (d).

When the Saints Go Marching In
Blue Bossa
Why Indianapolis—Why Not Indianapolis?
Misty
Confirmation
Quintergy

[291] October 27, 1988   Belgium
      J.J. Johnson Quintet   Nita Club
                                    Radio broadcast (Holland)

J.J. Johnson (tb), Ralph Moore (ts, ss), Renee Rosnes (p), Rufus Reid (b), Victor Lewis (d).

Shortcake
Quintergy
My Funny Valentine
Commutation
Doc Was Here
Rhythm-a-ning

Note: An additional title, "Old Folks," features Renee Rosnes with Reid and Lewis.

[292] 1988   New York, New York
      Milt Jackson: Bebop   Studio performance

Milt Jackson (v), Jon Faddis (tp), J.J. Johnson (tb), Jimmy Heath (ts), Cedar Walton (p), John Clayton (b), Mickey Roker (d).

> Au Privave
> Good Bait
> Now's the Time
> Ornithology
> Groovin' High
> Birk's Works
> Salt Peanuts
> I Waited for You

Note: All titles issued on the CD WEA/Atlantic 7-90991-2.

[293] February 24–25, 1992   New York, New York
     Abbey Lincoln: Devil's Got Your Tongue   BMG Studios
                                                  Studio performance

Abbey Lincoln (voc), J.J. Johnson (tb), Maxine Roach (va), Rodney
Kendrick (p), Marcus McLaurine (b), Grady Tate (d).

> The Legend of Evalina Coffey

Omit Maxine Roach (va):

> A Child Is Born

Add Stanley Turrentine (ts):

> Spring Will Be a Little Late This Year

Note: Of the eleven tracks recorded for the compact disc, only these three include
J.J. Johnson in the ensemble. All titles issued on the CD Verve 314-513-574-2.

[294] June 2–3, 1992   New York, New York
     J.J. Johnson Quintet: Vivian   Penny Lane Studios
                                                  Studio performance

J.J. Johnson (tb), Rob Schneiderman (p), Ted Dunbar (g), Rufus
Reid (b), Akira Tana (d).

> Alone Together
> Frankie and Johnnie
> I Thought about You
> I Love You
> What's New
> How Deep Is the Ocean

But Not for Me
There Will Never Be Another You
Azure-Té
You Don't Know What Love Is

Note: All titles issued on the CD Concord CCD-4523.

[295] December 7, 1992   New York, New York
   J.J. Johnson: Let's Hang Out   BMG Studios
                                                    Studio performance

J.J. Johnson (tb), Ralph Moore (ts), Terence Blanchard (tp), Stanley
Cowell (p), Rufus Reid (b), Victor Lewis (d).

            Kenya
            Hasten Jason
            Stir Fry

Omit Ralph Moore (ts), add Jimmy Heath (ts):

            It's You or No One

Note: All titles issued on the CD EmArcy 514-454-2. Discographical data were
obtained from J.J. Johnson's production notes.

[296] December 8, 1992   New York, New York
   J.J. Johnson: Let's Hang Out   BMG Studios
                                                    Studio performance

J.J. Johnson (tb), Jimmy Heath (ts), Renee Rosnes (p), Rufus Reid
(b), Lewis Nash (d).

            Friendship Suite: Ode To G.T., Let's Hang
               Out, Love You Nana, Reunion

            It Never Entered My Mind

Omit Jimmy Heath (ts):

            I Got It Bad (And That Ain't Good)

Note: All titles issued on the CD EmArcy 514-454-2. Discographical data were
obtained from J.J. Johnson's production notes.

[297] December 9, 1992   New York, New York
      J.J. Johnson: Let's Hang Out   BMG Studios
                                                                Studio performance

J.J. Johnson (tb), Ralph Moore (ss), Renee Rosnes (p), Rufus Reid
(b), Lewis Nash (d).

> May I Have Dis Dance?
> Syntax (Bebop Song)

Omit all but J.J. Johnson (tb):

> Beautiful Love

Note: All titles issued on the CD EmArcy 514 454-2. Discographical data were
obtained from J.J. Johnson's production notes.

[298] May 1993   Bern, Switzerland
      J.J. Johnson Quintet   Bern Jazz Festival Concert
                                                       Television broadcast (Germany)

J.J. Johnson (tb), Ralph Moore (ts, ss), Renee Rosnes (p), Rufus Reid
(b), Billy Drummond (d).

> Autumn Leaves
> Hasten Jason
> Blue Bossa
> It Never Entered My Mind

[299] April 26, 1994   New York, New York
      Carnegie Hall Salutes The Jazz Masters   Carnegie Hall
                                                              Concert performance

J.J. Johnson (tb), Joe Henderson (ts), Kenny Burrell (g), Herbie
Hancock (p), Ray Brown (b), Kenny Washington (d).

> Tea for Two

Note: This title segues into a big band version featuring Vanessa Williams (voc),
with the Carnegie Hall Jazz Band: Don Sickler (cond), Randy Brecker, Earl
Gardner, Lew Soloff, Byron Stripling (tp), Slide Hampton, Douglas Purviance,
Steve Turré, Dennis Wilson (tb), Jerry Dodgion, Frank Wess (as), Alex Foster,
Willie Williams (ts), Gary Smulyan (bs), Don Alias (per), with the small group
rhythm section of Kenny Burrell (g), Herbie Hancock (p), Ray Brown (b), Kenny
Washington (d).

Dee Dee Bridgewater (voc), J.J. Johnson (tb), with the Carnegie Hall Jazz Band: Don Sickler (cond),Randy Brecker, Earl Gardner, Lew Soloff, Byron Stripling (tp), Slide Hampton, Douglas Purviance, Steve Turre, Dennis Wilson (tb), Jerry Dodgion, Frank Wess (as), Alex Foster, Willie Williams (ts), Gary Smulyan (bs), Renee Rosnes (p), Kenny Burrell (g), Dennis Irwin (b), Don Alias (per).

Shiny Stockings

J.J. Johnson (tb), Abbey Lincoln (voc), Hank Jones (p), Charlie Haden (b), Al Foster (d).

I Must Have That Man

J.J. Johnson (tb), Roy Hargrove (tp), Jackie McLean (as), Joe Henderson (ts), Kenny Burrel (g), Herbie Hancock, Hank Jones (p), Ray Brown, Christian McBride (b), Kenny Washington (d), Dee Dee Bridgewater, Betty Carter, Vanessa Williams (voc).

Now's the Time

Note: All titles issued on the CD, Verve 314-523-150-2This concert, a benefit for Carnegia Hall and its *Jazzed* education program for high school students, also celebrated Verve Records' fiftieth anniversary. It presented—in the jam-session tradition of *Jazz at the Philharmonic*—a variety of artists on each tune. Additional titles performed and recorded include "Tangerine," "Willow Weep for Me," "Desafinado," "Manteca," "Parisian Thoroughfare," "How High the Moon," "Turn out the Stars," "The Eternal Triangle," "How Insensitive," "Down by the Riverside," "Yellowstone," and "It's About That Time." The concert was also recorded for a ninety-minute broadcast by the Public Broadcasting Service on its *Great Performances* program on May 18, 1994.

[300] July 13–15, 1994   Wembley, England
       J.J. Johnson with the   Studio performance
       Robert Farnon Orchestra: Tangence

J.J. Johnson (tb), Robert Farnon (arr, cond), Nigel Carter, Ronnie Hughes, Derek Healey, Simon Gardner, Kenny Baker (tp), Don Lusher, Gordon Campbell, Colin Sheen, Bill Geldard (tb), John Pignegny, Jeff Bryant, Nick Busch, Richard Watkins (hn), Ray Swinfield, Tommy Whittle, Robin Kennard, Joseph Sanders, Roy Willox, Peter Hughes, Denis Walton (reeds), Rachel Cohen, Derek Collier, Maurice Brett, Marc Berrow, Gillian Cohen, Levine Andrade, Geoffrey Grey, Michael De Saulles, Joan Edwards, Homi Kanga, David Randall, Beatrice Harper, P.J. Dale (vn), Ken Essex,

George Turnland, John Graham, Michael Ponder (va), Ursula Hess,
Caroline Dale, Norman Jones, Anthony Pleeth (vc), Chris Laurence,
Peter Cullington, Allen Walley (b), Laurie Holloway (p, kb), Louis
Stewart (g), Hugh Webb (hp), Terry Jenkins (d), Eric Allen (per).

> People Time
> The Meaning of the Blues
> Dinner for One, Please, James
> Lament
> The Very Thought of You
> Amazing Grace
> End of a Love Affair
> Malaga Moon

Add Wynton Marsalis (tp):

> Two's Company
> Malagueña

Omit Robert Farnon (arr, cond), orchestra, and rhythm section;
Personnel are J.J. Johnson (tb), Wynton Marsalis (tp) only:

> For Dancers Only

Personnel are J.J. Johnson (tb), Chris Laurence (b) only:

> Opus De Focus

Note: All titles issued on the CD, Verve 314-526-588-2. Discographical data were
obtained from J.J. Johnson's production notes although specific recording dates were
unavailable.

[301] August 28, 1994   Japan
       J.J. Johnson Quintet   Mount Fuji Jazz Festival Concert
                                                         Audience tape

J.J. Johnson (tb), Ralph Moore (ts), Renee Rosnes (p), Todd Coolman
(b), Billy Drummond (d).

> Kenya
> Why Indianapolis—Why Not Indianapolis?
> Friendship Suite

[302] November 18, 1994   Paris, France
       J.J. Johnson Quintet   Concert performance
                                           Audience tape

J.J. Johnson (tb), Ralph Moore (ts, ss), Renee Rosnes (p), Rufus Reid (b), George Brown (d).

         Shortcake
         Lament
         See See Rider
         When the Saints Go Marching In

[303] December 20, 1994   New York, New York
       J.J. Johnson Quintet   Concert performance

J.J. Johnson (tb), Ralph Moore (ts, ss), Renee Rosnes (p), Rufus Reid (b), George Brown (d).

         Nina Mae
         Mom, Are You Listening?

Note: Remainder of titles recorded are unknown. Trombonist Steve Turré and additional unknown personnel (Jamaican steel drums, conch shells, harp, celesta) participate in this session; however, additional discographical data were unavailable. The session remains unreleased.

[304] 1995   New York, New York
       J.J. Johnson Quintet   Iridium Jazz Club
                                             Audience tape

J.J. Johnson (tb), Dan Faulk (ts, ss), Renee Rosnes (p), Rufus Reid (b), Bruce Cox (d).

         Just Friends
         Will You Still Be Mine
         Road Song
         Quintergy
         It Never Entered My Mind
         Blue Bossa
         Hasten Jason
         Autumn Leaves

[305] May 7, June 20, 1996   Astoria, New York
       Steve Turré   Master Sound Astoria Studios
                                                            Studio performance

Steve Turré, J.J. Johnson (tb), John Faddis (tp), Robin Eubanks,
Jimmy Bosch, Frank Lacy, Douglas Purviance (tb), Stephen Scott
(p), Andy Gonzalez (b), Victor Lewis (d), Stefon Harris, Milton
Cardona, Kimati Dinizulu (per), Akua Dixon (cond).

The Emperor

Steve Turré, J.J. Johnson (tb), John Faddis (tp), Robin Eubanks,
Jimmy Bosch, Frank Lacy (tb), Douglas Purviance (bt), Stephen Scott
(p), Andy Gonzalez (b), Victor Lewis (d), Milton Cardona (per),
Akua Dixon (cond).

Steve's Blues

Note: In addition, Turré solos on natural shells, and Eubanks and Bosch double on
ensemble shells in "The Emperor" and "Steve's Blues"; Purviance doubles on
ensemble shells in "The Emperor." Both titles issued on the CD, Verve 314-537-
133-2.

[306] September 24, 1996   New York, New York
       J.J. Johnson: The Brass Orchestra   Clinton Recording Studio
                                                            Studio performance

J.J. Johnson (tb, arr[1]), Slide Hampton (comp, arr,[2] cond), Jon Faddis,
Lew Soloff, Earl Gardner, Byron Stripling, Joe Wilder, Danny Cahn
(tp), John Clark, Bob Carlisle, Chris Komer, Marshall Sealy (hn),
Jim Pugh, Steve Turré, Douglas Purviance (tb), Dave Taylor (bt),
Bruce Bonvissuto, Alan Raph (eu), Howard Johnson, Andy Rodgers
(tu), Francesca Corsi (hp), Renee Rosnes (p), Rufus Reid (b), Victor
Lewis (d), Freddie Santiago, Milton Cardona, Kevin Johnson (per).

Gingerbread Boy (Jimmy Heath, comp)[1]

Add soloists Eddie Henderson (tp), Robin Eubanks (tb), Dan Faulk (ts):

Comfort Zone (Slide Hampton, comp)[2]

J.J. Johnson (tb, comp, arr), Eddie Henderson (tp), Dan Faulk (ts),
Slide Hampton (cond), Jon Faddis, Lew Soloff, Earl Gardner, Byron
Stripling, Joe Wilder, Danny Cahn (tp), John Clark, Bob Carlisle,

Chris Komer, Marshall Sealy (hn), Jim Pugh, Steve Turré, Douglas Purviance (tb), Dave Taylor (bt), Bruce Bonvissuto, Alan Raph (eu), Howard Johnson, Andy Rodgers (tu), Renee Rosnes (ep), Rufus Reid (b), Victor Lewis (d), Freddie Santiago (per).

Night Flight (unissued)

J.J. Johnson (tb, comp), Dan Faulk (ts), Slide Hampton (arr, cond), Jon Faddis, Lew Soloff (fg), John Clark, Bob Carlisle, Chris Komer, Marshall Sealy (hn), Jim Pugh, Steve Turré, Douglas Purviance (tb), Dave Taylor (bt), Bruce Bonvissuto, Alan Raph (eu), Howard Johnson (tu), Francesca Corsi (hp), Renee Rosnes (p), Rufus Reid (b), Victor Lewis (d), Freddie Santiago (per).

Enigma

Note: All issued titles on the CD Verve 314-537-321-2. Discographical data were obtained from J.J. Johnson's production notes.

[307]   September 25, 1996   New York, New York
        J.J. Johnson: The Brass Orchestra   Clinton Recording Studio
                                                            Studio performance

J.J. Johnson (tb, comp, arr), Dan Faulk (ts), Slide Hampton (cond), Jon Faddis, Lew Soloff, Earl Gardner, Byron Stripling, Joe Wilder, Joe Shepley (tp), John Clark, Bob Carlisle, Chris Komer, Marshall Sealy (hn), Jim Pugh, Steve Turré, Douglas Purviance (tb), Dave Taylor (bt), Bruce Bonvissuto, Alan Raph (eu), Howard Johnson, Andy Rodgers (tu), Renee Rosnes (p), Rufus Reid (b), Kevin Johnson (d), Freddie Santiago (v).

Brass TMX Suite—Part 2 (unissued)

J.J. Johnson (tb, comp, arr), Eddie Henderson (tp), Dan Faulk (ts), Slide Hampton (cond), Jon Faddis, Lew Soloff, Earl Gardner, Byron Stripling, Joe Wilder, Joe Shepley (tp), John Clark, Bob Carlisle (hn), Jim Pugh, Steve Turré, Douglas Purviance (tb), Dave Taylor (bt), Bruce Bonvissuto, Alan Raph (eu), Howard Johnson (tu), Renee Rosnes (p), Rufus Reid (b), Victor Lewis (d).

Four Plus Four (unissued)

J.J. Johnson (tb, comp, arr), Eddie Henderson (tp), Dan Faulk (ss), Slide Hampton (cond), Jon Faddis, Lew Soloff, Earl Gardner, Byron

Stripling, Joe Wilder, Joe Shepley (tp), John Clark, Bob Carlisle, Chris Komer, Marshall Sealy (hn), Jim Pugh, Steve Turré, Douglas Purviance (tb), Dave Taylor (bt), Bruce Bonvissuto, Alan Raph (eu), Howard Johnson, Andy Rodgers (tu), Renee Rosnes (p), Rufus Reid (b), Victor Lewis (d), Kevin Johnson, Freddie Santiago (per).

If I Hit the Lottery

Note: All issued titles on the CD Verve 314-537-321-2. Discographical data were obtained from J.J. Johnson's production notes.

[308] September 26, 1996   New York, New York
J.J. Johnson: The Brass Orchestra   Clinton Recording Studios
                                                        Studio performance

J.J. Johnson (tb), Thomas Everett (cond), Robert Farnon (arr), Jon Faddis, Lew Soloff (fg), John Clark, Bob Carlisle, Chris Komer, Marshall Sealy (hn), Jim Pugh, Steve Turré, Douglas Purviance (tb), Dave Taylor (bt), Bruce Bonvissuto, Alan Raph (eu), Howard Johnson (tu), Francesca Corsi (hp), Renee Rosnes (p), Rufus Reid (b), Victor Lewis (d), Freddie Santiago (per).

Wild Is the Wind (Dmitri Tiomkin, comp)

Add soloists Robin Eubanks (tb, comp, arr), Dan Faulk (ts):

Cross Currents

Omit all personnel except J.J. Johnson (tb, arr), Thomas Everett (cond), John Clark (hn), Bruce Bonvissuto (eu), Howard Johnson (tu):

Deep River (brass quartet version, unissued)

Omit J.J. Johnson (tb):

Deep River (brass trio version, unissued)

J.J. Johnson (tb, comp, arr), Dan Faulk (ts), Thomas Everett (cond), Jon Faddis, Lew Soloff, Earl Gardner, Byron Stripling, Joe Wilder, Danny Cahn (tp), John Clark, Bob Carlisle, Chris Komer, Marshall Sealy (hn), Jim Pugh, Steve Turré, Douglas Purviance, Joseph Alessi (tb), Dave Taylor (bt), Bruce Bonvissuto, Alan Raph (eu), Howard Johnson, Andy Rodgers (tu), Francesca Corsi (hp), Renee Rosnes (p),

Rufus Reid (b), Victor Lewis (d), Freddie Santiago (per).

Why Indianapolis—Why Not Indianapolis?

Omit Dan Faulk (ts), add soloists Eddie Henderson, Joe Wilder (tp):

Ballad for Joe

Omit soloists Eddie Henderson, Joe Wilder (tp):

El Camino Real

Omit J.J. Johnson (tb):

Fiesta Fanfare (unissued)

Omit all personnel except Danny Cahn, Byron Stripling (tp), John Clark (hn), Joseph Alessi (tb).

Morgenmusik (Paul Hindemith, comp) (unissued)

Note: All issued titles on the CD Verve 314-537-321-2. Discographical data were obtained from J.J. Johnson's production notes.

[309] September 27, 1996   New York, New York
       J.J. Johnson: The Brass Orchestra   Clinton Recording Studios
                                                    Studio performance

J.J. Johnson (tb, comp, arr), Thomas Everett (cond), Jon Faddis, Lew Soloff, Earl Gardner, Byron Stripling, Joe Wilder, Danny Cahn, Joe Shepley (tp), John Clark, Bob Carlisle, Chris Komer, Marshall Sealy (hn), Jim Pugh, Steve Turré, Douglas Purviance, Joseph Alessi (tb), Dave Taylor (bt), Bruce Bonvissuto, Alan Raph (eu), Howard Johnson, Andy Rodgers (tu), Francesca Corsi (hp), Renee Rosnes (p), Rufus Reid (b), Victor Lewis (d), Freddie Santiago (per).

Canonn for Bela

Omit J.J. Johnson (tb), Joe Shepley (tp), Joseph Alessi (tb):

Brass TMX Suite—Part 1 (unissued)

Brass TMX Suite—Part 1A (unissued)

J.J. Johnson (tb, arr), Dan Faulk (ss), Jon Faddis, Earl Gardner, Danny Cahn (tp), Steve Turré, Jim Pugh, Douglas Purviance (tb), Bruce Bonvissuto, Alan Raph (eu), Howard Johnson (tu), Renee Rosnes (p), Rufus Reid (b), Victor Lewis (d).

Swing Spring

Mohawk (Miles Davis, comp) (unissued)

J.J. Johnson (comp, arr), Jon Faddis (tp), Thomas Everett (cond), Lew Soloff, Earl Gardner, Byron Stripling, Joe Wilder, Danny Cahn, Joe Shepley (tp), John Clark, Bob Carlisle, Chris Komer, Marshall Sealy (hn), Jim Pugh, Joseph Alessi, Steve Turré, Douglas Purviance (tb), Dave Taylor (bt), Howard Johnson, Andy Rodgers (tu), Francesca Corsi (hp), Renee Rosnes (p), Rufus Reid (b), Victor Lewis (d).

"Horn of Plenty" from *Perceptions*

"Ballade" from *Perceptions*

Note: All issued titles on the CD Verve 314-537-321-2. Discographical data were obtained from J.J. Johnson's production notes. When queried about the unusual spelling of the title, "Canonn for Bela," Johnson's tongue-in-cheek reply recalled the title of a tune issued on the *Quintergy* album: "Why the spelling for Canonn— Why not the spelling for Canonn?"

[310] October 1–4, 1996   New York, New York
      J.J. Johnson: Heroes   Clinton Recording Studio
                                                           Studio performance

J.J. Johnson (tb), Dan Faulk (ts), Renee Rosnes (p), Rufus Reid (b), Victor Lewis (d).

Carolyn (In the Morning)
Ten-85

Personnel same except Dan Faulk (ss, ts):

Thelonious the Onliest

Personnel changes to J.J. Johnson (tb), Renee Rosnes (p):

Better Days

Personnel changes to J.J. Johnson (tb), Dan Faulk (ss), Don Sickler (fg), Renee Rosnes (p), Rufus Reid (b), Victor Lewis (d):

>Blue in Green

Personnel changes to J.J. Johnson (tb), Dan Faulk (ts), Renee Rosnes (p), Rufus Reid (b), Victor Lewis (d):

>Blue Train
>Carolyn (In the Evening)

Note: On the title "Ten-85," Johnson recorded a second trombone track to give the effect of two trombones in the ensemble. An additional title, "Vista," is a feature for pianist Renee Rosnes. All titles issued on the CD Verve 528-864-2.

[311] November 18, 1996   New York, New York
  J.J. Johnson: Heroes   Studio performance

J.J. Johnson (tb), Wayne Shorter (ts), Renee Rosnes (p), Rufus Reid (b), Victor Lewis (d).

>In Walked Wayne

Notes: According to Johnson, Shorter's track on "In Walked Wayne" was dubbed onto the master tape recorded during the October 1–4 sessions. Dan Faulk (ts) recorded the original track (for ensemble purposes), which was omitted from the mixdown.

[312] October 1997   Washington, D.C.
  National Public Radio: Jazz Profiles Series   Radio broadcast

Program number 971002.
55–minute documentary; includes interviews with J.J. Johnson, David N. Baker, Robin Eubanks, Slide Hampton, Dick Katz, Max Roach, Mary Ann Topper, Steve Turré, Thomas Everett, and Bill Watrous, interspersed with recordings.

Note: Written by David Tarnow with special assistance from the Smithsonian Institution Jazz Oral History Program, Joshua Berrett, and Louis G. Bourgois III; the NPR Jazz Profiles Series is a weekly jazz documentary program narrated by vocalist Nancy Wilson and broadcast on over 200 NPR-affiliated stations across the United States. See the World Wide Web page at <http://www.npr.org/programs/jazzprofiles/jjohnson.html> for additional information.

Index

431

About the Authors

Joshua Berrett (B.A., University of Cape Town; M.A., Columbia University; Ph.D., The University of Michigan) is professor of music at Mercy College, Dobbs Ferry, New York. A specialist in nineteenth- and twentieth-century music, he has published on a wide array of topics, including two volumes on the symphony and articles on jazz and contemporary music in such journals as the *Journal of Jazz Studies*, *The Musical Quarterly*, and *American Music*. His book, *The Louis Armstrong Companion: Eight Decades of Commentary* has been published by Schirmer Books/Simon & Schuster Macmillan. Another jazz book is under contract with Yale University Press.

Louis G. Bourgois III (B.Mus.Ed., Murray State University; M.M., University of Louisville; D.M.A., The Ohio State University) is professor of music at Kentucky State University, Frankfort, Kentucky. He is a specialist in jazz history and discography. His research on J.J. Johnson began in 1973 during his undergraduate studies and resulted in his doctoral dissertation, *Jazz Trombonist J.J. Johnson: A Comprehensive Discography and Study of the Early Evolution of His Style* (The Ohio State University, 1986). As a professional bass trombonist, he performs with the Lexington Brass Band, Lexington Philharmonic Orchestra, Vincent DiMartino Jazz Big Band, and Kentucky Jazz Repertory Orchestra.

441

DEMCO

AUG 1 1 2008